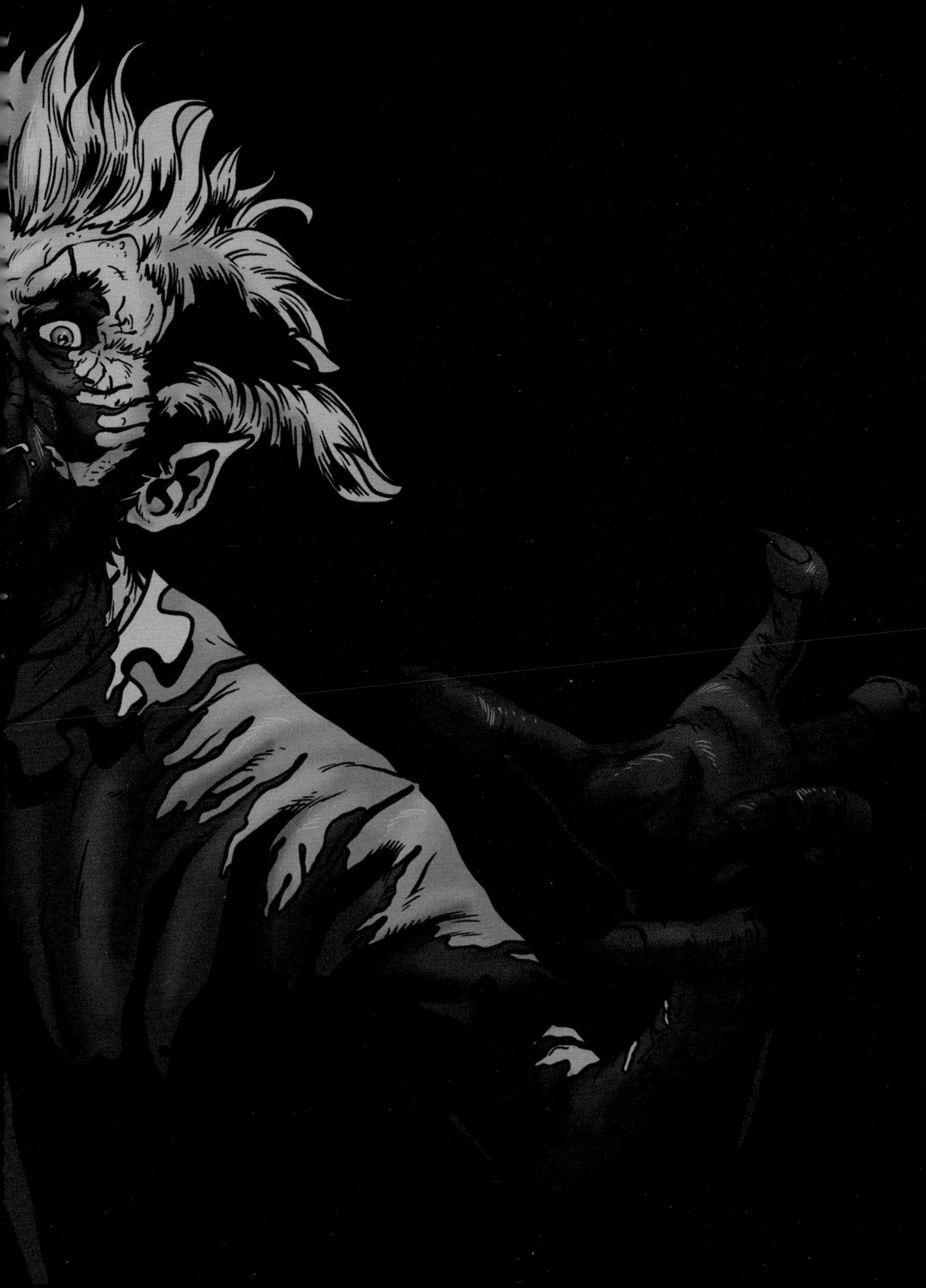

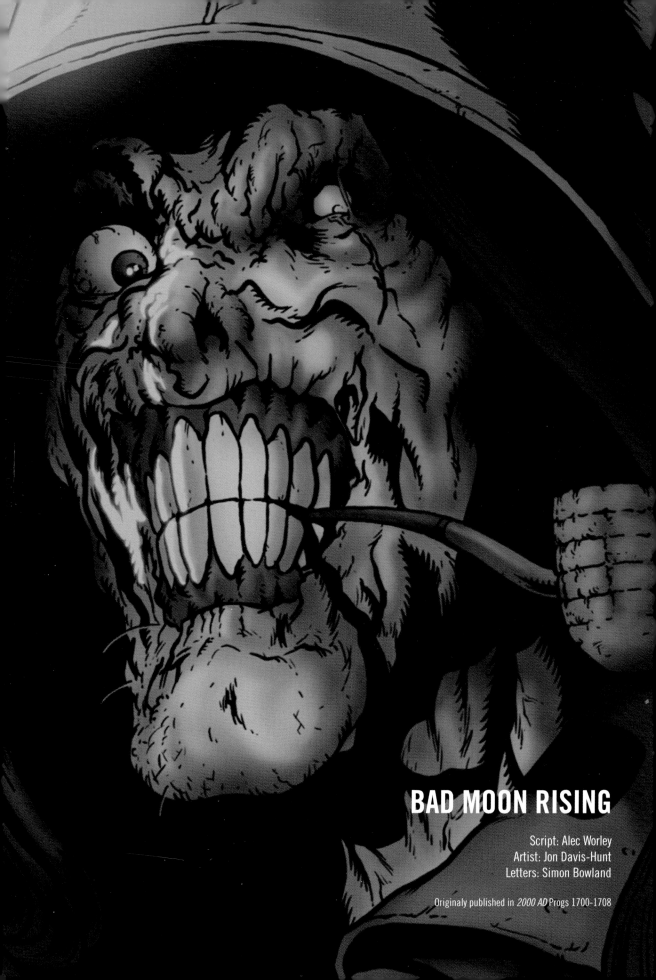

BAD MOON RISING

Script: Alec Worley
Artist: Jon Davis-Hunt
Letters: Simon Bowland

Originaly published in *2000 AD* Progs 1700-1708

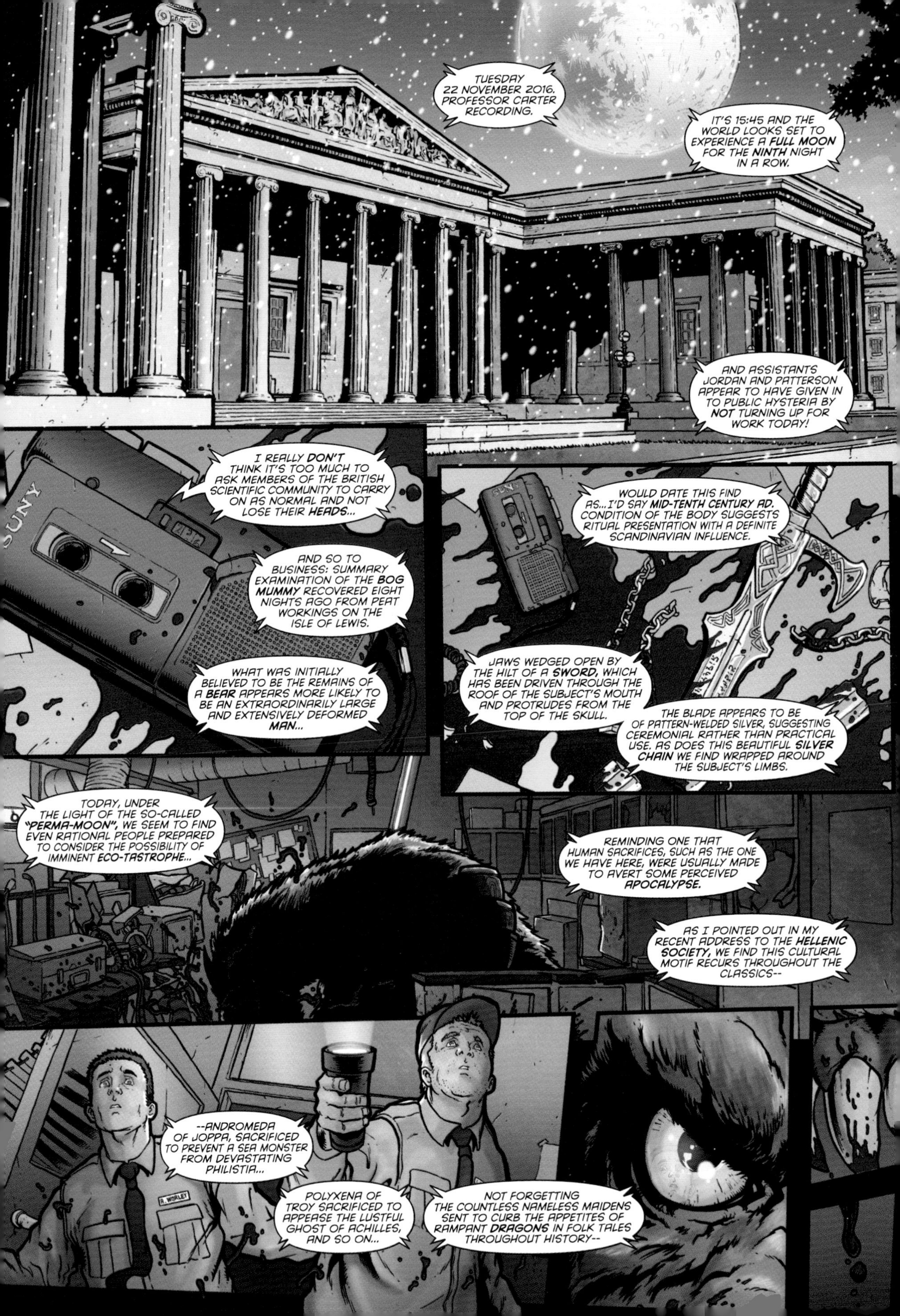
TUESDAY 22 NOVEMBER 2016. PROFESSOR CARTER RECORDING.
IT'S 15:45 AND THE WORLD LOOKS SET TO EXPERIENCE A FULL MOON FOR THE NINTH NIGHT IN A ROW.
AND ASSISTANTS JORDAN AND PATTERSON APPEAR TO HAVE GIVEN IN TO PUBLIC HYSTERIA BY NOT TURNING UP FOR WORK TODAY!
I REALLY DON'T THINK IT'S TOO MUCH TO ASK MEMBERS OF THE BRITISH SCIENTIFIC COMMUNITY TO CARRY ON AS NORMAL AND NOT LOSE THEIR HEADS...
AND SO TO BUSINESS: SUMMARY EXAMINATION OF THE BOG MUMMY RECOVERED EIGHT NIGHTS AGO FROM PEAT WORKINGS ON THE ISLE OF LEWIS.
WHAT WAS INITIALLY BELIEVED TO BE THE REMAINS OF A BEAR APPEARS MORE LIKELY TO BE AN EXTRAORDINARILY LARGE AND EXTENSIVELY DEFORMED MAN...
WOULD DATE THIS FIND AS...I'D SAY MID-TENTH CENTURY AD. CONDITION OF THE BODY SUGGESTS RITUAL PRESENTATION WITH A DEFINITE SCANDINAVIAN INFLUENCE.
JAWS WEDGED OPEN BY THE HILT OF A SWORD, WHICH HAS BEEN DRIVEN THROUGH THE ROOF OF THE SUBJECT'S MOUTH AND PROTRUDES FROM THE TOP OF THE SKULL.
THE BLADE APPEARS TO BE OF PATTERN-WELDED SILVER, SUGGESTING CEREMONIAL RATHER THAN PRACTICAL USE. AS DOES THIS BEAUTIFUL SILVER CHAIN WE FIND WRAPPED AROUND THE SUBJECT'S LIMBS.
TODAY, UNDER THE LIGHT OF THE SO-CALLED "PERMA-MOON", WE SEEM TO FIND EVEN RATIONAL PEOPLE PREPARED TO CONSIDER THE POSSIBILITY OF IMMINENT ECO-TASTROPHE...
REMINDING ONE THAT HUMAN SACRIFICES, SUCH AS THE ONE WE HAVE HERE, WERE USUALLY MADE TO AVERT SOME PERCEIVED APOCALYPSE.
AS I POINTED OUT IN MY RECENT ADDRESS TO THE HELLENIC SOCIETY, WE FIND THIS CULTURAL MOTIF RECURS THROUGHOUT THE CLASSICS--
--ANDROMEDA OF JOPPA, SACRIFICED TO PREVENT A SEA MONSTER FROM DEVASTATING PHILISTIA...
POLYXENA OF TROY SACRIFICED TO APPEASE THE LUSTFUL GHOST OF ACHILLES, AND SO ON...
NOT FORGETTING THE COUNTLESS NAMELESS MAIDENS SENT TO CURB THE APPETITES OF RAMPANT DRAGONS IN FOLK TALES THROUGHOUT HISTORY--

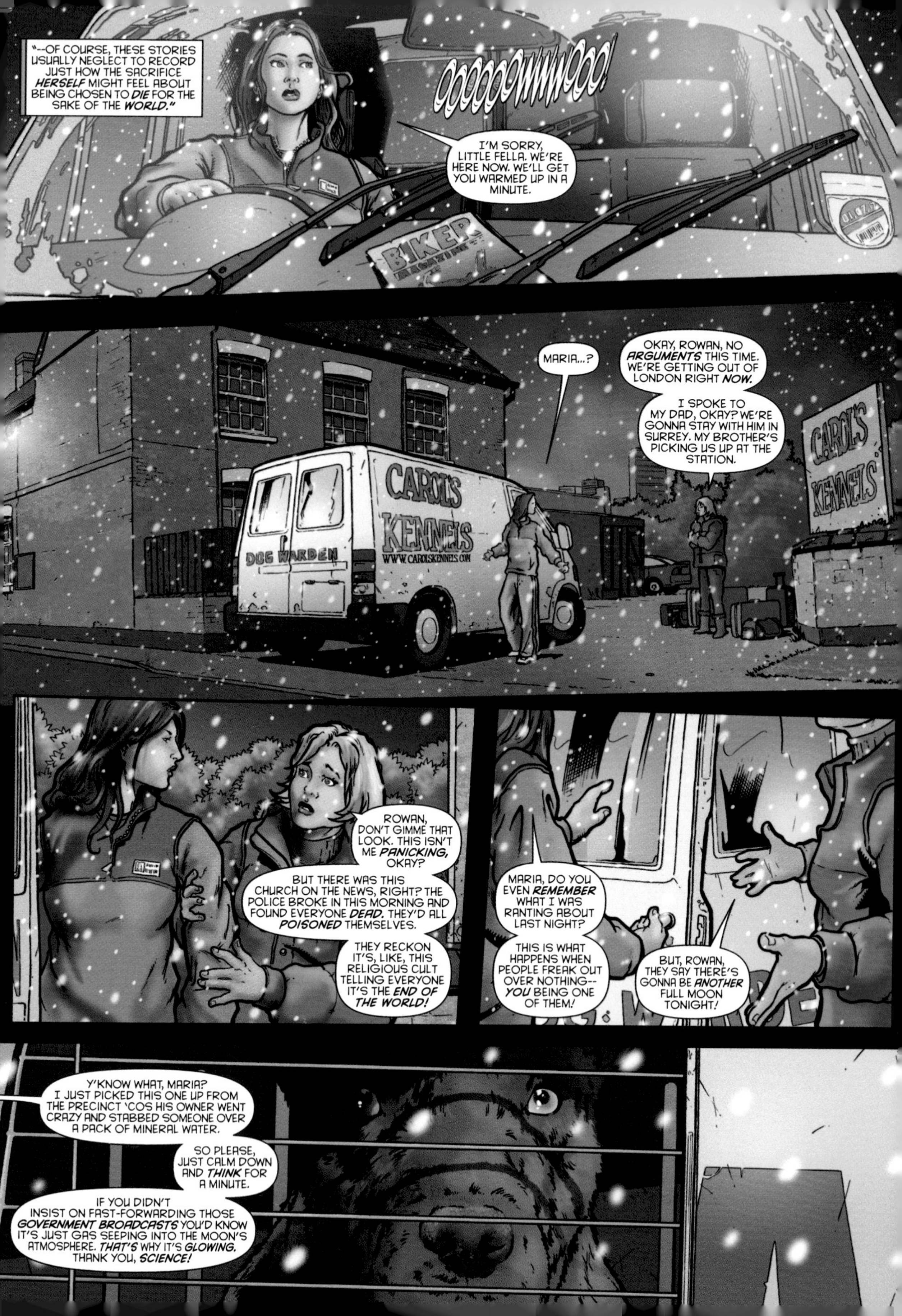

"--OF COURSE, THESE STORIES USUALLY NEGLECT TO RECORD JUST HOW THE SACRIFICE *HERSELF* MIGHT FEEL ABOUT BEING CHOSEN TO *DIE* FOR THE SAKE OF THE *WORLD*."
OOOOOOWWWOOO!
I'M SORRY, LITTLE FELLA. WE'RE HERE NOW. WE'LL GET YOU WARMED UP IN A MINUTE.
BIKER
CAROL'S KENNELS
DOG WARDEN
WWW.CAROLSKENNELS.COM
MARIA...?
OKAY, ROWAN, NO *ARGUMENTS* THIS TIME. WE'RE GETTING OUT OF LONDON RIGHT *NOW*.
I SPOKE TO MY DAD, OKAY? WE'RE GONNA STAY WITH HIM IN SURREY. MY BROTHER'S PICKING US UP AT THE STATION.
CAROL'S KENNELS
ROWAN, DON'T GIMME THAT LOOK. THIS ISN'T ME *PANICKING*, OKAY?
BUT THERE WAS THIS CHURCH ON THE NEWS, RIGHT? THE POLICE BROKE IN THIS MORNING AND FOUND EVERYONE *DEAD*. THEY'D ALL *POISONED* THEMSELVES.
THEY RECKON IT'S, LIKE, THIS RELIGIOUS CULT TELLING EVERYONE IT'S THE *END OF THE WORLD!*
MARIA, DO YOU EVEN *REMEMBER* WHAT I WAS RANTING ABOUT LAST NIGHT?
THIS IS WHAT HAPPENS WHEN PEOPLE FREAK OUT OVER NOTHING-- *YOU* BEING ONE OF THEM!
BUT, ROWAN, THEY SAY THERE'S GONNA BE *ANOTHER* FULL MOON TONIGHT!
Y'KNOW WHAT, MARIA? I JUST PICKED THIS ONE UP FROM THE PRECINCT 'COS HIS OWNER WENT CRAZY AND STABBED SOMEONE OVER A PACK OF MINERAL WATER.
SO PLEASE, JUST CALM DOWN AND *THINK* FOR A MINUTE.
IF YOU DIDN'T INSIST ON FAST-FORWARDING THOSE *GOVERNMENT BROADCASTS* YOU'D KNOW IT'S JUST GAS SEEPING INTO THE MOON'S ATMOSPHERE. *THAT'S* WHY IT'S *GLOWING*. THANK YOU, *SCIENCE!*

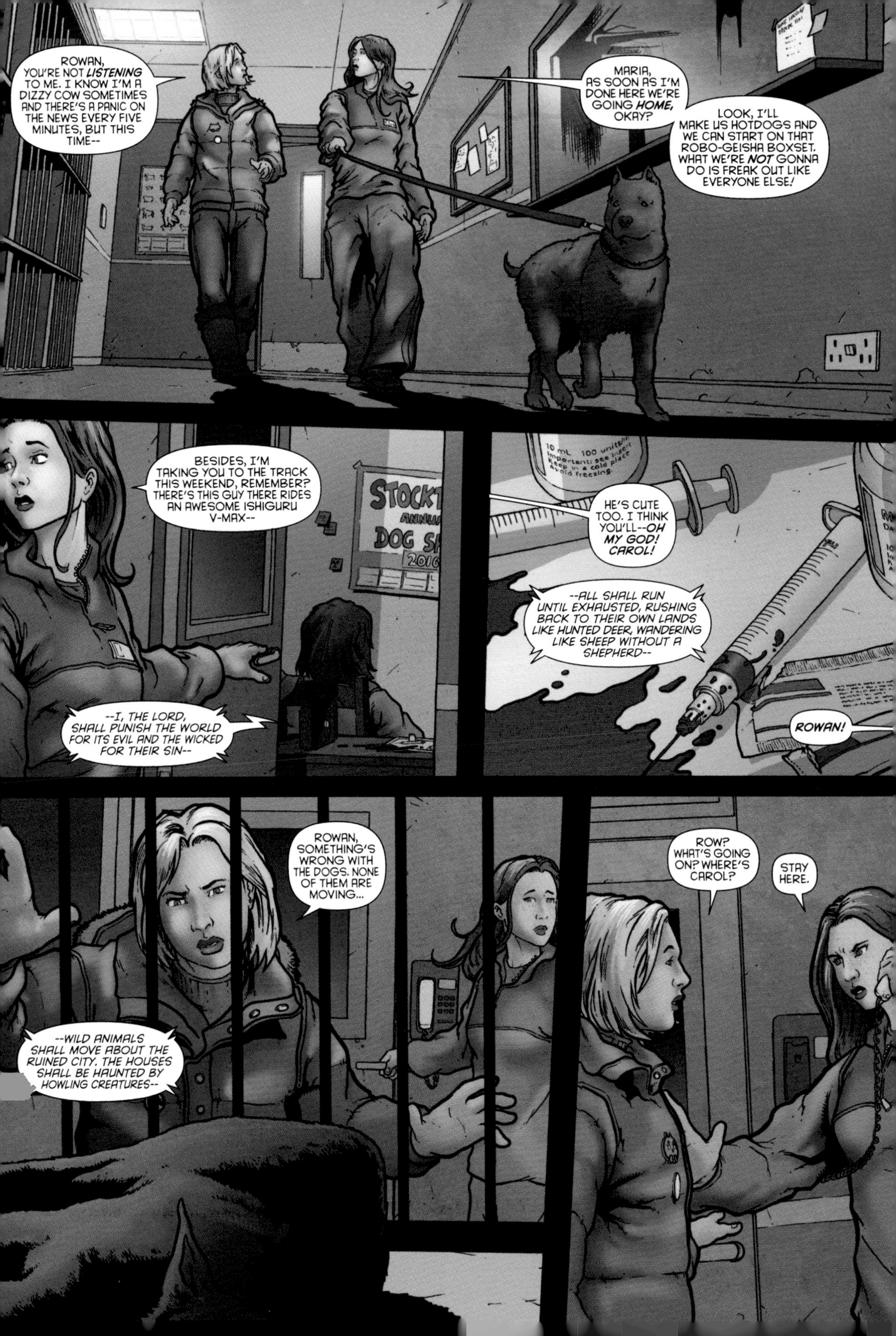
ROWAN, YOU'RE NOT LISTENING TO ME. I KNOW I'M A DIZZY COW SOMETIMES AND THERE'S A PANIC ON THE NEWS EVERY FIVE MINUTES, BUT THIS TIME--
MARIA, AS SOON AS I'M DONE HERE WE'RE GOING HOME, OKAY?
LOOK, I'LL MAKE US HOTDOGS AND WE CAN START ON THAT ROBO-GEISHA BOXSET. WHAT WE'RE NOT GONNA DO IS FREAK OUT LIKE EVERYONE ELSE!
BESIDES, I'M TAKING YOU TO THE TRACK THIS WEEKEND, REMEMBER? THERE'S THIS GUY THERE RIDES AN AWESOME ISHIGURU V-MAX--
--I, THE LORD, SHALL PUNISH THE WORLD FOR ITS EVIL AND THE WICKED FOR THEIR SIN--
HE'S CUTE TOO. I THINK YOU'LL--OH MY GOD! CAROL!
--ALL SHALL RUN UNTIL EXHAUSTED, RUSHING BACK TO THEIR OWN LANDS LIKE HUNTED DEER, WANDERING LIKE SHEEP WITHOUT A SHEPHERD--
ROWAN!
ROWAN, SOMETHING'S WRONG WITH THE DOGS. NONE OF THEM ARE MOVING...
--WILD ANIMALS SHALL MOVE ABOUT THE RUINED CITY. THE HOUSES SHALL BE HAUNTED BY HOWLING CREATURES--
ROW? WHAT'S GOING ON? WHERE'S CAROL?
STAY HERE.

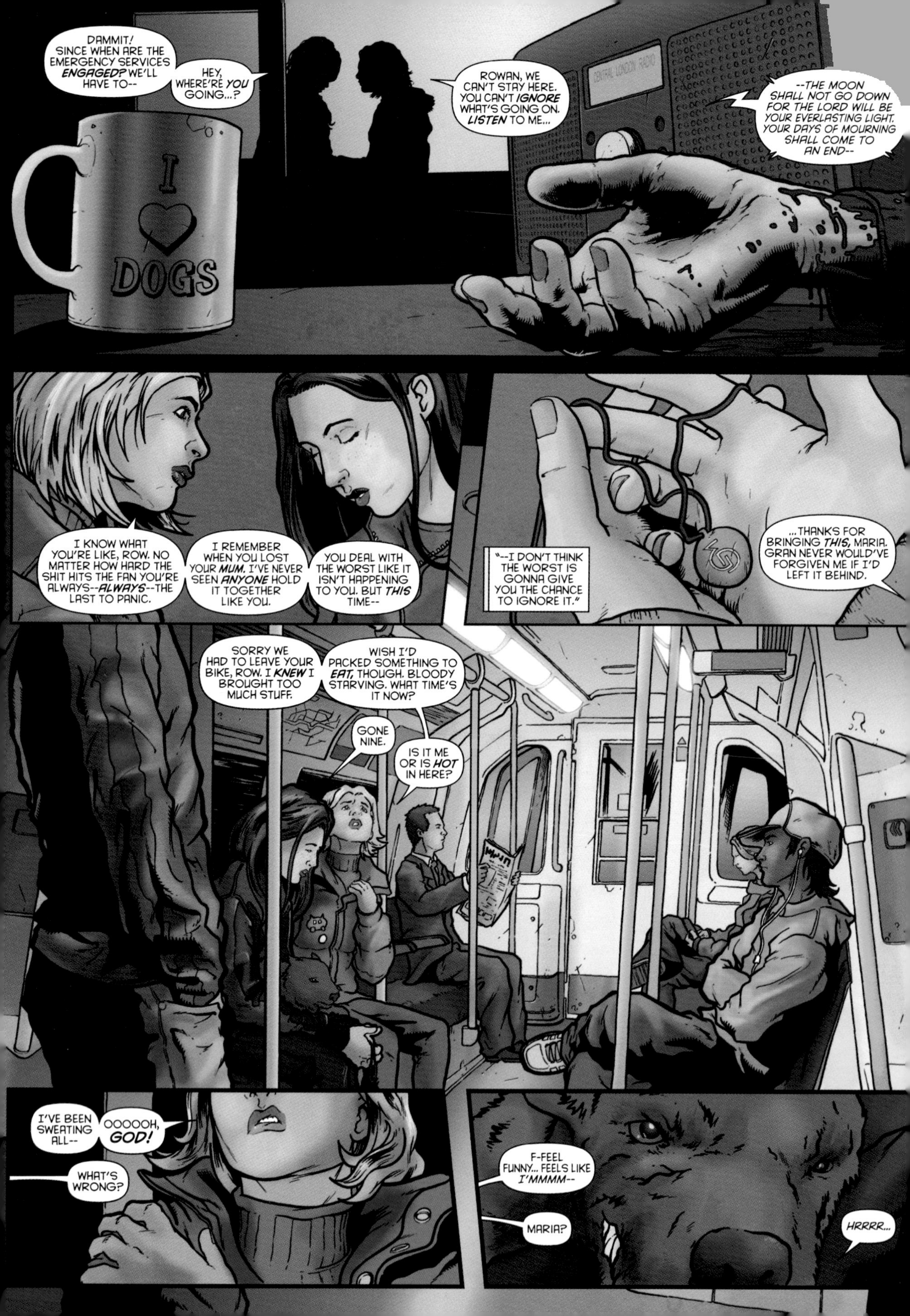
DAMMIT! SINCE WHEN ARE THE EMERGENCY SERVICES *ENGAGED?* WE'LL HAVE TO--
HEY, WHERE'RE *YOU* GOING...?
ROWAN, WE CAN'T STAY HERE. YOU CAN'T *IGNORE* WHAT'S GOING ON. *LISTEN* TO ME...
CENTRAL LONDON RADIO
--THE MOON SHALL NOT GO DOWN FOR THE LORD WILL BE YOUR EVERLASTING LIGHT. YOUR DAYS OF MOURNING SHALL COME TO AN END--
I ❤ DOGS
I KNOW WHAT YOU'RE LIKE, ROW. NO MATTER HOW HARD THE SHIT HITS THE FAN YOU'RE ALWAYS--*ALWAYS*--THE LAST TO PANIC.
I REMEMBER WHEN YOU LOST YOUR *MUM*. I'VE NEVER SEEN *ANYONE* HOLD IT TOGETHER LIKE YOU.
YOU DEAL WITH THE WORST LIKE IT ISN'T HAPPENING TO YOU. BUT *THIS* TIME--
"--I DON'T THINK THE WORST IS GONNA GIVE YOU THE CHANCE TO IGNORE IT."
...THANKS FOR BRINGING *THIS,* MARIA. GRAN NEVER WOULD'VE FORGIVEN ME IF I'D LEFT IT BEHIND.
SORRY WE HAD TO LEAVE YOUR BIKE, ROW. I *KNEW* I BROUGHT TOO MUCH STUFF.
WISH I'D PACKED SOMETHING TO *EAT,* THOUGH. BLOODY STARVING. WHAT TIME'S IT NOW?
GONE NINE.
IS IT ME OR IS *HOT* IN HERE?
I'VE BEEN SWEATING ALL--
OOOOOH, *GOD!*
WHAT'S WRONG?
F-FEEL FUNNY... FEELS LIKE *I'MMMM--*
MARIA?
HRRRR...

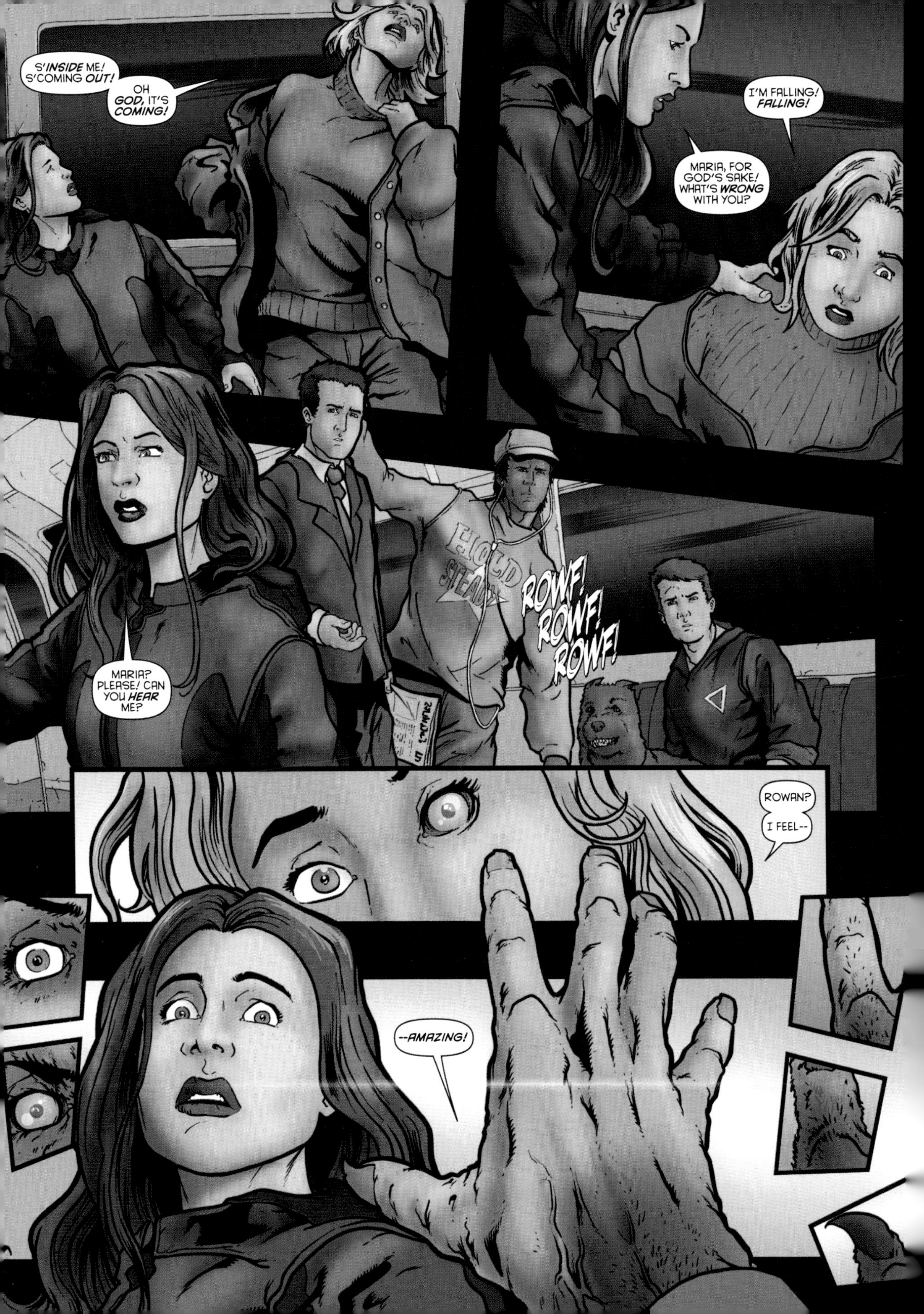
S'INSIDE ME! S'COMING OUT!
OH GOD, IT'S COMING!
I'M FALLING! FALLING!
MARIA, FOR GOD'S SAKE! WHAT'S WRONG WITH YOU?
HOLD STEADY
ROWF! ROWF! ROWF!
MARIA? PLEASE! CAN YOU HEAR ME?
ROWAN?
I FEEL--
--AMAZING!

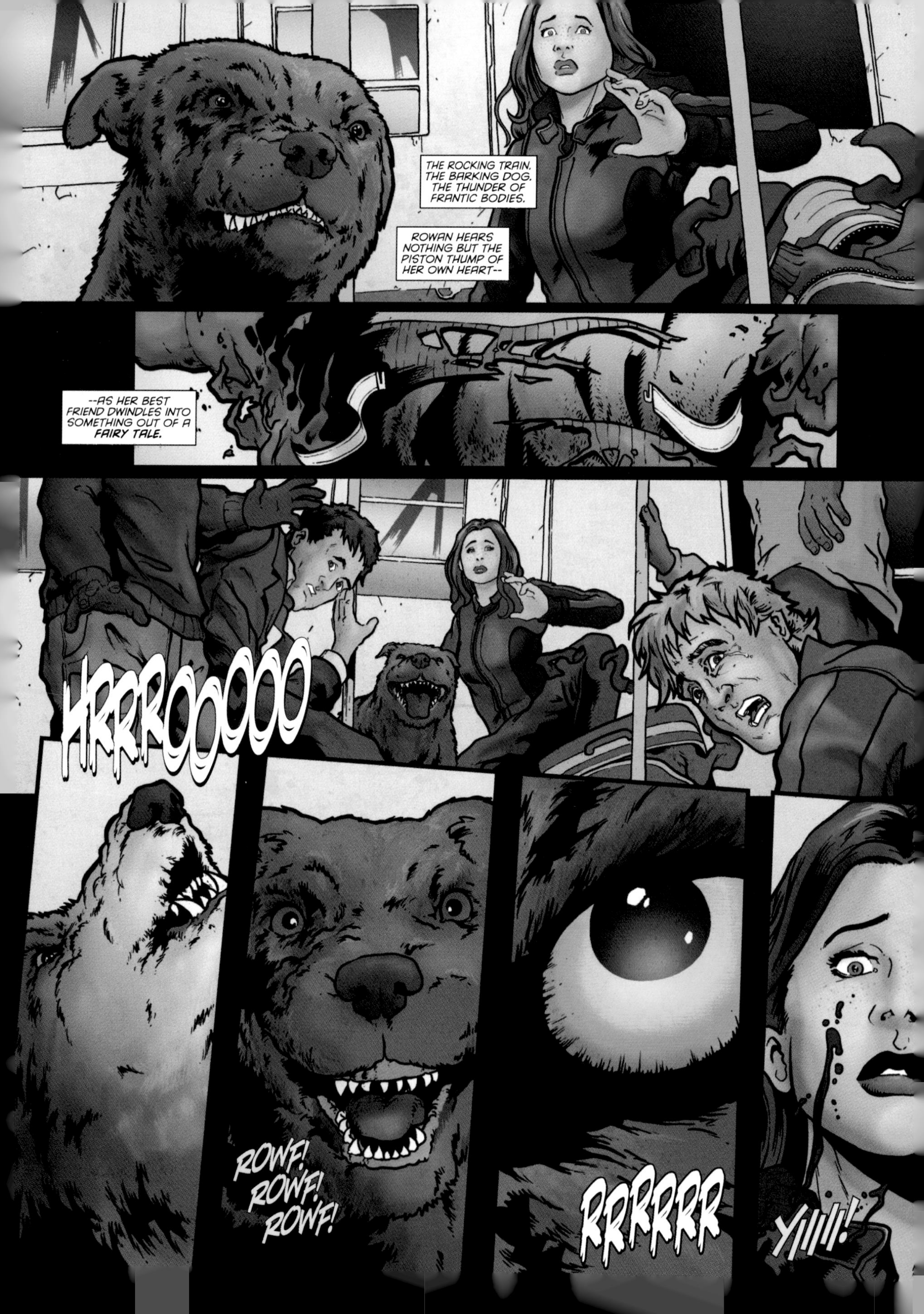
THE ROCKING TRAIN. THE BARKING DOG. THE THUNDER OF FRANTIC BODIES.
ROWAN HEARS NOTHING BUT THE PISTON THUMP OF HER OWN HEART--
--AS HER BEST FRIEND DWINDLES INTO SOMETHING OUT OF A FAIRY TALE.
HRRROOOOO
ROWF! ROWF! ROWF!
RRRRRR
YIIII!

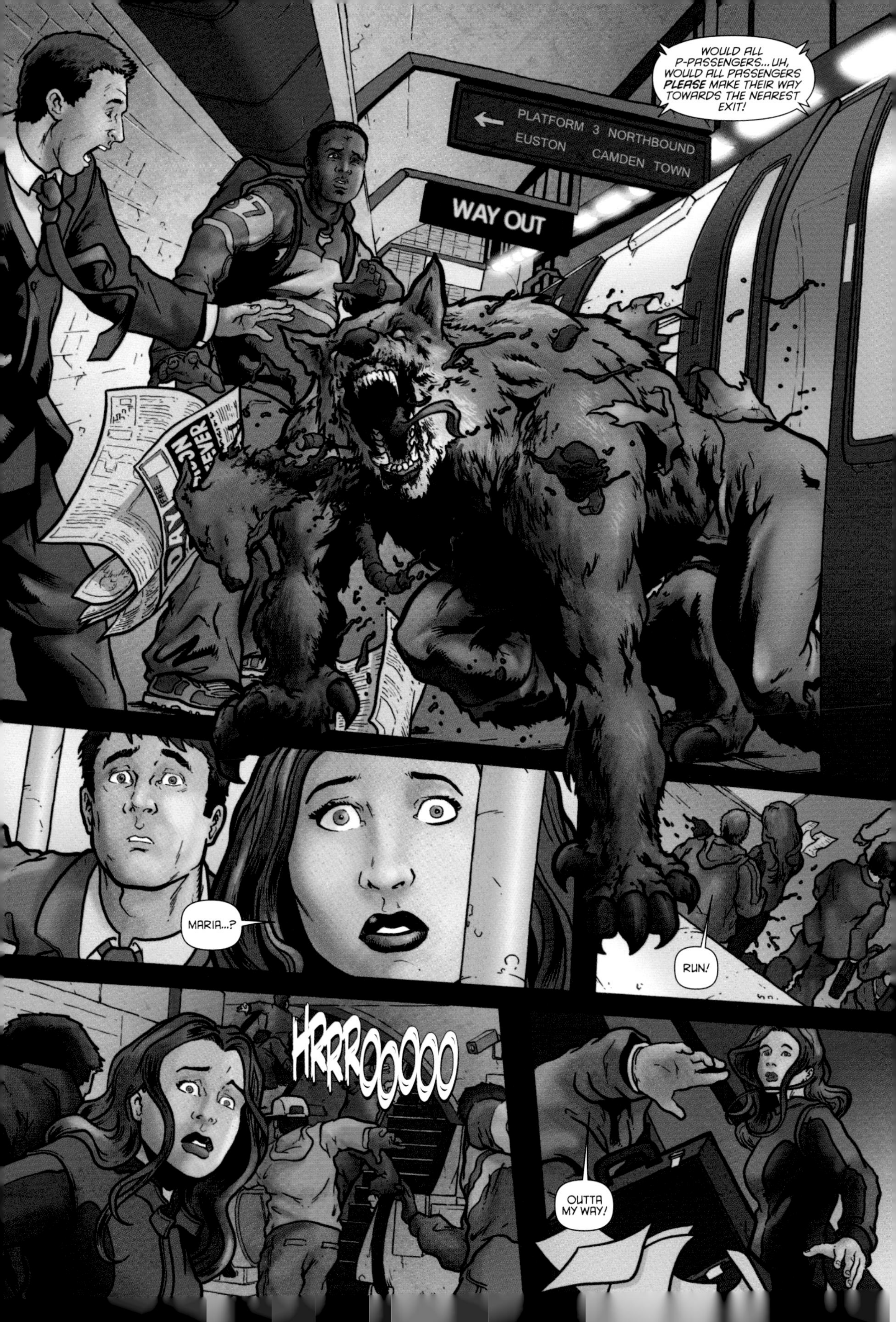

WOULD ALL P-PASSENGERS...UH, WOULD ALL PASSENGERS **PLEASE** MAKE THEIR WAY TOWARDS THE NEAREST EXIT!
PLATFORM 3 NORTHBOUND
EUSTON CAMDEN TOWN
WAY OUT
MARIA...?
RUN!
HRRROOOOO
OUTTA MY WAY!

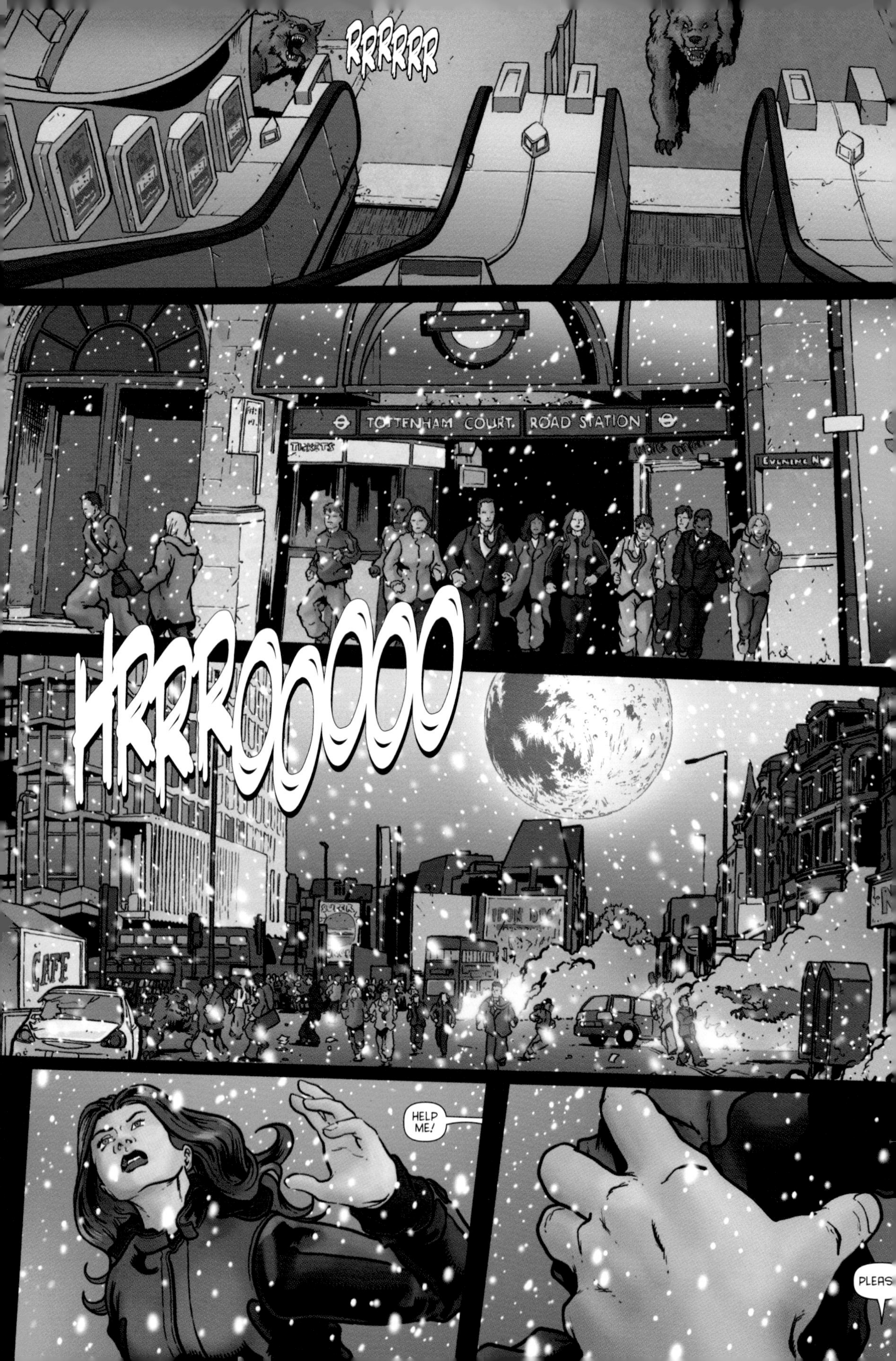
RRRRRR
TOTTENHAM COURT ROAD STATION
TICKETS
HRRROOOOO
CAFE
HELP ME!
PLEAS

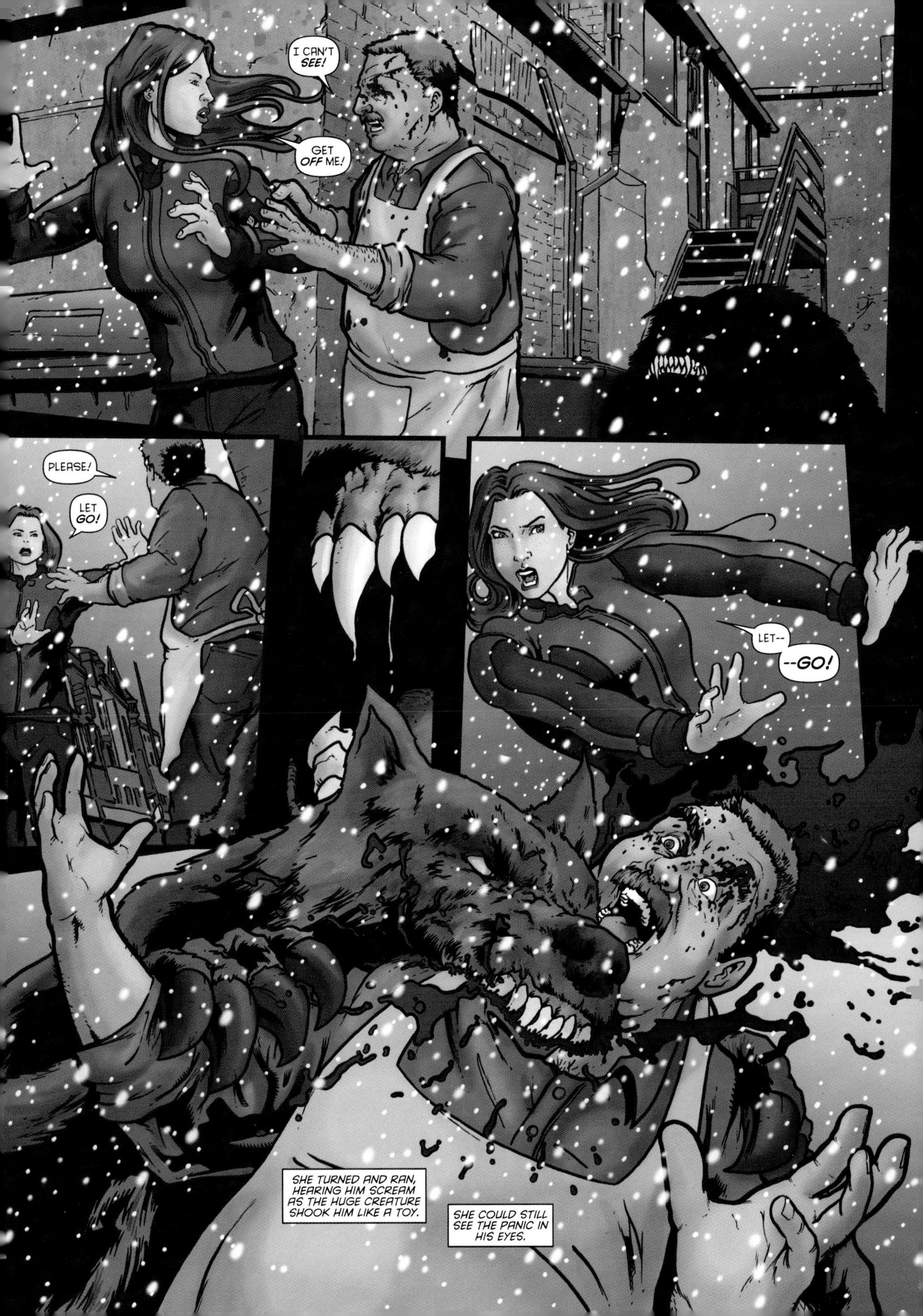
I CAN'T SEE!
GET OFF ME!
PLEASE!
LET GO!
LET--
--GO!
SHE TURNED AND RAN, HEARING HIM SCREAM AS THE HUGE CREATURE SHOOK HIM LIKE A TOY.
SHE COULD STILL SEE THE PANIC IN HIS EYES.

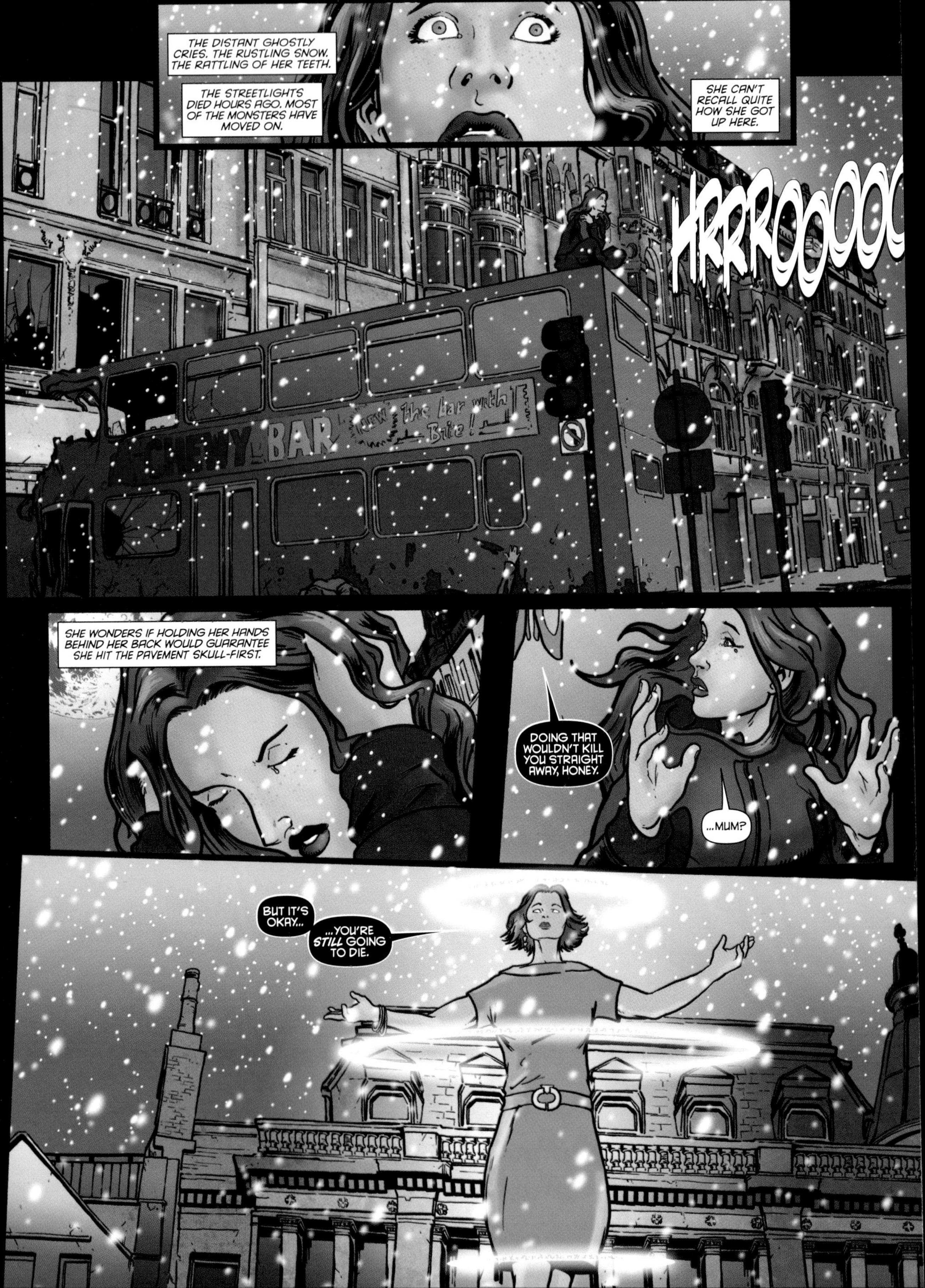
THE DISTANT GHOSTLY CRIES. THE RUSTLING SNOW. THE RATTLING OF HER TEETH.
THE STREETLIGHTS DIED HOURS AGO. MOST OF THE MONSTERS HAVE MOVED ON.
SHE CAN'T RECALL QUITE HOW SHE GOT UP HERE.
HRRROOOOO
BAR
NEW The bar with Bite!
SHE WONDERS IF HOLDING HER HANDS BEHIND HER BACK WOULD GUARANTEE SHE HIT THE PAVEMENT SKULL-FIRST.
DOING THAT WOULDN'T KILL YOU STRAIGHT AWAY, HONEY.
...MUM?
BUT IT'S OKAY...
...YOU'RE *STILL* GOING TO DIE.

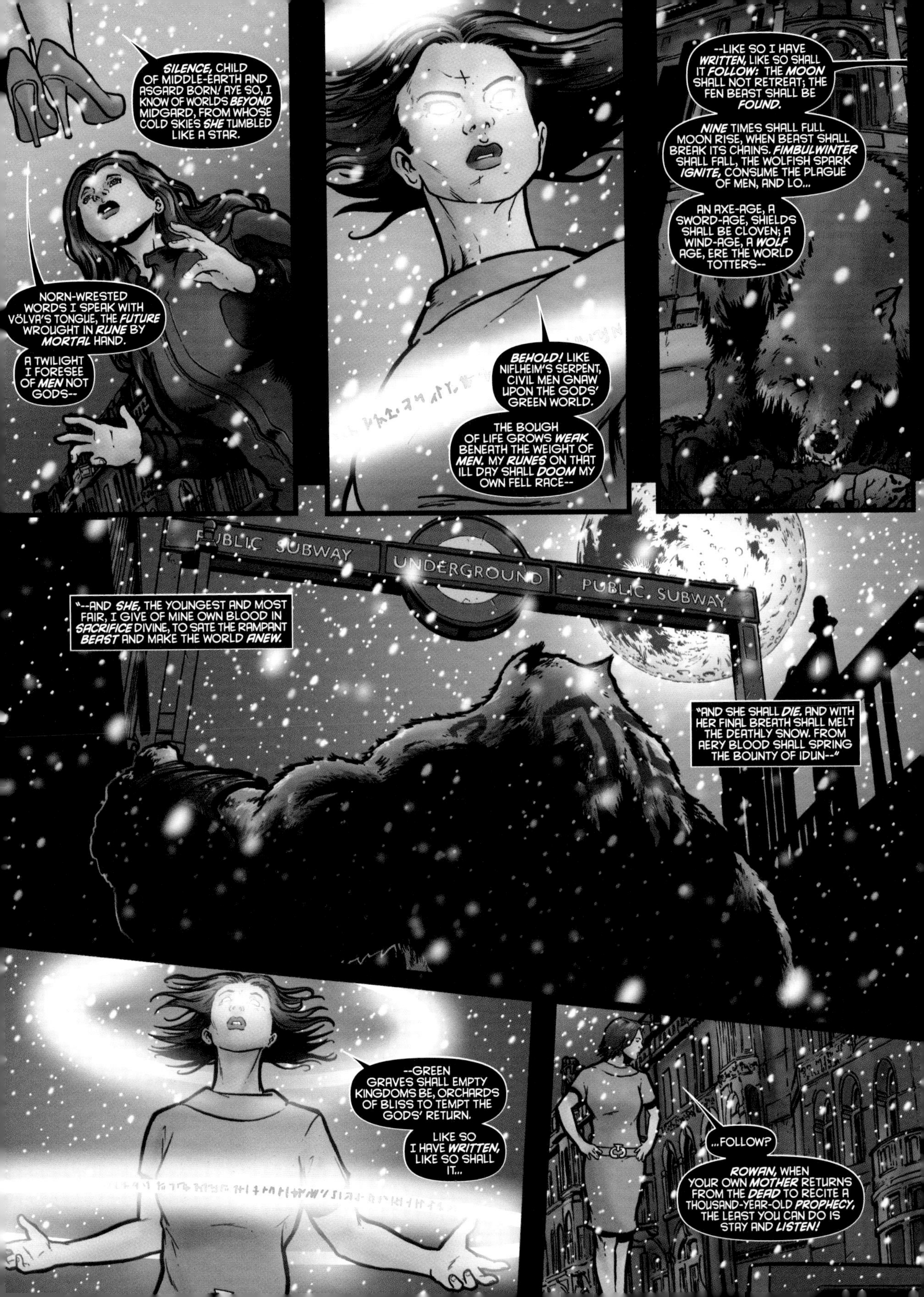
SILENCE, CHILD OF MIDDLE-EARTH AND ASGARD BORN! AYE SO, I KNOW OF WORLDS BEYOND MIDGARD, FROM WHOSE COLD SKIES SHE TUMBLED LIKE A STAR.
NORN-WRESTED WORDS I SPEAK WITH VÖLVA'S TONGUE, THE FUTURE WROUGHT IN RUNE BY MORTAL HAND.
A TWILIGHT I FORESEE OF MEN NOT GODS--
BEHOLD! LIKE NIFLHEIM'S SERPENT, CIVIL MEN GNAW UPON THE GODS' GREEN WORLD.
THE BOUGH OF LIFE GROWS WEAK BENEATH THE WEIGHT OF MEN. MY RUNES ON THAT ILL DAY SHALL DOOM MY OWN FELL RACE--
--LIKE SO I HAVE WRITTEN, LIKE SO SHALL IT FOLLOW: THE MOON SHALL NOT RETREAT; THE FEN BEAST SHALL BE FOUND.
NINE TIMES SHALL FULL MOON RISE, WHEN BEAST SHALL BREAK ITS CHAINS. FIMBULWINTER SHALL FALL, THE WOLFISH SPARK IGNITE, CONSUME THE PLAGUE OF MEN, AND LO...
AN AXE-AGE, A SWORD-AGE, SHIELDS SHALL BE CLOVEN; A WIND-AGE, A WOLF AGE, ERE THE WORLD TOTTERS--
PUBLIC SUBWAY
UNDERGROUND
PUBLIC SUBWAY
"--AND SHE, THE YOUNGEST AND MOST FAIR, I GIVE OF MINE OWN BLOOD IN SACRIFICE DIVINE, TO SATE THE RAMPANT BEAST AND MAKE THE WORLD ANEW.
"AND SHE SHALL DIE. AND WITH HER FINAL BREATH SHALL MELT THE DEATHLY SNOW. FROM AERY BLOOD SHALL SPRING THE BOUNTY OF IDUN--"
--GREEN GRAVES SHALL EMPTY KINGDOMS BE, ORCHARDS OF BLISS TO TEMPT THE GODS' RETURN.
LIKE SO I HAVE WRITTEN, LIKE SO SHALL IT...
...FOLLOW?
ROWAN, WHEN YOUR OWN MOTHER RETURNS FROM THE DEAD TO RECITE A THOUSAND-YEAR-OLD PROPHECY, THE LEAST YOU CAN DO IS STAY AND LISTEN!

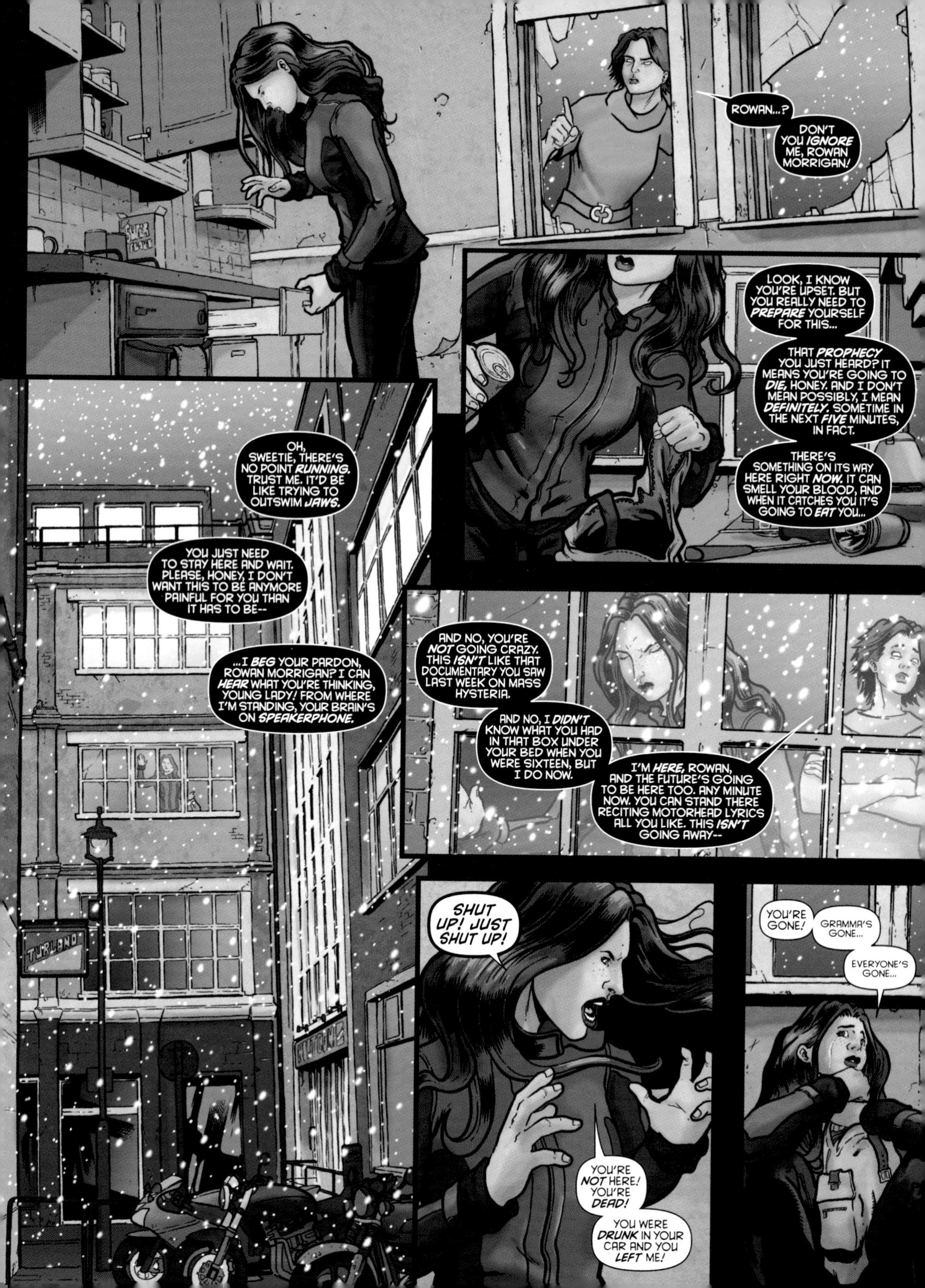

ROWAN...?
DON'T YOU IGNORE ME, ROWAN MORRIGAN!
LOOK, I KNOW YOU'RE UPSET. BUT YOU REALLY NEED TO PREPARE YOURSELF FOR THIS...
THAT PROPHECY YOU JUST HEARD? IT MEANS YOU'RE GOING TO DIE, HONEY. AND I DON'T MEAN POSSIBLY, I MEAN DEFINITELY. SOMETIME IN THE NEXT FIVE MINUTES, IN FACT.
THERE'S SOMETHING ON ITS WAY HERE RIGHT NOW. IT CAN SMELL YOUR BLOOD, AND WHEN IT CATCHES YOU IT'S GOING TO EAT YOU...
OH, SWEETIE, THERE'S NO POINT RUNNING. TRUST ME. IT'D BE LIKE TRYING TO OUTSWIM JAWS.
YOU JUST NEED TO STAY HERE AND WAIT. PLEASE, HONEY, I DON'T WANT THIS TO BE ANYMORE PAINFUL FOR YOU THAN IT HAS TO BE--
...I BEG YOUR PARDON, ROWAN MORRIGAN? I CAN HEAR WHAT YOU'RE THINKING, YOUNG LADY! FROM WHERE I'M STANDING, YOUR BRAIN'S ON SPEAKERPHONE.
TURLAND
AND NO, YOU'RE NOT GOING CRAZY. THIS ISN'T LIKE THAT DOCUMENTARY YOU SAW LAST WEEK ON MASS HYSTERIA.
AND NO, I DIDN'T KNOW WHAT YOU HAD IN THAT BOX UNDER YOUR BED WHEN YOU WERE SIXTEEN, BUT I DO NOW.
I'M HERE, ROWAN, AND THE FUTURE'S GOING TO BE HERE TOO. ANY MINUTE NOW. YOU CAN STAND THERE RECITING MOTORHEAD LYRICS ALL YOU LIKE. THIS ISN'T GOING AWAY--
SHUT UP! JUST SHUT UP!
YOU'RE NOT HERE! YOU'RE DEAD!
YOU WERE DRUNK IN YOUR CAR AND YOU LEFT ME!
YOU'RE GONE!
GRAMMA'S GONE...
EVERYONE'S GONE...

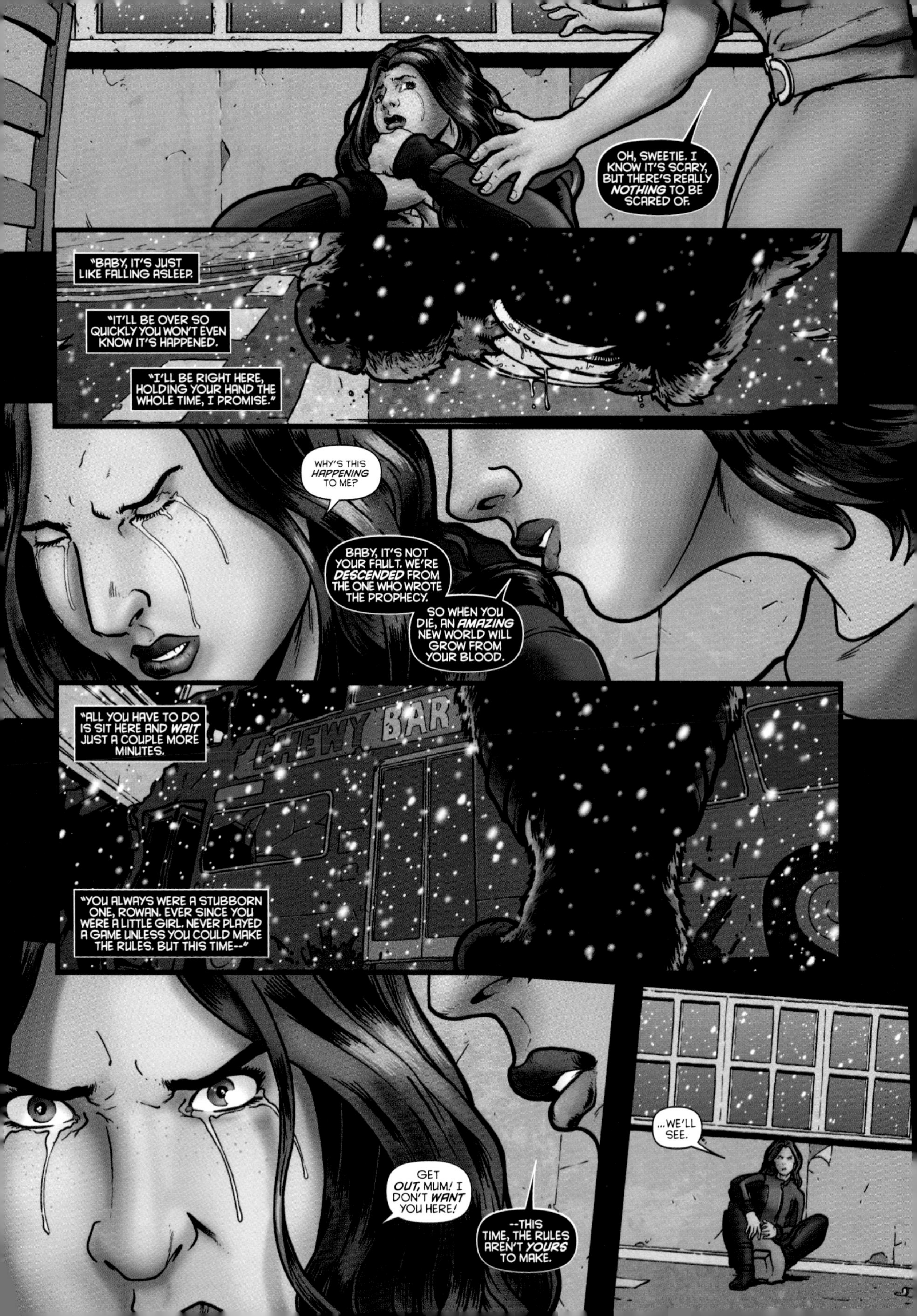
OH, SWEETIE. I KNOW IT'S SCARY, BUT THERE'S REALLY *NOTHING* TO BE SCARED OF.
"BABY, IT'S JUST LIKE FALLING ASLEEP.
"IT'LL BE OVER SO QUICKLY YOU WON'T EVEN KNOW IT'S HAPPENED.
"I'LL BE RIGHT HERE, HOLDING YOUR HAND THE WHOLE TIME, I PROMISE."
WHY'S THIS *HAPPENING* TO ME?
BABY, IT'S NOT YOUR FAULT. WE'RE *DESCENDED* FROM THE ONE WHO WROTE THE PROPHECY.
SO WHEN YOU DIE, AN *AMAZING* NEW WORLD WILL GROW FROM YOUR BLOOD.
"ALL YOU HAVE TO DO IS SIT HERE AND *WAIT* JUST A COUPLE MORE MINUTES.
CHEWY BAR
"YOU ALWAYS WERE A STUBBORN ONE, ROWAN. EVER SINCE YOU WERE A LITTLE GIRL. NEVER PLAYED A GAME UNLESS YOU COULD MAKE THE RULES. BUT THIS TIME--"
GET *OUT,* MUM! I DON'T *WANT* YOU HERE!
--THIS TIME, THE RULES AREN'T *YOURS* TO MAKE.
...WE'LL SEE.

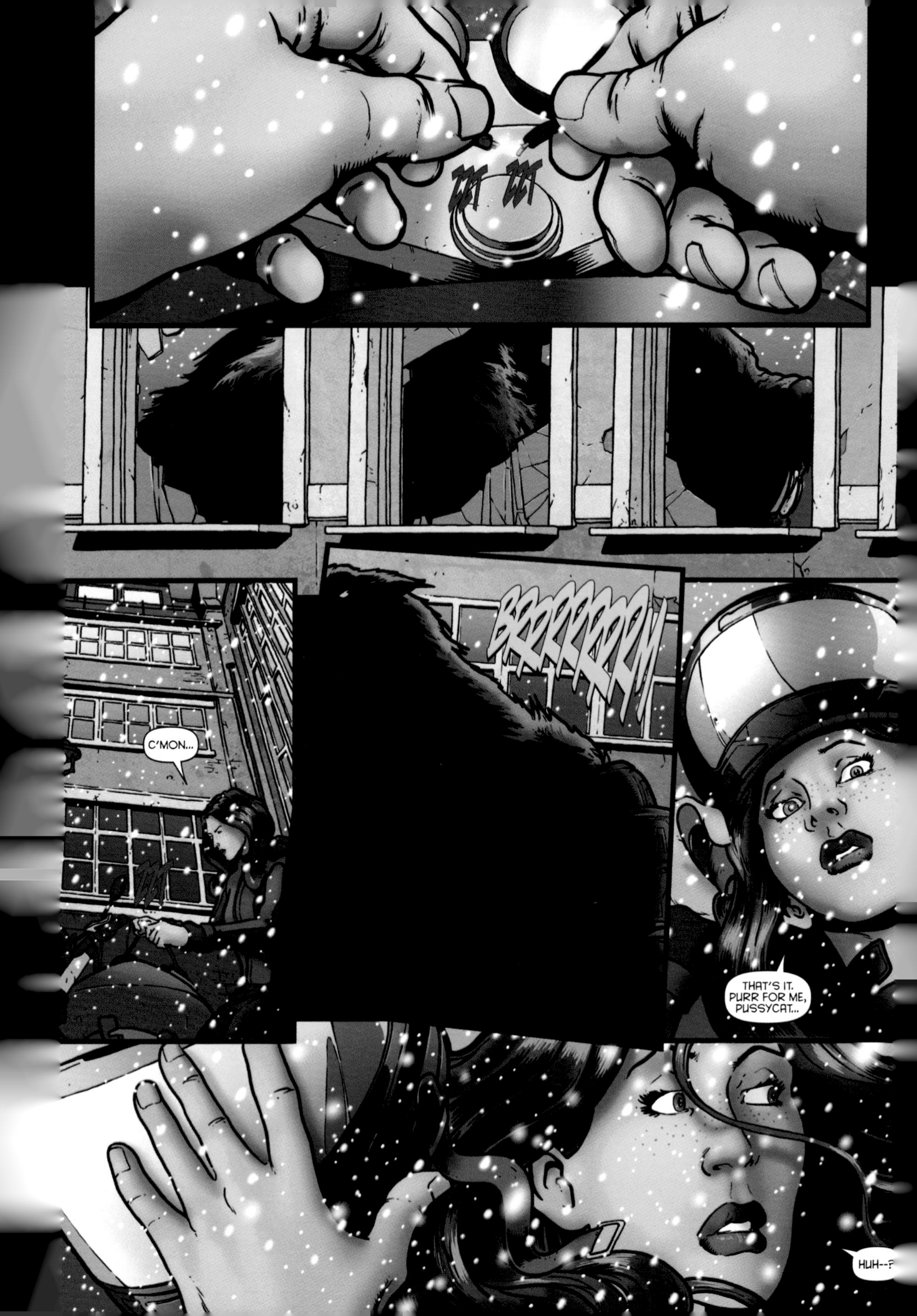
ZZT ZZT
BRRRRRRM
C'MON...
THAT'S IT. PURR FOR ME, PUSSYCAT...
HUH--?

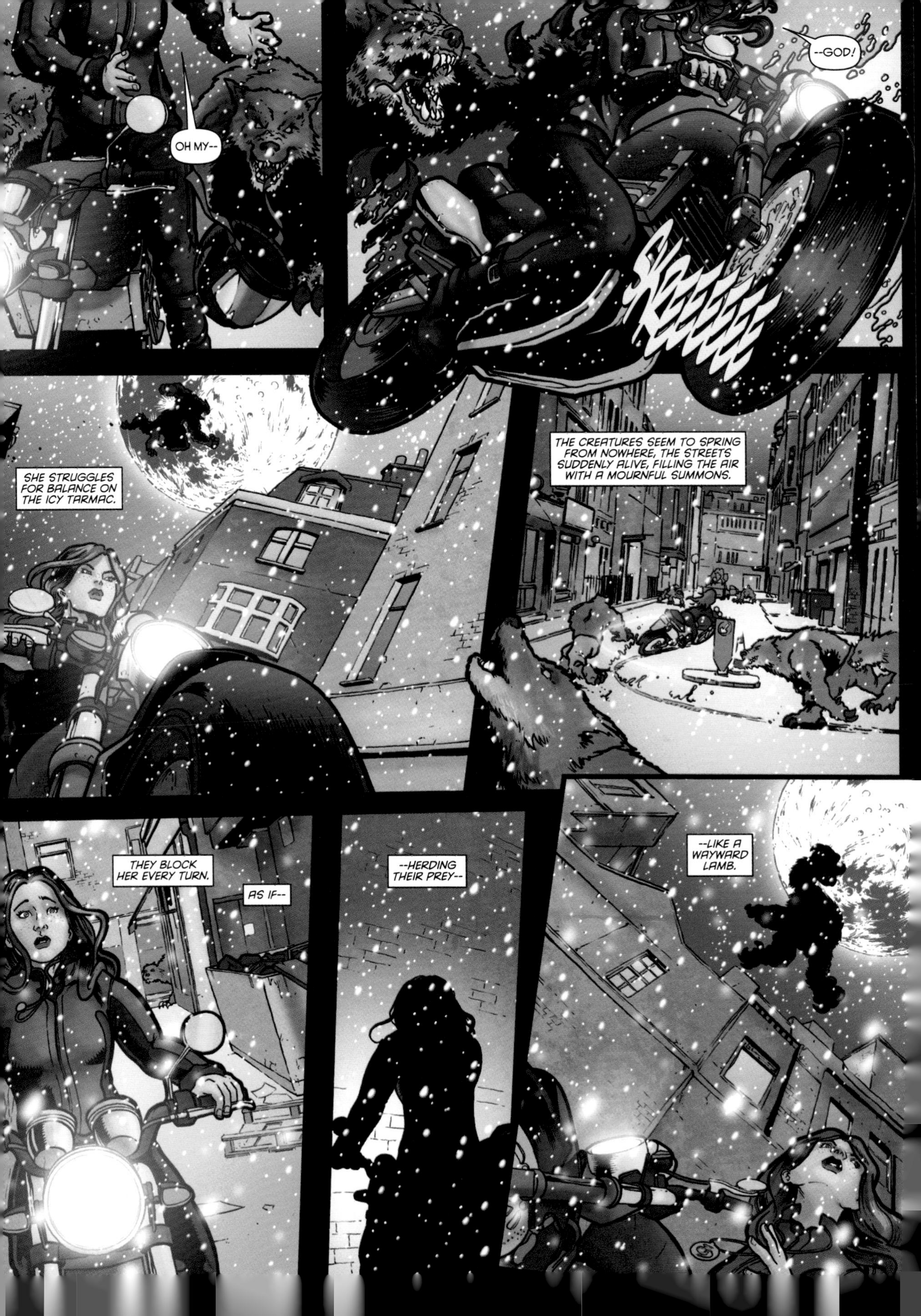
OH MY--
--GOD!
SKREEEEE
SHE STRUGGLES FOR BALANCE ON THE ICY TARMAC.
THE CREATURES SEEM TO SPRING FROM NOWHERE, THE STREETS SUDDENLY ALIVE, FILLING THE AIR WITH A MOURNFUL SUMMONS.
THEY BLOCK HER EVERY TURN.
AS IF--
--HERDING THEIR PREY--
--LIKE A WAYWARD LAMB.

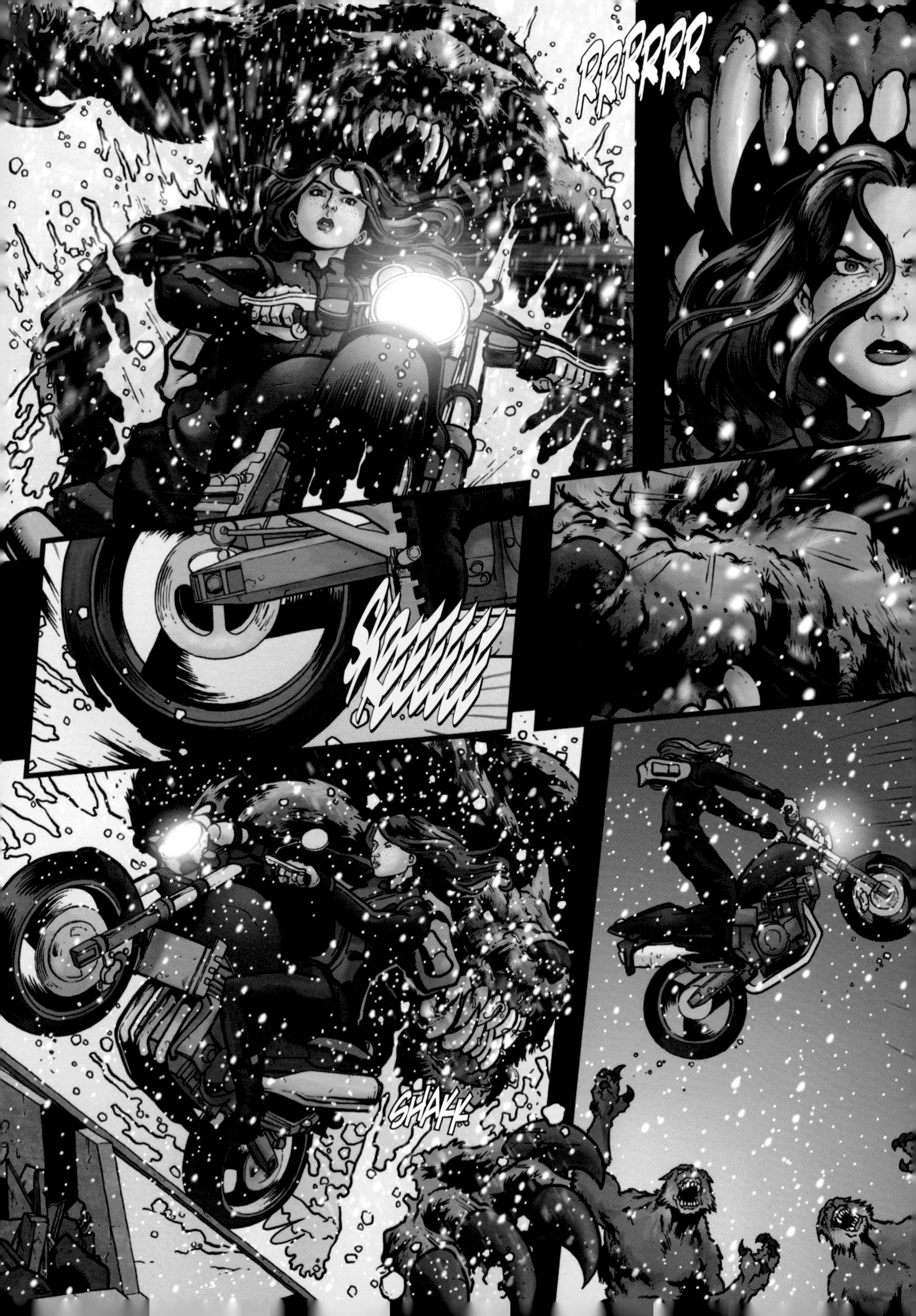
RRRRRR
SKREEEEEE
SHAKK

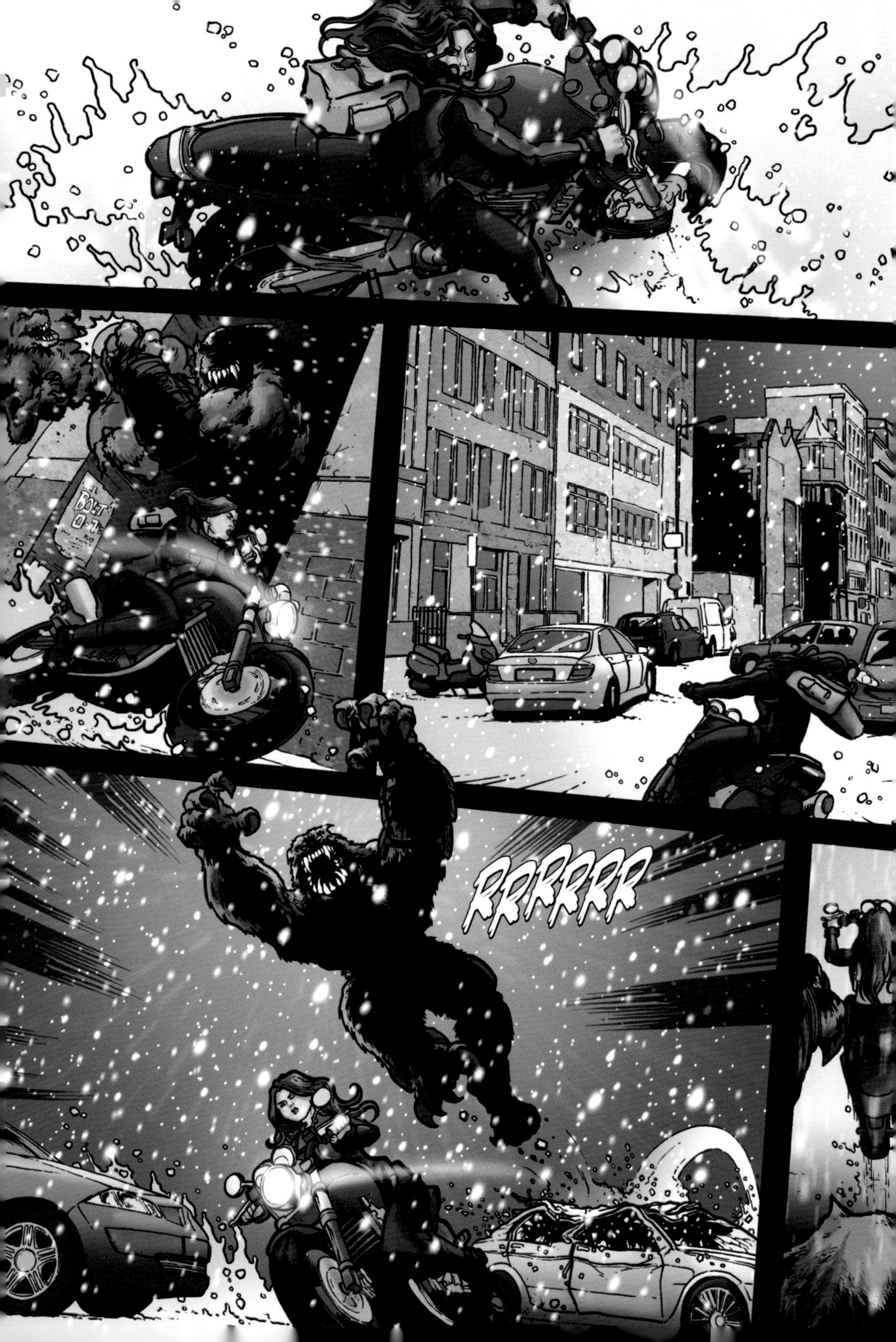
BOLT
RRRRRR

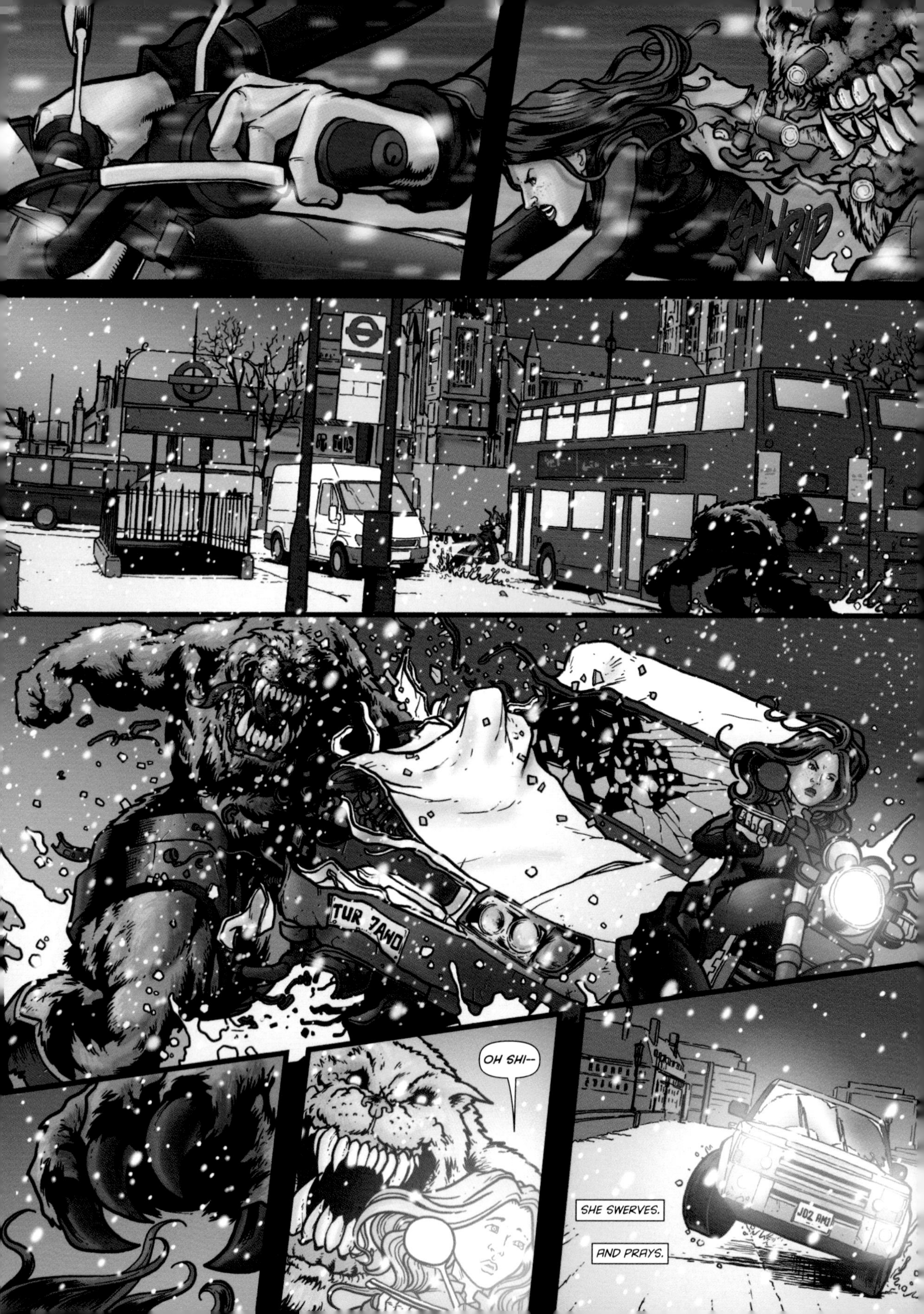
SHHRIP
TUR 7ANO
OH SHI--
JD2 AM1
SHE SWERVES.
AND PRAYS.

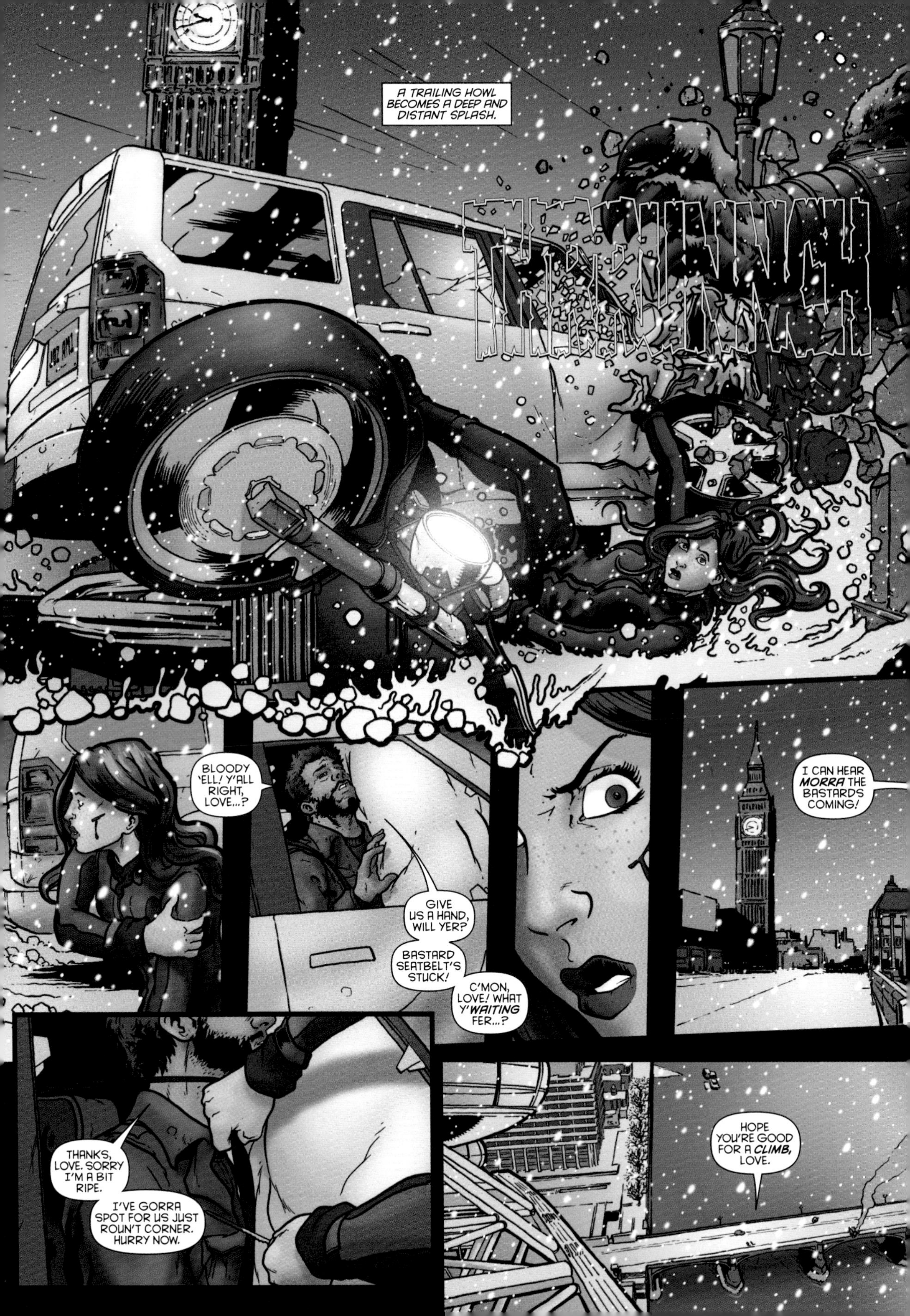
A TRAILING HOWL BECOMES A DEEP AND DISTANT SPLASH.
BLOODY 'ELL! Y'ALL RIGHT, LOVE...?
GIVE US A HAND, WILL YER?
BASTARD SEATBELT'S STUCK!
C'MON, LOVE! WHAT Y'*WAITING* FER...?
I CAN HEAR *MORRA* THE BASTARDS COMING!
THANKS, LOVE. SORRY I'M A BIT RIPE.
I'VE GORRA SPOT FOR US JUST ROUN'T CORNER. HURRY NOW.
HOPE YOU'RE GOOD FOR A *CLIMB,* LOVE.

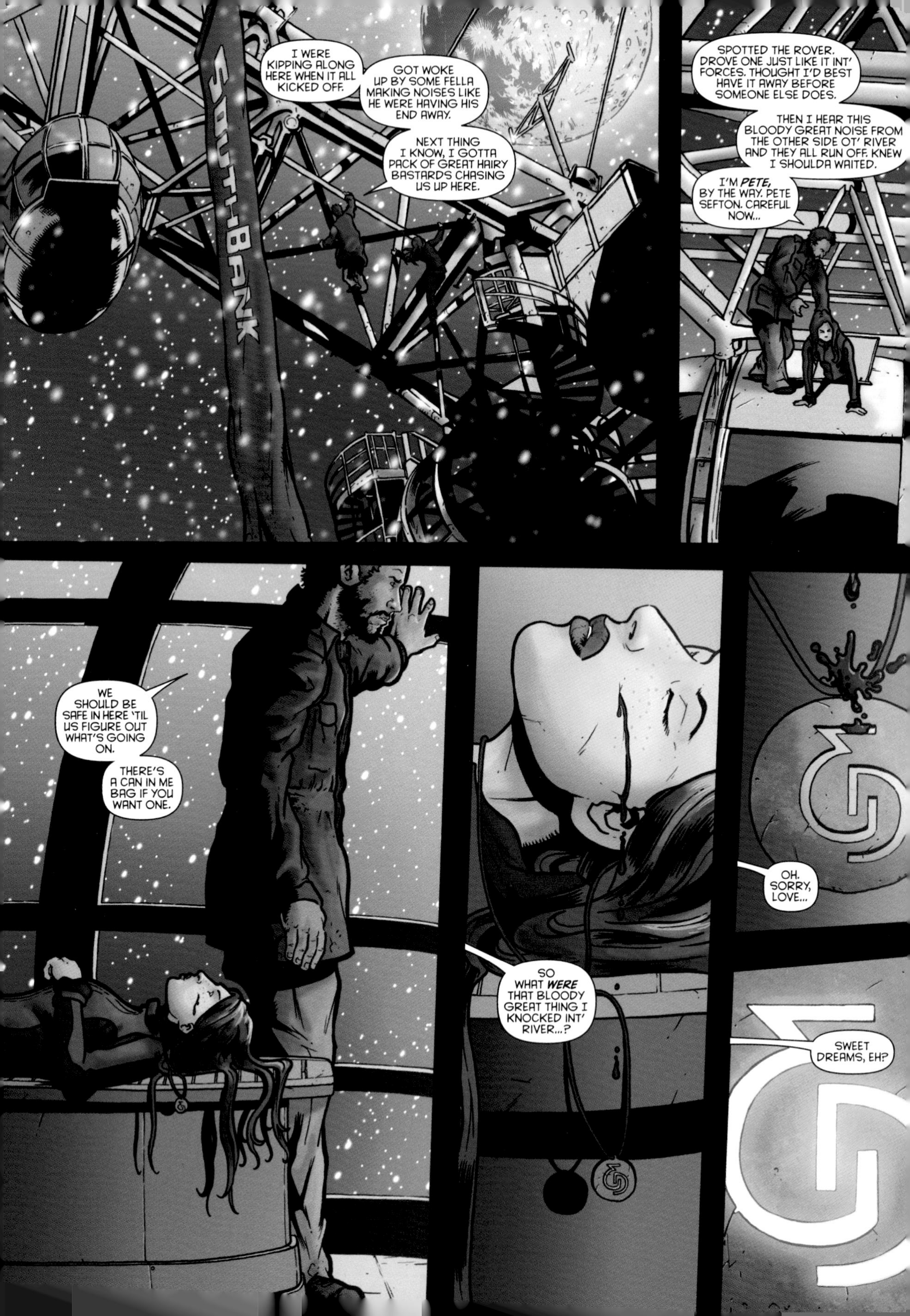
SOUTHBANK
I WERE KIPPING ALONG HERE WHEN IT ALL KICKED OFF.
GOT WOKE UP BY SOME FELLA MAKING NOISES LIKE HE WERE HAVING HIS END AWAY.
NEXT THING I KNOW, I GOTTA PACK OF GREAT HAIRY BASTARDS CHASING US UP HERE.
SPOTTED THE ROVER. DROVE ONE JUST LIKE IT INT' FORCES. THOUGHT I'D BEST HAVE IT AWAY BEFORE SOMEONE ELSE DOES.
THEN I HEAR THIS BLOODY GREAT NOISE FROM THE OTHER SIDE OT' RIVER AND THEY ALL RUN OFF. KNEW I SHOULDA WAITED.
I'M **PETE**, BY THE WAY. PETE SEFTON. CAREFUL NOW...
WE SHOULD BE SAFE IN HERE 'TIL US FIGURE OUT WHAT'S GOING ON.
THERE'S A CAN IN ME BAG IF YOU WANT ONE.
SO WHAT **WERE** THAT BLOODY GREAT THING I KNOCKED INT' RIVER...?
OH. SORRY, LOVE...
SWEET DREAMS, EH?

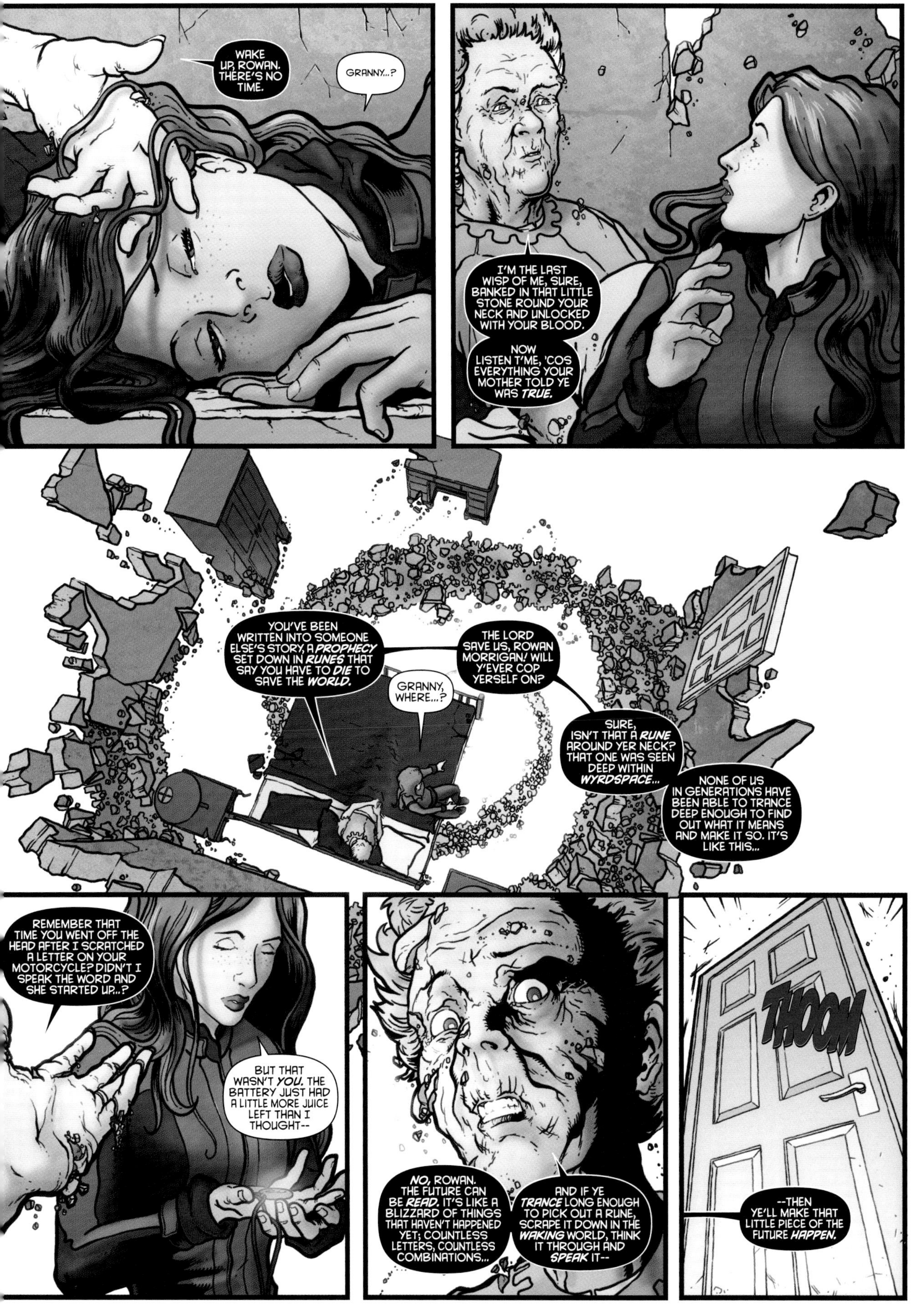
WAKE UP, ROWAN. THERE'S NO TIME.
GRANNY...?
I'M THE LAST WISP OF ME, SURE, BANKED IN THAT LITTLE STONE ROUND YOUR NECK AND UNLOCKED WITH YOUR BLOOD.
NOW LISTEN T'ME, 'COS EVERYTHING YOUR MOTHER TOLD YE WAS *TRUE.*
YOU'VE BEEN WRITTEN INTO SOMEONE ELSE'S STORY, A *PROPHECY* SET DOWN IN *RUNES* THAT SAY YOU HAVE TO *DIE* TO SAVE THE *WORLD.*
GRANNY, WHERE...?
THE LORD SAVE US, ROWAN MORRIGAN! WILL Y'EVER COP YERSELF ON?
SURE, ISN'T THAT A *RUNE* AROUND YER NECK? THAT ONE WAS SEEN DEEP WITHIN *WYRDSPACE*...
NONE OF US IN GENERATIONS HAVE BEEN ABLE TO TRANCE DEEP ENOUGH TO FIND OUT WHAT IT MEANS AND MAKE IT SO. IT'S LIKE THIS...
REMEMBER THAT TIME YOU WENT OFF THE HEAD AFTER I SCRATCHED A LETTER ON YOUR MOTORCYCLE? DIDN'T I SPEAK THE WORD AND SHE STARTED UP...?
BUT THAT WASN'T *YOU.* THE BATTERY JUST HAD A LITTLE MORE JUICE LEFT THAN I THOUGHT--
NO, ROWAN. THE FUTURE CAN BE *READ.* IT'S LIKE A BLIZZARD OF THINGS THAT HAVEN'T HAPPENED YET; COUNTLESS LETTERS, COUNTLESS COMBINATIONS...
AND IF YE *TRANCE* LONG ENOUGH TO PICK OUT A RUNE, SCRAPE IT DOWN IN THE *WAKING* WORLD, THINK IT THROUGH AND *SPEAK* IT--
THOOM
--THEN YE'LL MAKE THAT LITTLE PIECE OF THE FUTURE *HAPPEN.*

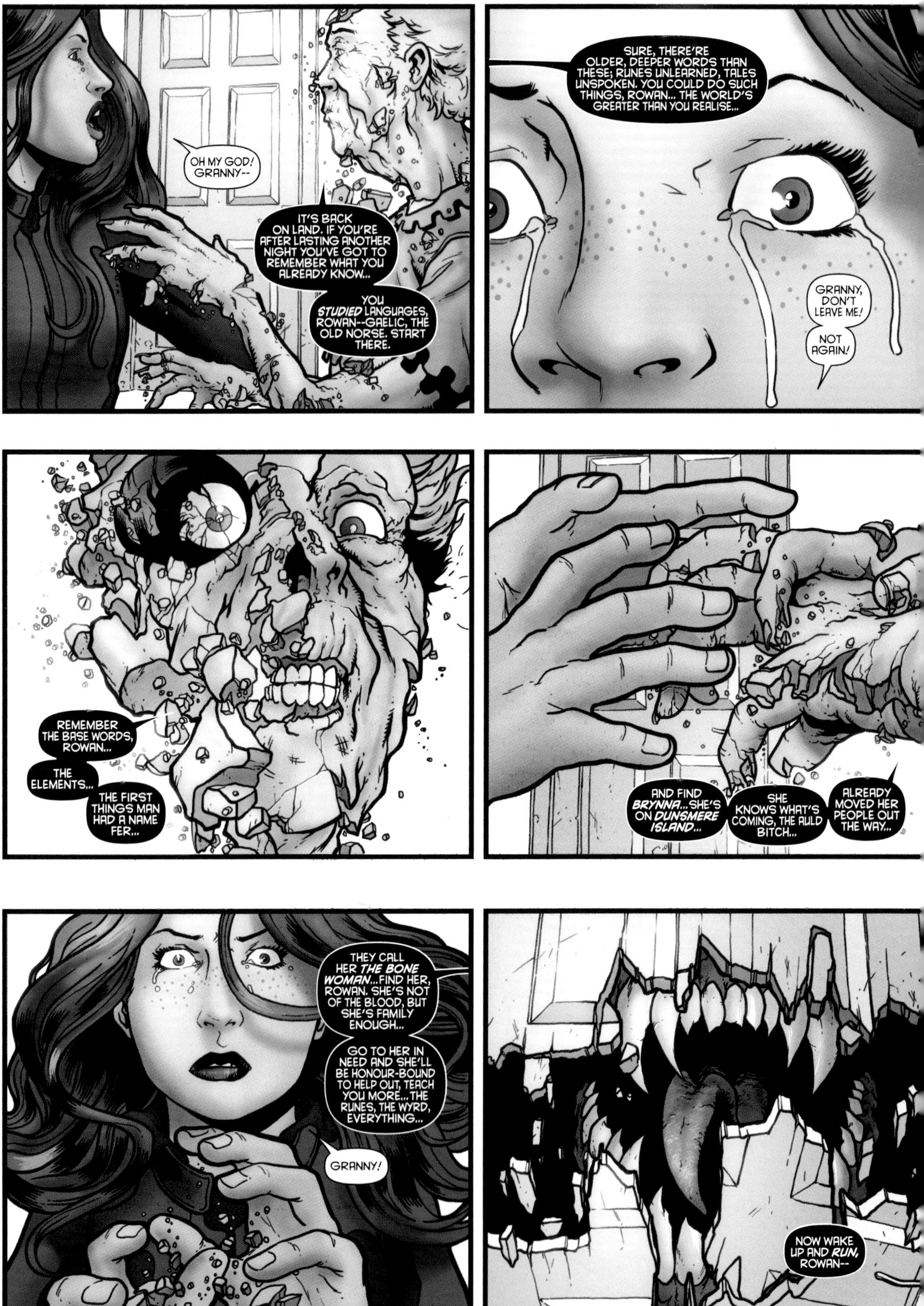
OH MY GOD! GRANNY--
IT'S BACK ON LAND. IF YOU'RE AFTER LASTING ANOTHER NIGHT YOU'VE GOT TO REMEMBER WHAT YOU ALREADY KNOW...
YOU STUDIED LANGUAGES, ROWAN--GAELIC, THE OLD NORSE. START THERE.
SURE, THERE'RE OLDER, DEEPER WORDS THAN THESE; RUNES UNLEARNED, TALES UNSPOKEN. YOU COULD DO SUCH THINGS, ROWAN... THE WORLD'S GREATER THAN YOU REALISE...
GRANNY, DON'T LEAVE ME!
NOT AGAIN!
REMEMBER THE BASE WORDS, ROWAN...
THE ELEMENTS...
THE FIRST THINGS MAN HAD A NAME FER...
AND FIND BRYNNA...SHE'S ON DUNSMERE ISLAND...
SHE KNOWS WHAT'S COMING, THE AULD BITCH...
ALREADY MOVED HER PEOPLE OUT THE WAY...
THEY CALL HER THE BONE WOMAN...FIND HER, ROWAN. SHE'S NOT OF THE BLOOD, BUT SHE'S FAMILY ENOUGH...
GO TO HER IN NEED AND SHE'LL BE HONOUR-BOUND TO HELP OUT, TEACH YOU MORE...THE RUNES, THE WYRD, EVERYTHING...
GRANNY!
NOW WAKE UP AND RUN, ROWAN--

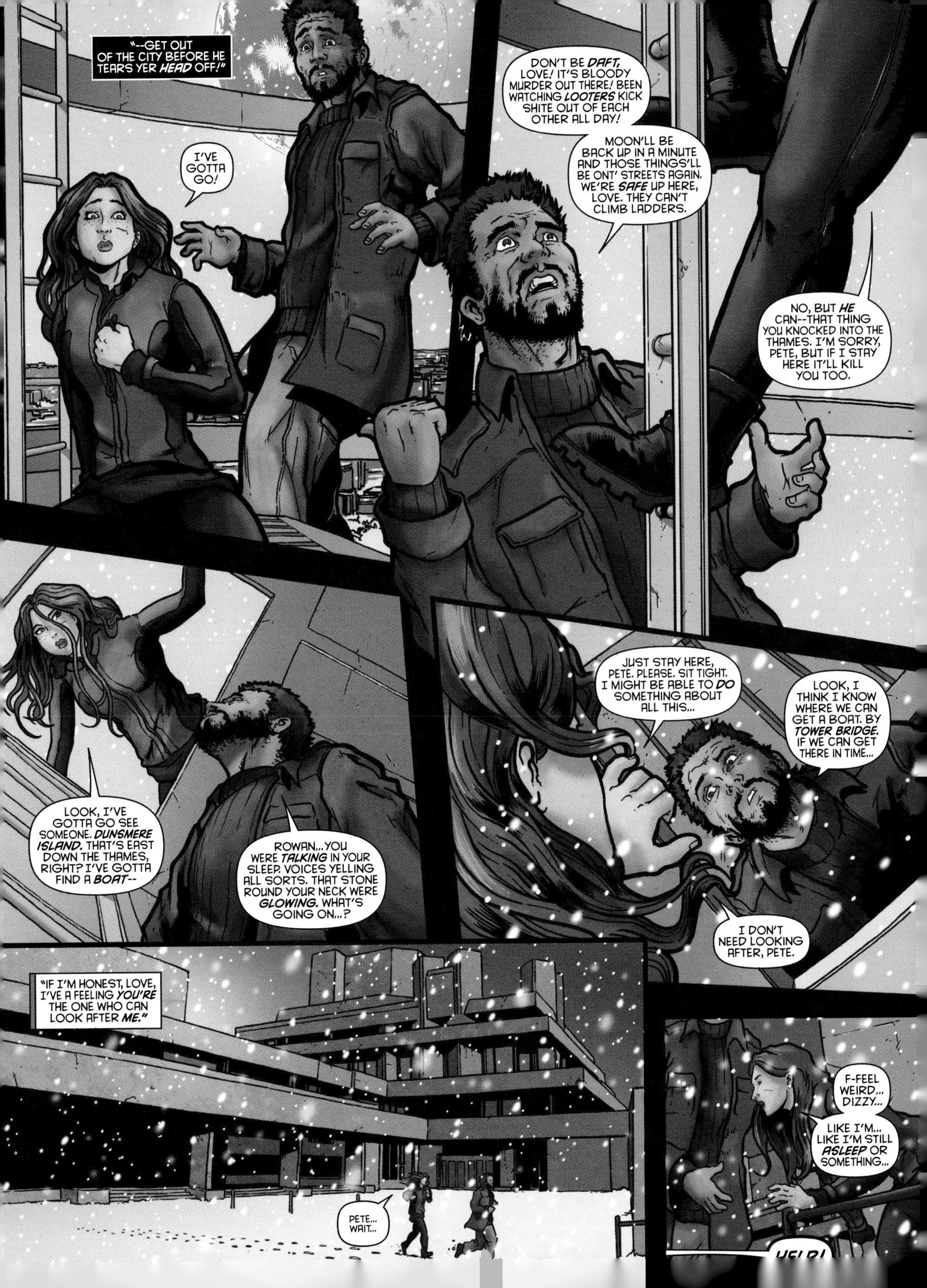
"--GET OUT OF THE CITY BEFORE HE TEARS YER HEAD OFF!"
I'VE GOTTA GO!
DON'T BE DAFT, LOVE! IT'S BLOODY MURDER OUT THERE! BEEN WATCHING LOOTERS KICK SHITE OUT OF EACH OTHER ALL DAY!
MOON'LL BE BACK UP IN A MINUTE AND THOSE THINGS'LL BE ONT' STREETS AGAIN. WE'RE SAFE UP HERE, LOVE. THEY CAN'T CLIMB LADDERS.
NO, BUT HE CAN--THAT THING YOU KNOCKED INTO THE THAMES. I'M SORRY, PETE, BUT IF I STAY HERE IT'LL KILL YOU TOO.
LOOK, I'VE GOTTA GO SEE SOMEONE. DUNSMERE ISLAND. THAT'S EAST DOWN THE THAMES, RIGHT? I'VE GOTTA FIND A BOAT--
ROWAN...YOU WERE TALKING IN YOUR SLEEP. VOICES YELLING ALL SORTS. THAT STONE ROUND YOUR NECK WERE GLOWING. WHAT'S GOING ON...?
JUST STAY HERE, PETE. PLEASE. SIT TIGHT. I MIGHT BE ABLE TO DO SOMETHING ABOUT ALL THIS...
LOOK, I THINK I KNOW WHERE WE CAN GET A BOAT. BY TOWER BRIDGE. IF WE CAN GET THERE IN TIME...
I DON'T NEED LOOKING AFTER, PETE.
"IF I'M HONEST, LOVE, I'VE A FEELING YOU'RE THE ONE WHO CAN LOOK AFTER ME."
PETE... WAIT...
F-FEEL WEIRD... DIZZY...
LIKE I'M... LIKE I'M STILL ASLEEP OR SOMETHING...

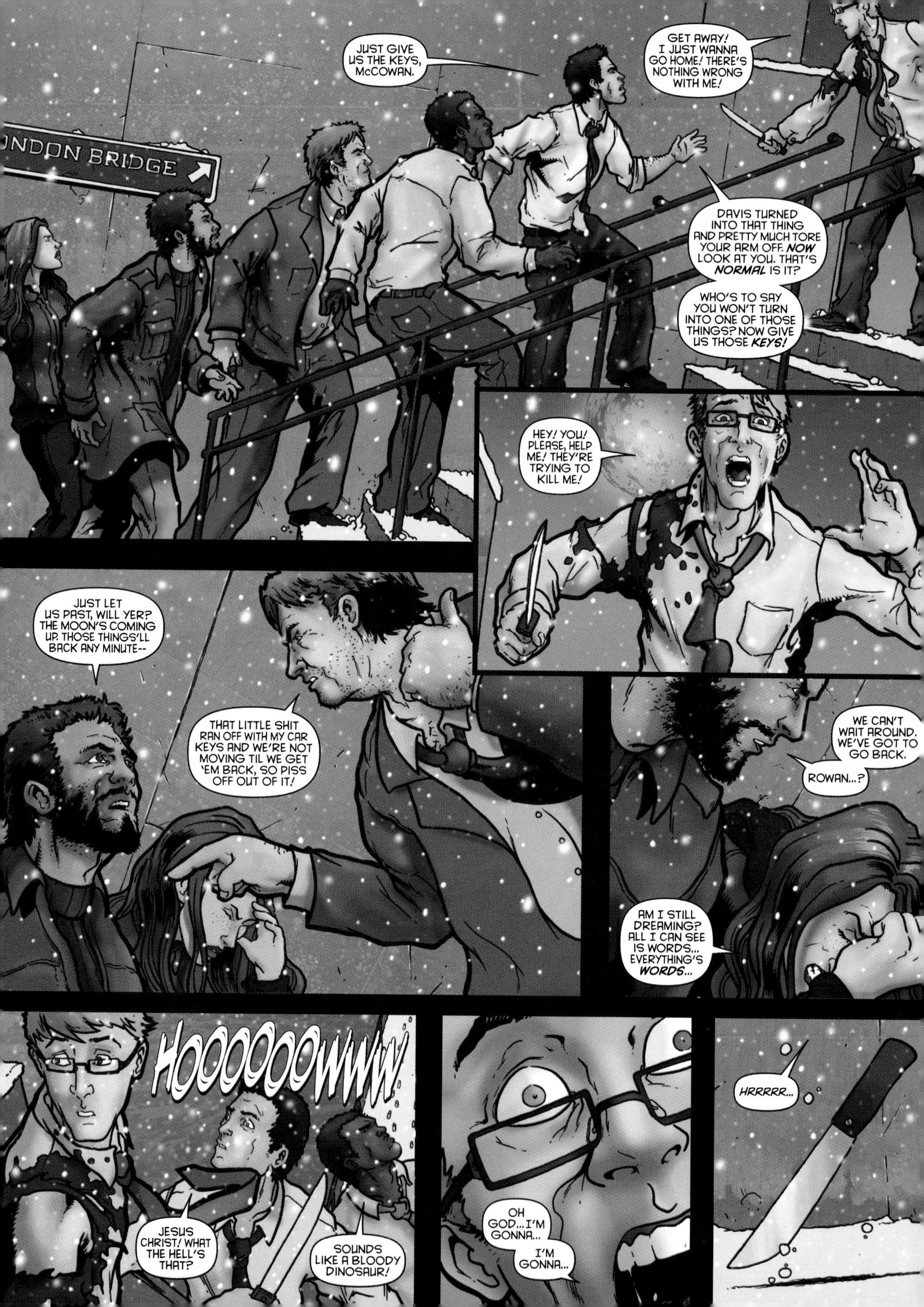
ONDON BRIDGE
JUST GIVE US THE KEYS, McCOWAN.
GET AWAY! I JUST WANNA GO HOME! THERE'S NOTHING WRONG WITH ME!
DAVIS TURNED INTO THAT THING AND PRETTY MUCH TORE YOUR ARM OFF. NOW LOOK AT YOU. THAT'S NORMAL IS IT?
WHO'S TO SAY YOU WON'T TURN INTO ONE OF THOSE THINGS? NOW GIVE US THOSE KEYS!
HEY! YOU! PLEASE, HELP ME! THEY'RE TRYING TO KILL ME!
JUST LET US PAST, WILL YER? THE MOON'S COMING UP. THOSE THINGS'LL BACK ANY MINUTE--
THAT LITTLE SHIT RAN OFF WITH MY CAR KEYS AND WE'RE NOT MOVING TIL WE GET 'EM BACK, SO PISS OFF OUT OF IT!
WE CAN'T WAIT AROUND. WE'VE GOT TO GO BACK.
ROWAN...?
AM I STILL DREAMING? ALL I CAN SEE IS WORDS... EVERYTHING'S WORDS...
HOOOOOOWWW
JESUS CHRIST! WHAT THE HELL'S THAT?
SOUNDS LIKE A BLOODY DINOSAUR!
OH GOD... I'M GONNA...
I'M GONNA...
HRRRRR...

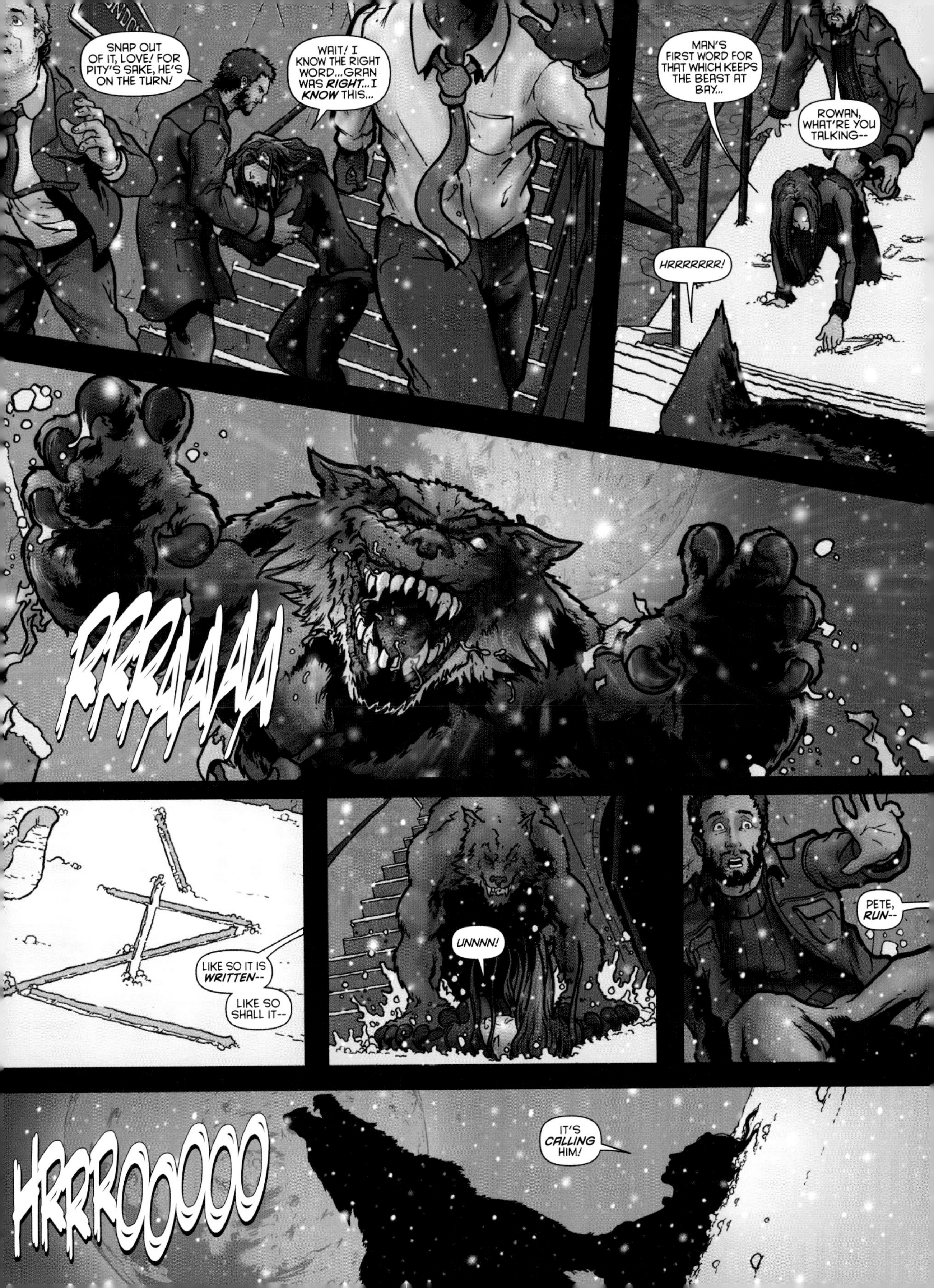
SNAP OUT OF IT, LOVE! FOR PITY'S SAKE, HE'S ON THE TURN!
WAIT! I KNOW THE RIGHT WORD... GRAN WAS RIGHT... I KNOW THIS...
MAN'S FIRST WORD FOR THAT WHICH KEEPS THE BEAST AT BAY...
ROWAN, WHAT'RE YOU TALKING--
HRRRRRRR!
RRRAAAAA
LIKE SO IT IS WRITTEN--
LIKE SO SHALL IT--
UNNNN!
PETE, RUN--
HRRROOOOO
IT'S CALLING HIM!

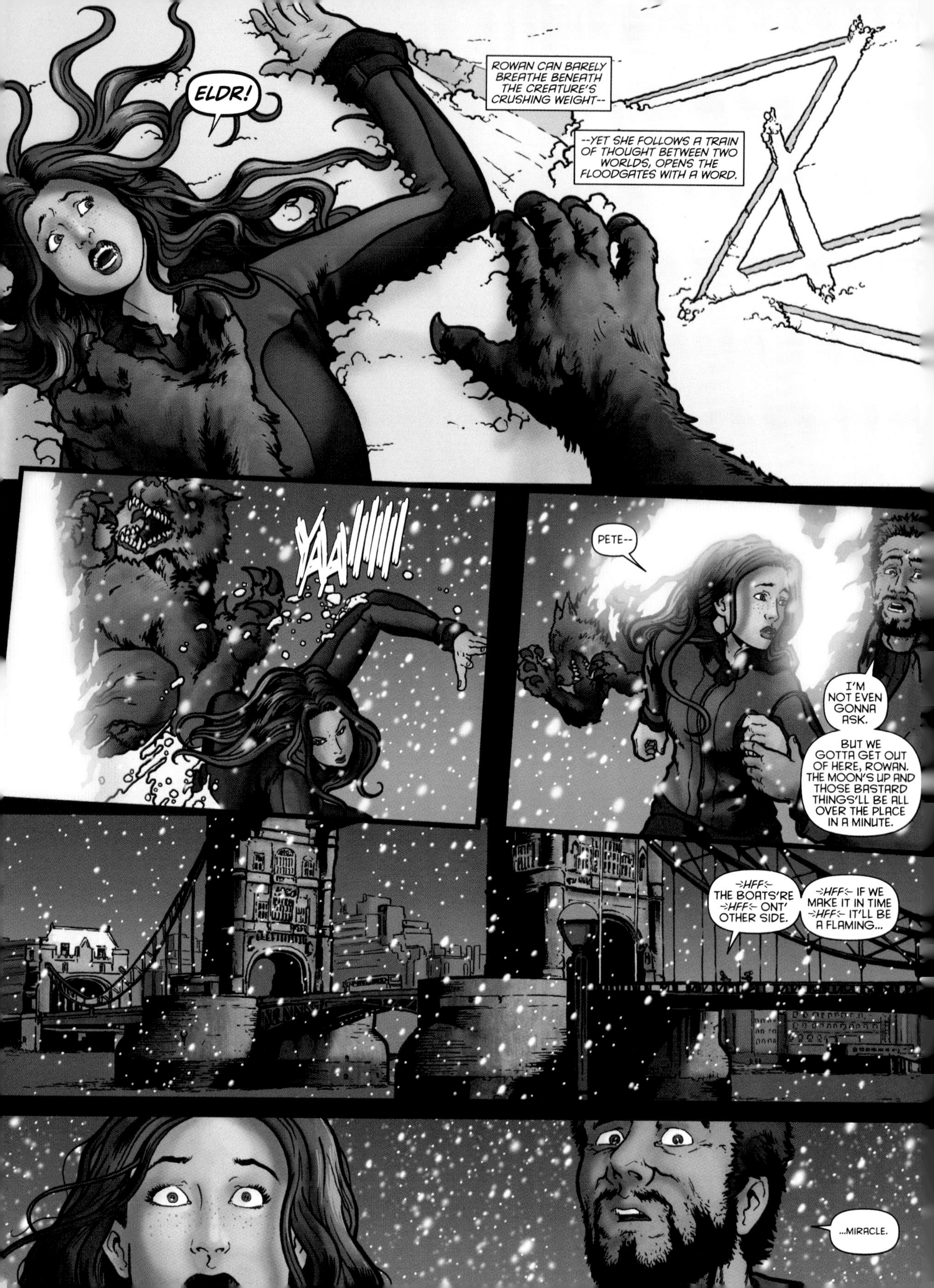

ELDR!
ROWAN CAN BARELY BREATHE BENEATH THE CREATURE'S CRUSHING WEIGHT--
--YET SHE FOLLOWS A TRAIN OF THOUGHT BETWEEN TWO WORLDS, OPENS THE FLOODGATES WITH A WORD.
YAA!!!!!!
PETE--
I'M NOT EVEN GONNA ASK.
BUT WE GOTTA GET OUT OF HERE, ROWAN. THE MOON'S UP AND THOSE BASTARD THINGS'LL BE ALL OVER THE PLACE IN A MINUTE.
-HFF- THE BOATS'RE -HFF- ONT' OTHER SIDE.
-HFF- IF WE MAKE IT IN TIME -HFF- IT'LL BE A FLAMING...
...MIRACLE.

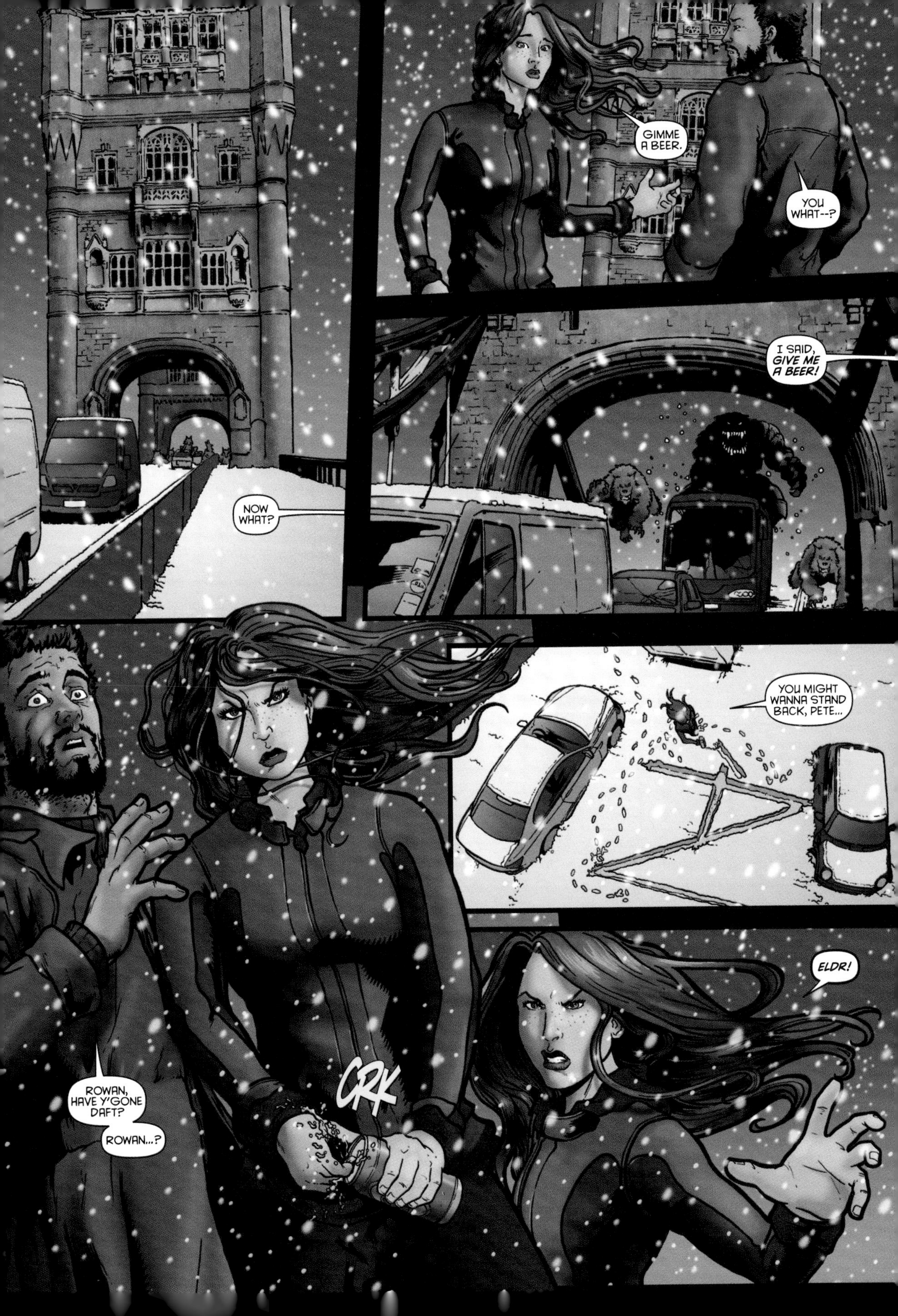
GIMME A BEER.
YOU WHAT--?
I SAID, *GIVE ME A BEER!*
NOW WHAT?
YOU MIGHT WANNA STAND BACK, PETE...
ROWAN, HAVE Y'GONE DAFT?
ROWAN...?
CRK
ELDR!

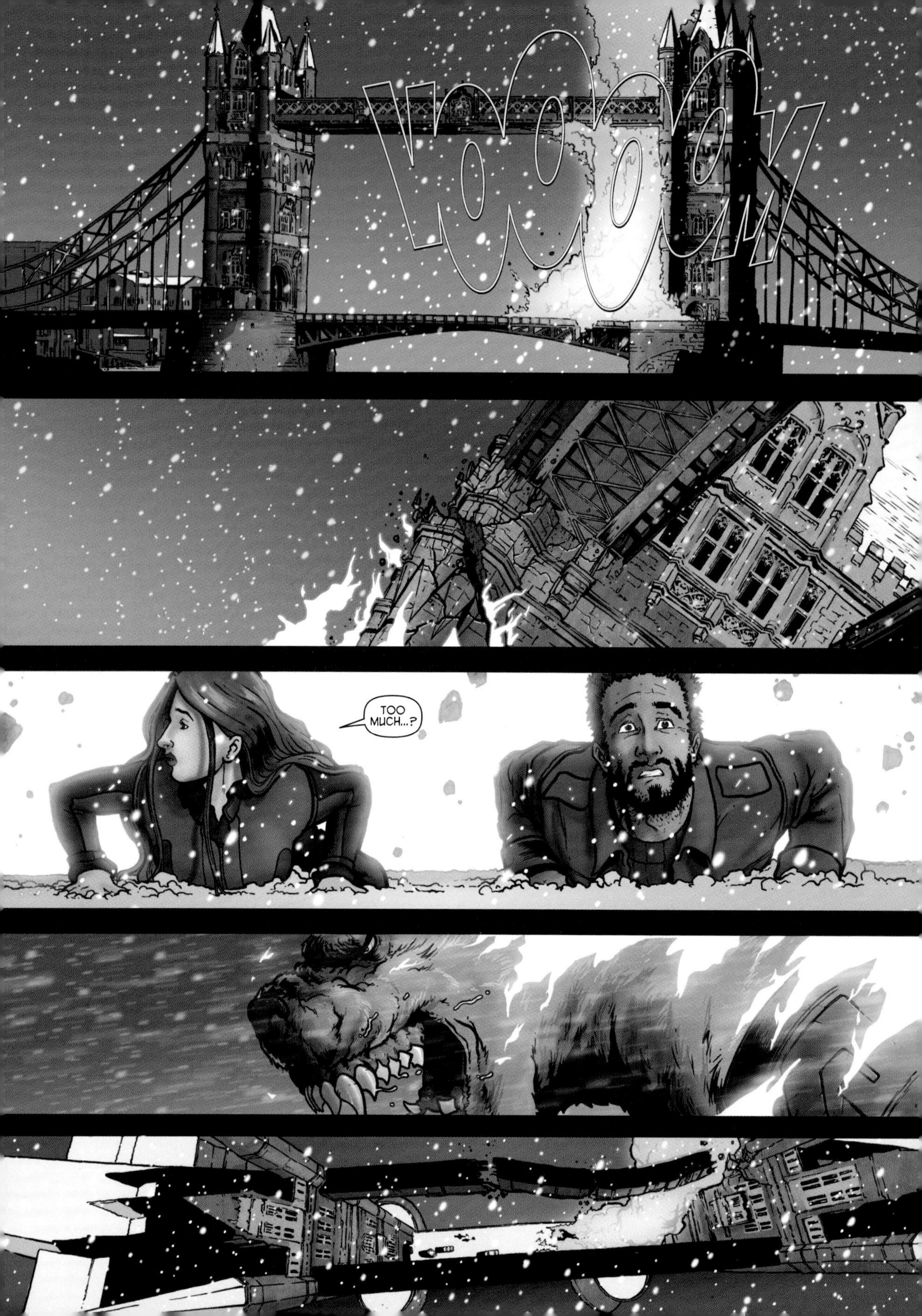
TOO MUCH...?

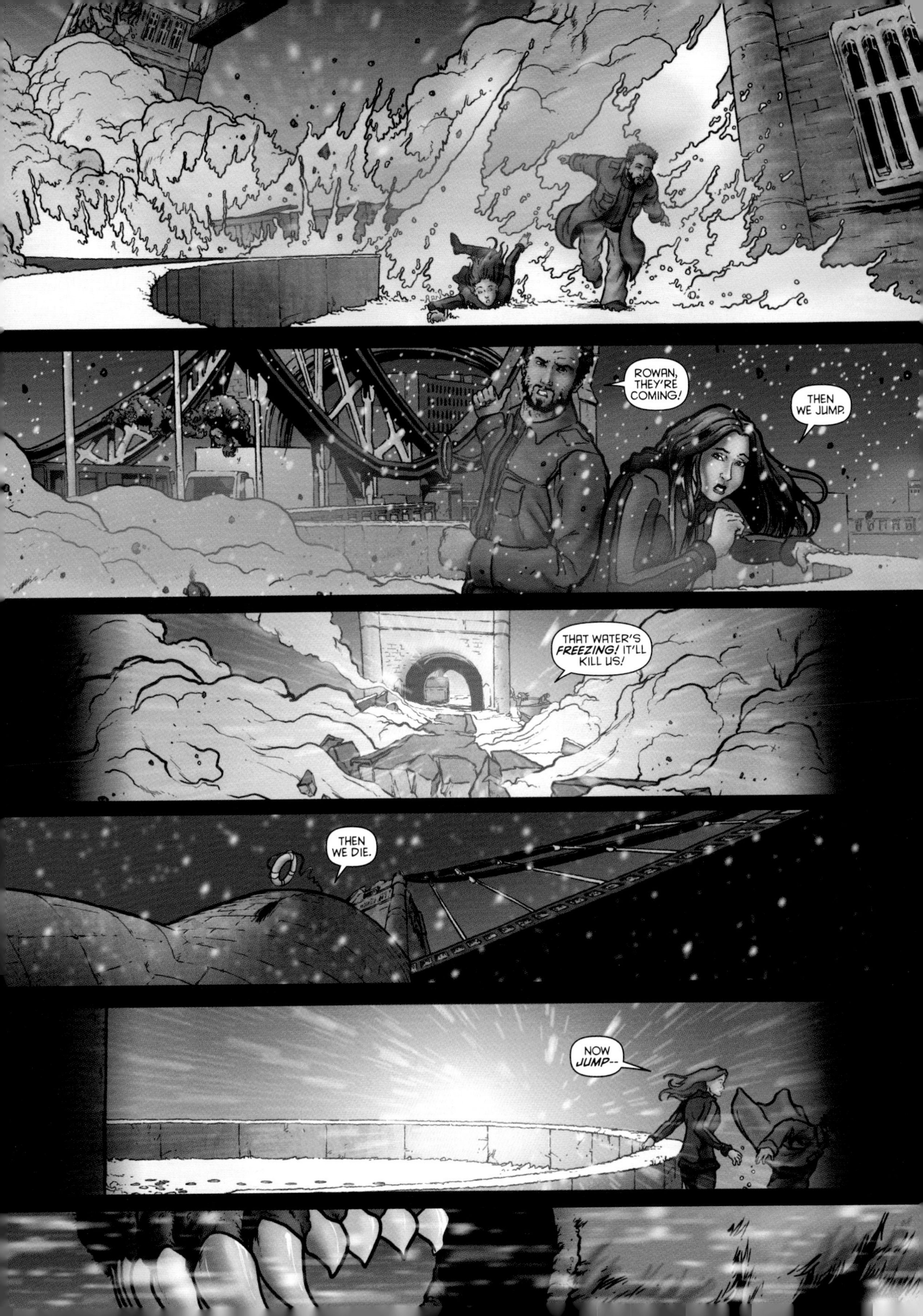
ROWAN, THEY'RE COMING!
THEN WE JUMP.
THAT WATER'S FREEZING! IT'LL KILL US!
THEN WE DIE.
NOW JUMP--

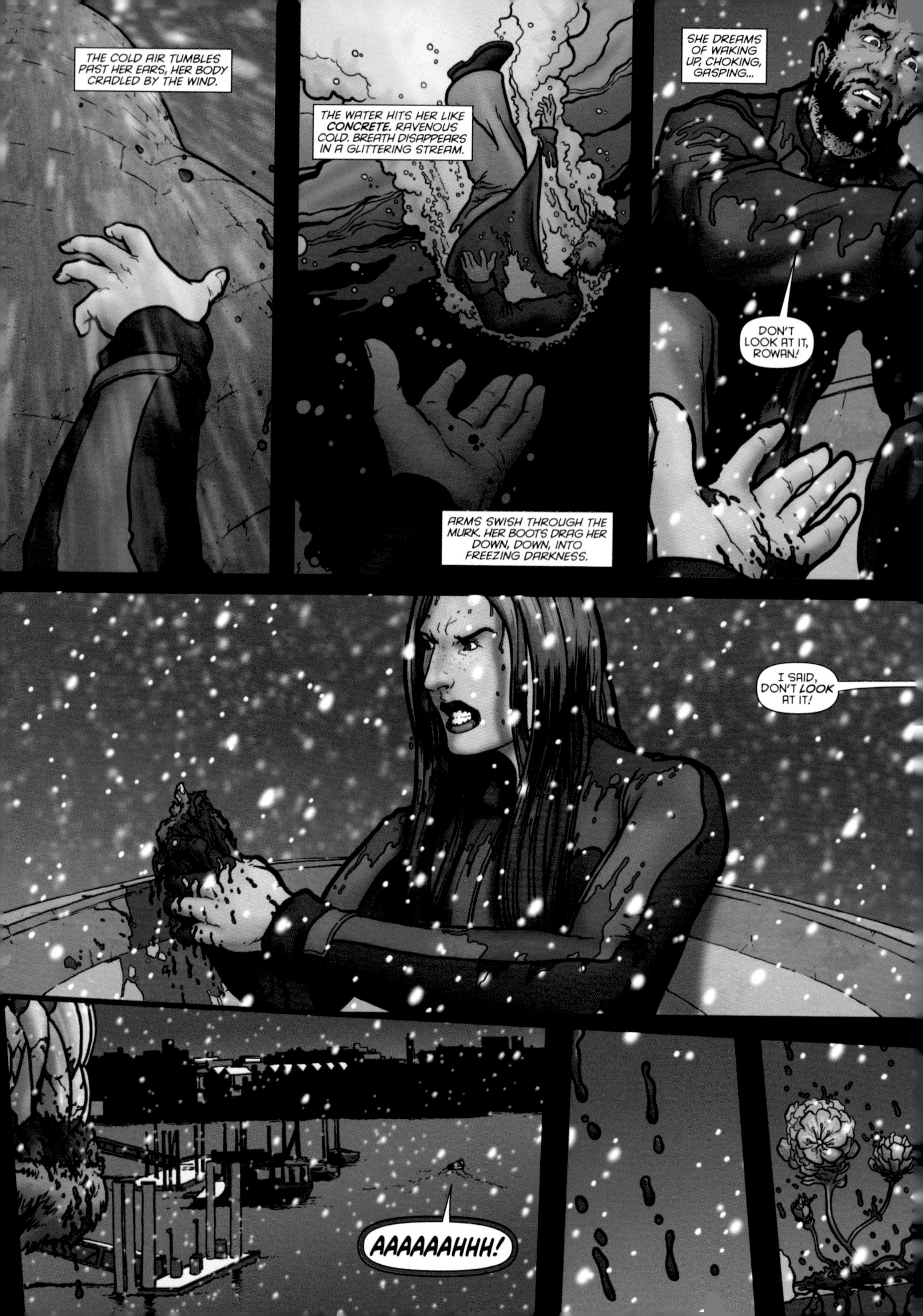
THE COLD AIR TUMBLES PAST HER EARS, HER BODY CRADLED BY THE WIND.
THE WATER HITS HER LIKE CONCRETE. RAVENOUS COLD. BREATH DISAPPEARS IN A GLITTERING STREAM.
ARMS SWISH THROUGH THE MURK. HER BOOTS DRAG HER DOWN, DOWN, INTO FREEZING DARKNESS.
SHE DREAMS OF WAKING UP, CHOKING, GASPING...
DON'T LOOK AT IT, ROWAN!
I SAID, DON'T LOOK AT IT!
AAAAAAHHH!

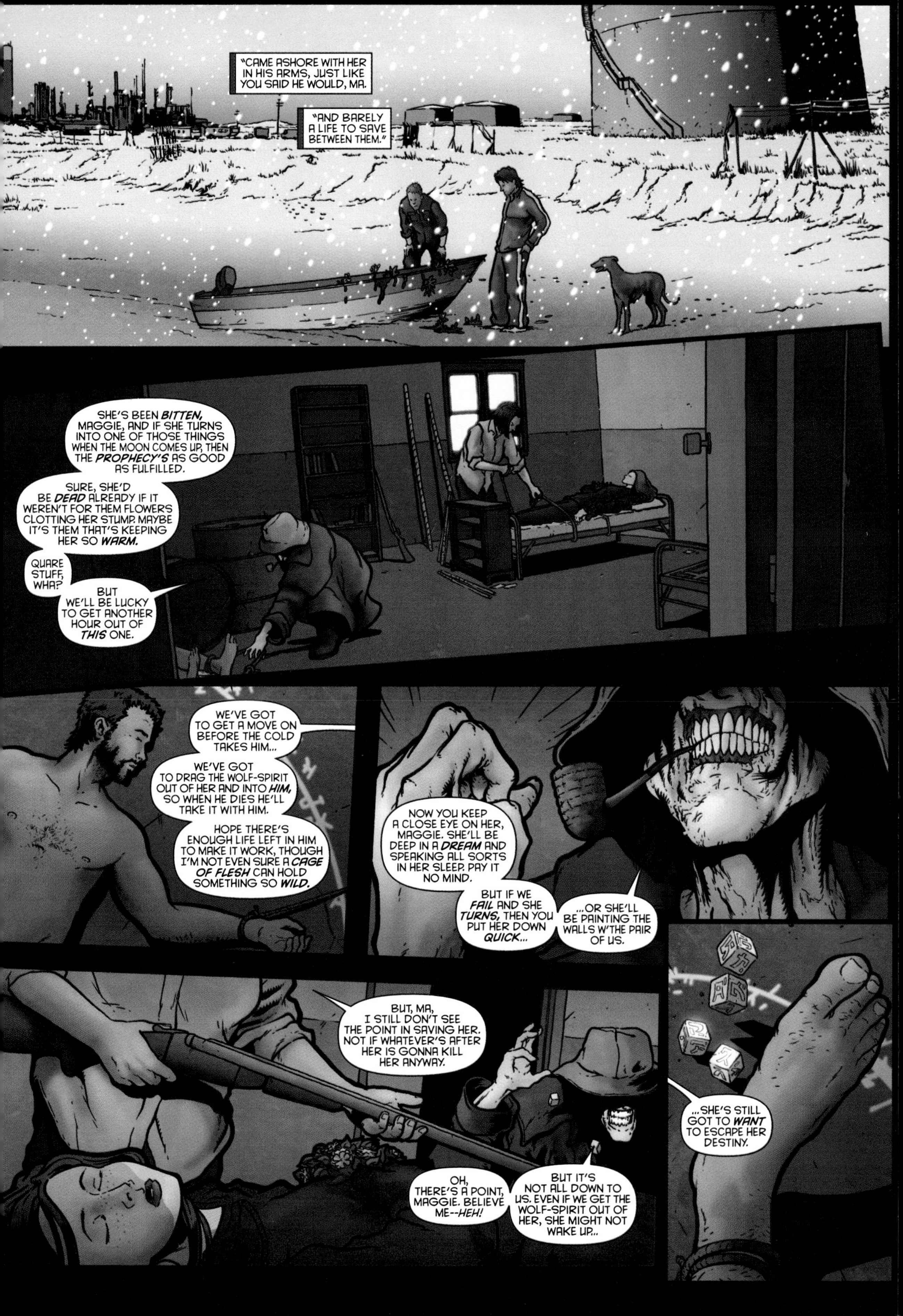

"CAME ASHORE WITH HER IN HIS ARMS, JUST LIKE YOU SAID HE WOULD, MA.
"AND BARELY A LIFE TO SAVE BETWEEN THEM."
SHE'S BEEN *BITTEN,* MAGGIE, AND IF SHE TURNS INTO ONE OF THOSE THINGS WHEN THE MOON COMES UP, THEN THE *PROPHECY'S* AS GOOD AS FULFILLED.
SURE, SHE'D BE *DEAD* ALREADY IF IT WEREN'T FOR THEM FLOWERS CLOTTING HER STUMP. MAYBE IT'S THEM THAT'S KEEPING HER SO *WARM.*
QUARE STUFF, WHA?
BUT WE'LL BE LUCKY TO GET ANOTHER HOUR OUT OF *THIS* ONE.
WE'VE GOT TO GET A MOVE ON BEFORE THE COLD TAKES HIM...
WE'VE GOT TO DRAG THE WOLF-SPIRIT OUT OF HER AND INTO *HIM,* SO WHEN HE DIES HE'LL TAKE IT WITH HIM.
HOPE THERE'S ENOUGH LIFE LEFT IN HIM TO MAKE IT WORK, THOUGH I'M NOT EVEN SURE A *CAGE OF FLESH* CAN HOLD SOMETHING SO *WILD.*
NOW YOU KEEP A CLOSE EYE ON HER, MAGGIE. SHE'LL BE DEEP IN A *DREAM* AND SPEAKING ALL SORTS IN HER SLEEP. PAY IT NO MIND.
BUT IF WE *FAIL* AND SHE *TURNS,* THEN YOU PUT HER DOWN *QUICK*...
...OR SHE'LL BE PAINTING THE WALLS W'THE PAIR OF US.
BUT, MA, I STILL DON'T SEE THE POINT IN SAVING HER. NOT IF WHATEVER'S AFTER HER IS GONNA KILL HER ANYWAY.
OH, THERE'S A POINT, MAGGIE. BELIEVE ME--*HEH!*
BUT IT'S NOT ALL DOWN TO US. EVEN IF WE GET THE WOLF-SPIRIT OUT OF HER, SHE MIGHT NOT WAKE UP...
...SHE'S STILL GOT TO *WANT* TO ESCAPE HER DESTINY.

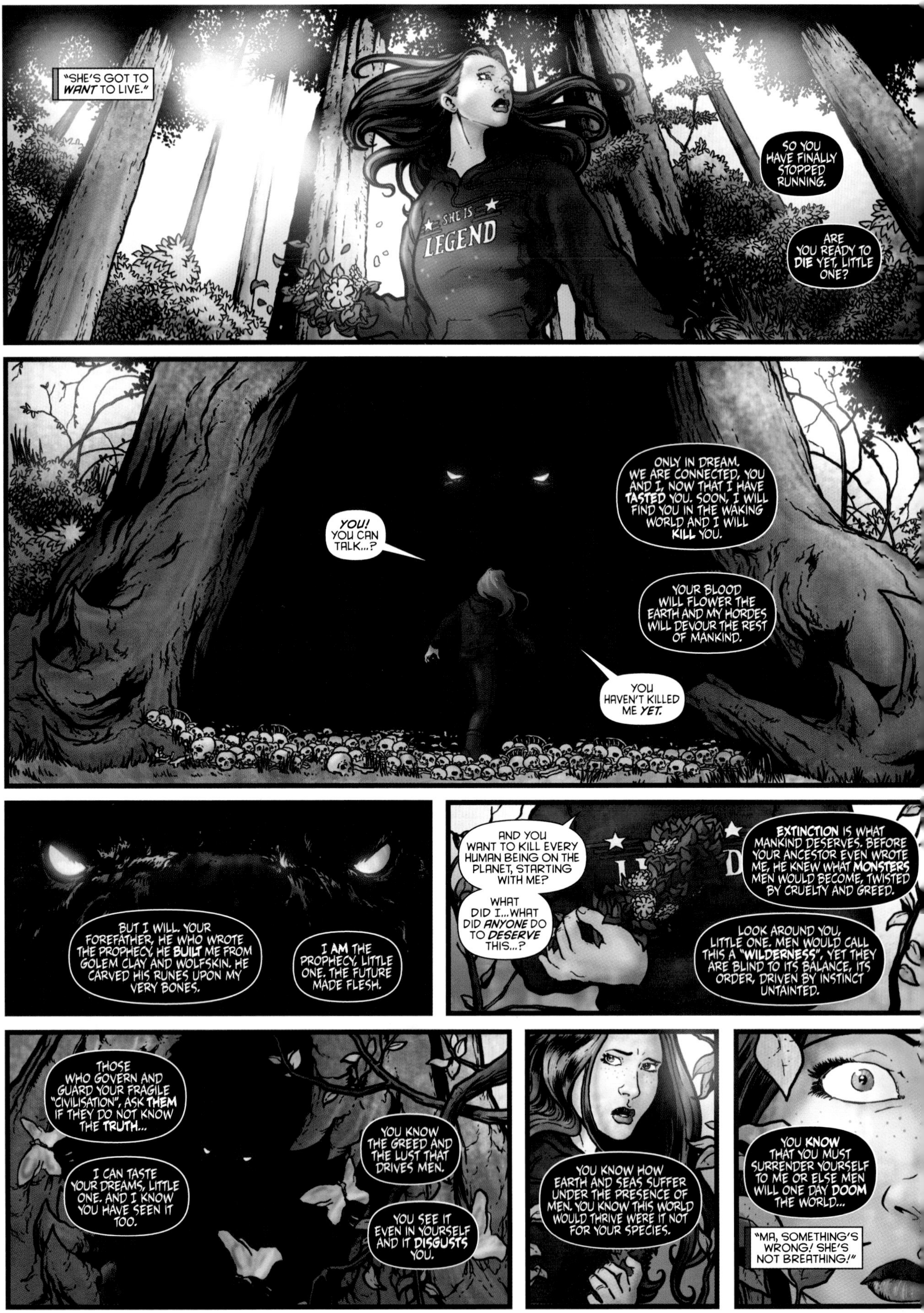
"SHE'S GOT TO WANT TO LIVE."
SHE IS LEGEND
SO YOU HAVE FINALLY STOPPED RUNNING.
ARE YOU READY TO DIE YET, LITTLE ONE?
YOU! YOU CAN TALK...?
ONLY IN DREAM. WE ARE CONNECTED, YOU AND I, NOW THAT I HAVE TASTED YOU. SOON, I WILL FIND YOU IN THE WAKING WORLD AND I WILL KILL YOU.
YOUR BLOOD WILL FLOWER THE EARTH AND MY HORDES WILL DEVOUR THE REST OF MANKIND.
YOU HAVEN'T KILLED ME YET.
BUT I WILL. YOUR FOREFATHER, HE WHO WROTE THE PROPHECY, HE BUILT ME FROM GOLEM CLAY AND WOLFSKIN. HE CARVED HIS RUNES UPON MY VERY BONES.
I AM THE PROPHECY, LITTLE ONE. THE FUTURE MADE FLESH.
AND YOU WANT TO KILL EVERY HUMAN BEING ON THE PLANET, STARTING WITH ME?
WHAT DID I...WHAT DID ANYONE DO TO DESERVE THIS...?
EXTINCTION IS WHAT MANKIND DESERVES. BEFORE YOUR ANCESTOR EVEN WROTE ME, HE KNEW WHAT MONSTERS MEN WOULD BECOME, TWISTED BY CRUELTY AND GREED.
LOOK AROUND YOU, LITTLE ONE. MEN WOULD CALL THIS A "WILDERNESS", YET THEY ARE BLIND TO ITS BALANCE, ITS ORDER, DRIVEN BY INSTINCT UNTAINTED.
THOSE WHO GOVERN AND GUARD YOUR FRAGILE "CIVILISATION", ASK THEM IF THEY DO NOT KNOW THE TRUTH...
I CAN TASTE YOUR DREAMS, LITTLE ONE. AND I KNOW YOU HAVE SEEN IT TOO.
YOU KNOW THE GREED AND THE LUST THAT DRIVES MEN.
YOU SEE IT EVEN IN YOURSELF AND IT DISGUSTS YOU.
YOU KNOW HOW EARTH AND SEAS SUFFER UNDER THE PRESENCE OF MEN. YOU KNOW THIS WORLD WOULD THRIVE WERE IT NOT FOR YOUR SPECIES.
YOU KNOW THAT YOU MUST SURRENDER YOURSELF TO ME OR ELSE MEN WILL ONE DAY DOOM THE WORLD...
"MA, SOMETHING'S WRONG! SHE'S NOT BREATHING!"

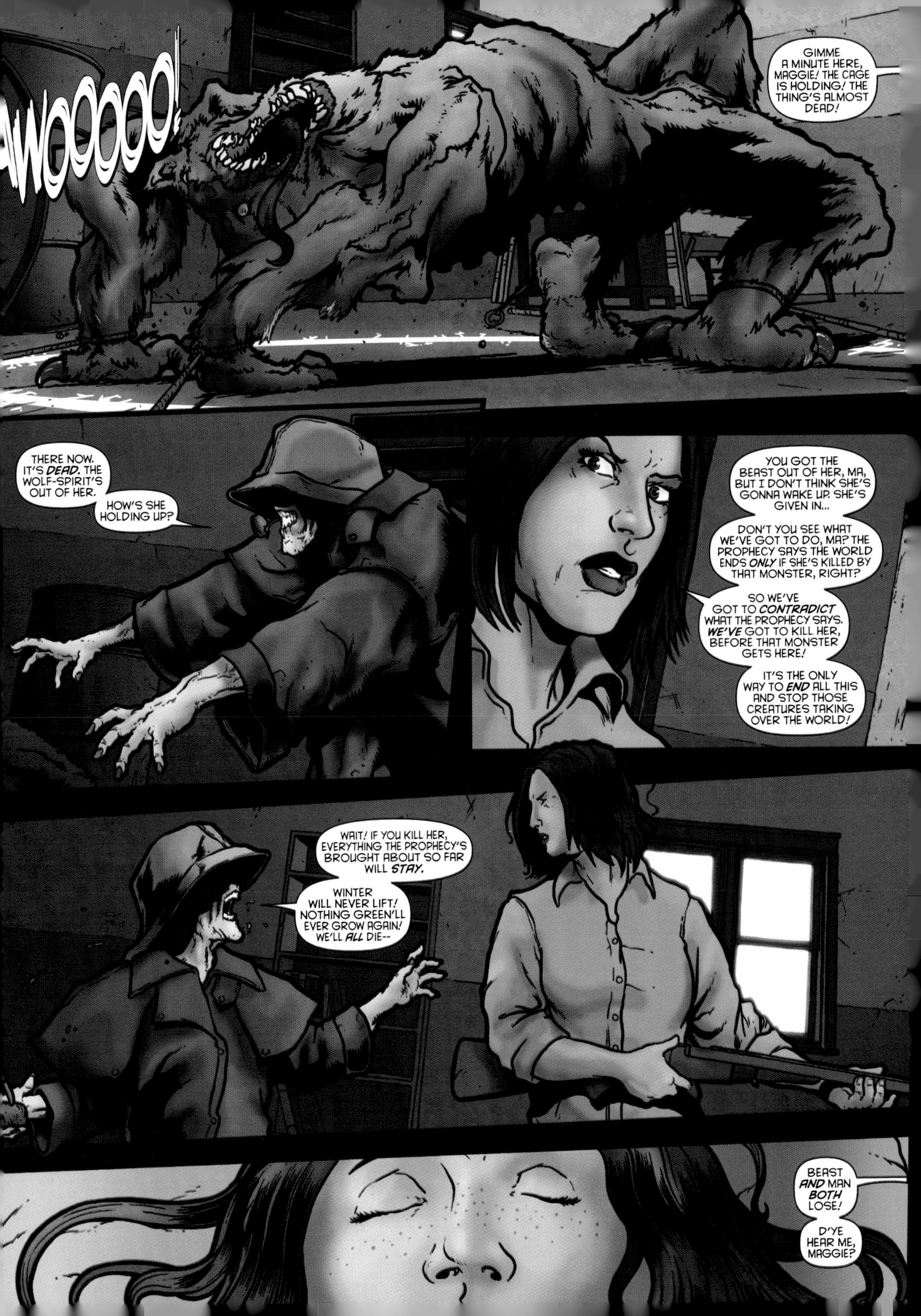
AWOOOOO!
GIMME A MINUTE HERE, MAGGIE! THE CAGE IS HOLDING! THE THING'S ALMOST DEAD!
THERE NOW. IT'S *DEAD*. THE WOLF-SPIRIT'S OUT OF HER.
HOW'S SHE HOLDING UP?
YOU GOT THE BEAST OUT OF HER, MA, BUT I DON'T THINK SHE'S GONNA WAKE UP. SHE'S GIVEN IN...
DON'T YOU SEE WHAT WE'VE GOT TO DO, MA? THE PROPHECY SAYS THE WORLD ENDS *ONLY* IF SHE'S KILLED BY THAT MONSTER, RIGHT?
SO WE'VE GOT TO ***CONTRADICT*** WHAT THE PROPHECY SAYS. ***WE'VE*** GOT TO KILL HER, BEFORE THAT MONSTER GETS HERE!
IT'S THE ONLY WAY TO ***END*** ALL THIS AND STOP THOSE CREATURES TAKING OVER THE WORLD!
WAIT! IF YOU KILL HER, EVERYTHING THE PROPHECY'S BROUGHT ABOUT SO FAR WILL ***STAY.***
WINTER WILL NEVER LIFT! NOTHING GREEN'LL EVER GROW AGAIN! WE'LL ***ALL*** DIE--
BEAST ***AND*** MAN ***BOTH*** LOSE!
D'YE HEAR ME, MAGGIE?

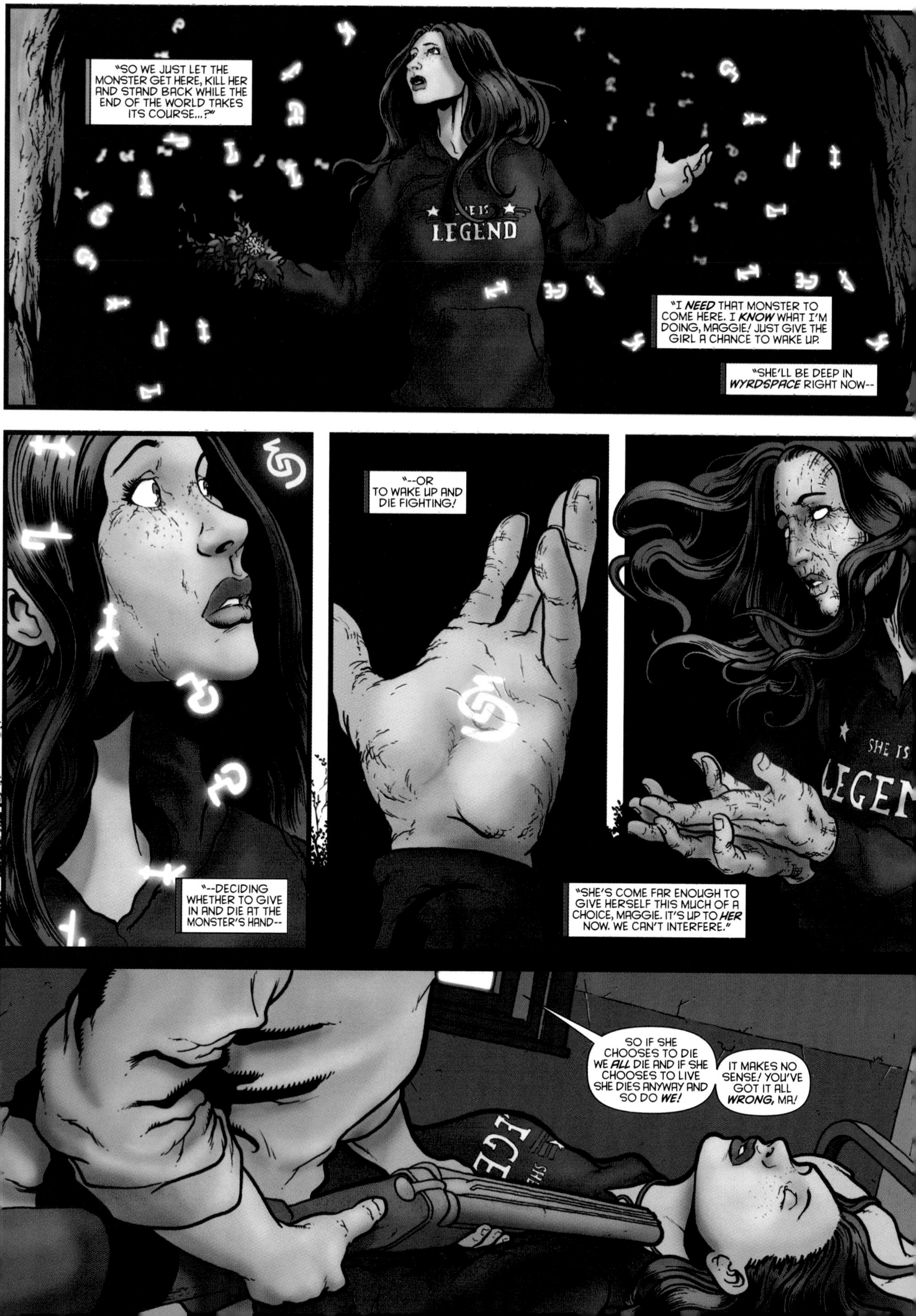
"SO WE JUST LET THE MONSTER GET HERE, KILL HER AND STAND BACK WHILE THE END OF THE WORLD TAKES ITS COURSE...?"
LEGEND
"I NEED THAT MONSTER TO COME HERE. I KNOW WHAT I'M DOING, MAGGIE! JUST GIVE THE GIRL A CHANCE TO WAKE UP.
"SHE'LL BE DEEP IN WYRDSPACE RIGHT NOW--
"--DECIDING WHETHER TO GIVE IN AND DIE AT THE MONSTER'S HAND--
"--OR TO WAKE UP AND DIE FIGHTING!
SHE IS LEGEN
"SHE'S COME FAR ENOUGH TO GIVE HERSELF THIS MUCH OF A CHOICE, MAGGIE. IT'S UP TO HER NOW. WE CAN'T INTERFERE."
SO IF SHE CHOOSES TO DIE WE ALL DIE AND IF SHE CHOOSES TO LIVE SHE DIES ANYWAY AND SO DO WE!
IT MAKES NO SENSE! YOU'VE GOT IT ALL WRONG, MA!

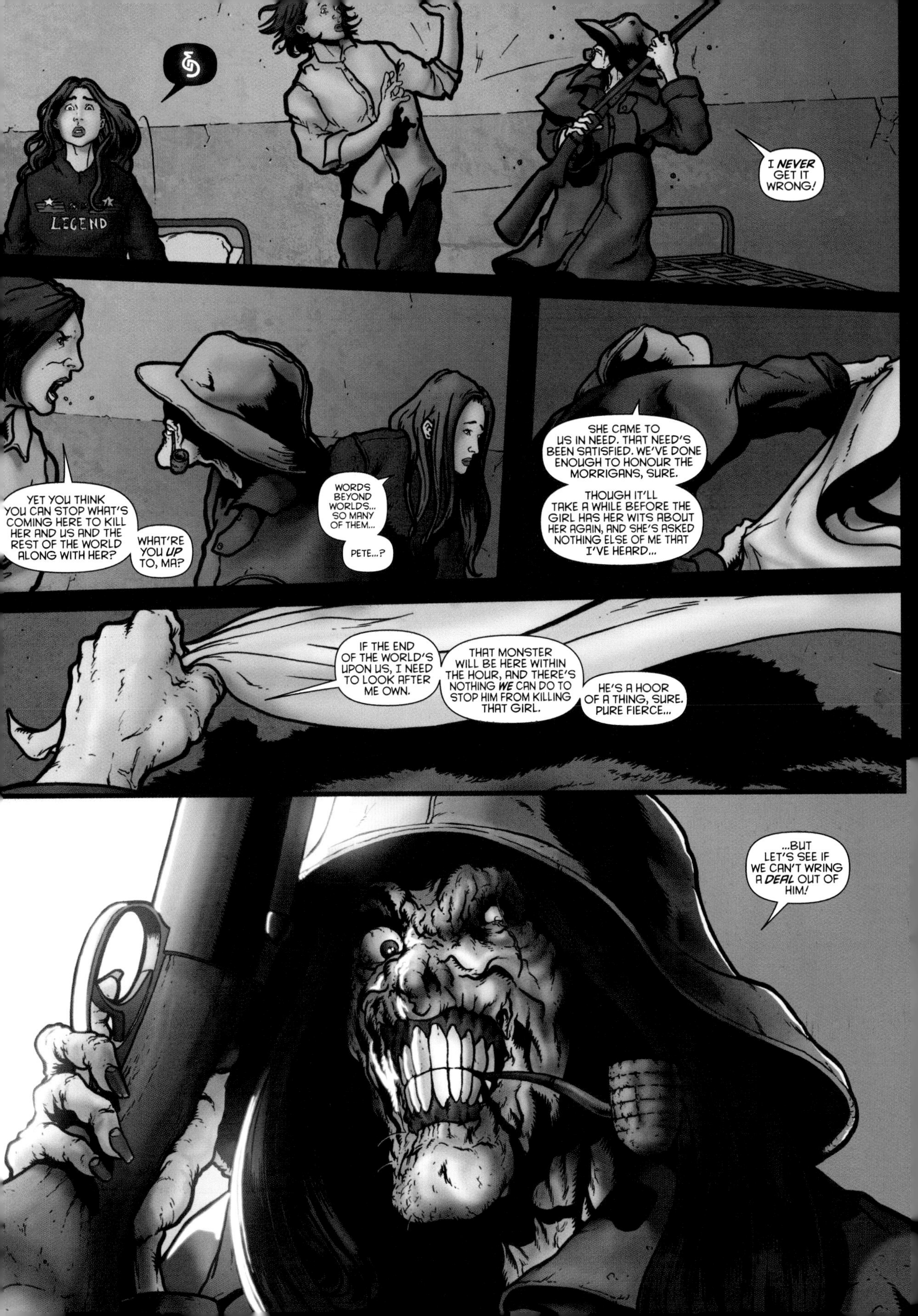
I NEVER GET IT WRONG!
YET YOU THINK YOU CAN STOP WHAT'S COMING HERE TO KILL HER AND US AND THE REST OF THE WORLD ALONG WITH HER?
WHAT'RE YOU UP TO, MA?
WORDS BEYOND WORLDS... SO MANY OF THEM...
PETE...?
SHE CAME TO US IN NEED. THAT NEED'S BEEN SATISFIED. WE'VE DONE ENOUGH TO HONOUR THE MORRIGANS, SURE.
THOUGH IT'LL TAKE A WHILE BEFORE THE GIRL HAS HER WITS ABOUT HER AGAIN, AND SHE'S ASKED NOTHING ELSE OF ME THAT I'VE HEARD...
IF THE END OF THE WORLD'S UPON US, I NEED TO LOOK AFTER ME OWN.
THAT MONSTER WILL BE HERE WITHIN THE HOUR, AND THERE'S NOTHING WE CAN DO TO STOP HIM FROM KILLING THAT GIRL.
HE'S A HOOR OF A THING, SURE. PURE FIERCE...
...BUT LET'S SEE IF WE CAN'T WRING A DEAL OUT OF HIM!

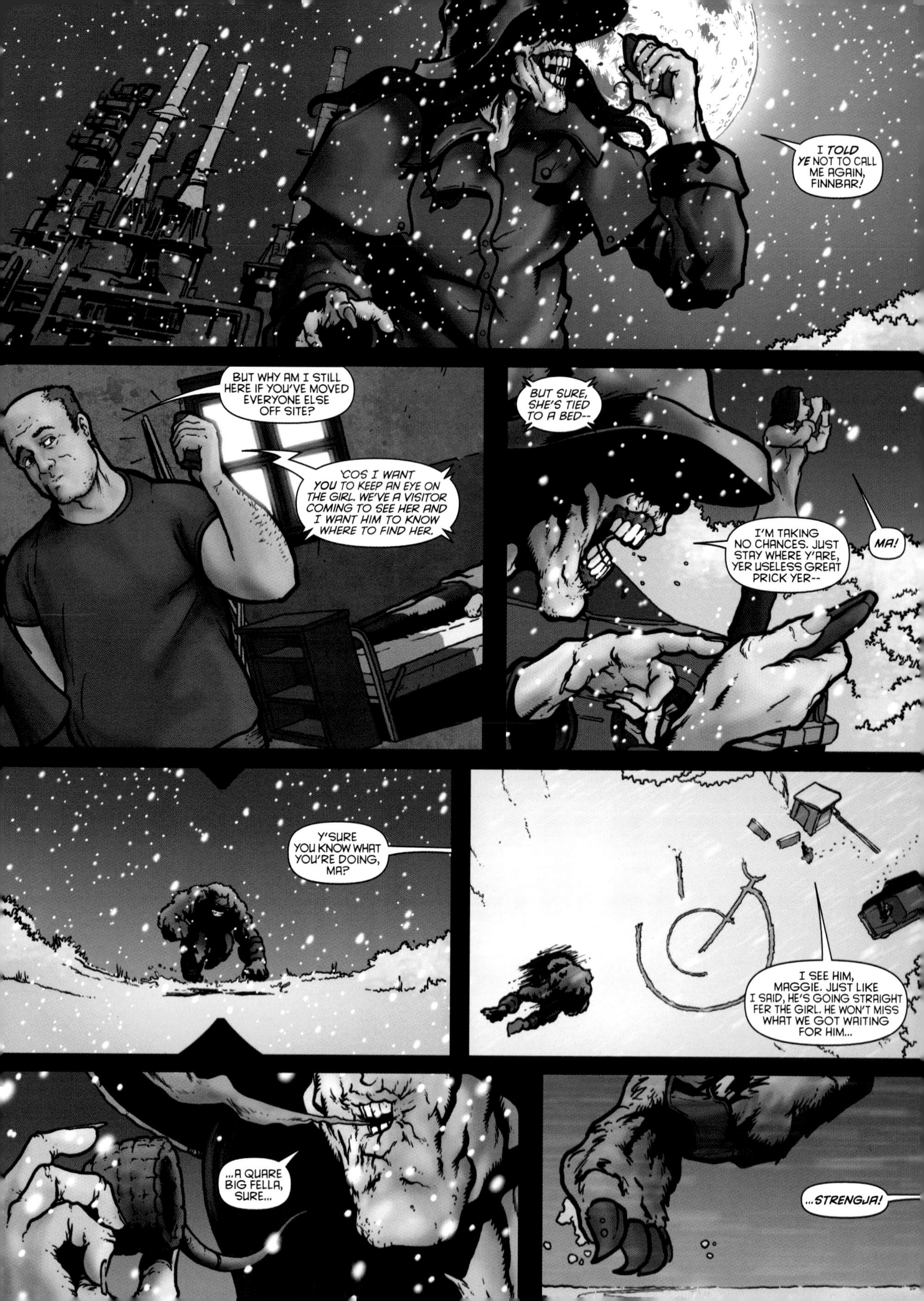

I *TOLD* *YE* NOT TO CALL ME AGAIN, FINNBAR!
BUT WHY AM I STILL HERE IF YOU'VE MOVED EVERYONE ELSE OFF SITE?
'COS I WANT *YOU* TO KEEP AN EYE ON THE GIRL. WE'VE A VISITOR COMING TO SEE HER AND I WANT HIM TO KNOW WHERE TO FIND HER.
BUT SURE, SHE'S TIED TO A BED--
I'M TAKING NO CHANCES. JUST STAY WHERE Y'ARE, YER USELESS GREAT PRICK YER--
MA!
Y'SURE YOU KNOW WHAT YOU'RE DOING, MA?
I SEE HIM, MAGGIE. JUST LIKE I SAID, HE'S GOING STRAIGHT FER THE GIRL. HE WON'T MISS WHAT WE GOT WAITING FOR HIM...
...A QUARE BIG FELLA, SURE...
...*STRENGJA!*

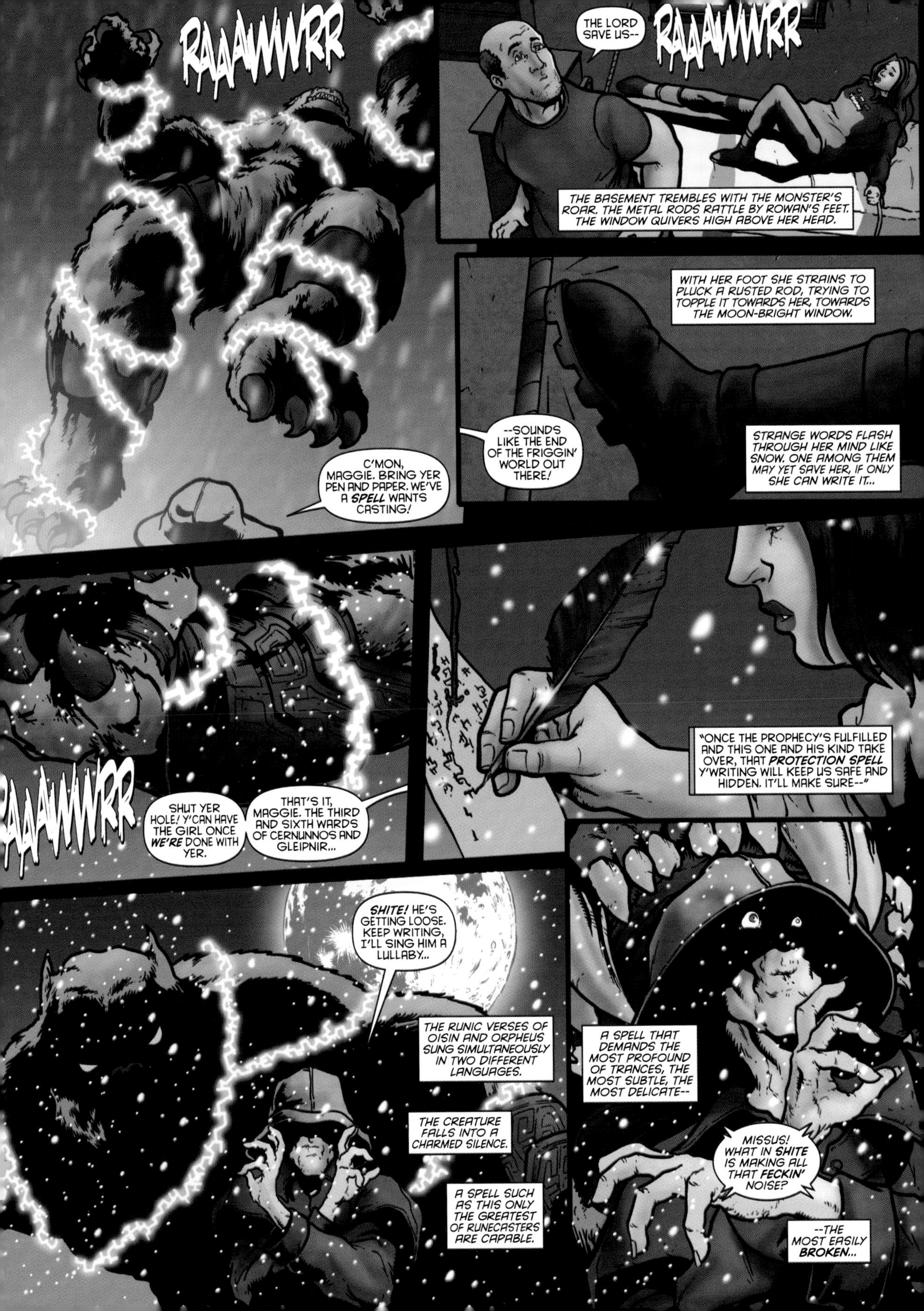
RAAAWWRR
THE LORD SAVE US--
RAAAWWRR
THE BASEMENT TREMBLES WITH THE MONSTER'S ROAR. THE METAL RODS RATTLE BY ROWAN'S FEET. THE WINDOW QUIVERS HIGH ABOVE HER HEAD.
C'MON, MAGGIE. BRING YER PEN AND PAPER. WE'VE A SPELL WANTS CASTING!
--SOUNDS LIKE THE END OF THE FRIGGIN' WORLD OUT THERE!
WITH HER FOOT SHE STRAINS TO PLUCK A RUSTED ROD, TRYING TO TOPPLE IT TOWARDS HER, TOWARDS THE MOON-BRIGHT WINDOW.
STRANGE WORDS FLASH THROUGH HER MIND LIKE SNOW. ONE AMONG THEM MAY YET SAVE HER, IF ONLY SHE CAN WRITE IT...
RAAAWWRR
SHUT YER HOLE! Y'CAN HAVE THE GIRL ONCE WE'RE DONE WITH YER.
THAT'S IT, MAGGIE. THE THIRD AND SIXTH WARDS OF CERNUNNOS AND GLEIPNIR...
"ONCE THE PROPHECY'S FULFILLED AND THIS ONE AND HIS KIND TAKE OVER, THAT PROTECTION SPELL Y'WRITING WILL KEEP US SAFE AND HIDDEN. IT'LL MAKE SURE--"
SHITE! HE'S GETTING LOOSE. KEEP WRITING, I'LL SING HIM A LULLABY...
THE RUNIC VERSES OF OISIN AND ORPHEUS SUNG SIMULTANEOUSLY IN TWO DIFFERENT LANGUAGES.
THE CREATURE FALLS INTO A CHARMED SILENCE.
A SPELL SUCH AS THIS ONLY THE GREATEST OF RUNECASTERS ARE CAPABLE.
A SPELL THAT DEMANDS THE MOST PROFOUND OF TRANCES, THE MOST SUBTLE, THE MOST DELICATE--
MISSUS! WHAT IN SHITE IS MAKING ALL THAT FECKIN' NOISE?
--THE MOST EASILY BROKEN...

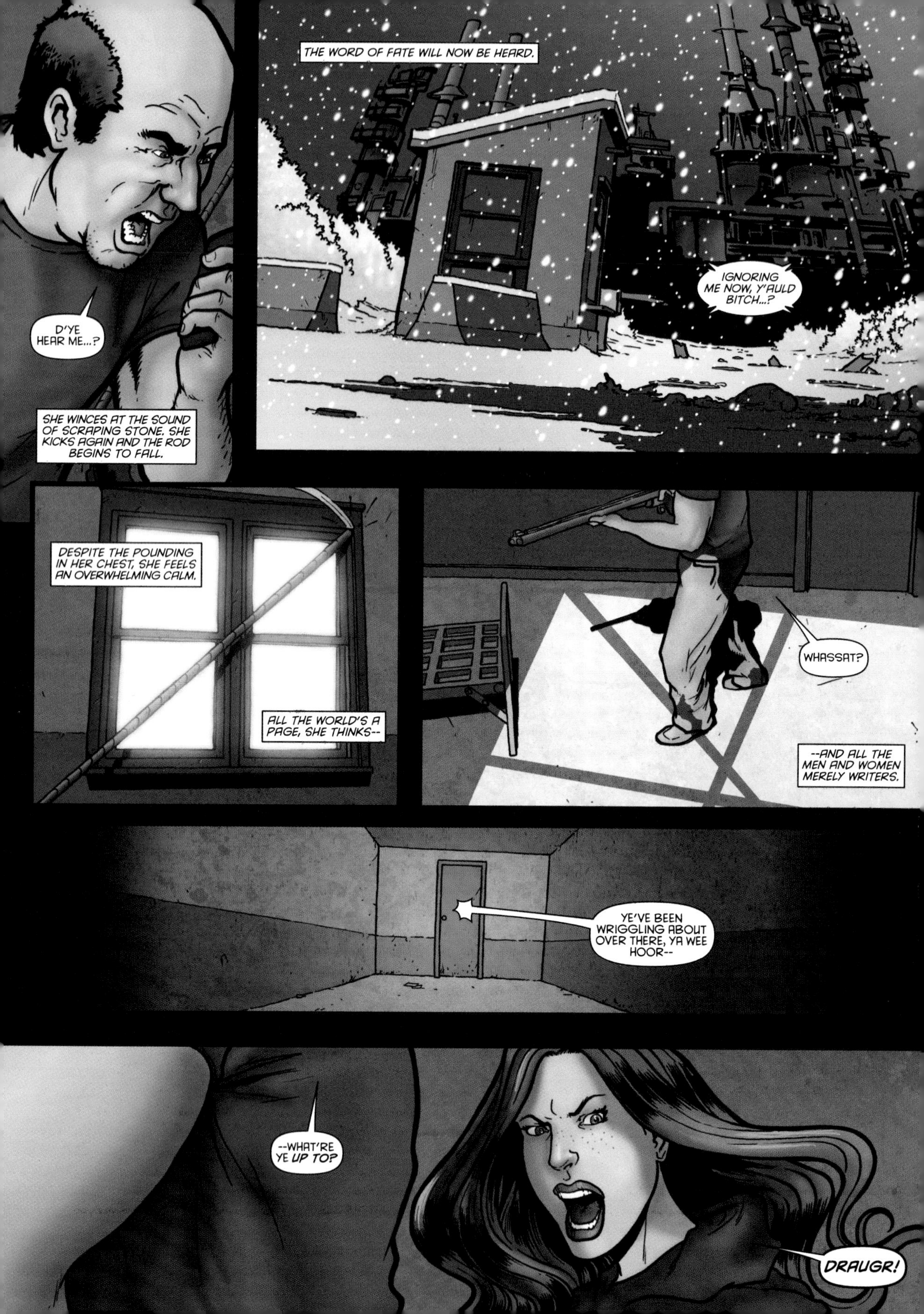
D'YE HEAR ME...?
THE WORD OF FATE WILL NOW BE HEARD.
IGNORING ME NOW, Y'AULD BITCH...?
SHE WINCES AT THE SOUND OF SCRAPING STONE. SHE KICKS AGAIN AND THE ROD BEGINS TO FALL.
DESPITE THE POUNDING IN HER CHEST, SHE FEELS AN OVERWHELMING CALM.
ALL THE WORLD'S A PAGE, SHE THINKS--
WHASSAT?
--AND ALL THE MEN AND WOMEN MERELY WRITERS.
YE'VE BEEN WRIGGLING ABOUT OVER THERE, YA WEE HOOR--
--WHAT'RE YE UP TO?
DRAUGR!

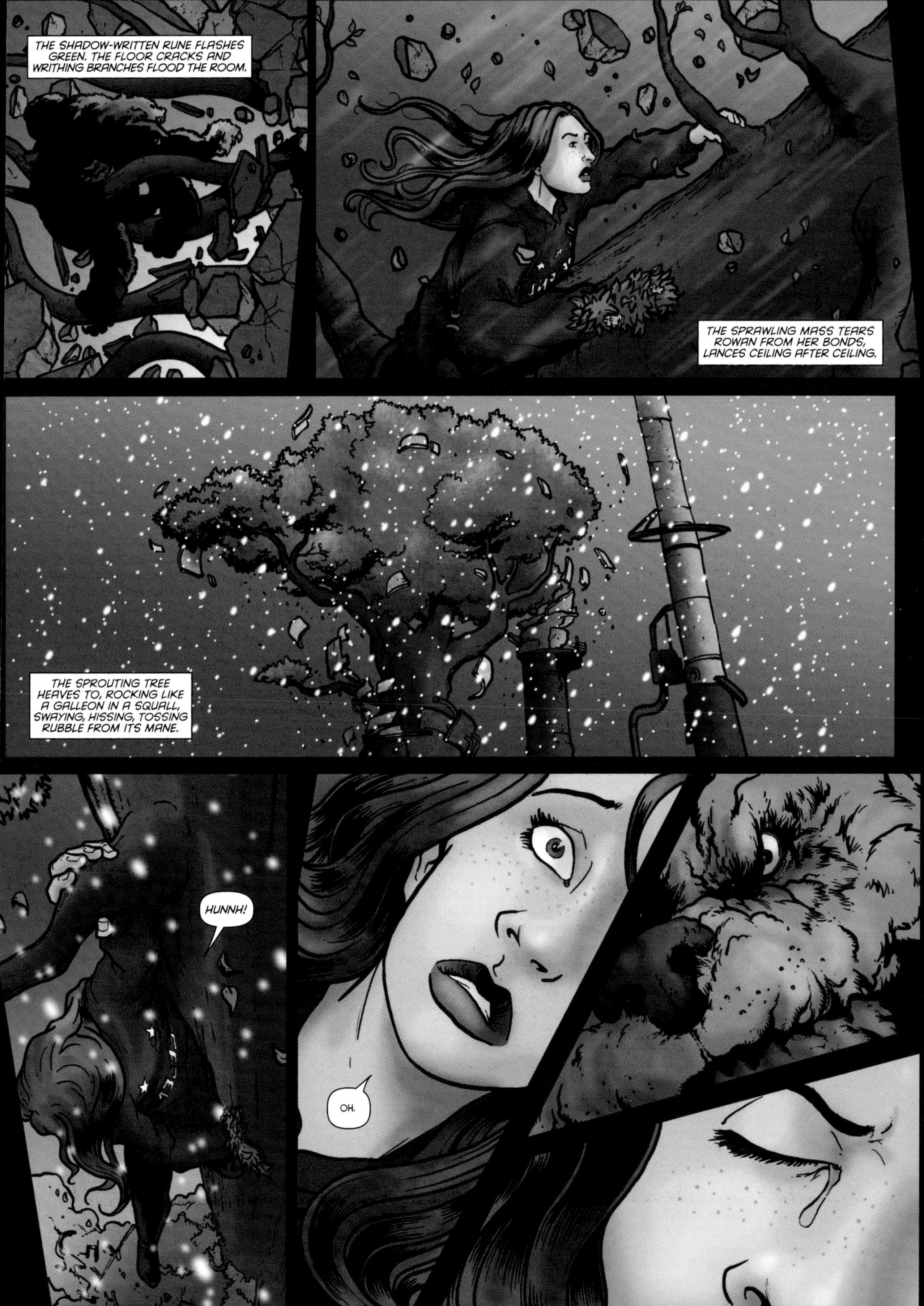
THE SHADOW-WRITTEN RUNE FLASHES GREEN. THE FLOOR CRACKS AND WRITHING BRANCHES FLOOD THE ROOM.
THE SPRAWLING MASS TEARS ROWAN FROM HER BONDS, LANCES CEILING AFTER CEILING.
THE SPROUTING TREE HEAVES TO, ROCKING LIKE A GALLEON IN A SQUALL, SWAYING, HISSING, TOSSING RUBBLE FROM ITS MANE.
HUNNH!
OH.

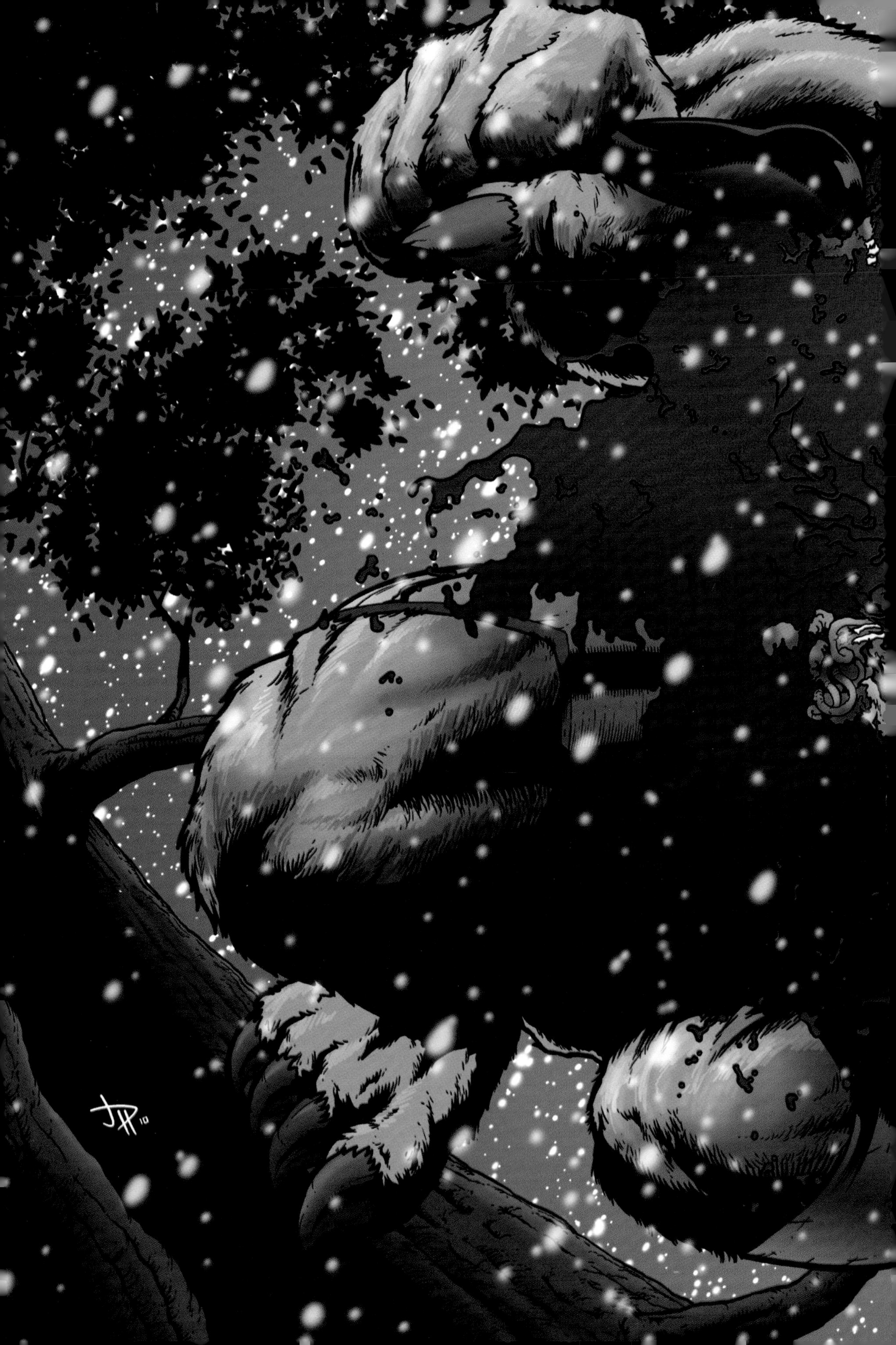

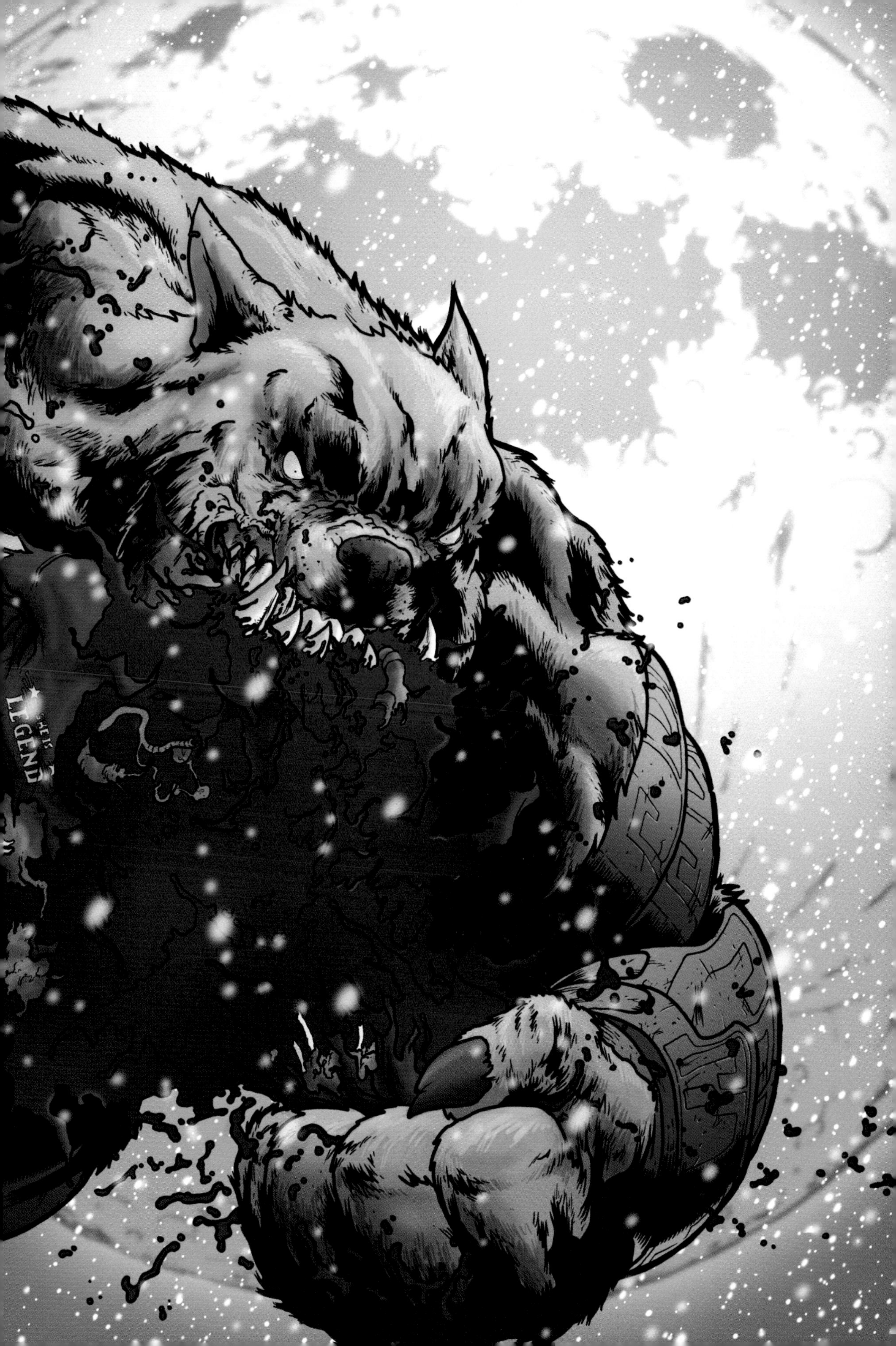
SHE IS
LEGEND

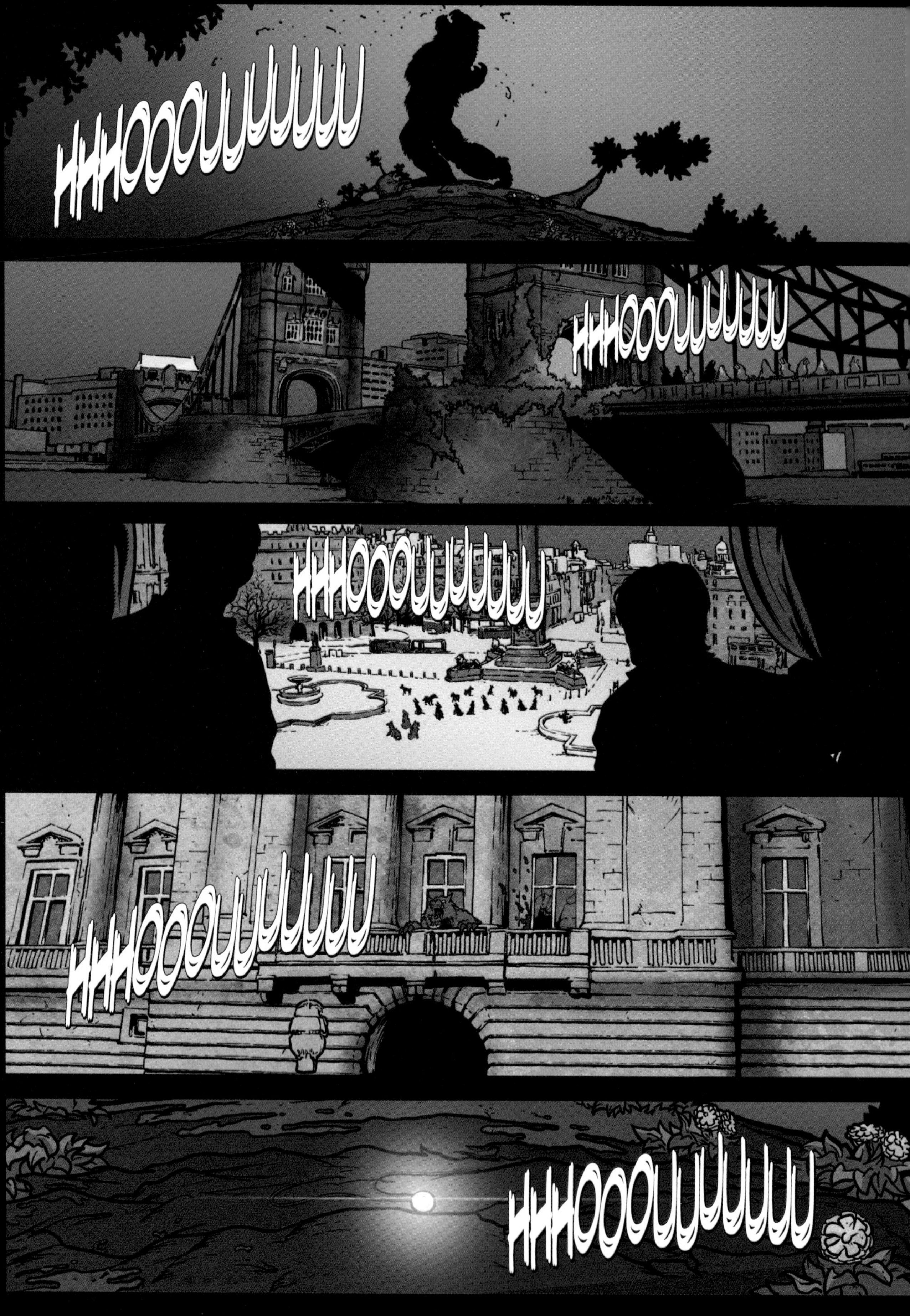
HHHOOOUUUUUUU
HHHOOOUUUUUUU
HHHOOOUUUUUUU
HHHOOOUUUUUUU
HHHOOOUUUUUUU

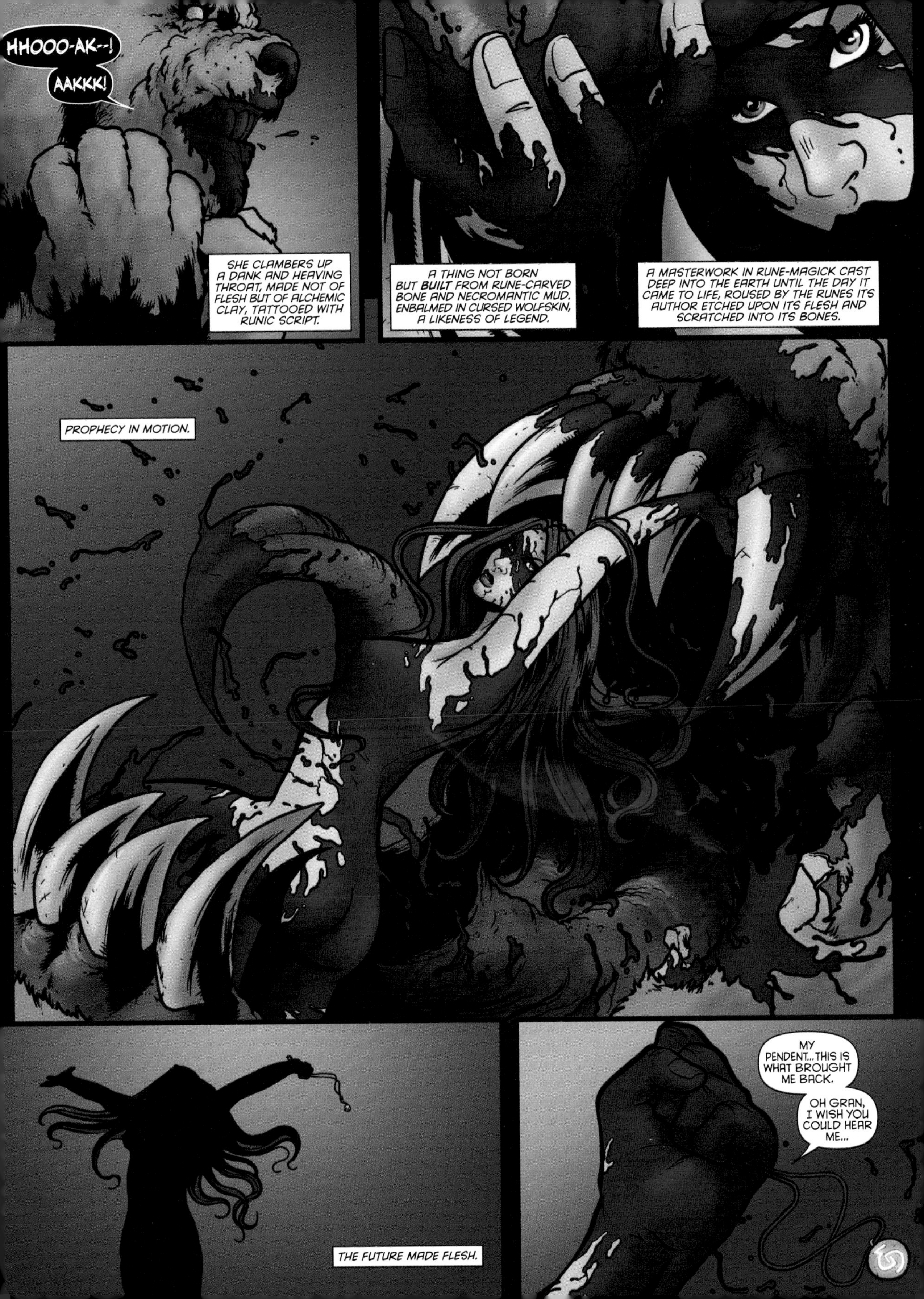
HHOOO-AK--!
AAKKK!
SHE CLAMBERS UP A DANK AND HEAVING THROAT, MADE NOT OF FLESH BUT OF ALCHEMIC CLAY, TATTOOED WITH RUNIC SCRIPT.
A THING NOT BORN BUT BUILT FROM RUNE-CARVED BONE AND NECROMANTIC MUD. ENBALMED IN CURSED WOLFSKIN, A LIKENESS OF LEGEND.
A MASTERWORK IN RUNE-MAGICK CAST DEEP INTO THE EARTH UNTIL THE DAY IT CAME TO LIFE, ROUSED BY THE RUNES ITS AUTHOR ETCHED UPON ITS FLESH AND SCRATCHED INTO ITS BONES.
PROPHECY IN MOTION.
THE FUTURE MADE FLESH.
MY PENDENT... THIS IS WHAT BROUGHT ME BACK.
OH GRAN, I WISH YOU COULD HEAR ME...

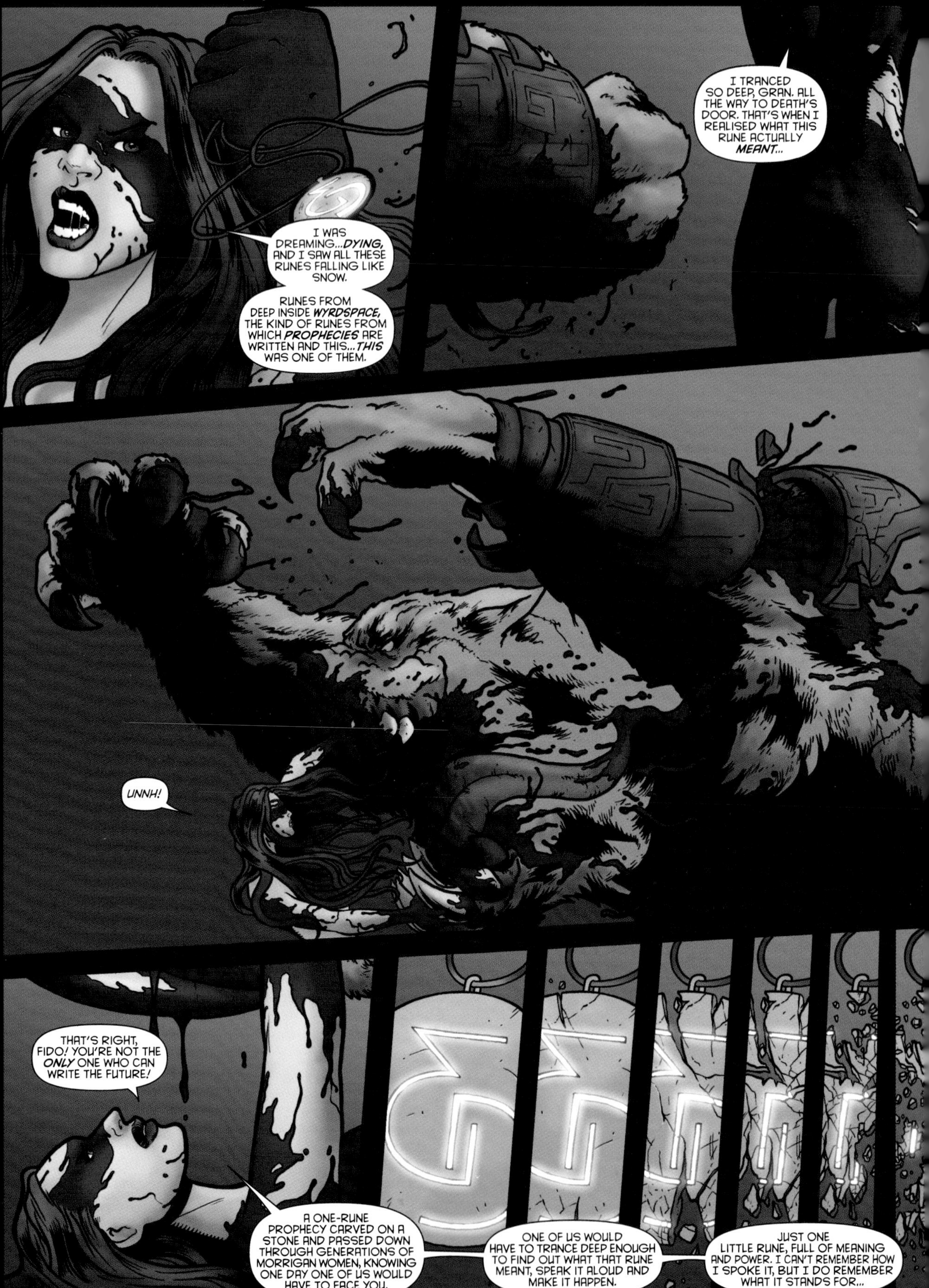
I WAS DREAMING...DYING, AND I SAW ALL THESE RUNES FALLING LIKE SNOW.
RUNES FROM DEEP INSIDE WYRDSPACE, THE KIND OF RUNES FROM WHICH PROPHECIES ARE WRITTEN AND THIS...THIS WAS ONE OF THEM.
I TRANCED SO DEEP, GRAN. ALL THE WAY TO DEATH'S DOOR. THAT'S WHEN I REALISED WHAT THIS RUNE ACTUALLY MEANT...
UNNH!
THAT'S RIGHT, FIDO! YOU'RE NOT THE ONLY ONE WHO CAN WRITE THE FUTURE!
A ONE-RUNE PROPHECY CARVED ON A STONE AND PASSED DOWN THROUGH GENERATIONS OF MORRIGAN WOMEN, KNOWING ONE DAY ONE OF US WOULD HAVE TO FACE YOU.
ONE OF US WOULD HAVE TO TRANCE DEEP ENOUGH TO FIND OUT WHAT THAT RUNE MEANT, SPEAK IT ALOUD AND MAKE IT HAPPEN.
JUST ONE LITTLE RUNE, FULL OF MEANING AND POWER. I CAN'T REMEMBER HOW I SPOKE IT, BUT I DO REMEMBER WHAT IT STANDS FOR...

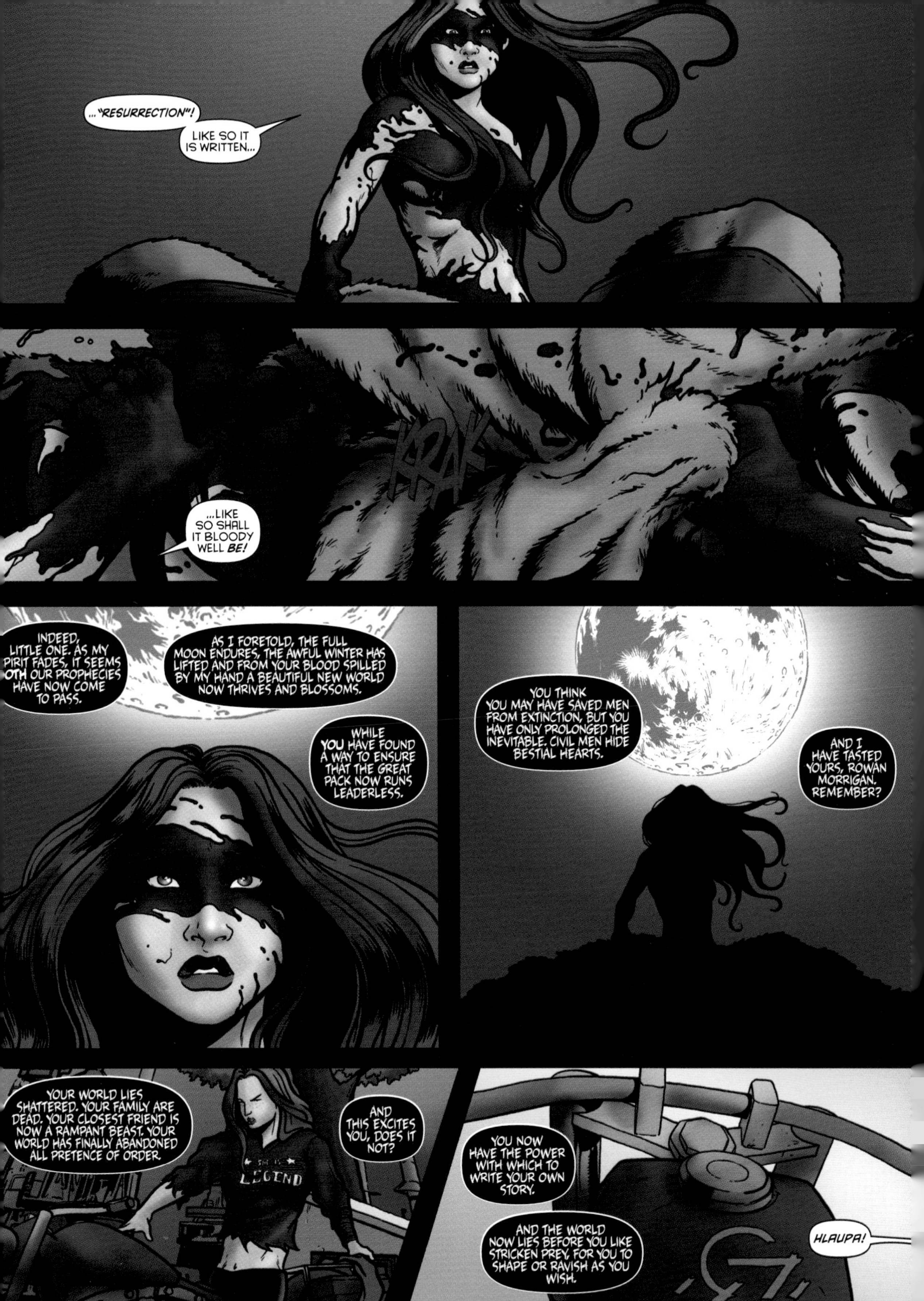

..."RESURRECTION"!
LIKE SO IT IS WRITTEN...
KRAK
...LIKE SO SHALL IT BLOODY WELL BE!
INDEED, LITTLE ONE. AS MY PIRIT FADES, IT SEEMS OTH OUR PROPHECIES HAVE NOW COME TO PASS.
AS I FORETOLD, THE FULL MOON ENDURES, THE AWFUL WINTER HAS LIFTED AND FROM YOUR BLOOD SPILLED BY MY HAND A BEAUTIFUL NEW WORLD NOW THRIVES AND BLOSSOMS.
WHILE YOU HAVE FOUND A WAY TO ENSURE THAT THE GREAT PACK NOW RUNS LEADERLESS.
YOU THINK YOU MAY HAVE SAVED MEN FROM EXTINCTION, BUT YOU HAVE ONLY PROLONGED THE INEVITABLE. CIVIL MEN HIDE BESTIAL HEARTS.
AND I HAVE TASTED YOURS, ROWAN MORRIGAN. REMEMBER?
YOUR WORLD LIES SHATTERED. YOUR FAMILY ARE DEAD. YOUR CLOSEST FRIEND IS NOW A RAMPANT BEAST. YOUR WORLD HAS FINALLY ABANDONED ALL PRETENCE OF ORDER.
AND THIS EXCITES YOU, DOES IT NOT?
LEGEND
YOU NOW HAVE THE POWER WITH WHICH TO WRITE YOUR OWN STORY.
AND THE WORLD NOW LIES BEFORE YOU LIKE STRICKEN PREY, FOR YOU TO SHAPE OR RAVISH AS YOU WISH.
HLAUPA!

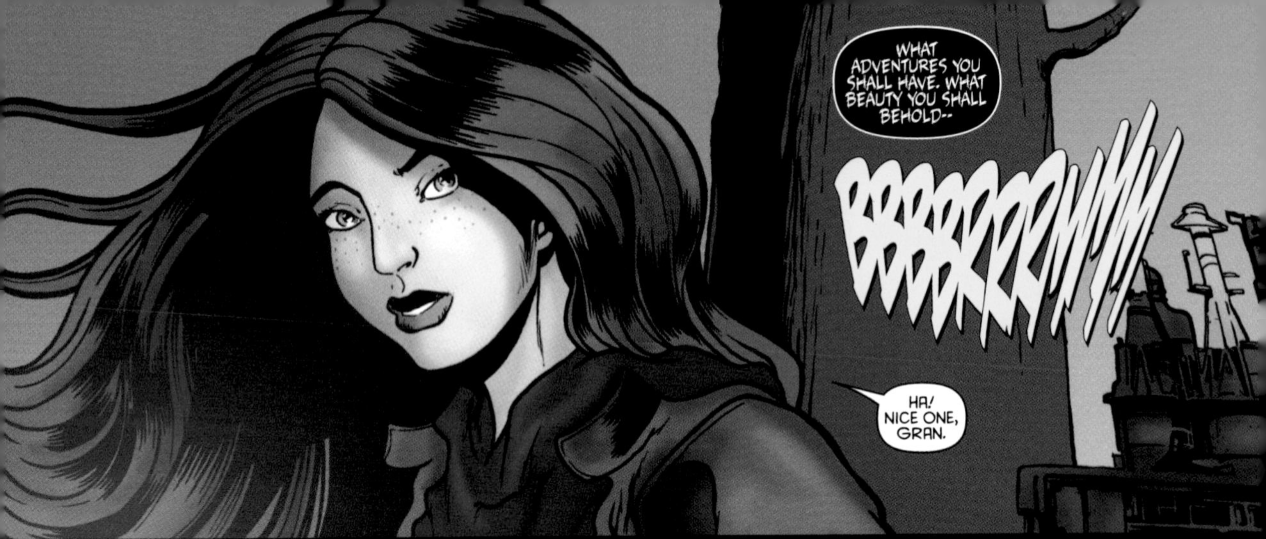
WHAT ADVENTURES YOU SHALL HAVE. WHAT BEAUTY YOU SHALL BEHOLD--
BBBBRRRRMMM
HA! NICE ONE, GRAN.

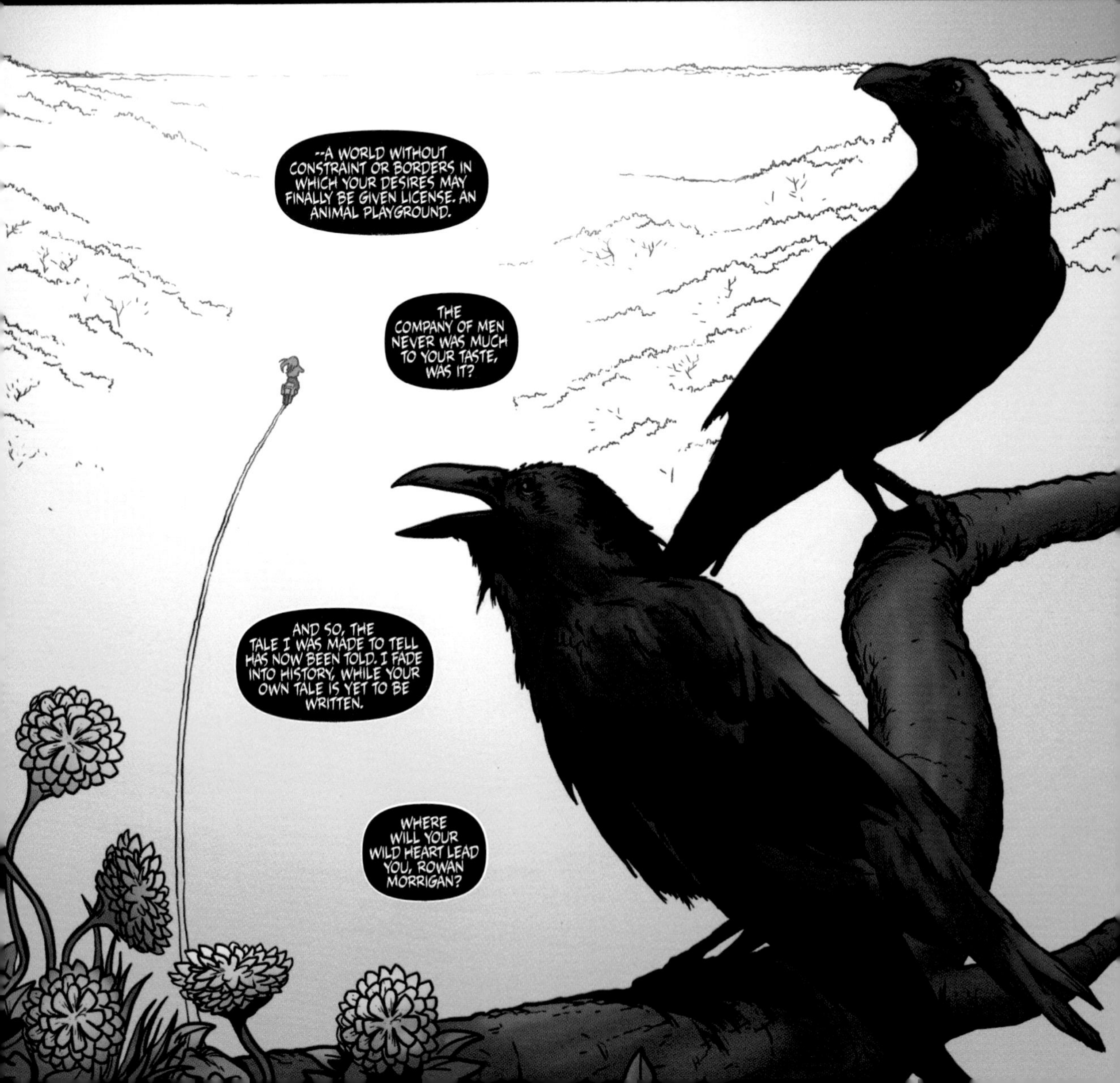
--A WORLD WITHOUT CONSTRAINT OR BORDERS IN WHICH YOUR DESIRES MAY FINALLY BE GIVEN LICENSE. AN ANIMAL PLAYGROUND.
THE COMPANY OF MEN NEVER WAS MUCH TO YOUR TASTE, WAS IT?
AND SO, THE TALE I WAS MADE TO TELL HAS NOW BEEN TOLD. I FADE INTO HISTORY, WHILE YOUR OWN TALE IS YET TO BE WRITTEN.
WHERE WILL YOUR WILD HEART LEAD YOU, ROWAN MORRIGAN?

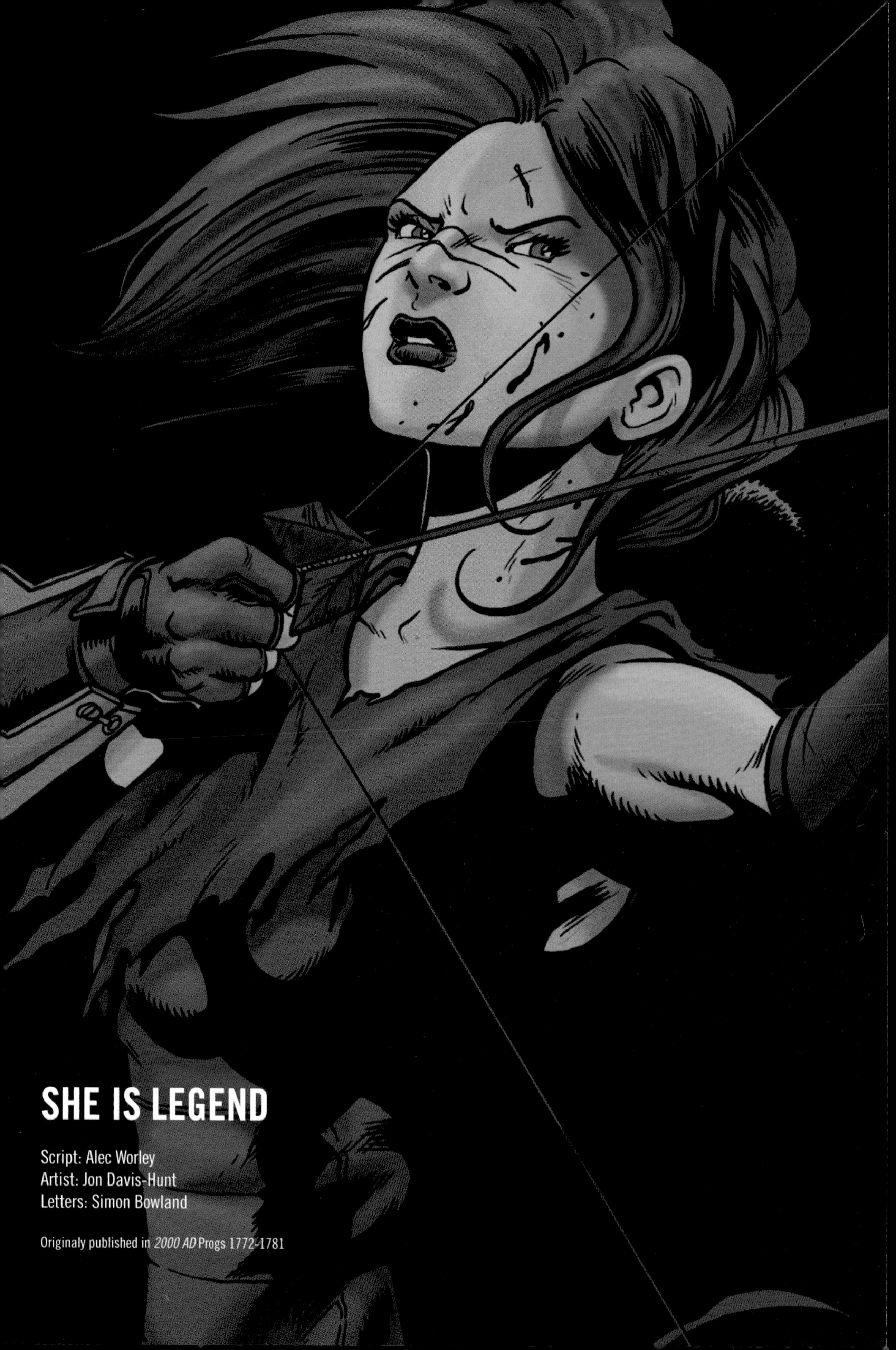

SHE IS LEGEND

Script: Alec Worley
Artist: Jon Davis-Hunt
Letters: Simon Bowland

Originaly published in *2000 AD* Progs 1772-1781

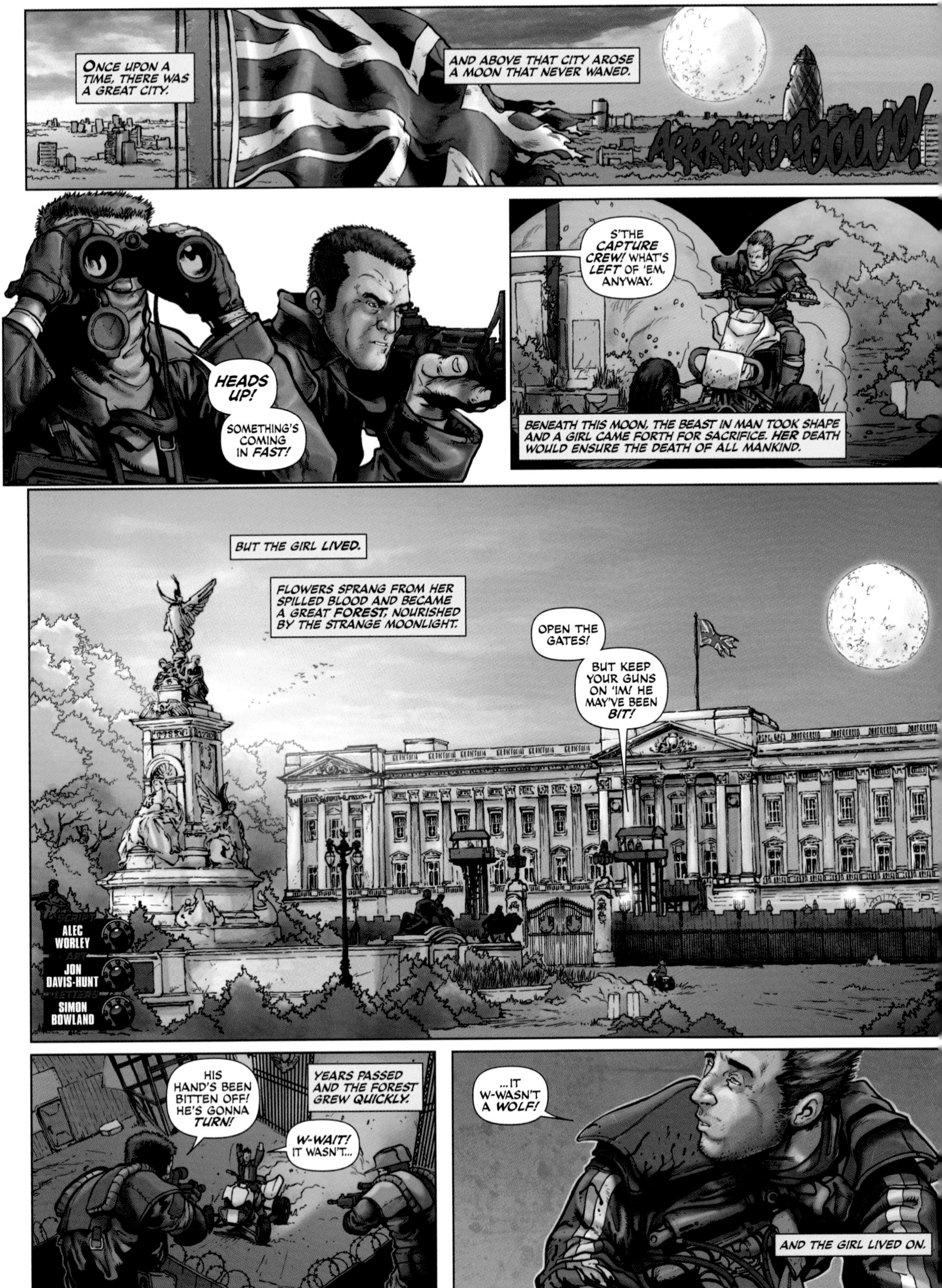
ONCE UPON A TIME, THERE WAS A GREAT CITY.
AND ABOVE THAT CITY AROSE A MOON THAT NEVER WANED.
ARRRRROOOOOOO!
HEADS UP!
SOMETHING'S COMING IN FAST!
S'THE CAPTURE CREW! WHAT'S LEFT OF 'EM, ANYWAY.
BENEATH THIS MOON, THE BEAST IN MAN TOOK SHAPE AND A GIRL CAME FORTH FOR SACRIFICE. HER DEATH WOULD ENSURE THE DEATH OF ALL MANKIND.
BUT THE GIRL LIVED.
FLOWERS SPRANG FROM HER SPILLED BLOOD AND BECAME A GREAT FOREST, NOURISHED BY THE STRANGE MOONLIGHT.
OPEN THE GATES!
BUT KEEP YOUR GUNS ON 'IM! HE MAY'VE BEEN BIT!
SCRIPT
ALEC WORLEY
ART
JON DAVIS-HUNT
LETTERS
SIMON BOWLAND
HIS HAND'S BEEN BITTEN OFF! HE'S GONNA TURN!
YEARS PASSED AND THE FOREST GREW QUICKLY.
W-WAIT! IT WASN'T...
...IT W-WASN'T A WOLF!
AND THE GIRL LIVED ON.

WAS IT *HER*? IS SHE *BACK*?

CAPTAIN SKINNER, WE NEED TO GET HIM INSIDE--

SIR, HE'S PASSING OUT!

WAKE UP, YOU MAGGOT!

UH!

I NEED TO KNOW WHAT YOU *SAW*, SOLDIER!

"WE...WE CRACKED THAT SUPERMARKET NEAR *WEMBLEY FALLS*. GOT FOUR ADULTS AND A KID...

"IT WASN'T 'TIL WE REACHED *KILBURN SWAMP* THAT WE NOTICED THE GUARDS WERE MISSING.

"THEN ARROWS STARTED COMING AT US LIKE BULLETS...

"SHE...SHE GOT INSIDE THE VAN SOMEHOW.

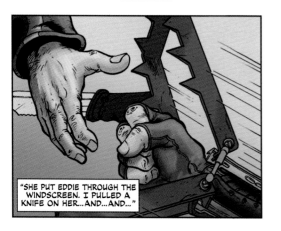

"SHE PUT EDDIE THROUGH THE WINDSCREEN. I PULLED A KNIFE ON HER...AND...AND..."

AND THEN... S-SHE WAS *GONE*...

THAT ANSWER YER QUESTION, HARRY?

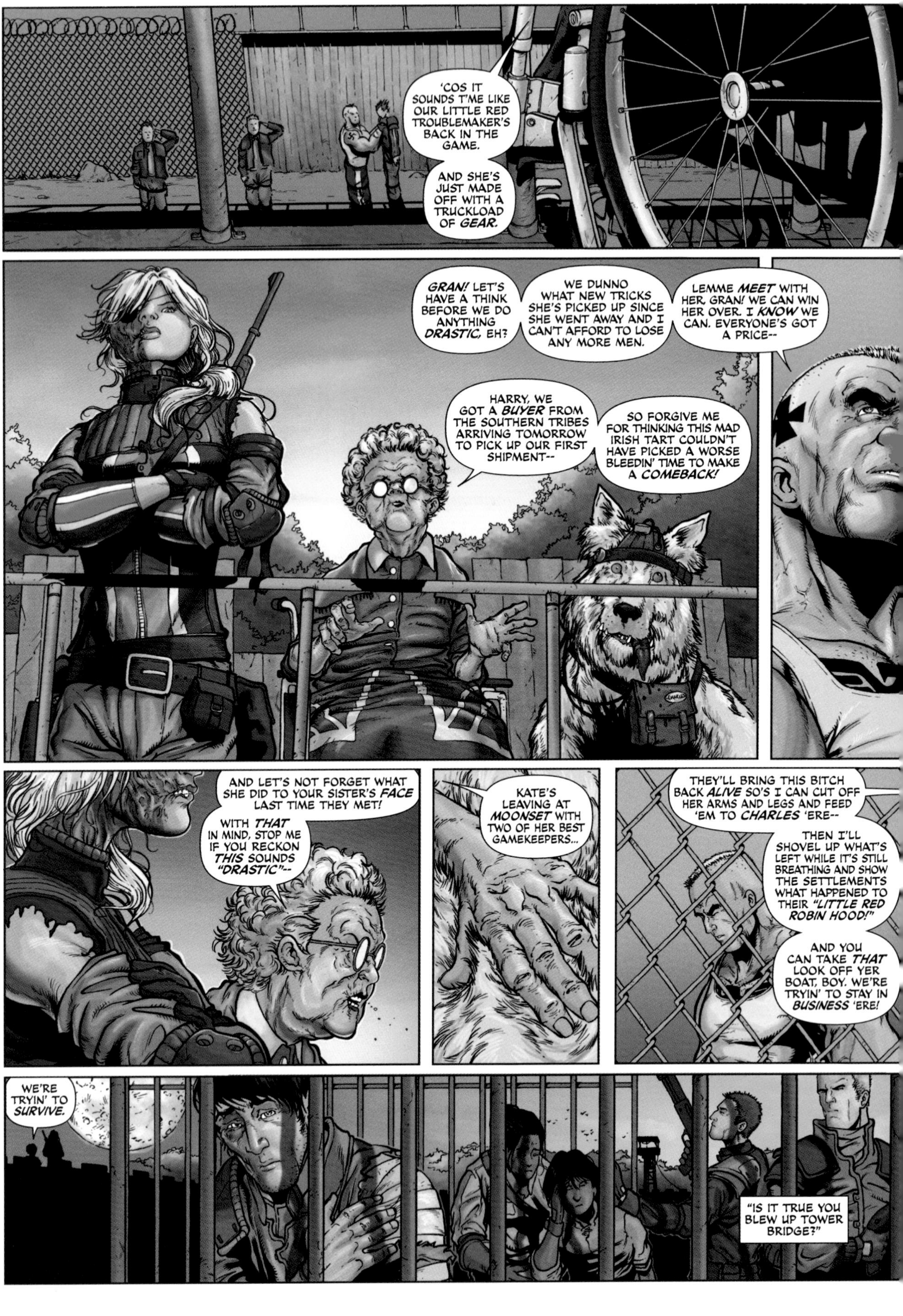
'COS IT SOUNDS T'ME LIKE OUR LITTLE RED TROUBLEMAKER'S BACK IN THE GAME.
AND SHE'S JUST MADE OFF WITH A TRUCKLOAD OF GEAR.
GRAN! LET'S HAVE A THINK BEFORE WE DO ANYTHING DRASTIC, EH?
WE DUNNO WHAT NEW TRICKS SHE'S PICKED UP SINCE SHE WENT AWAY AND I CAN'T AFFORD TO LOSE ANY MORE MEN.
LEMME MEET WITH HER, GRAN! WE CAN WIN HER OVER. I KNOW WE CAN. EVERYONE'S GOT A PRICE--
HARRY, WE GOT A BUYER FROM THE SOUTHERN TRIBES ARRIVING TOMORROW TO PICK UP OUR FIRST SHIPMENT--
SO FORGIVE ME FOR THINKING THIS MAD IRISH TART COULDN'T HAVE PICKED A WORSE BLEEDIN' TIME TO MAKE A COMEBACK!
AND LET'S NOT FORGET WHAT SHE DID TO YOUR SISTER'S FACE LAST TIME THEY MET!
WITH THAT IN MIND, STOP ME IF YOU RECKON THIS SOUNDS "DRASTIC"--
KATE'S LEAVING AT MOONSET WITH TWO OF HER BEST GAMEKEEPERS...
THEY'LL BRING THIS BITCH BACK ALIVE SO'S I CAN CUT OFF HER ARMS AND LEGS AND FEED 'EM TO CHARLES 'ERE--
THEN I'LL SHOVEL UP WHAT'S LEFT WHILE IT'S STILL BREATHING AND SHOW THE SETTLEMENTS WHAT HAPPENED TO THEIR "LITTLE RED ROBIN HOOD!"
AND YOU CAN TAKE THAT LOOK OFF YER BOAT, BOY. WE'RE TRYIN' TO STAY IN BUSINESS 'ERE!
WE'RE TRYIN' TO SURVIVE.
"IS IT TRUE YOU BLEW UP TOWER BRIDGE?"

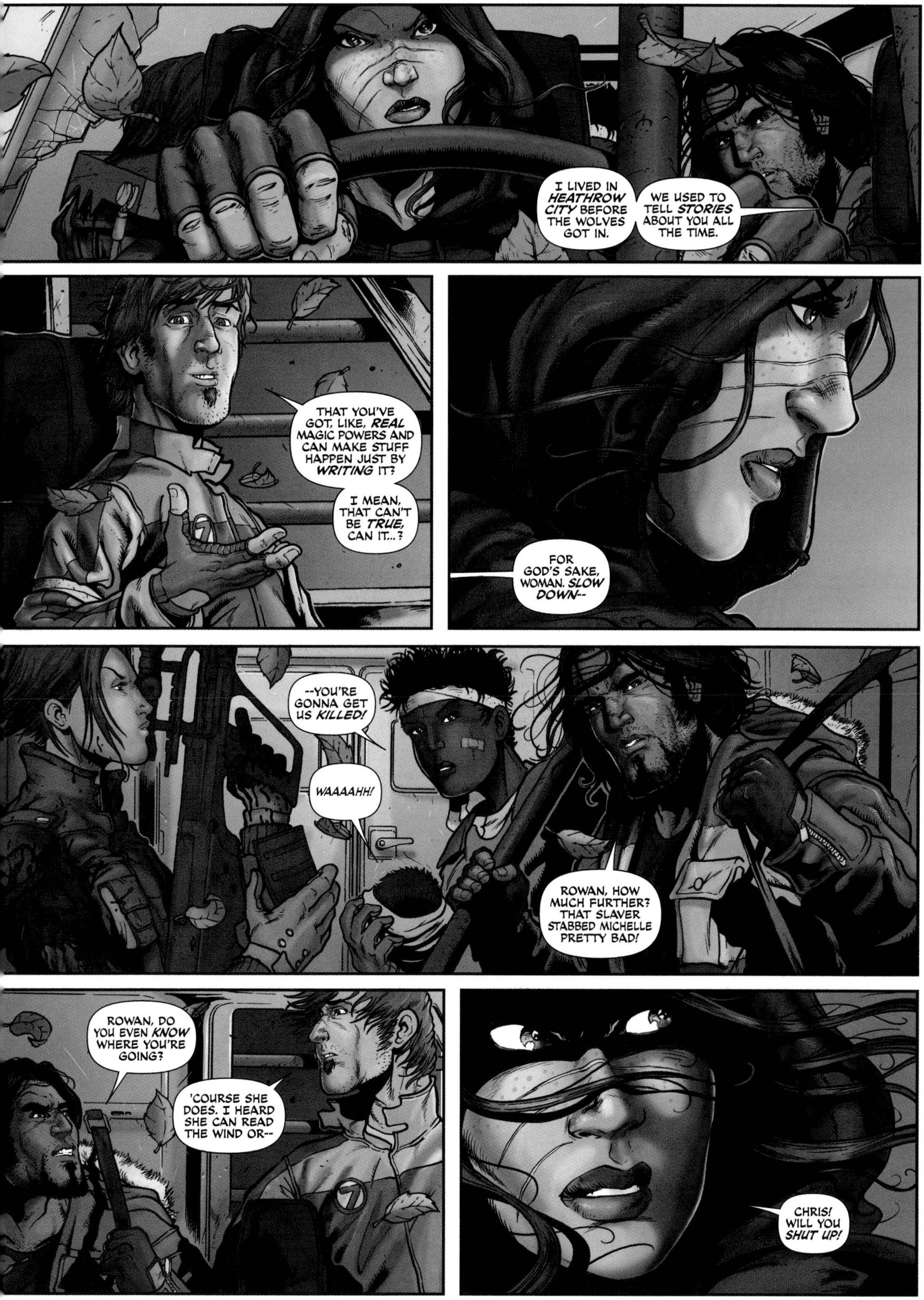
I LIVED IN HEATHROW CITY BEFORE THE WOLVES GOT IN.
WE USED TO TELL STORIES ABOUT YOU ALL THE TIME.
THAT YOU'VE GOT, LIKE, REAL MAGIC POWERS AND CAN MAKE STUFF HAPPEN JUST BY WRITING IT?
I MEAN, THAT CAN'T BE TRUE, CAN IT...?
FOR GOD'S SAKE, WOMAN. SLOW DOWN--
--YOU'RE GONNA GET US KILLED!
WAAAAHH!
ROWAN, HOW MUCH FURTHER? THAT SLAVER STABBED MICHELLE PRETTY BAD!
ROWAN, DO YOU EVEN KNOW WHERE YOU'RE GOING?
'COURSE SHE DOES. I HEARD SHE CAN READ THE WIND OR--
CHRIS! WILL YOU SHUT UP!

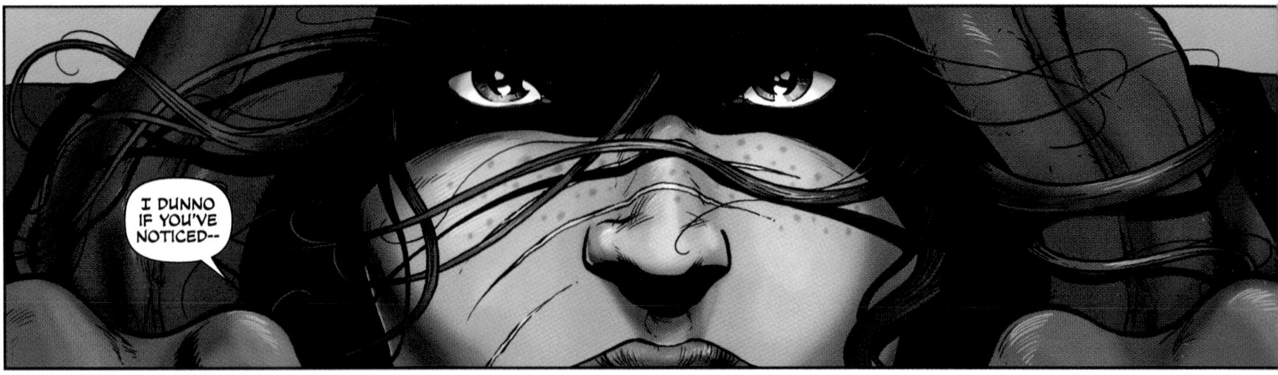
I DUNNO IF YOU'VE NOTICED--

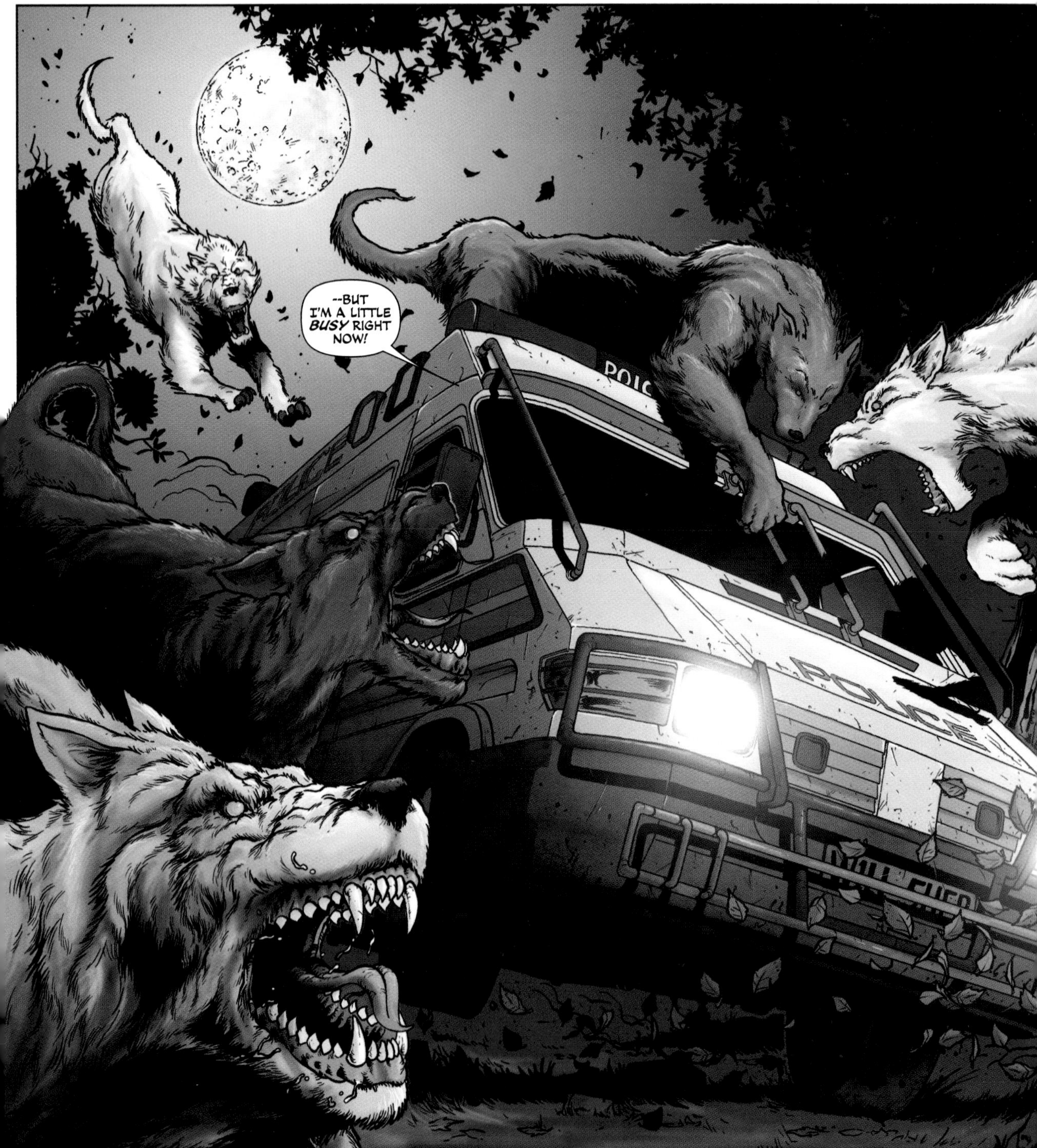
--BUT I'M A LITTLE *BUSY* RIGHT NOW!
POLICE
POLICE

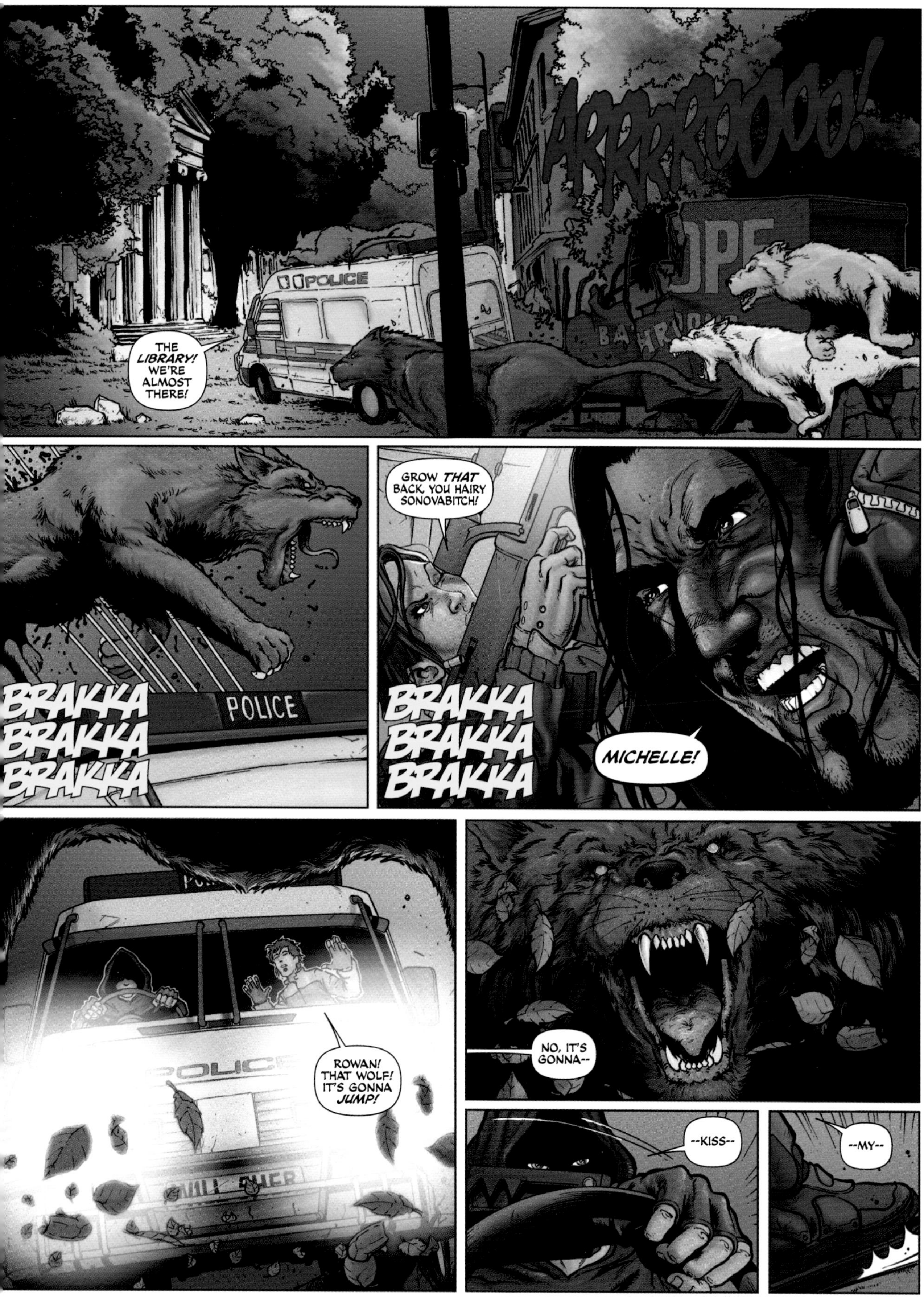
ARRRROOOO!
THE LIBRARY! WE'RE ALMOST THERE!
BRAKKA
BRAKKA
BRAKKA
POLICE
GROW THAT BACK, YOU HAIRY SONOVABITCH!
BRAKKA
BRAKKA
BRAKKA
MICHELLE!
ROWAN! THAT WOLF! IT'S GONNA JUMP!
NO, IT'S GONNA--
--KISS--
--MY--

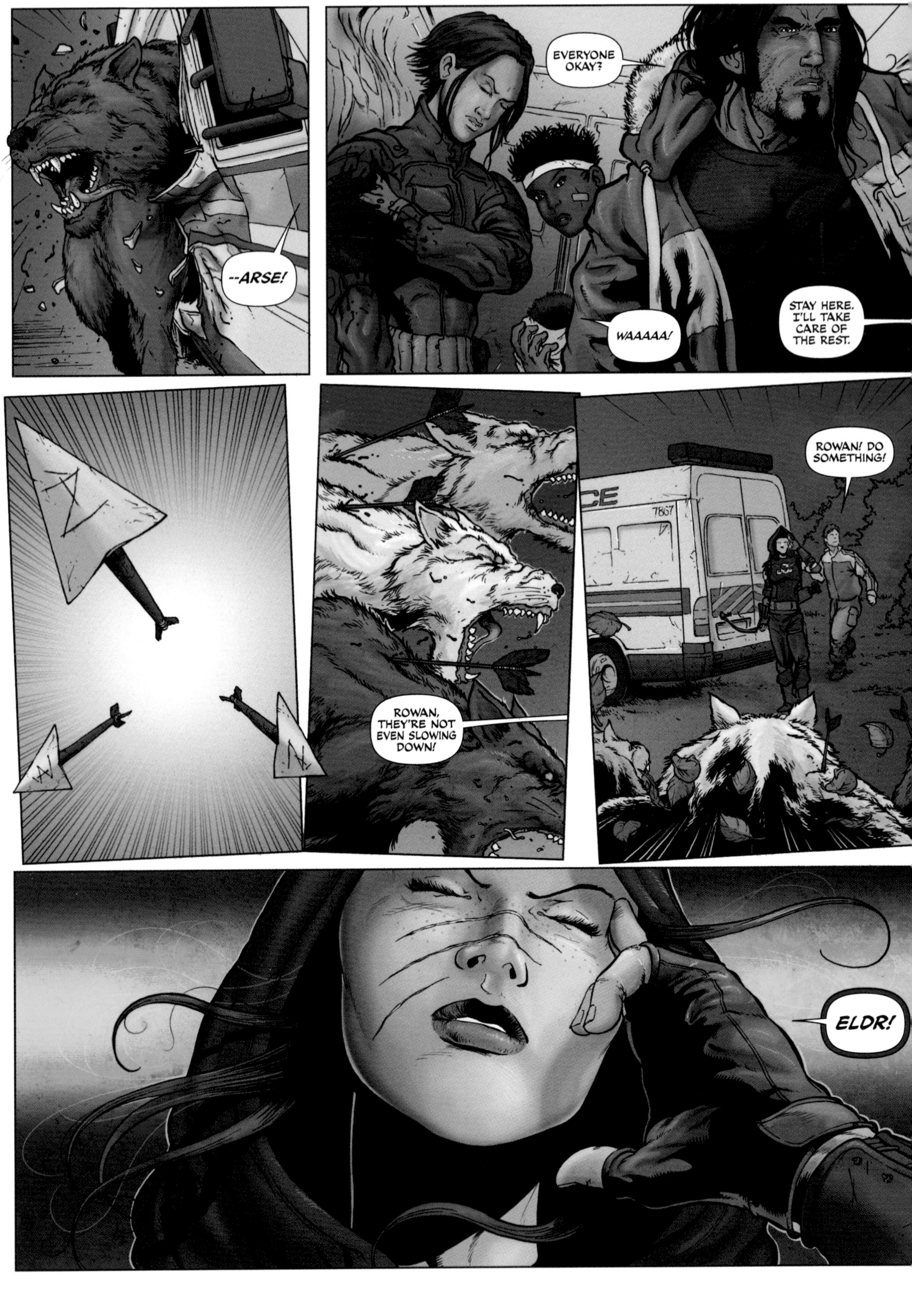
--ARSE!
EVERYONE OKAY?
WAAAAA!
STAY HERE. I'LL TAKE CARE OF THE REST.
ROWAN, THEY'RE NOT EVEN SLOWING DOWN!
ROWAN! DO SOMETHING!
ELDR!

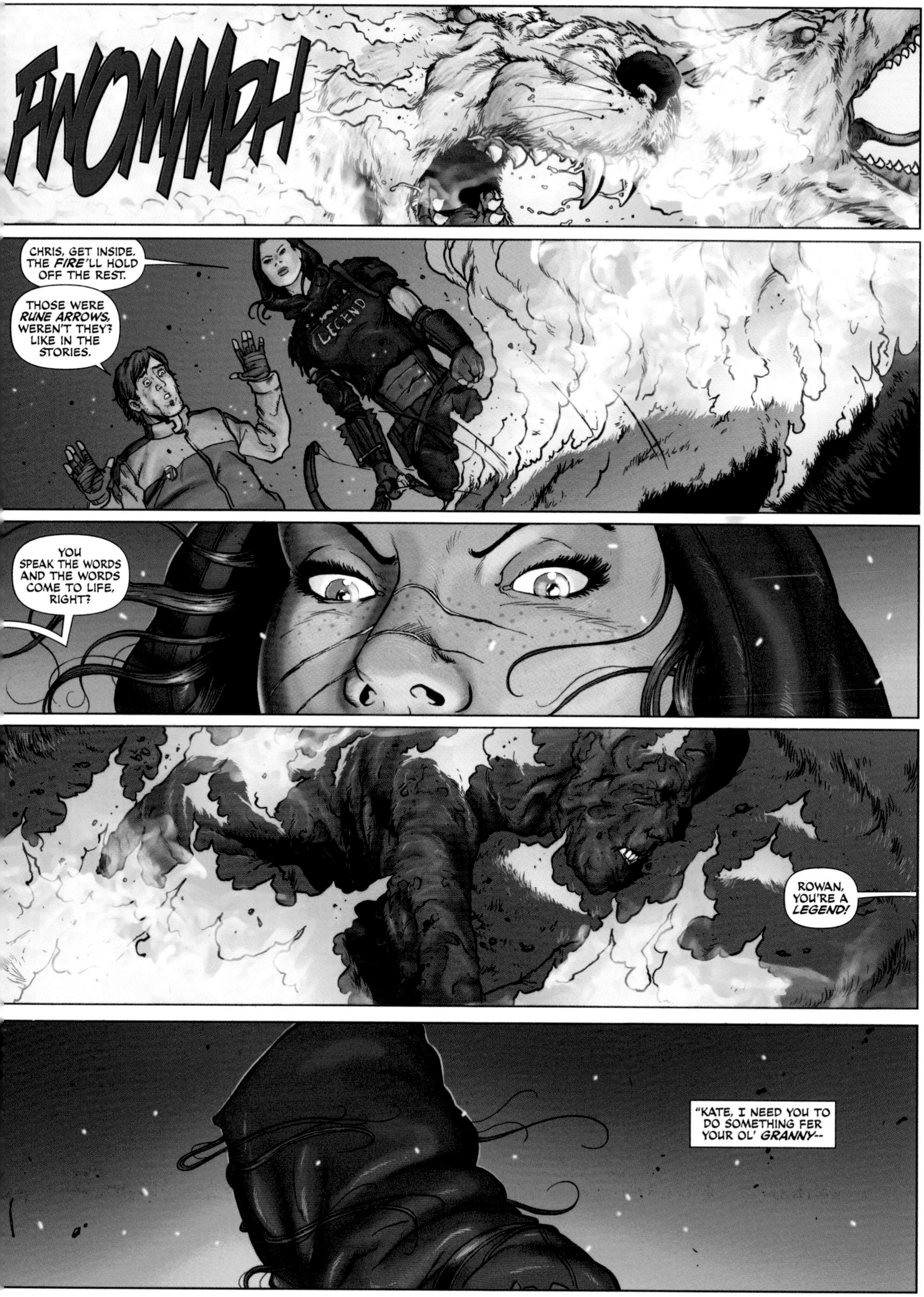
FWOMMPH
CHRIS, GET INSIDE. THE FIRE'LL HOLD OFF THE REST.
THOSE WERE RUNE ARROWS, WEREN'T THEY? LIKE IN THE STORIES.
LEGEND
YOU SPEAK THE WORDS AND THE WORDS COME TO LIFE, RIGHT?
ROWAN, YOU'RE A LEGEND!
"KATE, I NEED YOU TO DO SOMETHING FER YOUR OL' GRANNY--

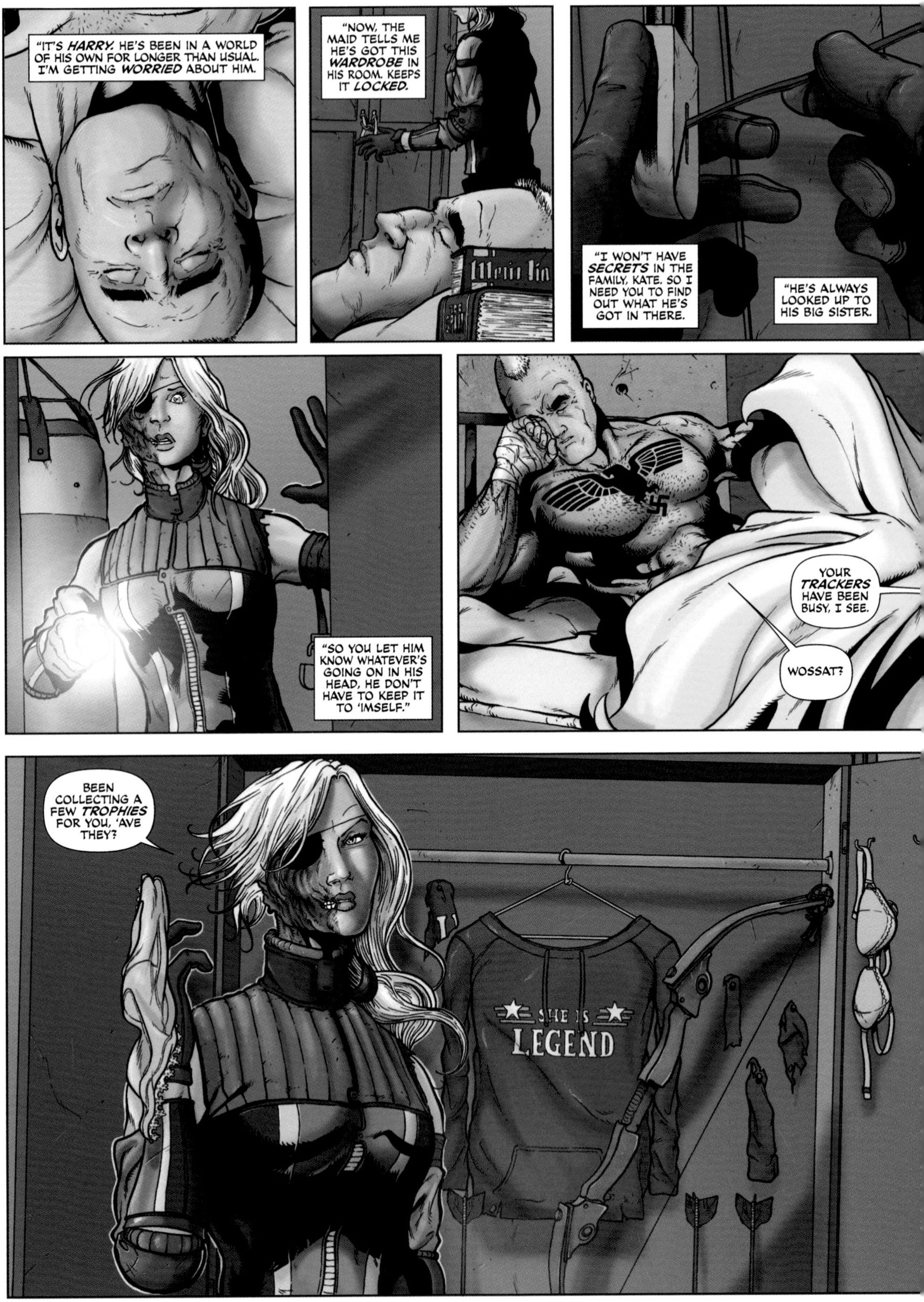
"IT'S HARRY. HE'S BEEN IN A WORLD OF HIS OWN FOR LONGER THAN USUAL. I'M GETTING WORRIED ABOUT HIM.
"NOW, THE MAID TELLS ME HE'S GOT THIS WARDROBE IN HIS ROOM. KEEPS IT LOCKED.
"I WON'T HAVE SECRETS IN THE FAMILY, KATE. SO I NEED YOU TO FIND OUT WHAT HE'S GOT IN THERE.
"HE'S ALWAYS LOOKED UP TO HIS BIG SISTER.
"SO YOU LET HIM KNOW WHATEVER'S GOING ON IN HIS HEAD, HE DON'T HAVE TO KEEP IT TO 'IMSELF."
YOUR TRACKERS HAVE BEEN BUSY, I SEE.
WOSSAT?
BEEN COLLECTING A FEW TROPHIES FOR YOU, 'AVE THEY?
SHE IS LEGEND

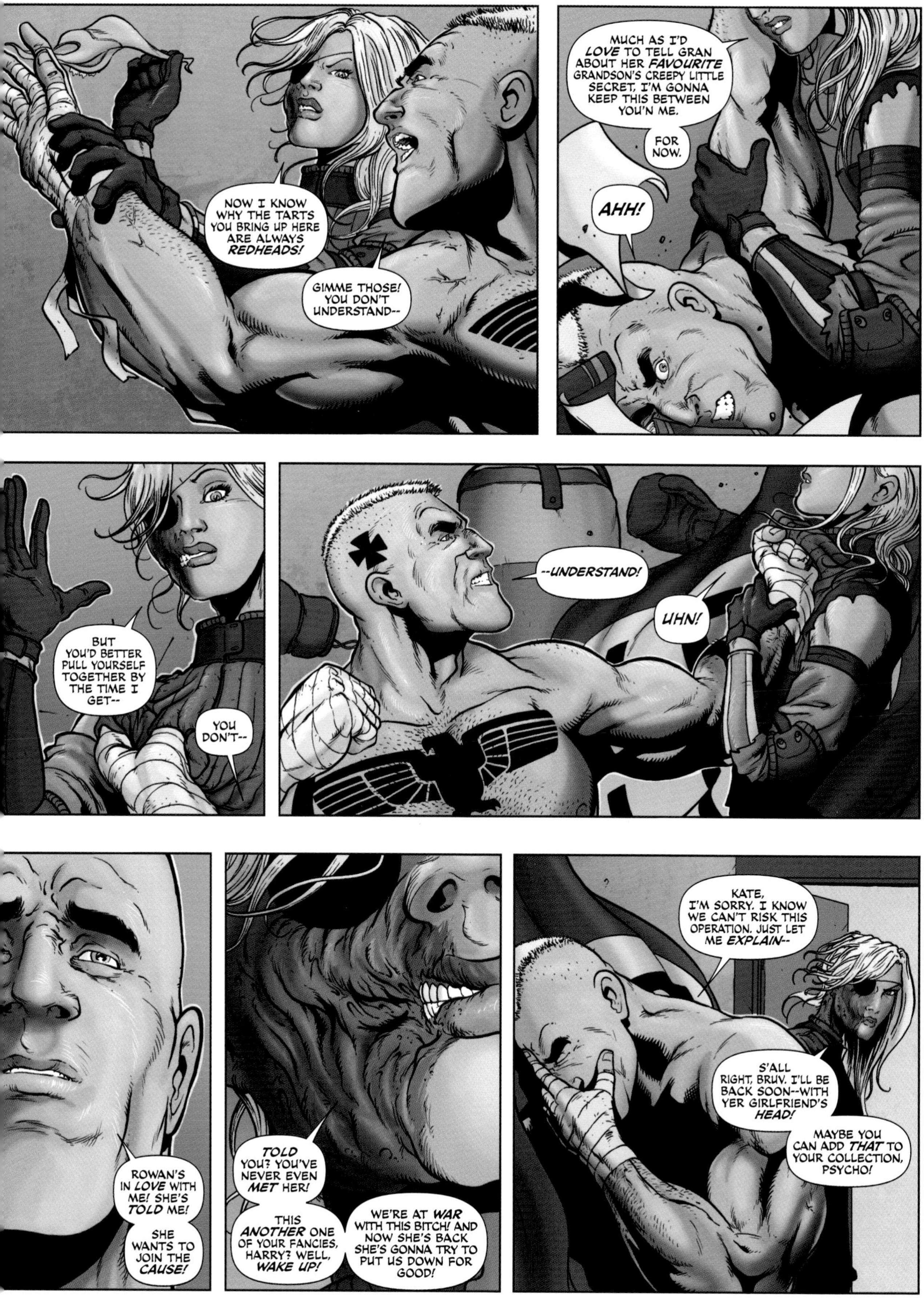
NOW I KNOW WHY THE TARTS YOU BRING UP HERE ARE ALWAYS *REDHEADS!*
GIMME THOSE! YOU DON'T UNDERSTAND--
MUCH AS I'D *LOVE* TO TELL GRAN ABOUT HER *FAVOURITE* GRANDSON'S CREEPY LITTLE SECRET, I'M GONNA KEEP THIS BETWEEN YOU'N ME.
FOR NOW.
AHH!
BUT YOU'D BETTER PULL YOURSELF TOGETHER BY THE TIME I GET--
YOU DON'T--
--UNDERSTAND!
UHN!
ROWAN'S IN *LOVE* WITH ME! SHE'S *TOLD* ME!
SHE WANTS TO JOIN THE *CAUSE!*
TOLD YOU? YOU'VE NEVER EVEN *MET* HER!
THIS *ANOTHER* ONE OF YOUR FANCIES, HARRY? WELL, *WAKE UP!*
WE'RE AT *WAR* WITH THIS BITCH! AND NOW SHE'S BACK SHE'S GONNA TRY TO PUT US DOWN FOR GOOD!
KATE, I'M SORRY. I KNOW WE CAN'T RISK THIS OPERATION. JUST LET ME *EXPLAIN--*
S'ALL RIGHT, BRUV. I'LL BE BACK SOON--WITH YER GIRLFRIEND'S *HEAD!*
MAYBE YOU CAN ADD *THAT* TO YOUR COLLECTION, PSYCHO!

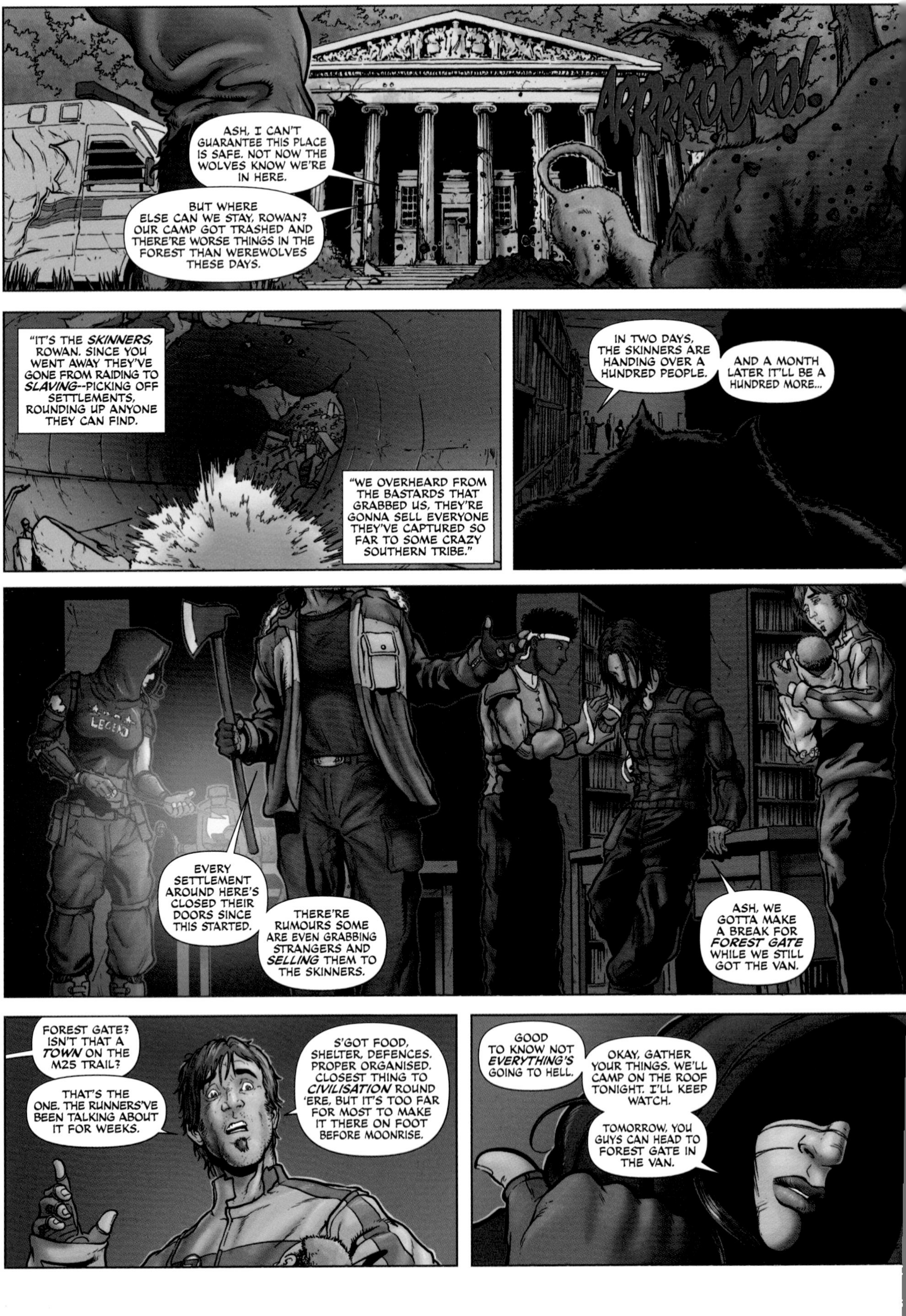
ARRRROOOOO!
ASH, I CAN'T GUARANTEE THIS PLACE IS SAFE. NOT NOW THE WOLVES KNOW WE'RE IN HERE.
BUT WHERE ELSE CAN WE STAY, ROWAN? OUR CAMP GOT TRASHED AND THERE'RE WORSE THINGS IN THE FOREST THAN WEREWOLVES THESE DAYS.
"IT'S THE *SKINNERS,* ROWAN. SINCE YOU WENT AWAY THEY'VE GONE FROM RAIDING TO *SLAVING*--PICKING OFF SETTLEMENTS, ROUNDING UP ANYONE THEY CAN FIND.
"WE OVERHEARD FROM THE BASTARDS THAT GRABBED US, THEY'RE GONNA SELL EVERYONE THEY'VE CAPTURED SO FAR TO SOME CRAZY SOUTHERN TRIBE."
IN TWO DAYS, THE SKINNERS ARE HANDING OVER A HUNDRED PEOPLE.
AND A MONTH LATER IT'LL BE A HUNDRED MORE...
EVERY SETTLEMENT AROUND HERE'S CLOSED THEIR DOORS SINCE THIS STARTED.
THERE'RE RUMOURS SOME ARE EVEN GRABBING STRANGERS AND *SELLING* THEM TO THE SKINNERS.
ASH, WE GOTTA MAKE A BREAK FOR *FOREST GATE* WHILE WE STILL GOT THE VAN.
FOREST GATE? ISN'T THAT A *TOWN* ON THE M25 TRAIL?
THAT'S THE ONE. THE RUNNERS'VE BEEN TALKING ABOUT IT FOR WEEKS.
S'GOT FOOD, SHELTER, DEFENCES. PROPER ORGANISED. CLOSEST THING TO *CIVILISATION* ROUND 'ERE, BUT IT'S TOO FAR FOR MOST TO MAKE IT THERE ON FOOT BEFORE MOONRISE.
GOOD TO KNOW NOT *EVERYTHING'S* GOING TO HELL.
OKAY, GATHER YOUR THINGS. WE'LL CAMP ON THE ROOF TONIGHT. I'LL KEEP WATCH.
TOMORROW, YOU GUYS CAN HEAD TO FOREST GATE IN THE VAN.

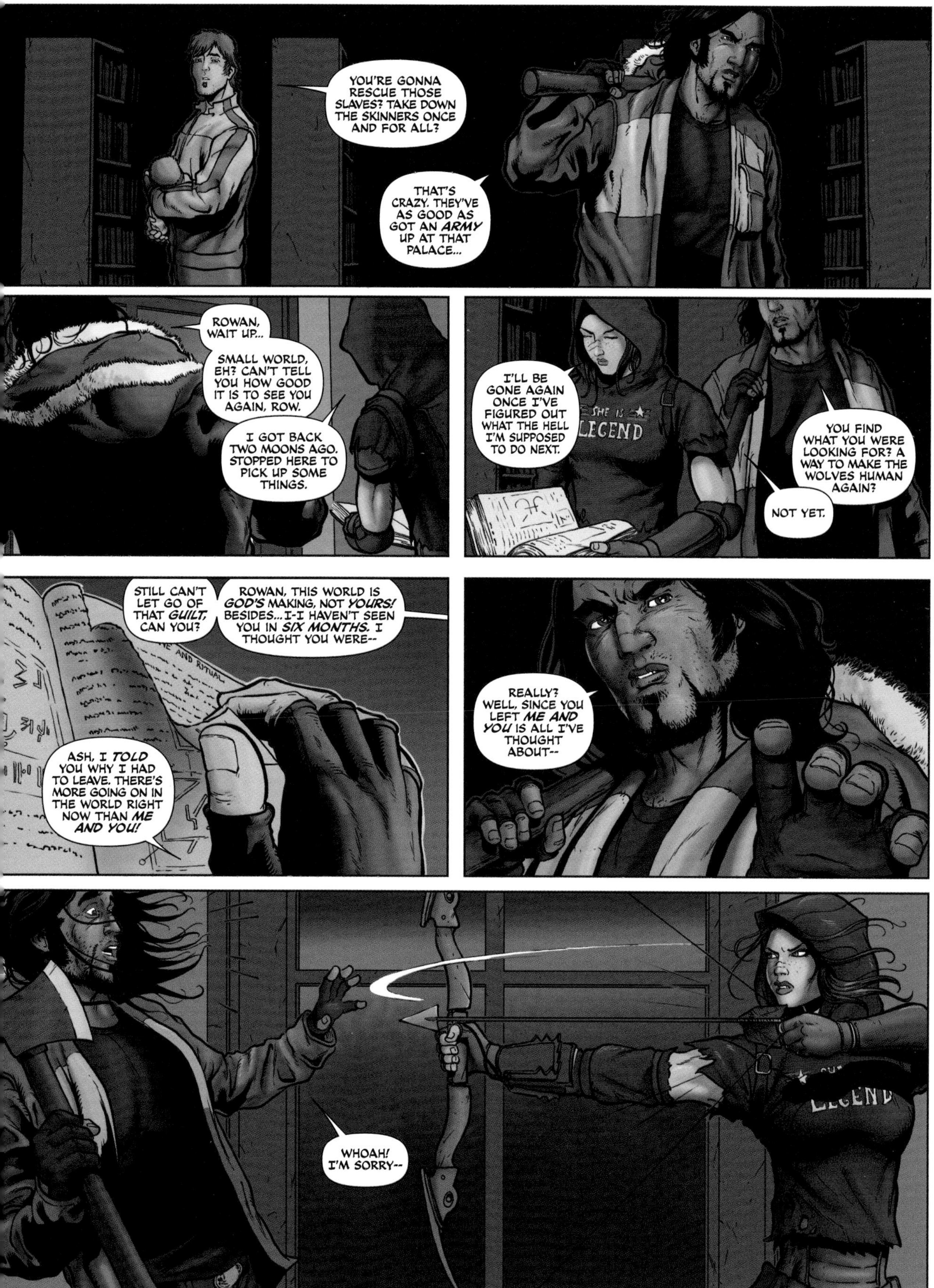
YOU'RE GONNA RESCUE THOSE SLAVES? TAKE DOWN THE SKINNERS ONCE AND FOR ALL?
THAT'S CRAZY. THEY'VE AS GOOD AS GOT AN ARMY UP AT THAT PALACE...
ROWAN, WAIT UP...
SMALL WORLD, EH? CAN'T TELL YOU HOW GOOD IT IS TO SEE YOU AGAIN, ROW.
I GOT BACK TWO MOONS AGO. STOPPED HERE TO PICK UP SOME THINGS.
I'LL BE GONE AGAIN ONCE I'VE FIGURED OUT WHAT THE HELL I'M SUPPOSED TO DO NEXT.
SHE IS LEGEND
YOU FIND WHAT YOU WERE LOOKING FOR? A WAY TO MAKE THE WOLVES HUMAN AGAIN?
NOT YET.
STILL CAN'T LET GO OF THAT GUILT, CAN YOU?
ROWAN, THIS WORLD IS GOD'S MAKING, NOT YOURS! BESIDES... I-I HAVEN'T SEEN YOU IN SIX MONTHS. I THOUGHT YOU WERE--
ASH, I TOLD YOU WHY I HAD TO LEAVE. THERE'S MORE GOING ON IN THE WORLD RIGHT NOW THAN ME AND YOU!
REALLY? WELL, SINCE YOU LEFT ME AND YOU IS ALL I'VE THOUGHT ABOUT--
WHOAH! I'M SORRY--
LEGEND

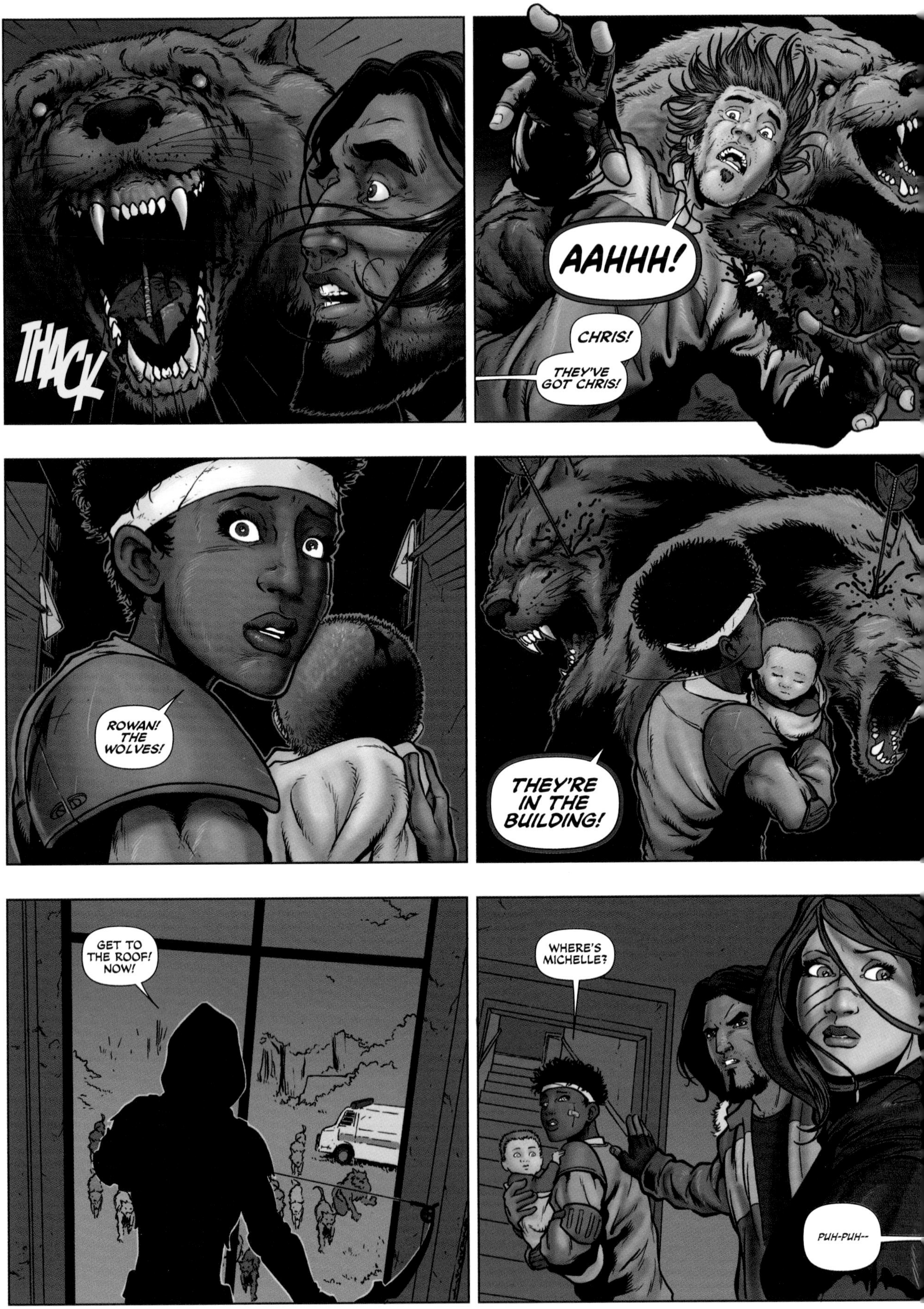
THACK
AAHHH!
CHRIS!
THEY'VE GOT CHRIS!
ROWAN! THE WOLVES!
THEY'RE IN THE BUILDING!
GET TO THE ROOF! NOW!
WHERE'S MICHELLE?
PUH-PUH--

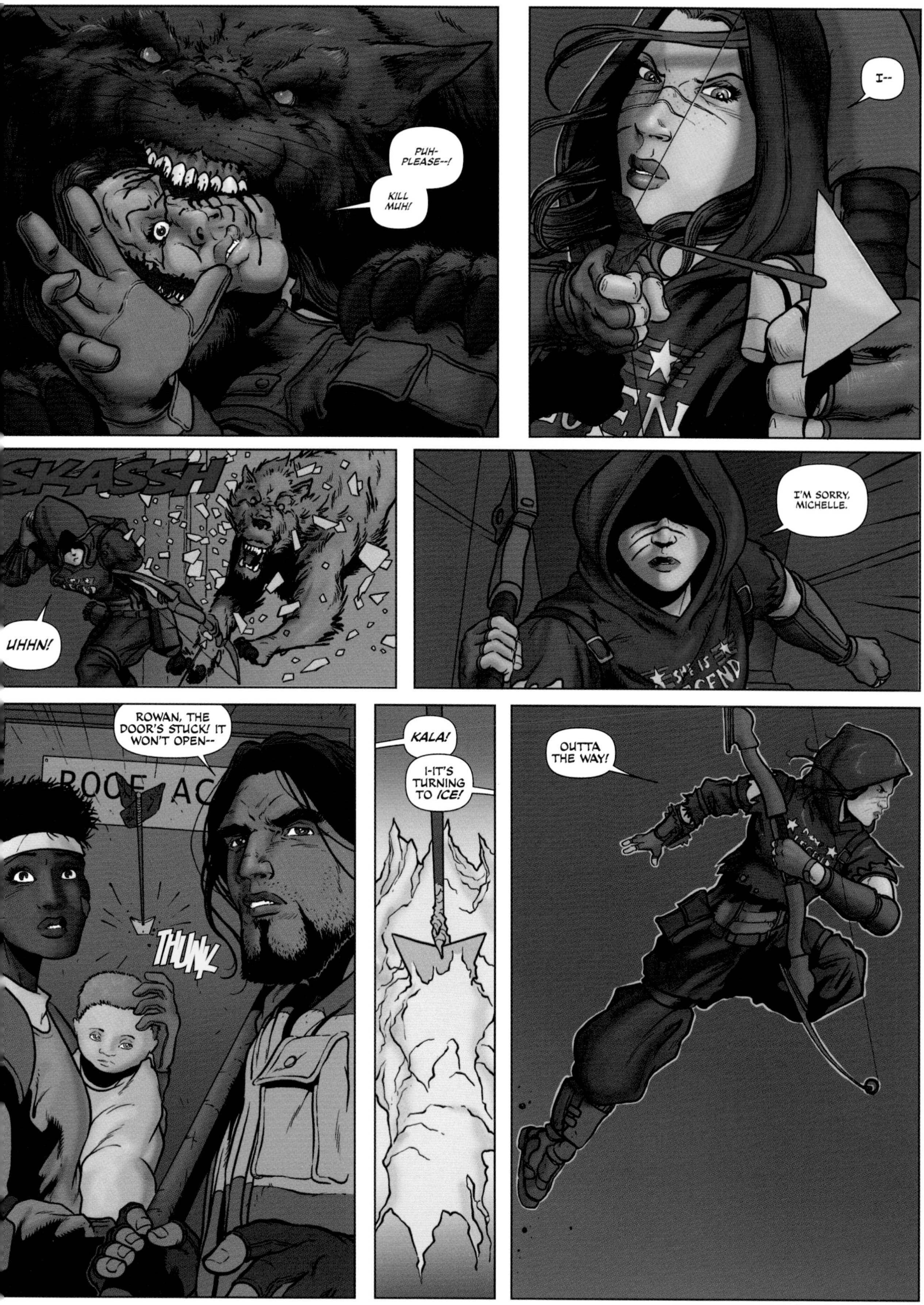
PUH-PLEASE--!
KILL MUH!
I--
SKASSH
UHHN!
I'M SORRY, MICHELLE.
ROWAN, THE DOOR'S STUCK! IT WON'T OPEN--
THUNK
KALA!
I-IT'S TURNING TO ICE!
OUTTA THE WAY!

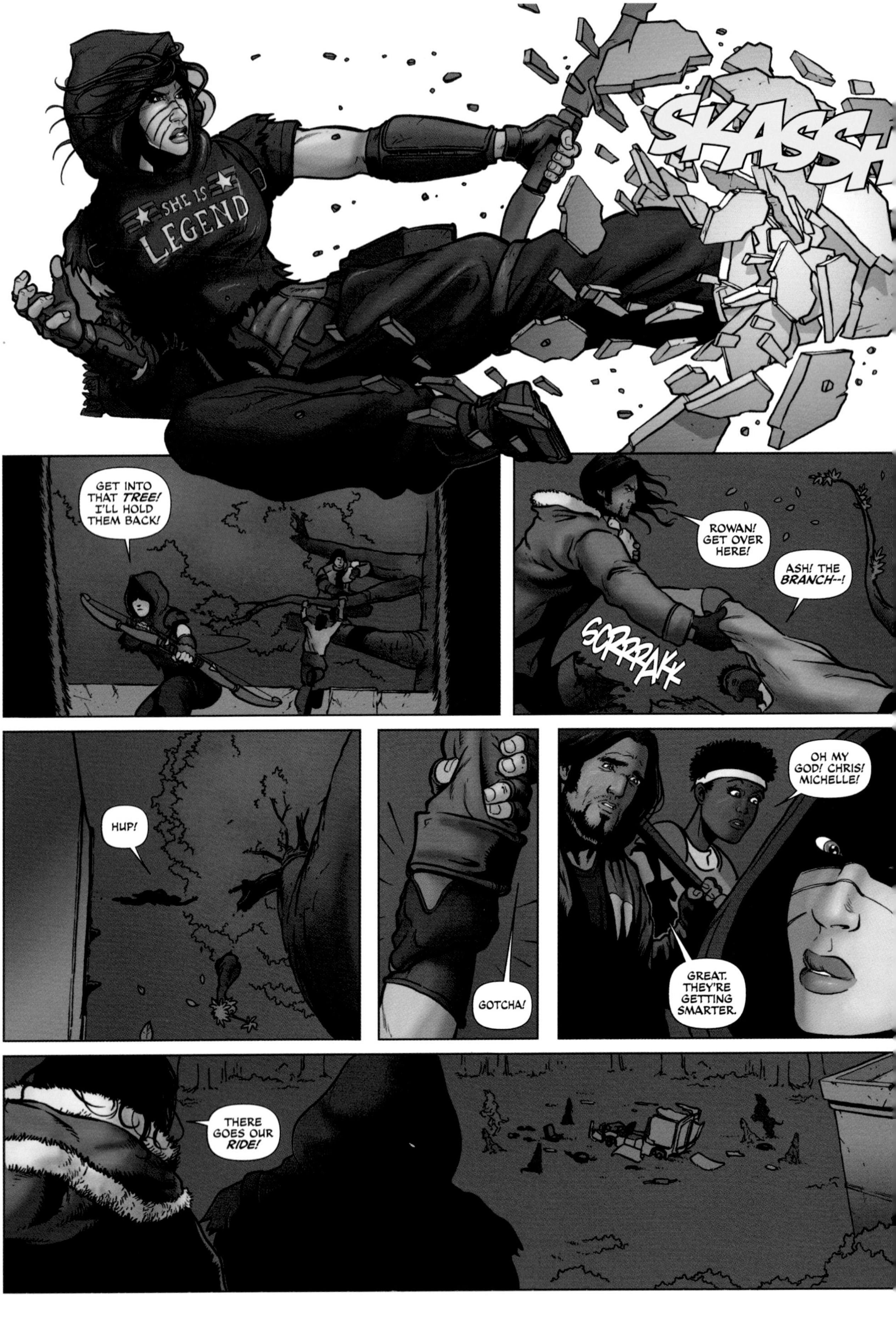
SKASSH
SHE IS LEGEND
GET INTO THAT TREE! I'LL HOLD THEM BACK!
ROWAN! GET OVER HERE!
ASH! THE BRANCH--!
SCRRRAKK
HUP!
GOTCHA!
OH MY GOD! CHRIS! MICHELLE!
GREAT. THEY'RE GETTING SMARTER.
THERE GOES OUR RIDE!

THE GREAT EXTRANEOUS, GRAND-BRUTE OF THE COASTAL TRIBES, SHALL BE PLEASED WITH YOUR OFFERING OF FLESH. AS SOON AS WE HAVE REPAIRED OUR TRANSPORT I SHALL--

I'M SORRY, SWEETHEART, I CAN ONLY 'OLD ME MANNERS FER SO LONG.

IS YOUR GAFFER ON A WIND-UP SENDING YOU 'ERE DRESSED LIKE THAT?

...IT-IT'S TRIBAL. THE CHIEF INSISTS ON IT...

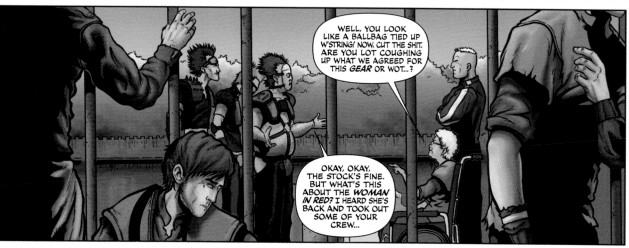

WELL, YOU LOOK LIKE A BALLBAG TIED UP W'STRING! NOW, CUT THE SHIT. ARE YOU LOT COUGHING UP WHAT WE AGREED FOR THIS GEAR OR WOT...?

OKAY, OKAY, THE STOCK'S FINE. BUT WHAT'S THIS ABOUT THE WOMAN IN RED? I HEARD SHE'S BACK AND TOOK OUT SOME OF YOUR CREW...

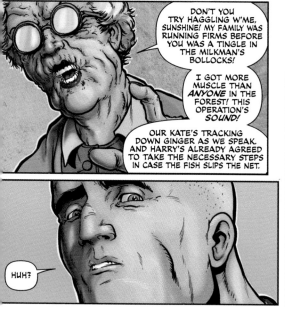

DON'T YOU TRY HAGGLING W'ME, SUNSHINE! MY FAMILY WAS RUNNING FIRMS BEFORE YOU WAS A TINGLE IN THE MILKMAN'S BOLLOCKS!

I GOT MORE MUSCLE THAN ANYONE IN THE FOREST! THIS OPERATION'S SOUND!

OUR KATE'S TRACKING DOWN GINGER AS WE SPEAK. AND HARRY'S ALREADY AGREED TO TAKE THE NECESSARY STEPS IN CASE THE FISH SLIPS THE NET.

HUH?

DIDN'T I MENTION? I GOT A MESSAGE WANTS DELIVERING TO THE LOCAL SETTLEMENTS. WE'RE TREBLING THE REWARD FOR THE CAPTURE OF LITTLE RED ROBIN HOOD.

THIS IS GINGER'S DEATH WARRANT. YOU'LL MAKE SURE IT'S DELIVERED, WON'T YOU, 'ARRY...?

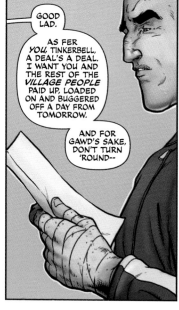

GOOD LAD.

AS FER YOU, TINKERBELL, A DEAL'S A DEAL. I WANT YOU AND THE REST OF THE VILLAGE PEOPLE PAID UP, LOADED ON AND BUGGERED OFF A DAY FROM TOMORROW.

AND FOR GAWD'S SAKE, DON'T TURN 'ROUND--

"--I'VE JUST 'AD ME TEA."

OKAY, THE VAN'S WRECKED, BUT I THINK I CAN STILL GET YOU TO *FOREST GATE.*

HOW? IT'S MILES NORTH OF HERE. WE NEED TO FIND SOMEWHERE SAFE BY MOONRISE *TONIGHT.*

LISTEN, THE *PICCADILLY RIVER* RUNS ALL THE WAY THERE. IT'S AN OBVIOUS ROUTE IF YOU'RE BEING FOLLOWED, BUT WE HAVEN'T MUCH CHOICE.

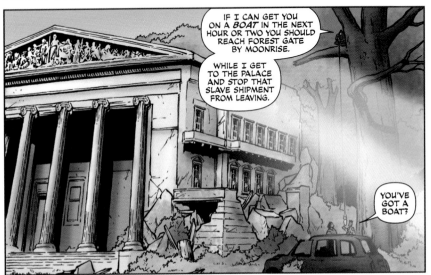

IF I CAN GET YOU ON A *BOAT* IN THE NEXT HOUR OR TWO YOU SHOULD REACH FOREST GATE BY MOONRISE.

WHILE I GET TO THE PALACE AND STOP THAT SLAVE SHIPMENT FROM LEAVING.

YOU'VE GOT A BOAT?

NO, BUT I KNOW WHERE I CAN GET ONE.

"YOU EVER HEARD OF THE *K9 KREW?*"

I DUNNO *WHAT* THEY'RE SAYING, KASS. I THINK IT'S SOME SORT OF *PRE-MOON* LANGUAGE.

GT 404. WE'RE BZ.

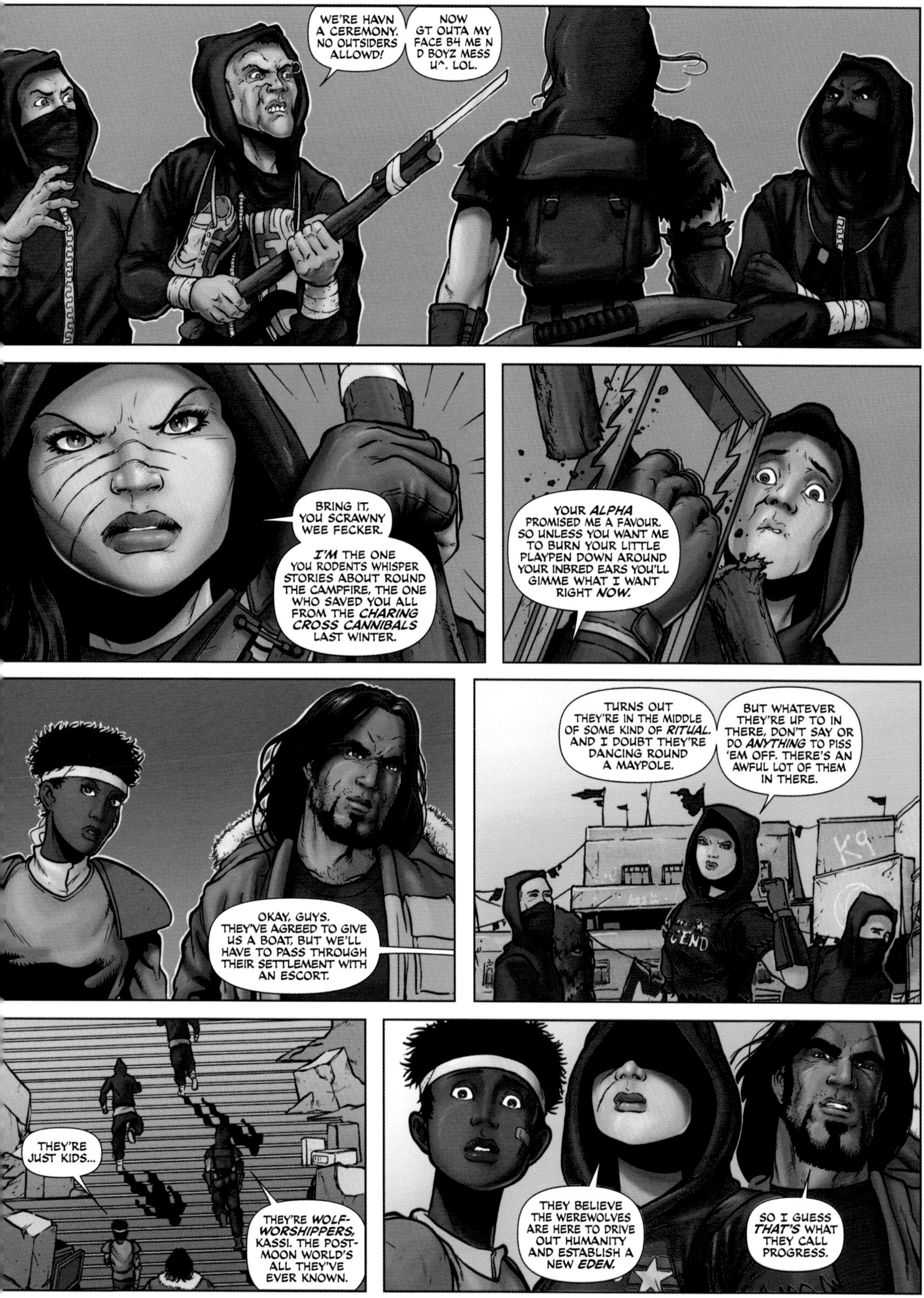
WE'RE HAVN A CEREMONY. NO OUTSIDERS ALLOWD!
NOW GT OUTA MY FACE B4 ME N D BOYZ MESS U^. LOL.
BRING IT, YOU SCRAWNY WEE FECKER.
I'M THE ONE YOU RODENTS WHISPER STORIES ABOUT ROUND THE CAMPFIRE, THE ONE WHO SAVED YOU ALL FROM THE CHARING CROSS CANNIBALS LAST WINTER.
YOUR ALPHA PROMISED ME A FAVOUR. SO UNLESS YOU WANT ME TO BURN YOUR LITTLE PLAYPEN DOWN AROUND YOUR INBRED EARS YOU'LL GIMME WHAT I WANT RIGHT NOW.
OKAY, GUYS. THEY'VE AGREED TO GIVE US A BOAT, BUT WE'LL HAVE TO PASS THROUGH THEIR SETTLEMENT WITH AN ESCORT.
TURNS OUT THEY'RE IN THE MIDDLE OF SOME KIND OF RITUAL. AND I DOUBT THEY'RE DANCING ROUND A MAYPOLE.
BUT WHATEVER THEY'RE UP TO IN THERE, DON'T SAY OR DO ANYTHING TO PISS 'EM OFF. THERE'S AN AWFUL LOT OF THEM IN THERE.
K9
THEY'RE JUST KIDS...
THEY'RE WOLF-WORSHIPPERS, KASSI. THE POST-MOON WORLD'S ALL THEY'VE EVER KNOWN.
THEY BELIEVE THE WEREWOLVES ARE HERE TO DRIVE OUT HUMANITY AND ESTABLISH A NEW EDEN.
SO I GUESS THAT'S WHAT THEY CALL PROGRESS.

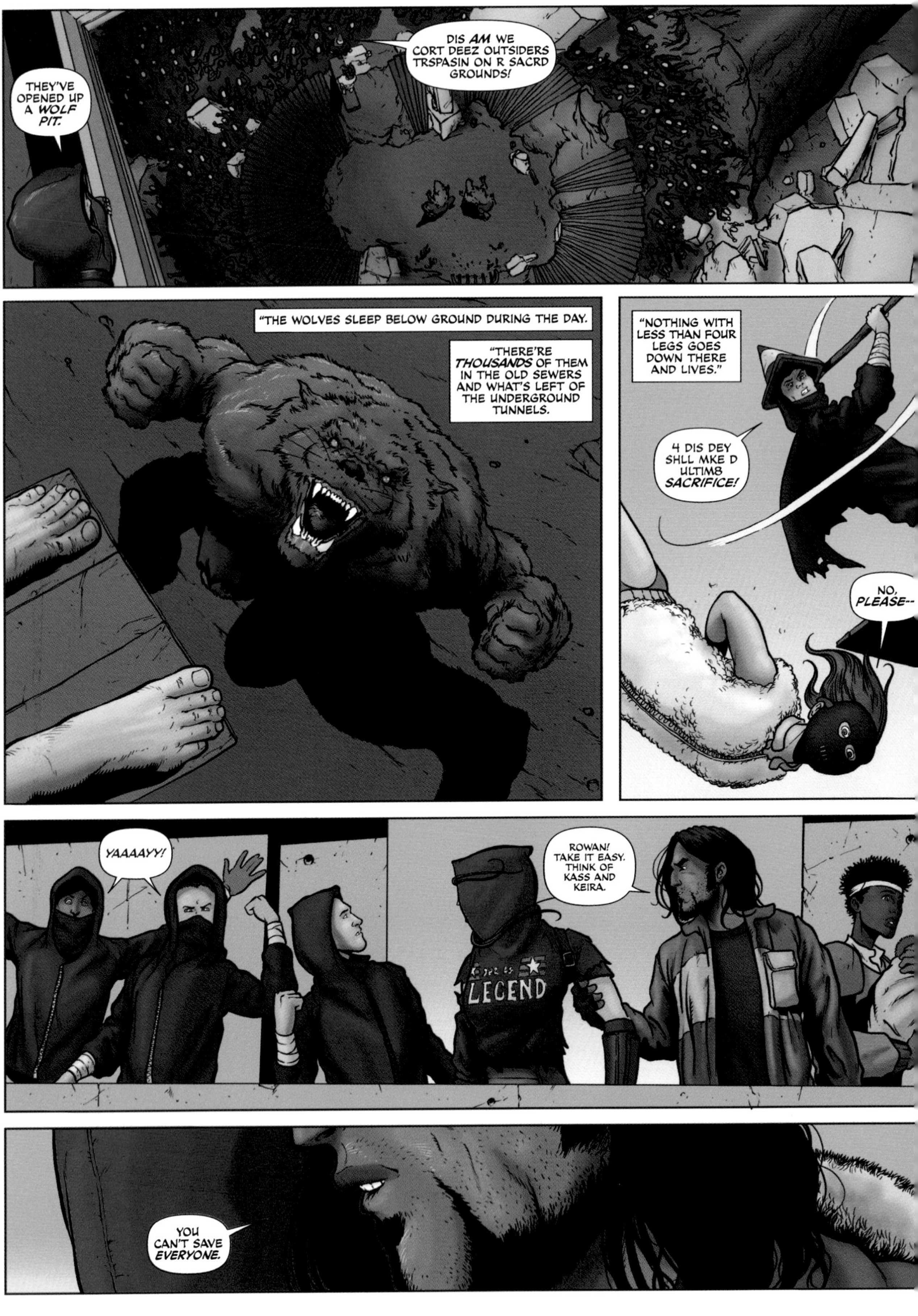
THEY'VE OPENED UP A WOLF PIT.
DIS AM WE CORT DEEZ OUTSIDERS TRSPASIN ON R SACRD GROUNDS!
"THE WOLVES SLEEP BELOW GROUND DURING THE DAY.
"THERE'RE THOUSANDS OF THEM IN THE OLD SEWERS AND WHAT'S LEFT OF THE UNDERGROUND TUNNELS.
"NOTHING WITH LESS THAN FOUR LEGS GOES DOWN THERE AND LIVES."
4 DIS DEY SHLL MKE D ULTIM8 SACRIFICE!
NO, PLEASE--
YAAAAYY!
ROWAN! TAKE IT EASY. THINK OF KASS AND KEIRA.
LEGEND
YOU CAN'T SAVE EVERYONE.

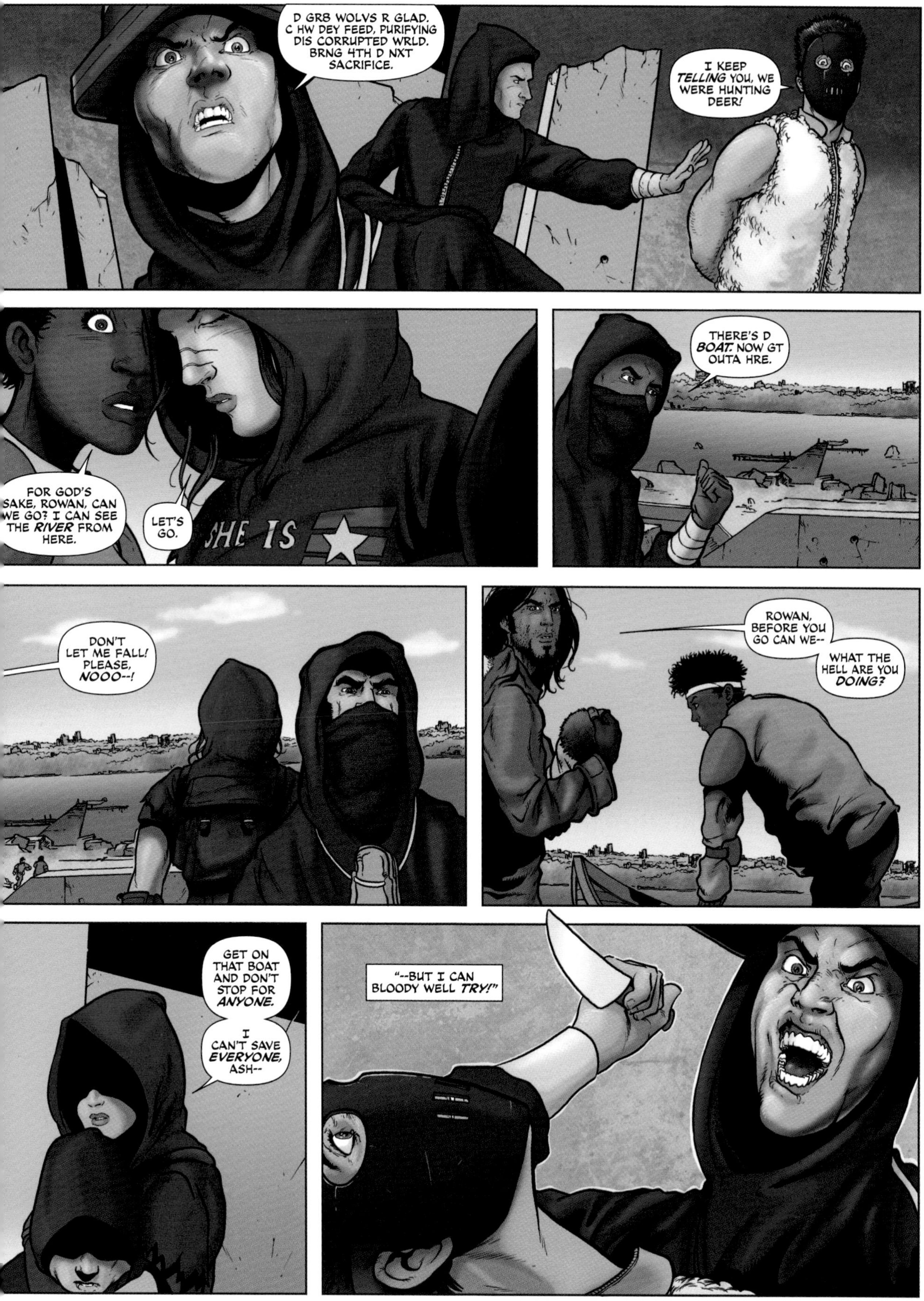
D GR8 WOLVS R GLAD. C HW DEY FEED, PURIFYING DIS CORRUPTED WRLD. BRNG 4TH D NXT SACRIFICE.
I KEEP TELLING YOU, WE WERE HUNTING DEER!
FOR GOD'S SAKE, ROWAN, CAN WE GO? I CAN SEE THE RIVER FROM HERE.
LET'S GO.
SHE IS
THERE'S D BOAT. NOW GT OUTA HRE.
DON'T LET ME FALL! PLEASE, NOOO--!
ROWAN, BEFORE YOU GO CAN WE--
WHAT THE HELL ARE YOU DOING?
GET ON THAT BOAT AND DON'T STOP FOR ANYONE.
I CAN'T SAVE EVERYONE, ASH--
"--BUT I CAN BLOODY WELL TRY!"

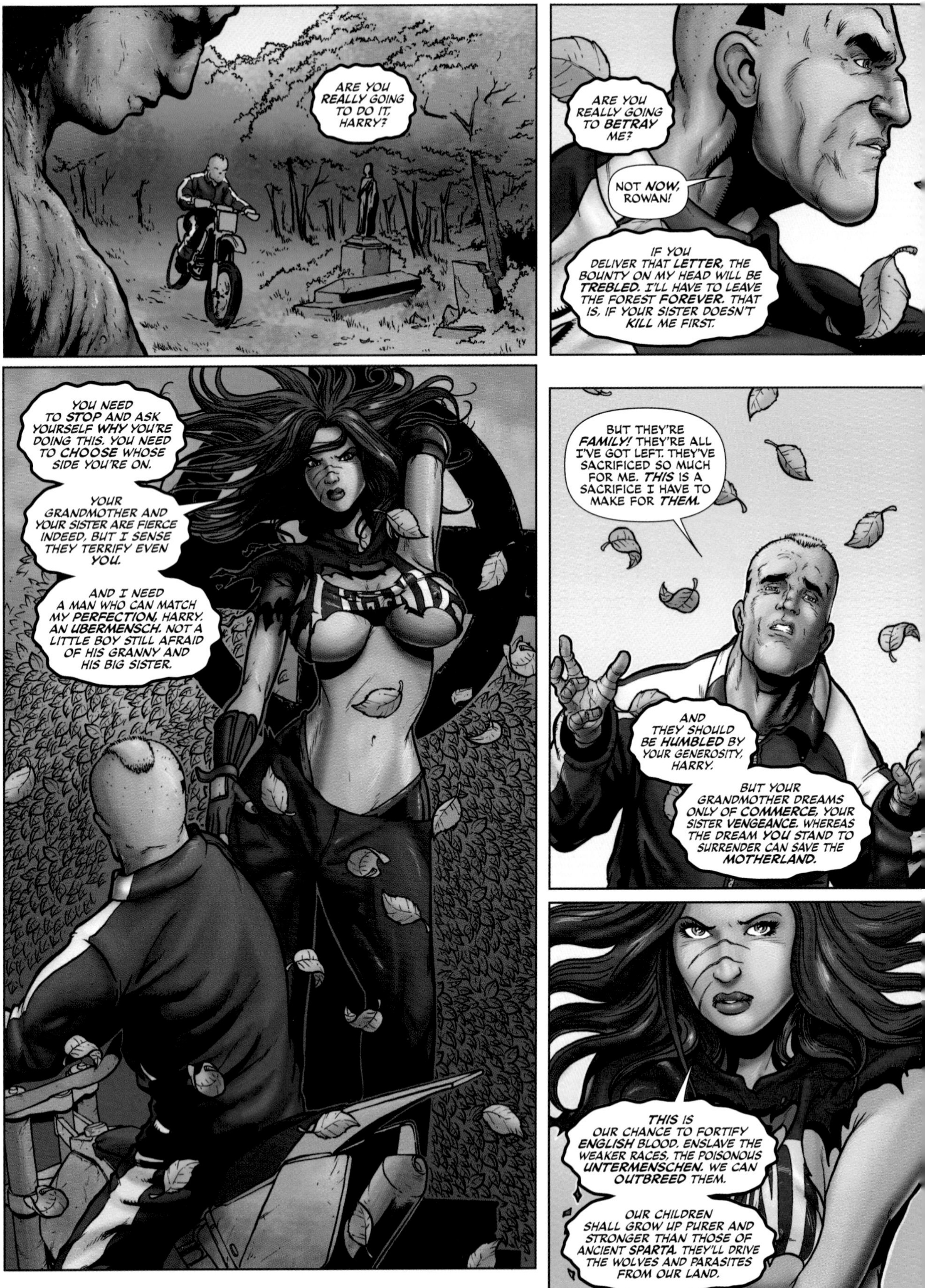
ARE YOU REALLY GOING TO DO IT, HARRY?
ARE YOU REALLY GOING TO BETRAY ME?
NOT NOW, ROWAN!
IF YOU DELIVER THAT LETTER, THE BOUNTY ON MY HEAD WILL BE TREBLED. I'LL HAVE TO LEAVE THE FOREST FOREVER. THAT IS, IF YOUR SISTER DOESN'T KILL ME FIRST.
YOU NEED TO STOP AND ASK YOURSELF WHY YOU'RE DOING THIS. YOU NEED TO CHOOSE WHOSE SIDE YOU'RE ON.
YOUR GRANDMOTHER AND YOUR SISTER ARE FIERCE INDEED, BUT I SENSE THEY TERRIFY EVEN YOU.
AND I NEED A MAN WHO CAN MATCH MY PERFECTION, HARRY. AN UBERMENSCH. NOT A LITTLE BOY STILL AFRAID OF HIS GRANNY AND HIS BIG SISTER.
BUT THEY'RE FAMILY! THEY'RE ALL I'VE GOT LEFT. THEY'VE SACRIFICED SO MUCH FOR ME. THIS IS A SACRIFICE I HAVE TO MAKE FOR THEM.
AND THEY SHOULD BE HUMBLED BY YOUR GENEROSITY, HARRY.
BUT YOUR GRANDMOTHER DREAMS ONLY OF COMMERCE, YOUR SISTER VENGEANCE. WHEREAS THE DREAM YOU STAND TO SURRENDER CAN SAVE THE MOTHERLAND.
THIS IS OUR CHANCE TO FORTIFY ENGLISH BLOOD. ENSLAVE THE WEAKER RACES, THE POISONOUS UNTERMENSCHEN. WE CAN OUTBREED THEM.
OUR CHILDREN SHALL GROW UP PURER AND STRONGER THAN THOSE OF ANCIENT SPARTA. THEY'LL DRIVE THE WOLVES AND PARASITES FROM OUR LAND.

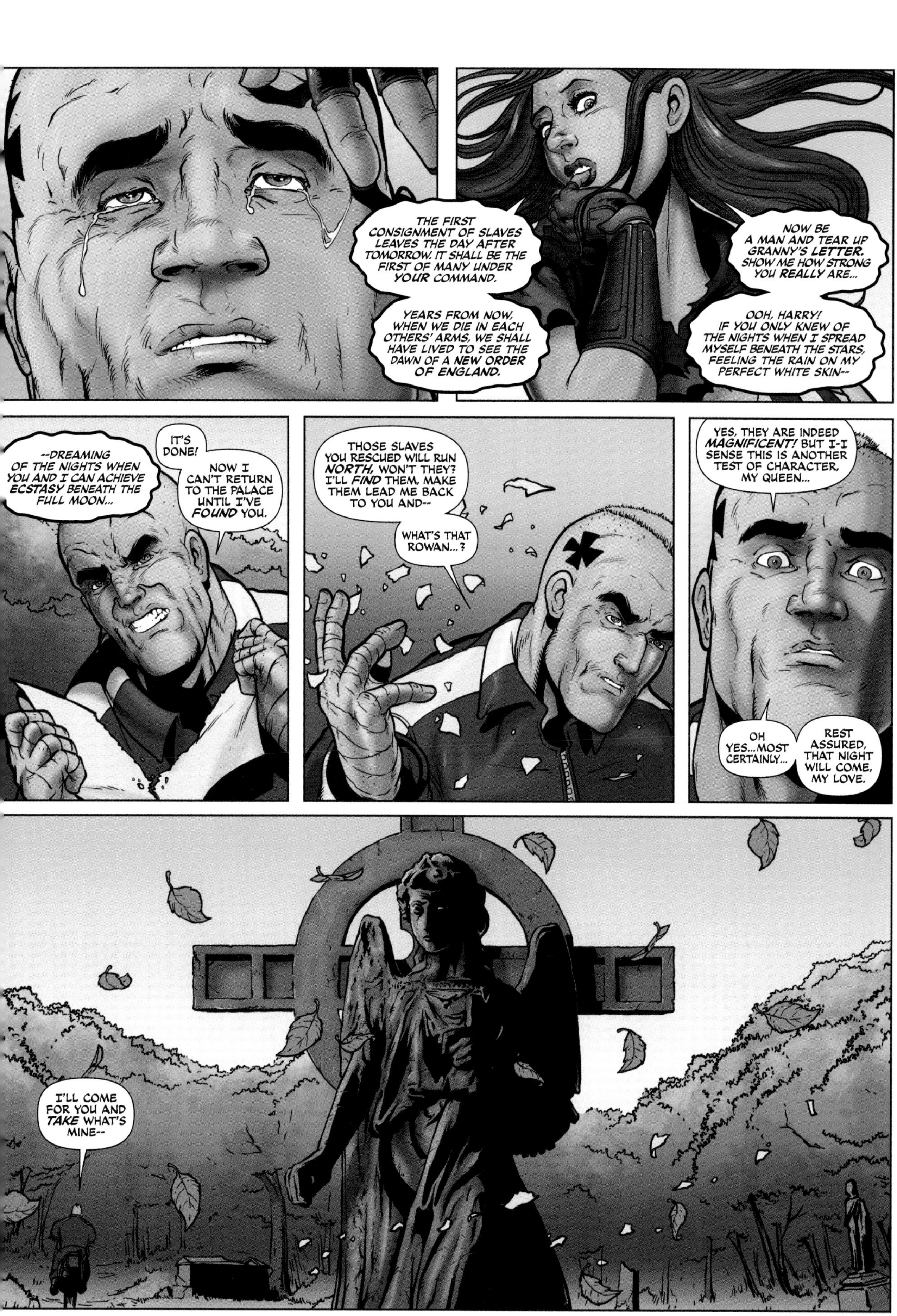
THE FIRST CONSIGNMENT OF SLAVES LEAVES THE DAY AFTER TOMORROW. IT SHALL BE THE FIRST OF MANY UNDER YOUR COMMAND.
YEARS FROM NOW, WHEN WE DIE IN EACH OTHERS' ARMS, WE SHALL HAVE LIVED TO SEE THE DAWN OF A NEW ORDER OF ENGLAND.
NOW BE A MAN AND TEAR UP GRANNY'S LETTER. SHOW ME HOW STRONG YOU REALLY ARE...
OOH, HARRY! IF YOU ONLY KNEW OF THE NIGHTS WHEN I SPREAD MYSELF BENEATH THE STARS, FEELING THE RAIN ON MY PERFECT WHITE SKIN--
--DREAMING OF THE NIGHTS WHEN YOU AND I CAN ACHIEVE ECSTASY BENEATH THE FULL MOON...
IT'S DONE!
NOW I CAN'T RETURN TO THE PALACE UNTIL I'VE FOUND YOU.
THOSE SLAVES YOU RESCUED WILL RUN NORTH, WON'T THEY? I'LL FIND THEM, MAKE THEM LEAD ME BACK TO YOU AND--
WHAT'S THAT ROWAN...?
YES, THEY ARE INDEED MAGNIFICENT! BUT I-I SENSE THIS IS ANOTHER TEST OF CHARACTER, MY QUEEN...
OH YES...MOST CERTAINLY...
REST ASSURED, THAT NIGHT WILL COME, MY LOVE.
I'LL COME FOR YOU AND TAKE WHAT'S MINE--

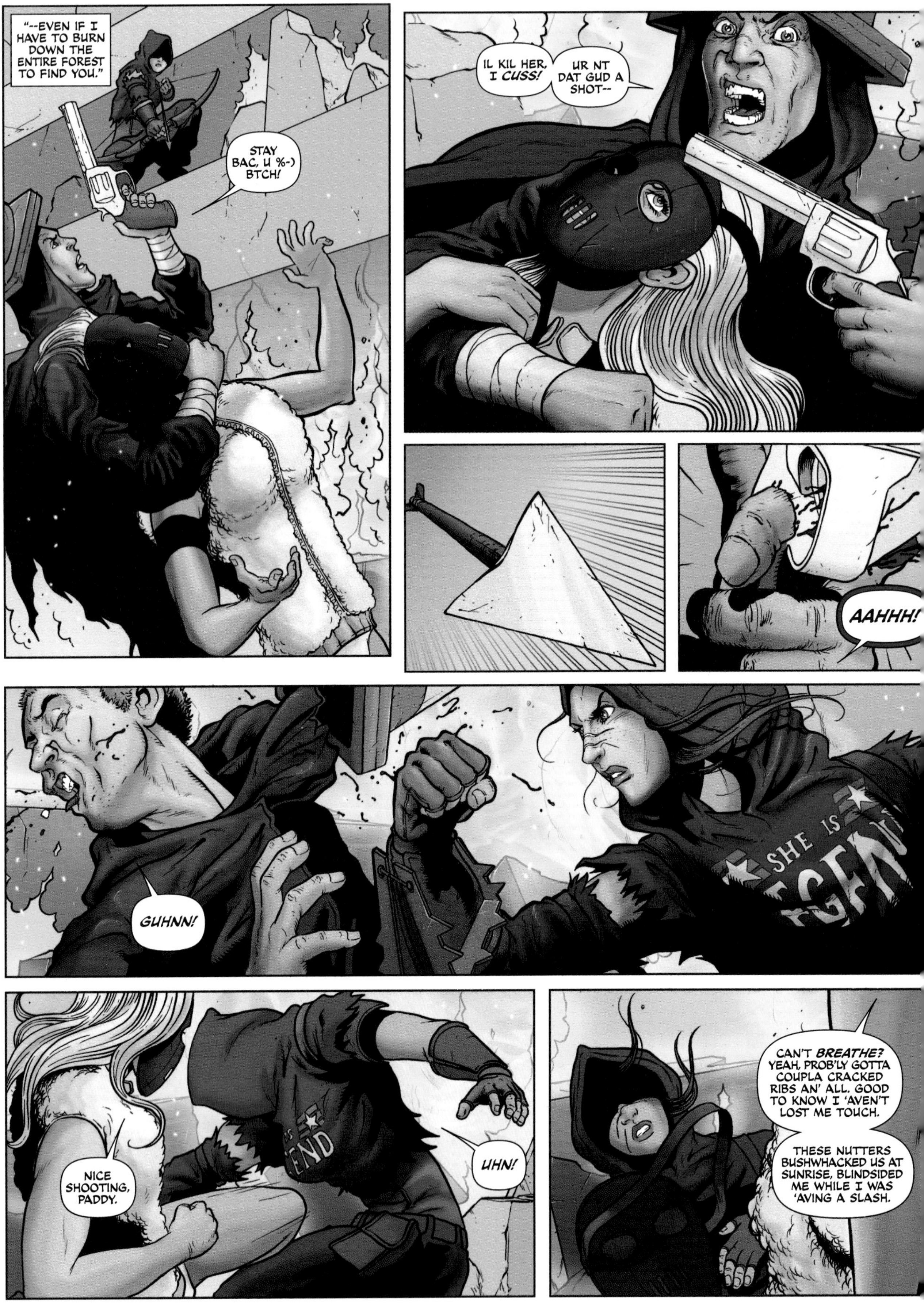
"--EVEN IF I HAVE TO BURN DOWN THE ENTIRE FOREST TO FIND YOU."
STAY BAC, U %-) BTCH!
IL KIL HER, I CUSS!
UR NT DAT GUD A SHOT--
AAHHH!
SHE IS
GUHNN!
NICE SHOOTING, PADDY.
UHN!
CAN'T BREATHE? YEAH, PROB'LY GOTTA COUPLA CRACKED RIBS AN' ALL. GOOD TO KNOW I 'AVEN'T LOST ME TOUCH.
THESE NUTTERS BUSHWHACKED US AT SUNRISE, BLINDSIDED ME WHILE I WAS 'AVING A SLASH.

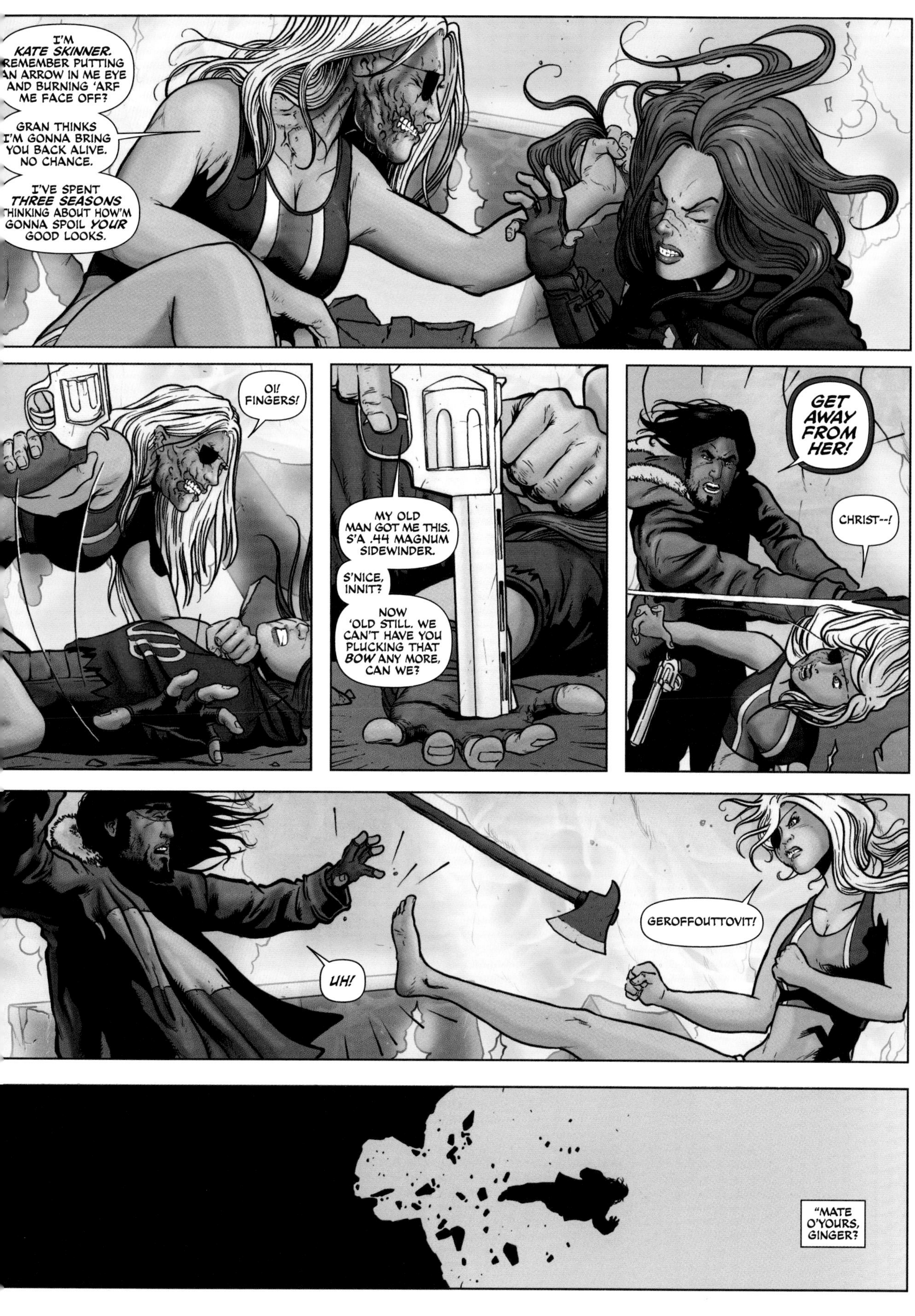
I'M KATE SKINNER. REMEMBER PUTTING AN ARROW IN ME EYE AND BURNING 'ARF ME FACE OFF?
GRAN THINKS I'M GONNA BRING YOU BACK ALIVE. NO CHANCE.
I'VE SPENT THREE SEASONS THINKING ABOUT HOW'M GONNA SPOIL YOUR GOOD LOOKS.
OI! FINGERS!
MY OLD MAN GOT ME THIS. S'A .44 MAGNUM SIDEWINDER.
S'NICE, INNIT?
NOW 'OLD STILL. WE CAN'T HAVE YOU PLUCKING THAT BOW ANY MORE, CAN WE?
GET AWAY FROM HER!
CHRIST--!
GEROFFOUTTOVIT!
UH!
"MATE O'YOURS, GINGER?

"WELL, NOT FER MUCH LONGER, EH?"

UHN!

S'ALL RIGHT, LUV. I GOT YOUR WINDPIPE. YOUR EYES'LL BE BULGING TOO MUCH TO MISS ANYTHING.

HKK!

G-GET BACK!

ASH!

STOP WRIGGLING--

--OR I'LL

AAAAAHH

YOU--

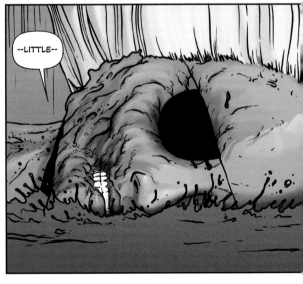

--LITTLE--

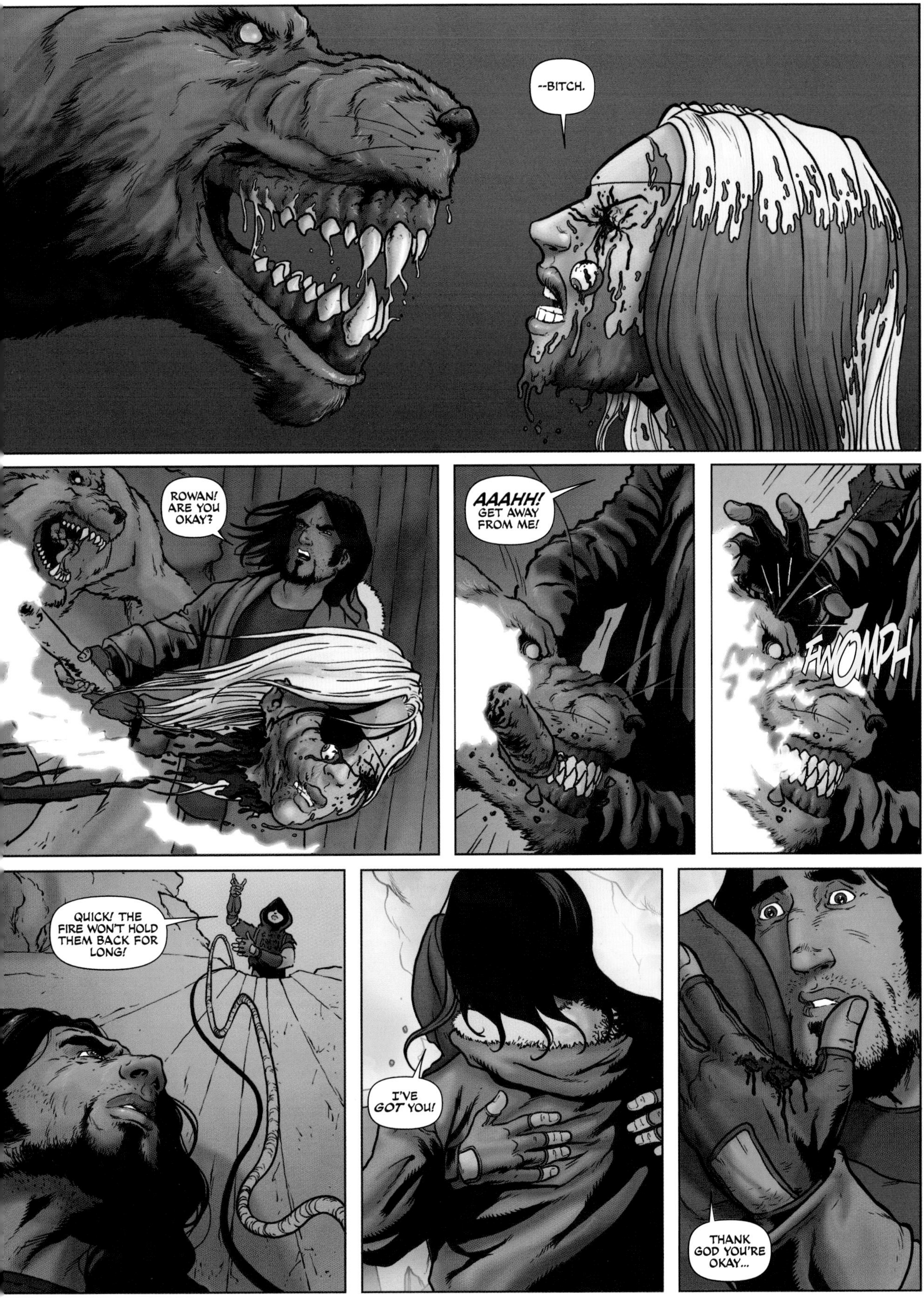
--BITCH.
ROWAN! ARE YOU OKAY?
AAAHH! GET AWAY FROM ME!
FWOMPH
QUICK! THE FIRE WON'T HOLD THEM BACK FOR LONG!
I'VE GOT YOU!
THANK GOD YOU'RE OKAY...

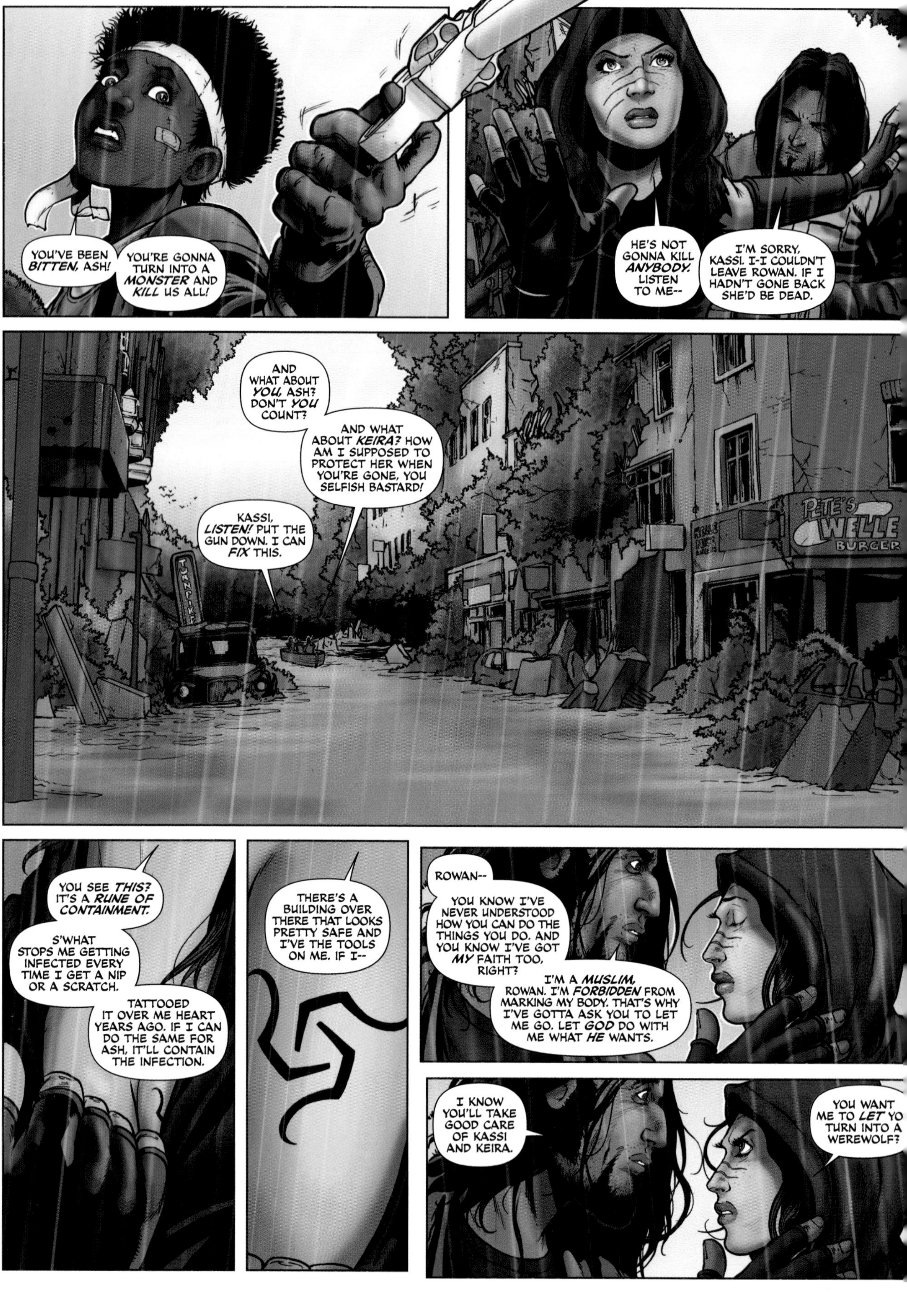

YOU'VE BEEN BITTEN, ASH!
YOU'RE GONNA TURN INTO A MONSTER AND KILL US ALL!
HE'S NOT GONNA KILL ANYBODY. LISTEN TO ME--
I'M SORRY, KASSI. I-I COULDN'T LEAVE ROWAN. IF I HADN'T GONE BACK SHE'D BE DEAD.
AND WHAT ABOUT YOU, ASH? DON'T YOU COUNT?
AND WHAT ABOUT KEIRA? HOW AM I SUPPOSED TO PROTECT HER WHEN YOU'RE GONE, YOU SELFISH BASTARD!
KASSI, LISTEN! PUT THE GUN DOWN. I CAN FIX THIS.
TURNPIKE
PETE'S WELLE BURGER
YOU SEE THIS? IT'S A RUNE OF CONTAINMENT.
S'WHAT STOPS ME GETTING INFECTED EVERY TIME I GET A NIP OR A SCRATCH.
TATTOOED IT OVER ME HEART YEARS AGO. IF I CAN DO THE SAME FOR ASH, IT'LL CONTAIN THE INFECTION.
THERE'S A BUILDING OVER THERE THAT LOOKS PRETTY SAFE AND I'VE THE TOOLS ON ME. IF I--
ROWAN--
YOU KNOW I'VE NEVER UNDERSTOOD HOW YOU CAN DO THE THINGS YOU DO. AND YOU KNOW I'VE GOT MY FAITH TOO, RIGHT?
I'M A MUSLIM, ROWAN. I'M FORBIDDEN FROM MARKING MY BODY. THAT'S WHY I'VE GOTTA ASK YOU TO LET ME GO. LET GOD DO WITH ME WHAT HE WANTS.
I KNOW YOU'LL TAKE GOOD CARE OF KASSI AND KEIRA.
YOU WANT ME TO LET YO TURN INTO A WEREWOLF?

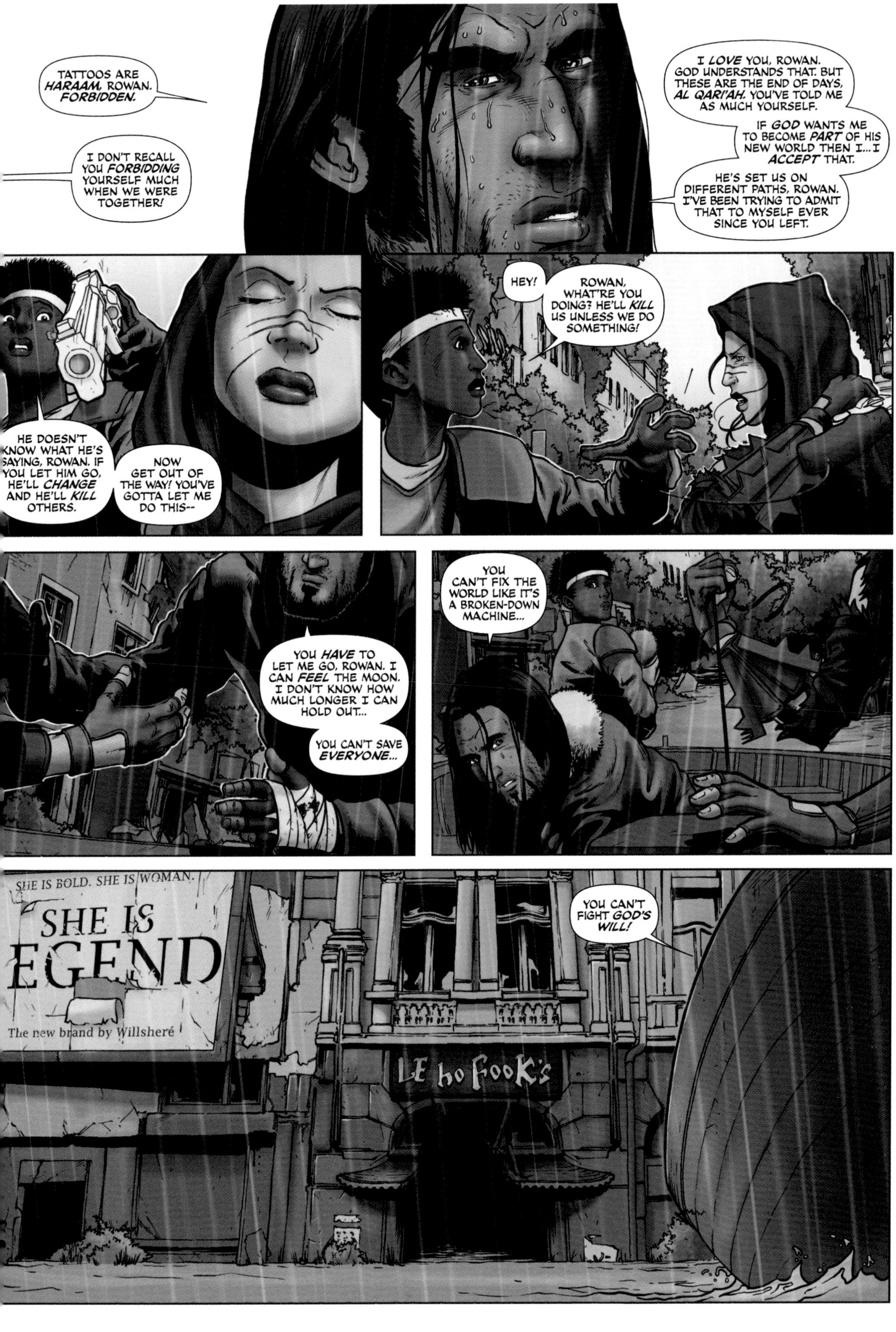
TATTOOS ARE HARAAM, ROWAN. FORBIDDEN.
I DON'T RECALL YOU FORBIDDING YOURSELF MUCH WHEN WE WERE TOGETHER!
I LOVE YOU, ROWAN. GOD UNDERSTANDS THAT. BUT THESE ARE THE END OF DAYS, AL QARI'AH. YOU'VE TOLD ME AS MUCH YOURSELF.
IF GOD WANTS ME TO BECOME PART OF HIS NEW WORLD THEN I... I ACCEPT THAT.
HE'S SET US ON DIFFERENT PATHS, ROWAN. I'VE BEEN TRYING TO ADMIT THAT TO MYSELF EVER SINCE YOU LEFT.
HE DOESN'T KNOW WHAT HE'S SAYING, ROWAN. IF YOU LET HIM GO, HE'LL CHANGE AND HE'LL KILL OTHERS.
NOW GET OUT OF THE WAY! YOU'VE GOTTA LET ME DO THIS--
HEY!
ROWAN, WHAT'RE YOU DOING? HE'LL KILL US UNLESS WE DO SOMETHING!
YOU HAVE TO LET ME GO, ROWAN. I CAN FEEL THE MOON. I DON'T KNOW HOW MUCH LONGER I CAN HOLD OUT...
YOU CAN'T SAVE EVERYONE...
YOU CAN'T FIX THE WORLD LIKE IT'S A BROKEN-DOWN MACHINE...
SHE IS BOLD. SHE IS WOMAN.
SHE IS
EGEND
The new brand by Willsheré
LE ho Fook's
YOU CAN'T FIGHT GOD'S WILL!

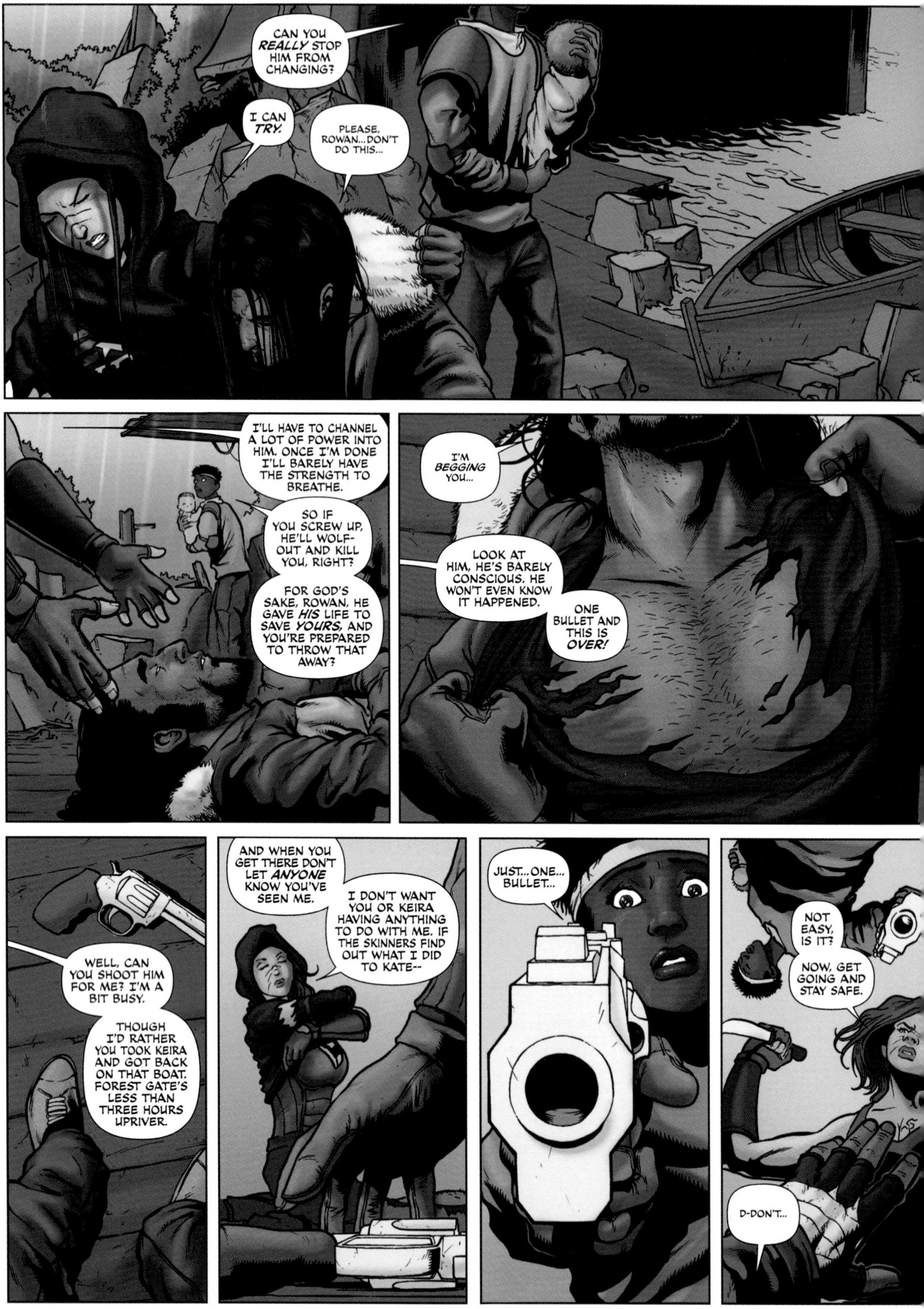
CAN YOU REALLY STOP HIM FROM CHANGING?
I CAN TRY.
PLEASE, ROWAN...DON'T DO THIS...
I'LL HAVE TO CHANNEL A LOT OF POWER INTO HIM. ONCE I'M DONE I'LL BARELY HAVE THE STRENGTH TO BREATHE.
SO IF YOU SCREW UP, HE'LL WOLF-OUT AND KILL YOU, RIGHT?
FOR GOD'S SAKE, ROWAN, HE GAVE HIS LIFE TO SAVE YOURS, AND YOU'RE PREPARED TO THROW THAT AWAY?
I'M BEGGING YOU...
LOOK AT HIM, HE'S BARELY CONSCIOUS. HE WON'T EVEN KNOW IT HAPPENED.
ONE BULLET AND THIS IS OVER!
WELL, CAN YOU SHOOT HIM FOR ME? I'M A BIT BUSY.
THOUGH I'D RATHER YOU TOOK KEIRA AND GOT BACK ON THAT BOAT. FOREST GATE'S LESS THAN THREE HOURS UPRIVER.
AND WHEN YOU GET THERE DON'T LET ANYONE KNOW YOU'VE SEEN ME.
I DON'T WANT YOU OR KEIRA HAVING ANYTHING TO DO WITH ME. IF THE SKINNERS FIND OUT WHAT I DID TO KATE--
JUST...ONE... BULLET...
NOT EASY, IS IT?
NOW, GET GOING AND STAY SAFE.
D-DON'T...

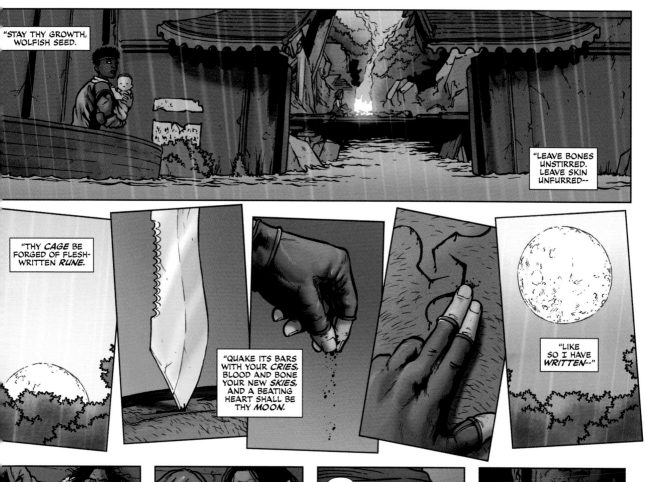

"STAY THY GROWTH, WOLFISH SEED.

"LEAVE BONES UNSTIRRED. LEAVE SKIN UNFURRED--

"THY *CAGE* BE FORGED OF FLESH-WRITTEN *RUNE*.

"QUAKE ITS BARS WITH YOUR *CRIES*, BLOOD AND BONE YOUR NEW *SKIES*, AND A BEATING HEART SHALL BE THY *MOON*.

"LIKE SO I HAVE *WRITTEN*--"

--LIKE SO SHALL IT *BE!*

UHHHH...

MM.

WHAT... WHAT'VE YOU *DONE*, ROWAN...?

"YOU CAN'T FIGHT *GOD'S WILL*...."

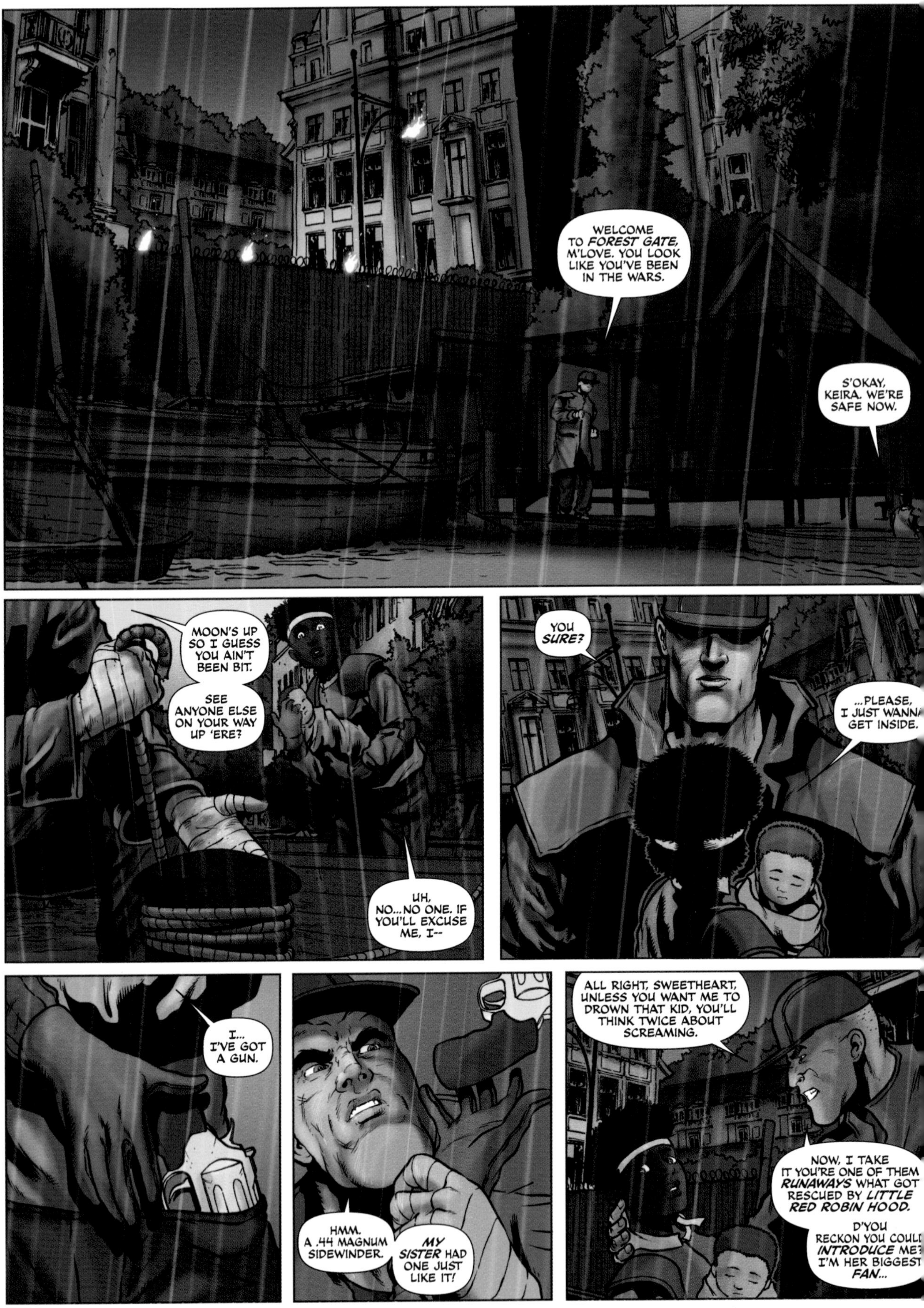

WELCOME TO FOREST GATE, M'LOVE. YOU LOOK LIKE YOU'VE BEEN IN THE WARS.
S'OKAY, KEIRA. WE'RE SAFE NOW.
MOON'S UP SO I GUESS YOU AIN'T BEEN BIT.
SEE ANYONE ELSE ON YOUR WAY UP 'ERE?
UH, NO...NO ONE. IF YOU'LL EXCUSE ME, I--
YOU SURE?
...PLEASE, I JUST WANNA GET INSIDE.
I... I'VE GOT A GUN.
HMM. A .44 MAGNUM SIDEWINDER.
MY SISTER HAD ONE JUST LIKE IT!
ALL RIGHT, SWEETHEART, UNLESS YOU WANT ME TO DROWN THAT KID, YOU'LL THINK TWICE ABOUT SCREAMING.
NOW, I TAKE IT YOU'RE ONE OF THEM RUNAWAYS WHAT GOT RESCUED BY LITTLE RED ROBIN HOOD.
D'YOU RECKON YOU COULD INTRODUCE ME? I'M HER BIGGEST FAN...

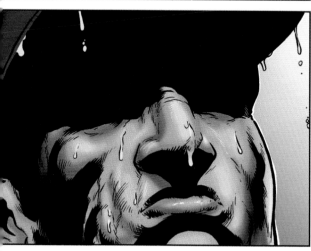

BLAM

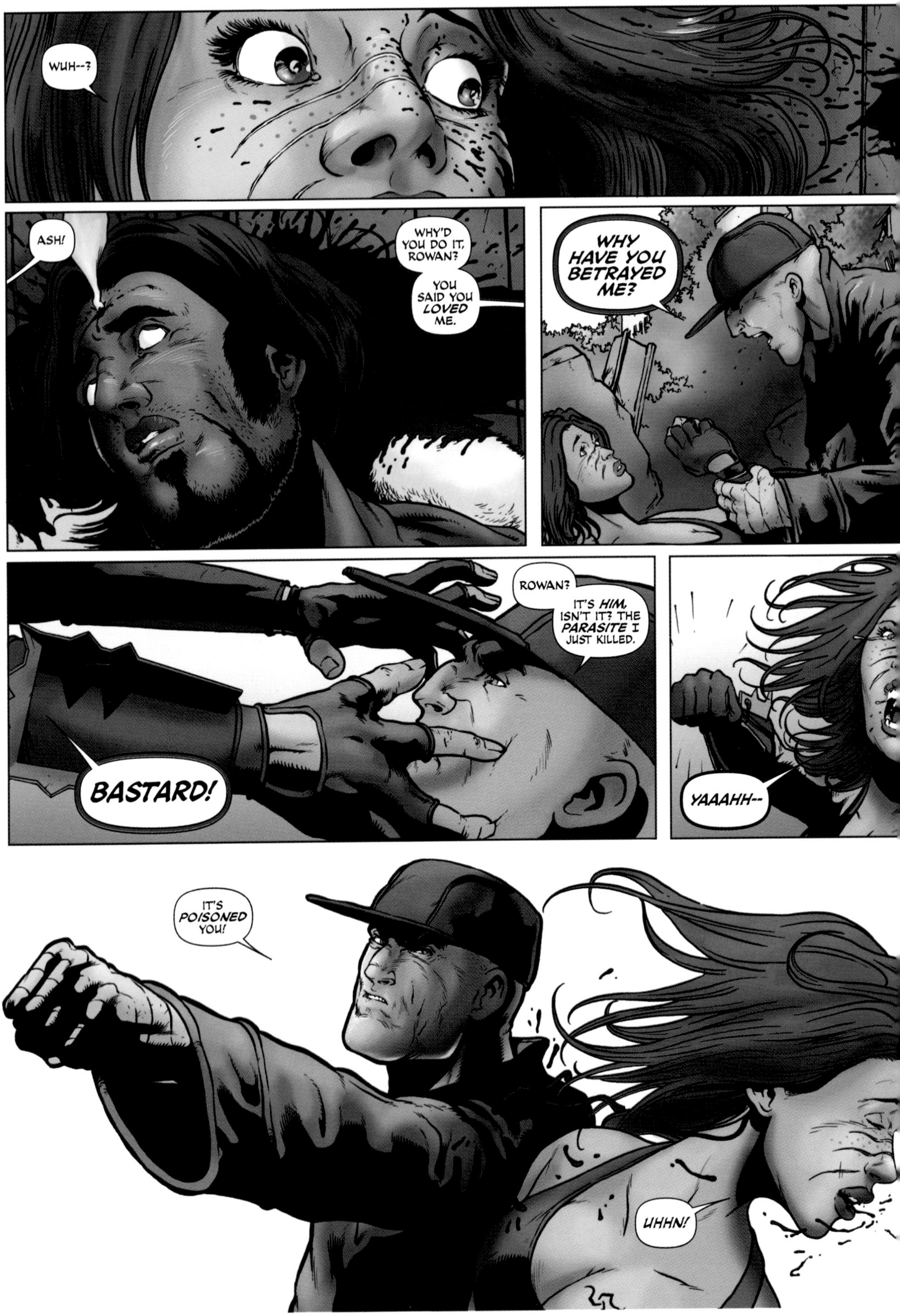
WUH--?
ASH!
WHY'D YOU DO IT, ROWAN?
YOU SAID YOU LOVED ME.
WHY HAVE YOU BETRAYED ME?
ROWAN?
IT'S HIM, ISN'T IT? THE PARASITE I JUST KILLED.
BASTARD!
YAAAHH--
IT'S POISONED YOU!
UHHN!

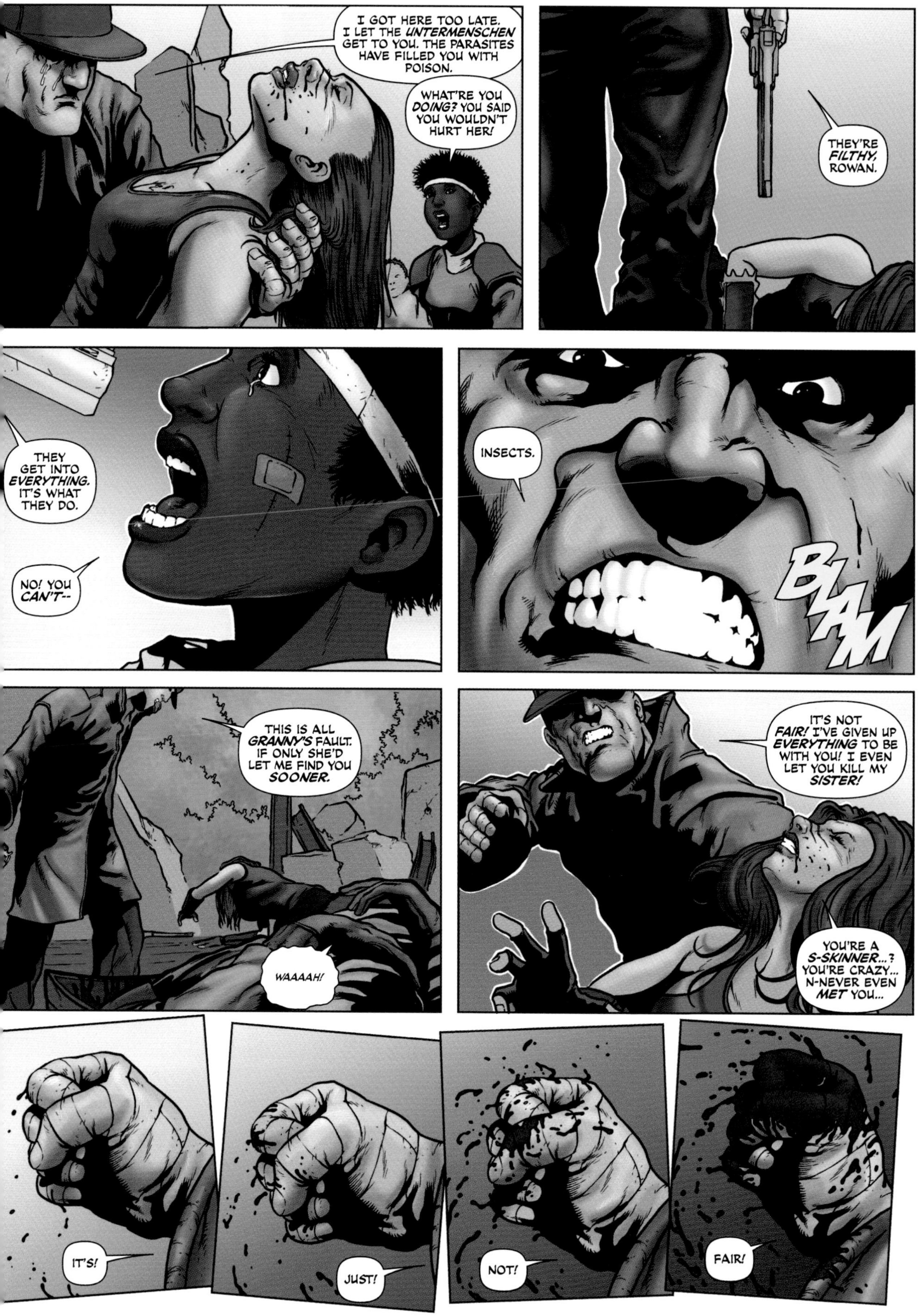
I GOT HERE TOO LATE. I LET THE *UNTERMENSCHEN* GET TO YOU. THE PARASITES HAVE FILLED YOU WITH POISON.
WHAT'RE YOU *DOING?* YOU SAID YOU WOULDN'T HURT HER!
THEY'RE *FILTHY,* ROWAN.
THEY GET INTO *EVERYTHING.* IT'S WHAT THEY DO.
NO! YOU *CAN'T*--
INSECTS.
BLAM
THIS IS ALL *GRANNY'S* FAULT. IF ONLY SHE'D LET ME FIND YOU *SOONER.*
WAAAAH!
IT'S NOT *FAIR!* I'VE GIVEN UP *EVERYTHING* TO BE WITH YOU! I EVEN LET YOU KILL MY *SISTER!*
YOU'RE A *S-SKINNER...?* YOU'RE CRAZY... N-NEVER EVEN *MET* YOU...
IT'S!
JUST!
NOT!
FAIR!

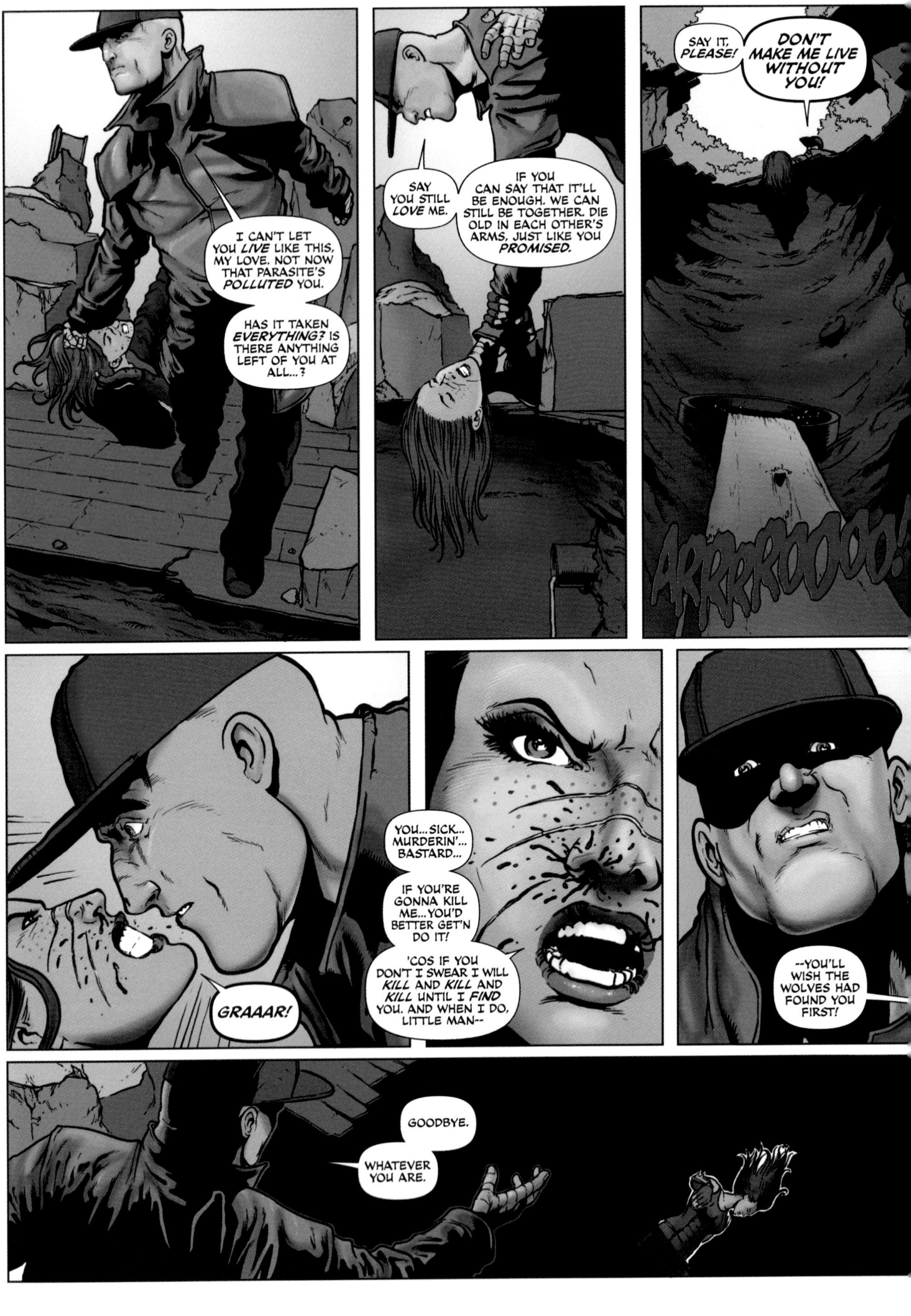

I CAN'T LET YOU LIVE LIKE THIS, MY LOVE. NOT NOW THAT PARASITE'S POLLUTED YOU.
HAS IT TAKEN EVERYTHING? IS THERE ANYTHING LEFT OF YOU AT ALL...?
SAY YOU STILL LOVE ME.
IF YOU CAN SAY THAT IT'LL BE ENOUGH. WE CAN STILL BE TOGETHER. DIE OLD IN EACH OTHER'S ARMS, JUST LIKE YOU PROMISED.
SAY IT, PLEASE!
DON'T MAKE ME LIVE WITHOUT YOU!
ARRRROOOO!
GRAAAR!
YOU...SICK... MURDERIN'... BASTARD...
IF YOU'RE GONNA KILL ME...YOU'D BETTER GET'N DO IT!
'COS IF YOU DON'T I SWEAR I WILL KILL AND KILL AND KILL UNTIL I FIND YOU. AND WHEN I DO, LITTLE MAN--
--YOU'LL WISH THE WOLVES HAD FOUND YOU FIRST!
GOODBYE.
WHATEVER YOU ARE.

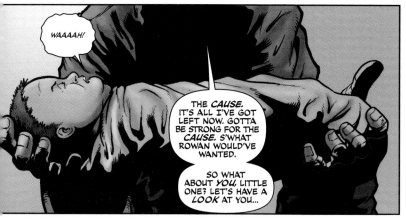

WAAAAH!

THE *CAUSE.* IT'S ALL I'VE GOT LEFT NOW. GOTTA BE STRONG FOR THE *CAUSE.* S'WHAT ROWAN WOULD'VE WANTED.

SO WHAT ABOUT *YOU,* LITTLE ONE? LET'S HAVE A *LOOK* AT YOU...

HMMM.

STRONG. NO DEFECTS. A PERFECT LITTLE *FRÄULEIN.*

LUCKY FOR *YOU,* EH?

NOW LET'S GET YOU HOME.

I'VE GOTTA HAVE A WORD W'GRANNY.

"AND WHEN I'M DONE, WE'LL PUT ALL THIS *BEHIND* US--

ARRRROOOO!

"WE WON'T LET THE *PARASITES* DRAG US DOWN--

"--AND WE'LL SEE IF YOU AN' ME CAN'T WIN ENGLAND BACK FROM THE *ANIMALS.*"

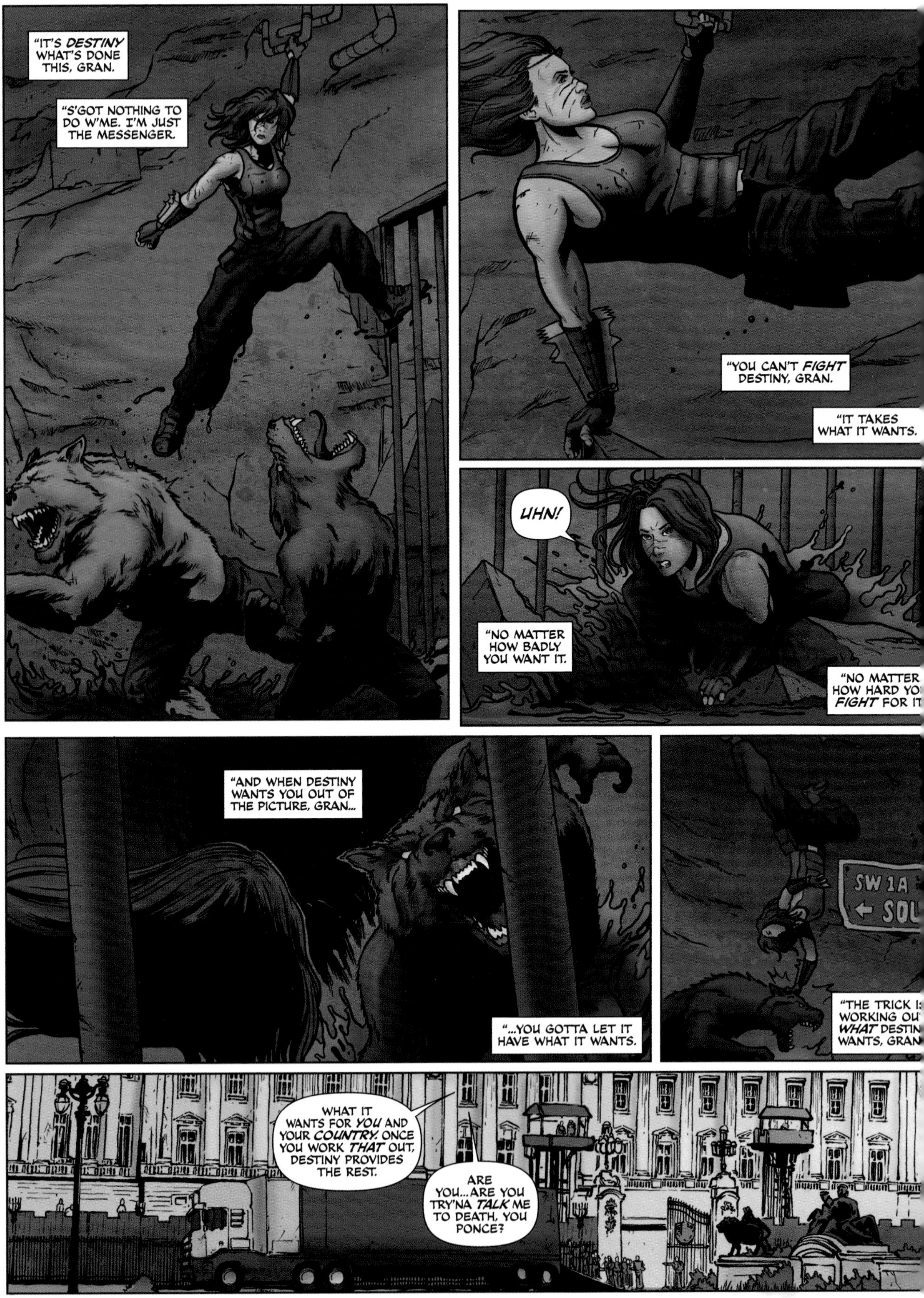

"IT'S DESTINY WHAT'S DONE THIS, GRAN.
"S'GOT NOTHING TO DO W'ME. I'M JUST THE MESSENGER.
"YOU CAN'T FIGHT DESTINY, GRAN.
"IT TAKES WHAT IT WANTS.
UHN!
"NO MATTER HOW BADLY YOU WANT IT.
"NO MATTER HOW HARD YO FIGHT FOR IT
"AND WHEN DESTINY WANTS YOU OUT OF THE PICTURE, GRAN...
"...YOU GOTTA LET IT HAVE WHAT IT WANTS.
SW1A
← SOU
"THE TRICK I WORKING OU WHAT DESTIN WANTS, GRAN
WHAT IT WANTS FOR YOU AND YOUR COUNTRY. ONCE YOU WORK THAT OUT, DESTINY PROVIDES THE REST.
ARE YOU...ARE YOU TRY'NA TALK ME TO DEATH, YOU PONCE?

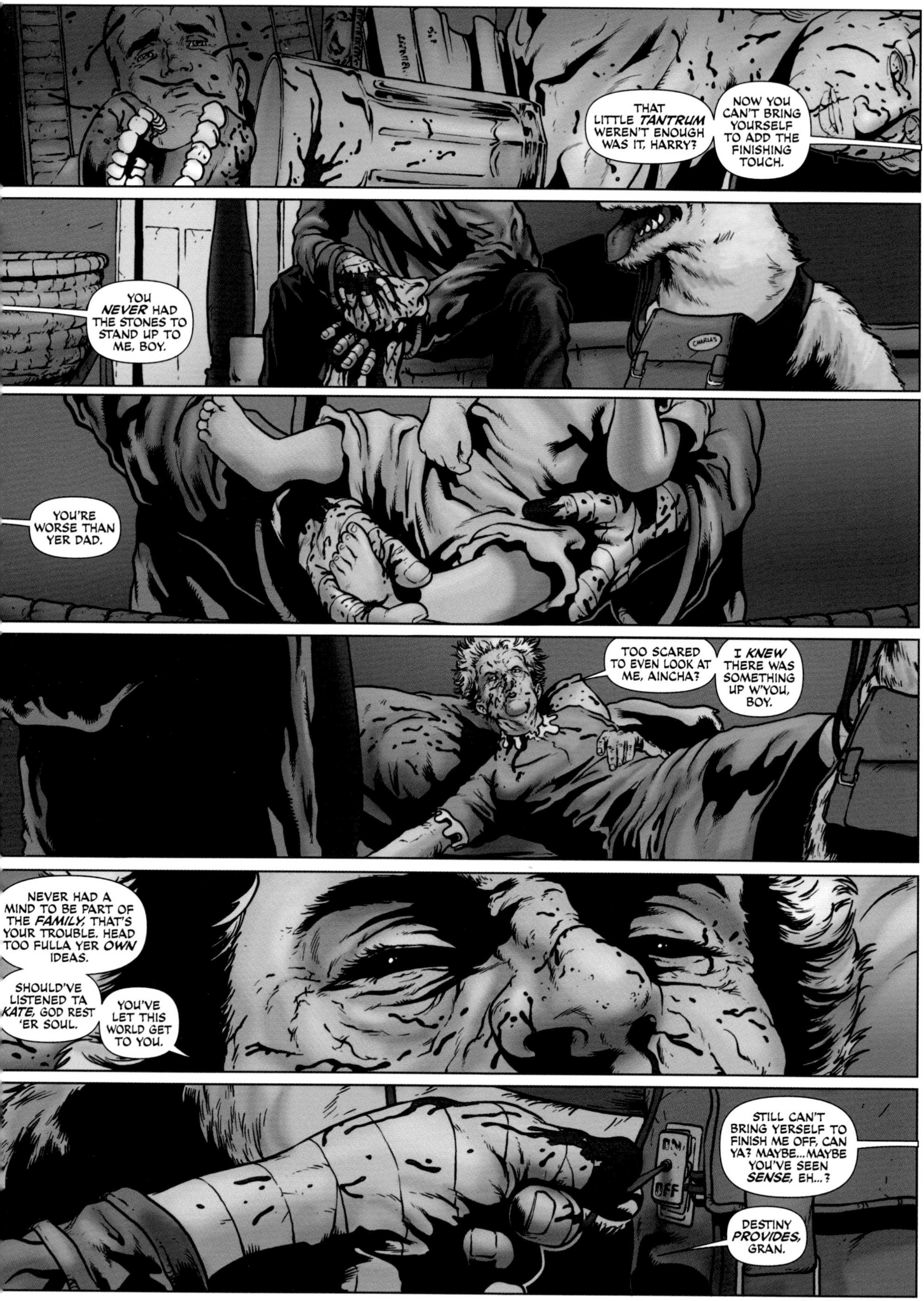
THAT LITTLE *TANTRUM* WEREN'T ENOUGH WAS IT, HARRY?
NOW YOU CAN'T BRING YOURSELF TO ADD THE FINISHING TOUCH.
YOU *NEVER* HAD THE STONES TO STAND UP TO ME, BOY.
YOU'RE WORSE THAN YER DAD.
TOO SCARED TO EVEN LOOK AT ME, AINCHA?
I *KNEW* THERE WAS SOMETHING UP W'YOU, BOY.
NEVER HAD A MIND TO BE PART OF THE *FAMILY,* THAT'S YOUR TROUBLE. HEAD TOO FULLA YER *OWN* IDEAS.
SHOULD'VE LISTENED TA *KATE,* GOD REST 'ER SOUL.
YOU'VE LET THIS WORLD GET TO YOU.
STILL CAN'T BRING YERSELF TO FINISH ME OFF, CAN YA? MAYBE...MAYBE YOU'VE SEEN *SENSE,* EH...?
DESTINY *PROVIDES,* GRAN.

I'M REMOVING CHARLES' *PACIFIER*, GRAN.

SHOULD TAKE ABOUT *TWO MINUTES* FOR HIS BRAIN TO IMPLODE, BY WHICH TIME HE'LL HAVE BEEN DRIVEN INTO A KILLING FRENZY.

I'D BETTER CHECK THEM SOUTHERNERS HAVE FIXED THEIR TRUCK. SHOULD BE LOADING UP THE SLAVES BY NOW, READY TO LEAVE IN THE MORNING.

I'LL BE BACK IN A BIT TO CLEAR UP THE MESS.

I LOVED YOU LIKE YOU WAS ME OWN *SON*, 'ARRY SKINNER!

YOU'VE BROKE MY HEART, YOU LITTLE BASTARD--

--AND WHEN I MEET YOU IN *HELL*, I'M GONNA BREAK YOUR *BALLS*!

NO! NO! *AAAHH!*

DON'T WORRY, LITTLE 'UN. SHE CAN'T HURT US NOW. ALL BARK EH? HOW'S ABOUT A LITTLE *SING-SONG*...

WHO'S AFRAID OF THE BIG BAD WOLF?

TRA-LA-LA-LA-LA!

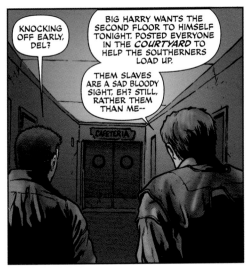

KNOCKING OFF EARLY, DEL?

BIG HARRY WANTS THE SECOND FLOOR TO HIMSELF TONIGHT. POSTED EVERYONE IN THE *COURTYARD* TO HELP THE SOUTHERNERS LOAD UP.

THEM SLAVES ARE A SAD BLOODY SIGHT, EH? STILL, RATHER THEM THAN ME--

JESUS CHRIST!

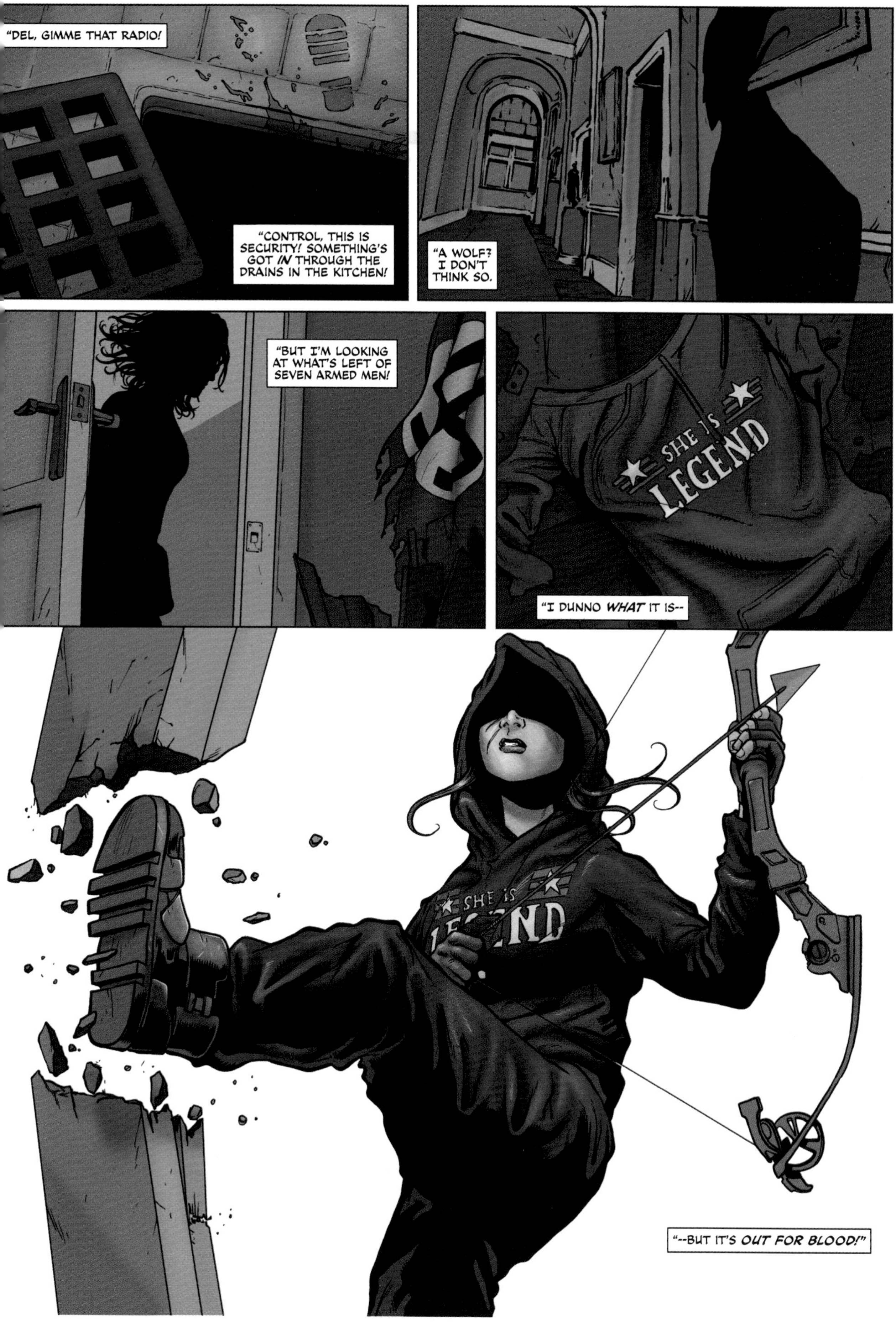
"DEL, GIMME THAT RADIO!
"CONTROL, THIS IS SECURITY! SOMETHING'S GOT IN THROUGH THE DRAINS IN THE KITCHEN!
"A WOLF? I DON'T THINK SO.
"BUT I'M LOOKING AT WHAT'S LEFT OF SEVEN ARMED MEN!
SHE IS LEGEND
"I DUNNO WHAT IT IS--
SHE IS LEGEND
"--BUT IT'S OUT FOR BLOOD!"

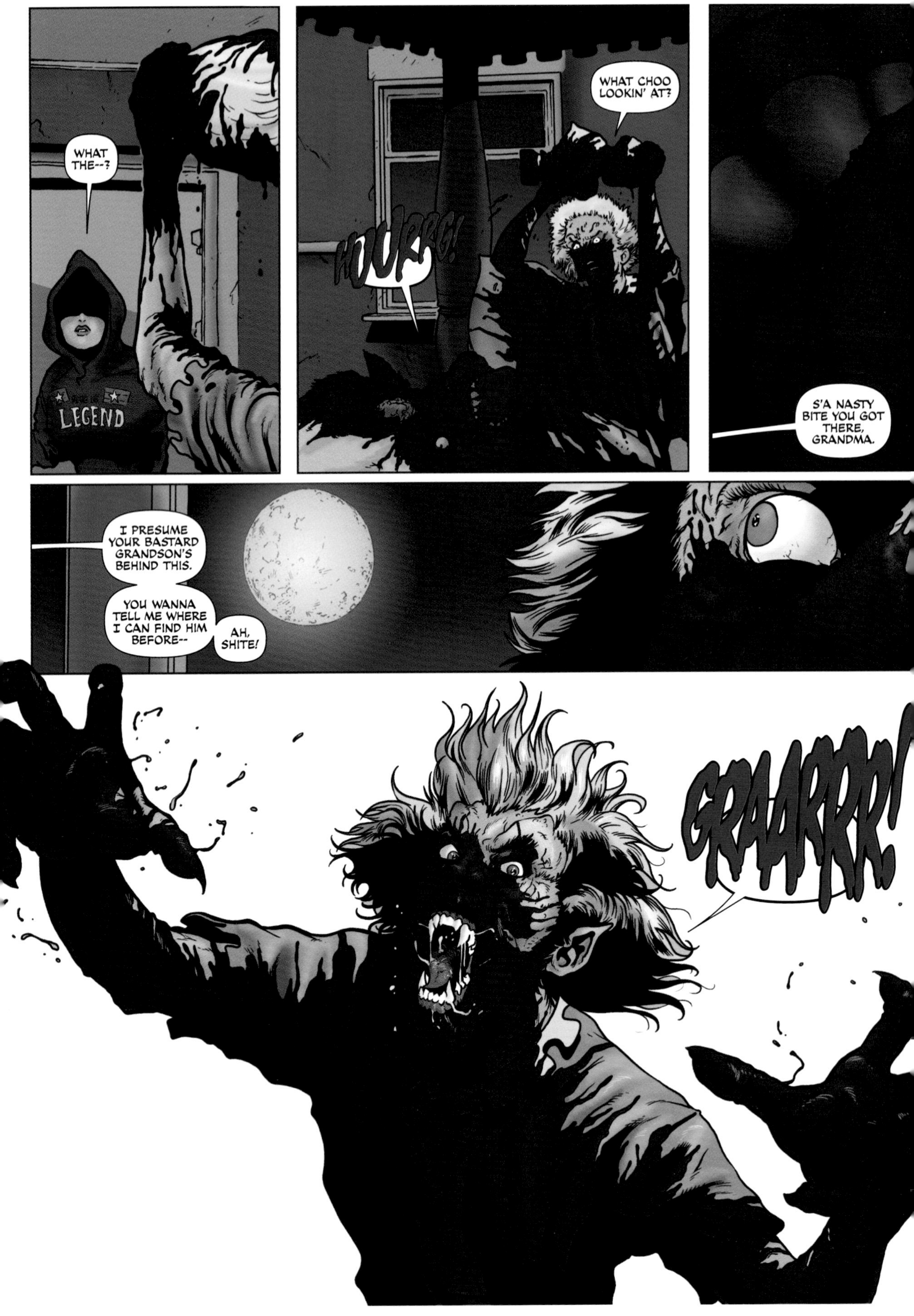
WHAT THE--?
LEGEND
WHAT CHOO LOOKIN' AT?
HOURRG!
S'A NASTY BITE YOU GOT THERE, GRANDMA.
I PRESUME YOUR BASTARD GRANDSON'S BEHIND THIS.
YOU WANNA TELL ME WHERE I CAN FIND HIM BEFORE--
AH, SHITE!
GRAARRR!

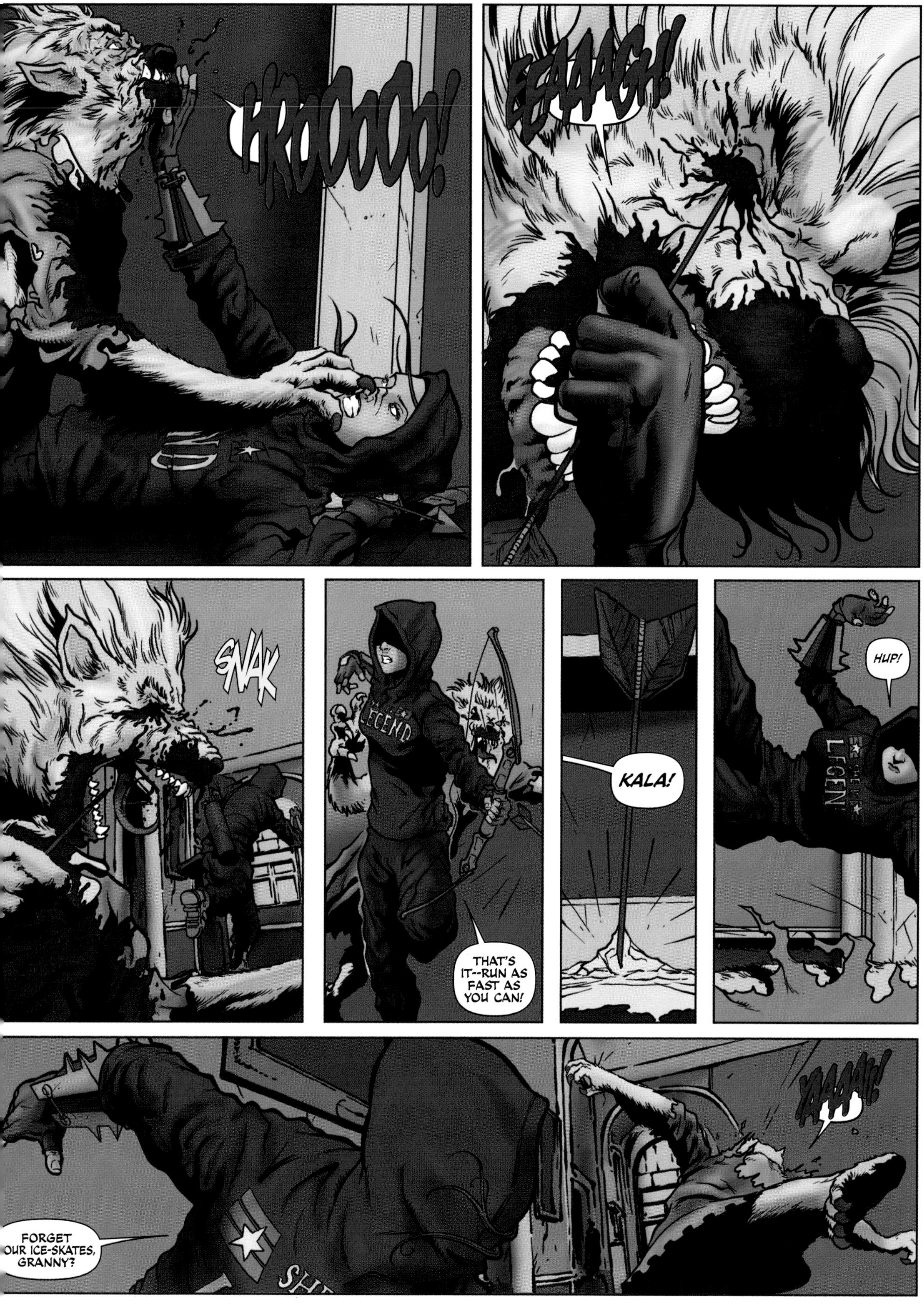
HROOOOO!
EEAAAGH!
SNAK
LEGEND
THAT'S IT--RUN AS FAST AS YOU CAN!
KALA!
HUP!
FORGET OUR ICE-SKATES, GRANNY?
YAAAAII!

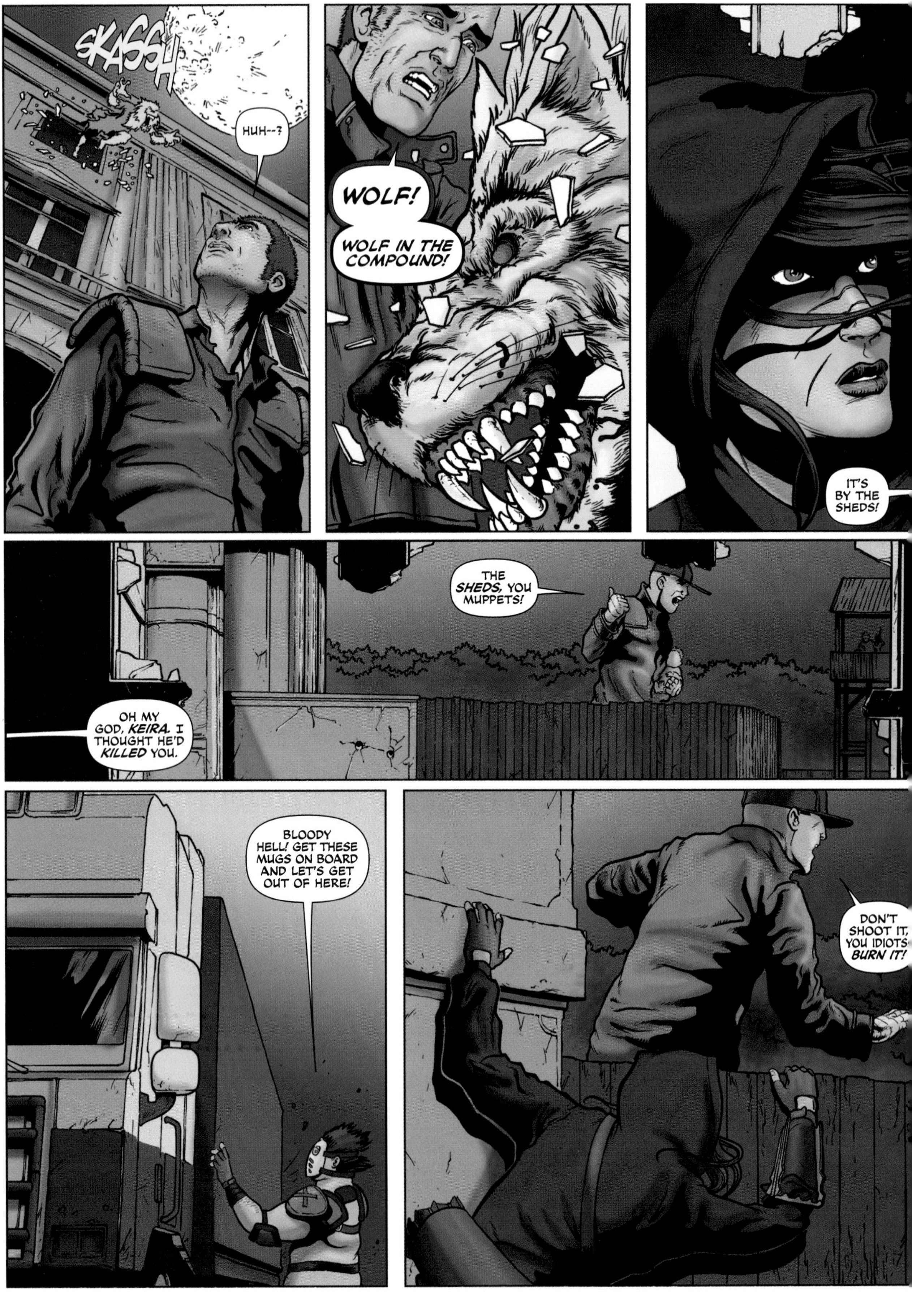
SKASSH
HUH--?
WOLF!
WOLF IN THE COMPOUND!
IT'S BY THE SHEDS!
THE SHEDS, YOU MUPPETS!
OH MY GOD, KEIRA. I THOUGHT HE'D KILLED YOU.
BLOODY HELL! GET THESE MUGS ON BOARD AND LET'S GET OUT OF HERE!
DON'T SHOOT IT, YOU IDIOTS BURN IT!

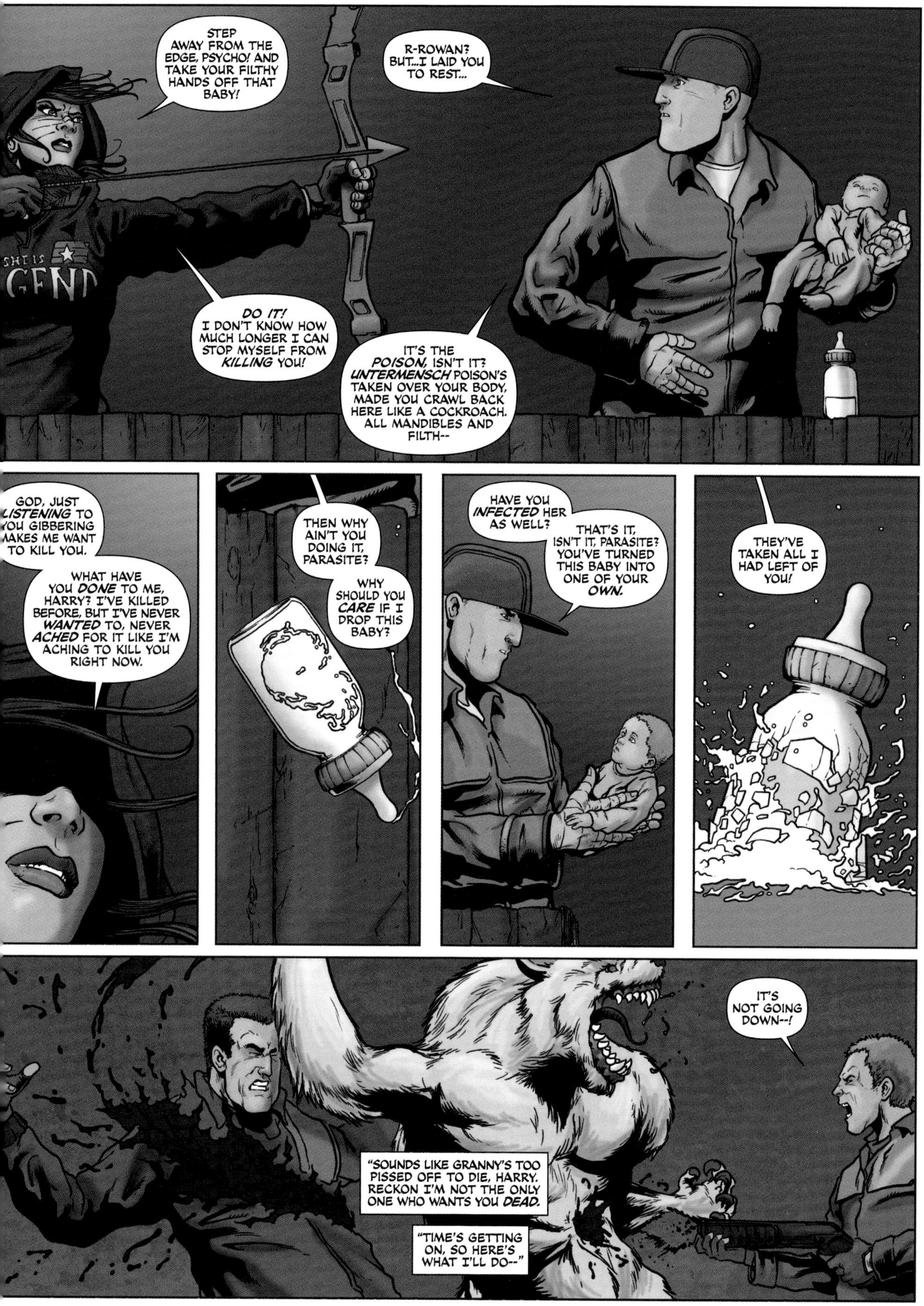
STEP AWAY FROM THE EDGE, PSYCHO! AND TAKE YOUR FILTHY HANDS OFF THAT BABY!
R-ROWAN? BUT...I LAID YOU TO REST...
DO IT! I DON'T KNOW HOW MUCH LONGER I CAN STOP MYSELF FROM KILLING YOU!
IT'S THE POISON, ISN'T IT? UNTERMENSCH POISON'S TAKEN OVER YOUR BODY, MADE YOU CRAWL BACK HERE LIKE A COCKROACH. ALL MANDIBLES AND FILTH--
GOD, JUST LISTENING TO GIBBERING AKES ME WANT TO KILL YOU.
WHAT HAVE YOU DONE TO ME, HARRY? I'VE KILLED BEFORE, BUT I'VE NEVER WANTED TO, NEVER ACHED FOR IT LIKE I'M ACHING TO KILL YOU RIGHT NOW.
THEN WHY AIN'T YOU DOING IT, PARASITE?
WHY SHOULD YOU CARE IF I DROP THIS BABY?
HAVE YOU INFECTED HER AS WELL?
THAT'S IT, ISN'T IT, PARASITE? YOU'VE TURNED THIS BABY INTO ONE OF YOUR OWN.
THEY'VE TAKEN ALL I HAD LEFT OF YOU!
IT'S NOT GOING DOWN--!
"SOUNDS LIKE GRANNY'S TOO PISSED OFF TO DIE, HARRY. RECKON I'M NOT THE ONLY ONE WHO WANTS YOU DEAD.
"TIME'S GETTING ON, SO HERE'S WHAT I'LL DO--"

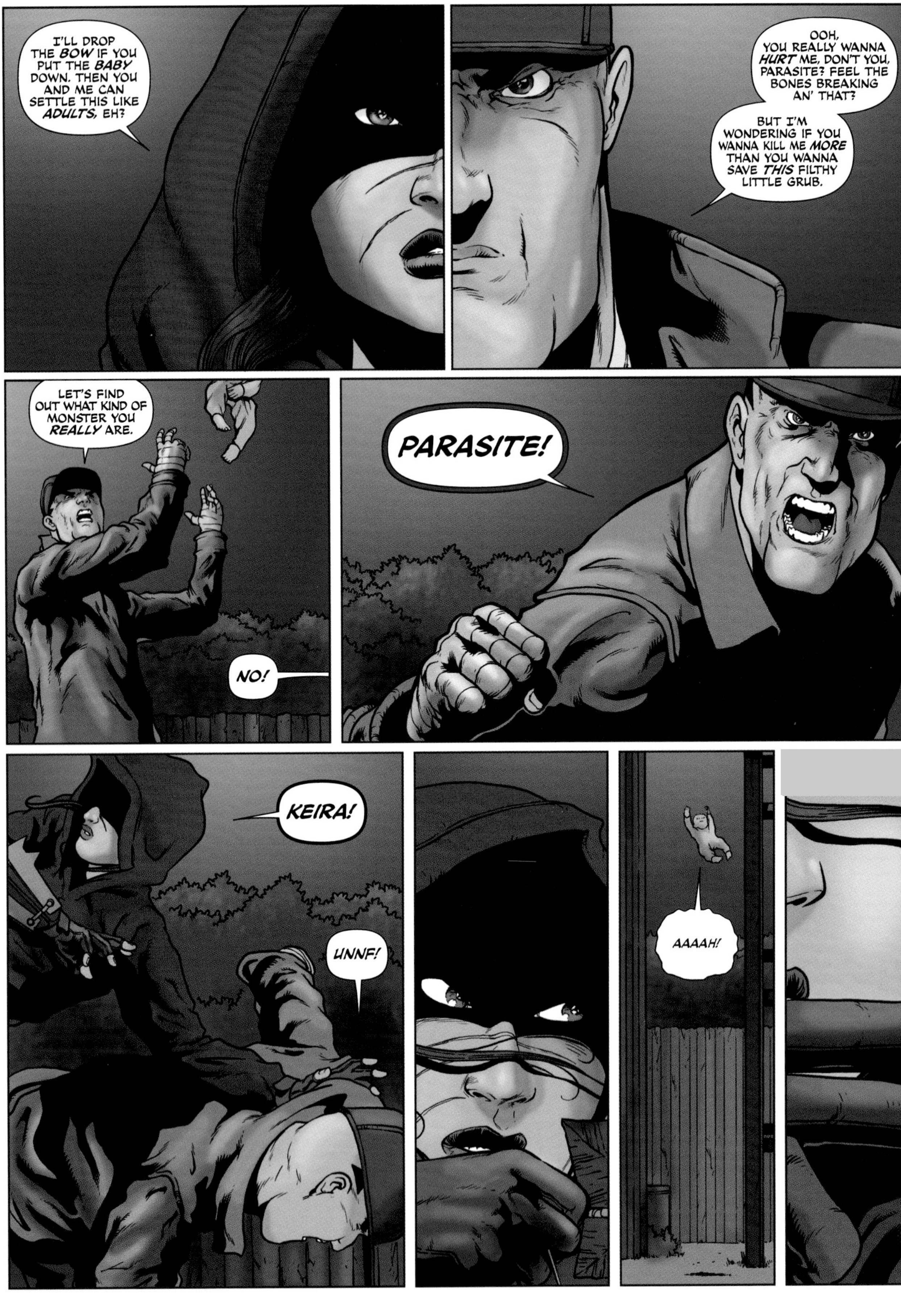
I'LL DROP THE BOW IF YOU PUT THE BABY DOWN. THEN YOU AND ME CAN SETTLE THIS LIKE ADULTS, EH?
OOH, YOU REALLY WANNA HURT ME, DON'T YOU, PARASITE? FEEL THE BONES BREAKING AN' THAT?
BUT I'M WONDERING IF YOU WANNA KILL ME MORE THAN YOU WANNA SAVE THIS FILTHY LITTLE GRUB.
LET'S FIND OUT WHAT KIND OF MONSTER YOU REALLY ARE.
NO!
PARASITE!
KEIRA!
UNNF!
AAAAH!

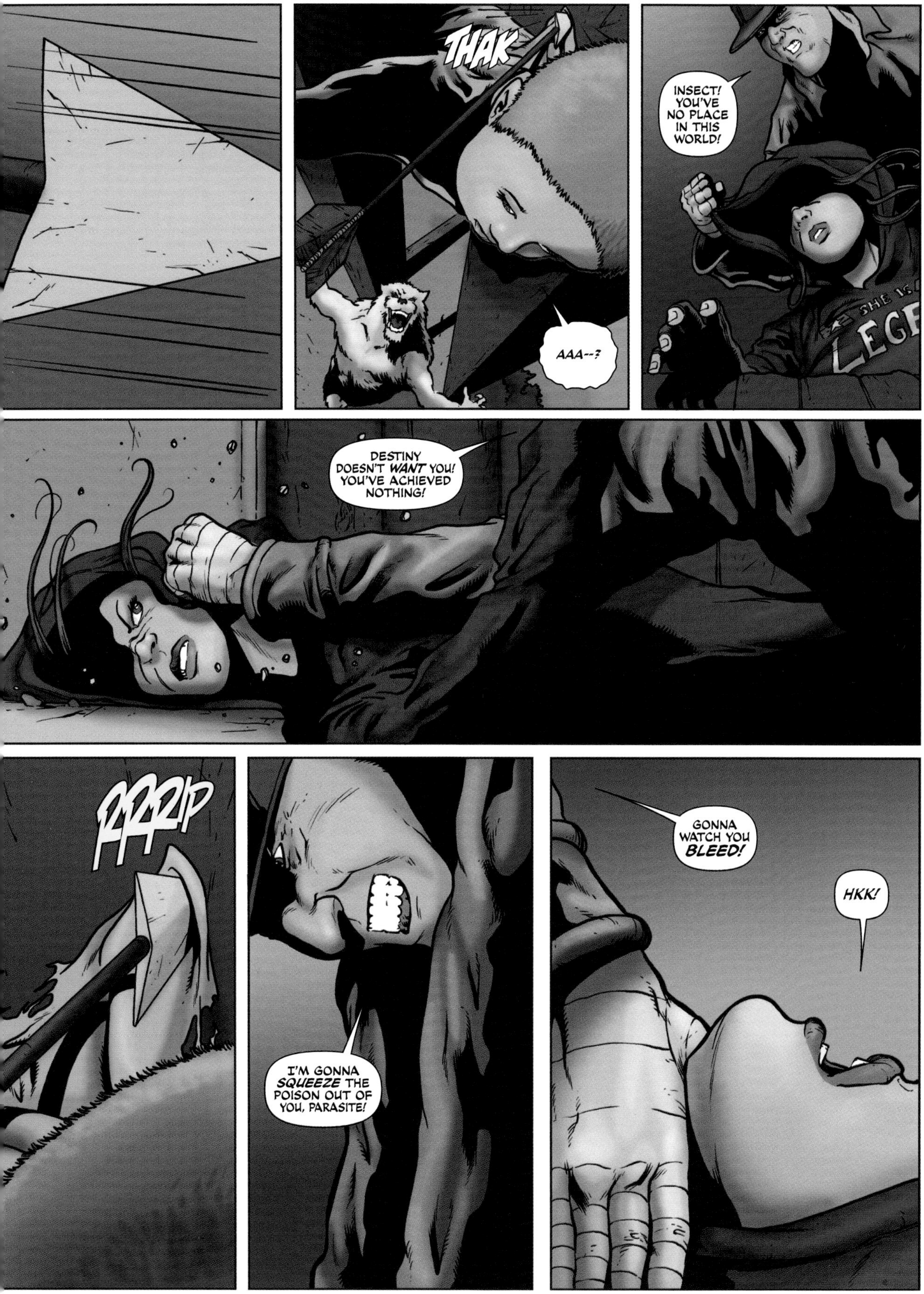
THAK
AAA--?
INSECT! YOU'VE NO PLACE IN THIS WORLD!
DESTINY DOESN'T *WANT* YOU! YOU'VE ACHIEVED NOTHING!
RRRIP
I'M GONNA *SQUEEZE* THE POISON OUT OF YOU, PARASITE!
GONNA WATCH YOU *BLEED!*
HKK!

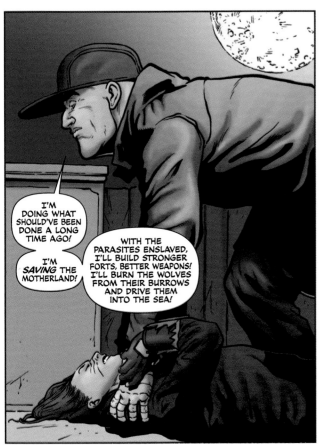

I'M DOING WHAT SHOULD'VE BEEN DONE A LONG TIME AGO!

I'M *SAVING* THE MOTHERLAND!

WITH THE PARASITES ENSLAVED, I'LL BUILD STRONGER FORTS, BETTER WEAPONS! I'LL BURN THE WOLVES FROM THEIR BURROWS AND DRIVE THEM INTO THE SEA!

I'LL SWEEP THE LAND CLEAN!

I'LL *FINALLY* ESTABLISH THE MASTER RACE!

THIS IS *DESTINY*, PARASITE! YOU CAN'T FIGHT IT! THE WORLD'S NO LONGER IN *YOUR* HANDS--

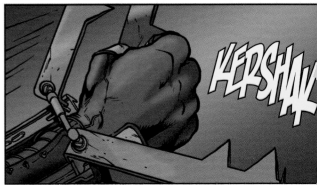

KERSHAK

AAIEEE!

JEEZ, YOU SCREAM LIKE A GIRL.

AND BY THE WAY--

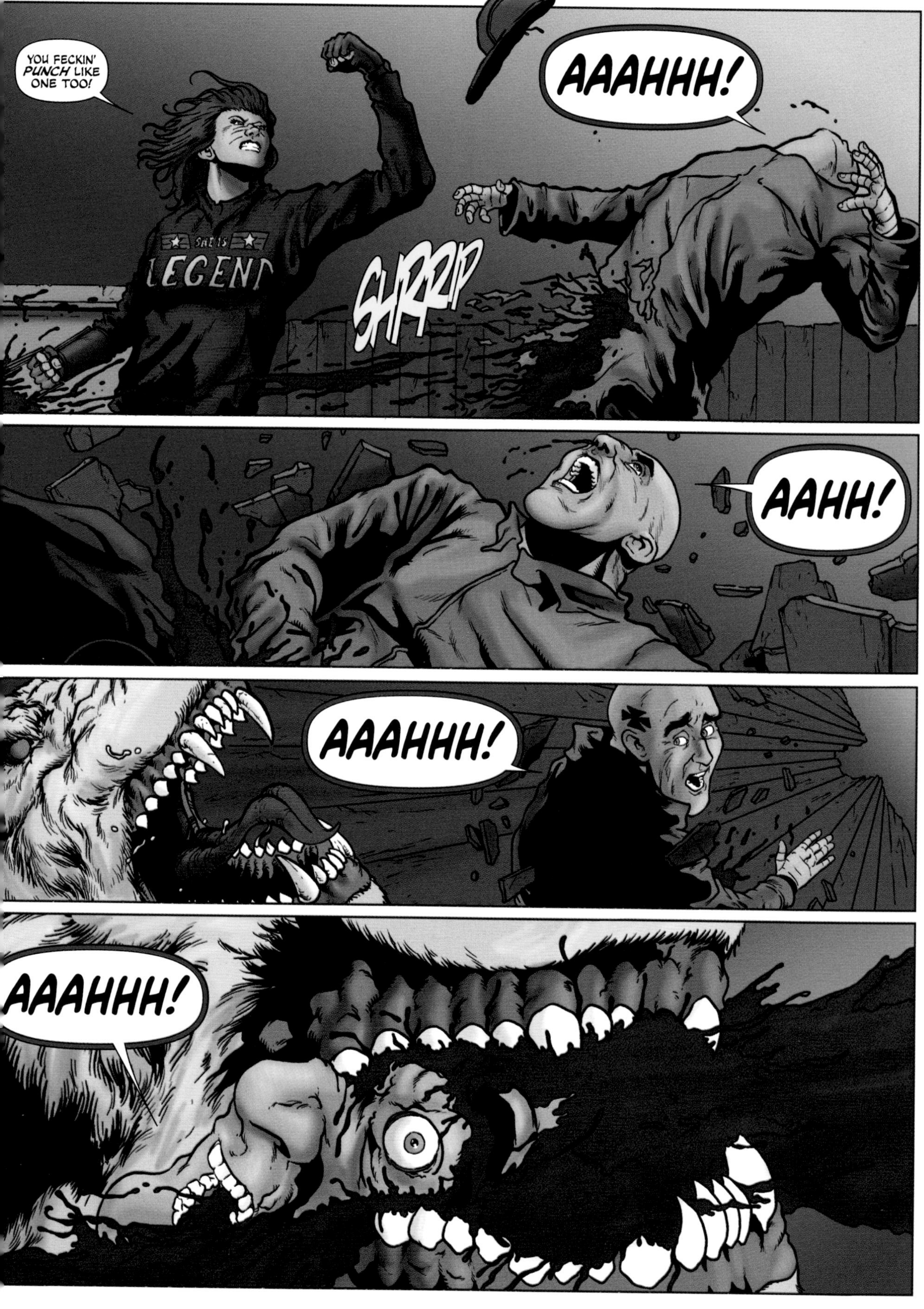
YOU FECKIN' *PUNCH* LIKE ONE TOO!
AAAHHH!
SHE IS LEGEND
SHRRIP
AAHH!
AAAHHH!
AAAHHH!

"ONCE UPON A TIME THERE WAS A *WOMAN.*

"A WOMAN WHO DROVE A GREAT *DARKNESS* FROM OUR LAND.

"SOME SAY SHE WAS A *WITCH.*

"SOME SAY SHE WAS MERELY A *LEGEND.*

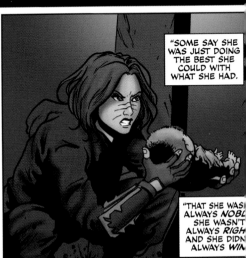

"SOME SAY SHE WAS JUST DOING THE BEST SHE COULD WITH WHAT SHE HAD.

"THAT SHE WAS ALWAYS *NOBL* SHE WASN'T ALWAYS *RIGH* AND SHE DIDN ALWAYS *WIN*

"BUT WHEN THE MONSTERS CLOSED IN...

"WHEN *FATE* ITSELF DECREED HER DEATH, THE WOMAN *ALWAYS* STOOD HER GROUND.

"AND HER *EYES* PROMISED ALL WHO CHALLENGED HER THAT SHE WOULD *FIGHT.*

"NOT BECAUSE IT WA WHAT SHE *WANTE* BUT BECAUSE IT WA *RIGHT.*

"AND SOMETIMES THOSE EYES WE ALL IT TOOK TO SEND THE MONSTE RUNNING BACK TO THE WOODS

THE SLAVES ARE IN AND I JUST SAW THAT WOLF LEG IT OVER THE PALACE WALL! WE'D BETTER--

"BUT BATTLING MONSTERS TAKES ITS TOLL.

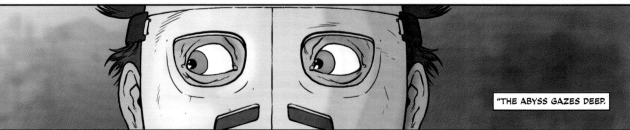

"THE ABYSS GAZES DEEP.

"SOME SAY SHE BECAME MORE *WOLF* THAN WOMAN.

"A SACRED KILLER.

P-PLEASE, DON'T--!

"BATTLING MONSTERS SO OTHERS MAY SLEEP.

"PITILESS.

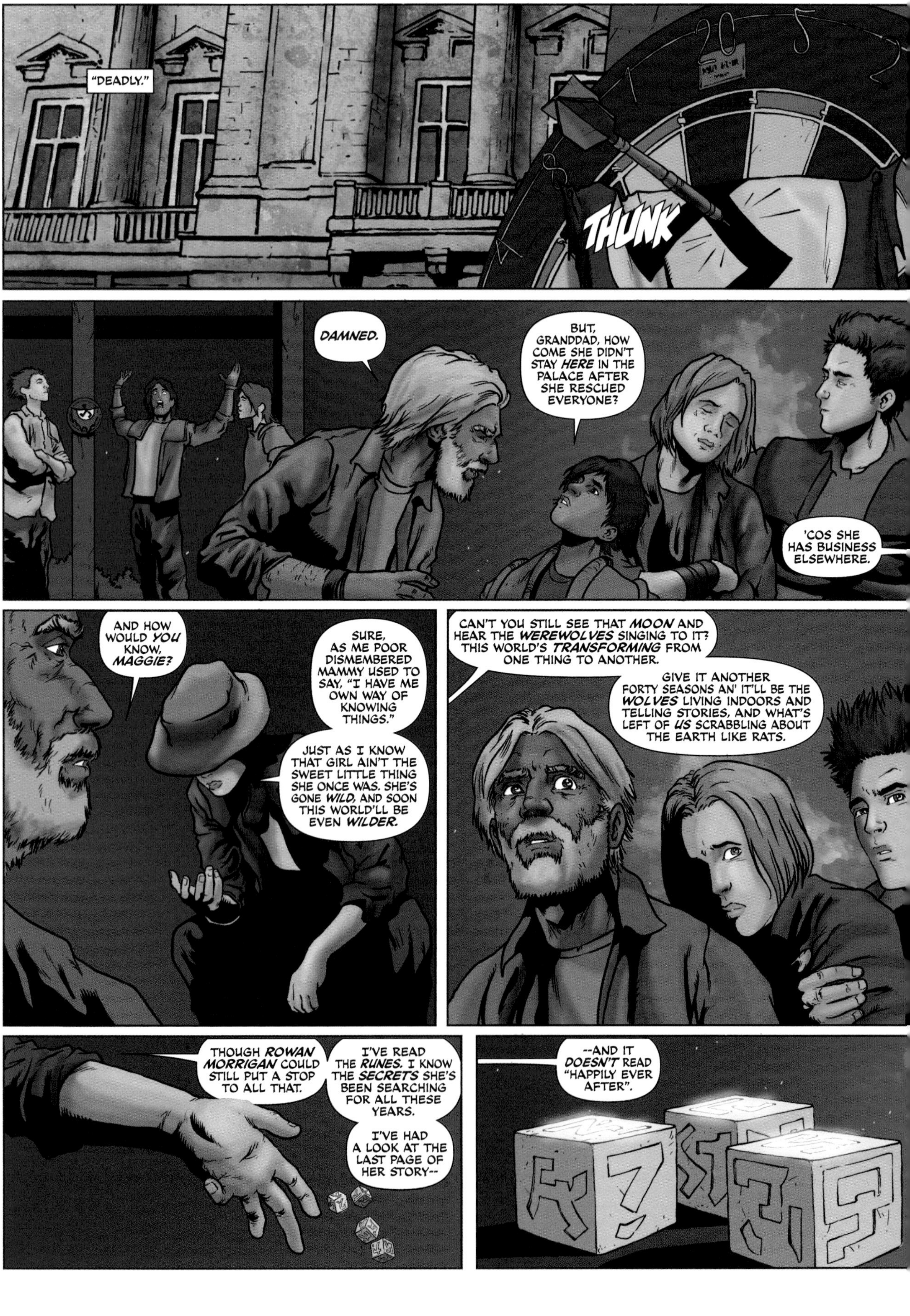
"DEADLY."
THUNK
DAMNED.
BUT, GRANDDAD, HOW COME SHE DIDN'T STAY HERE IN THE PALACE AFTER SHE RESCUED EVERYONE?
'COS SHE HAS BUSINESS ELSEWHERE.
AND HOW WOULD YOU KNOW, MAGGIE?
SURE, AS ME POOR DISMEMBERED MAMMY USED TO SAY, "I HAVE ME OWN WAY OF KNOWING THINGS."
JUST AS I KNOW THAT GIRL AIN'T THE SWEET LITTLE THING SHE ONCE WAS. SHE'S GONE WILD, AND SOON THIS WORLD'LL BE EVEN WILDER.
CAN'T YOU STILL SEE THAT MOON AND HEAR THE WEREWOLVES SINGING TO IT? THIS WORLD'S TRANSFORMING FROM ONE THING TO ANOTHER.
GIVE IT ANOTHER FORTY SEASONS AN' IT'LL BE THE WOLVES LIVING INDOORS AND TELLING STORIES, AND WHAT'S LEFT OF US SCRABBLING ABOUT THE EARTH LIKE RATS.
THOUGH ROWAN MORRIGAN COULD STILL PUT A STOP TO ALL THAT.
I'VE READ THE RUNES. I KNOW THE SECRETS SHE'S BEEN SEARCHING FOR ALL THESE YEARS.
I'VE HAD A LOOK AT THE LAST PAGE OF HER STORY--
--AND IT DOESN'T READ "HAPPILY EVER AFTER".

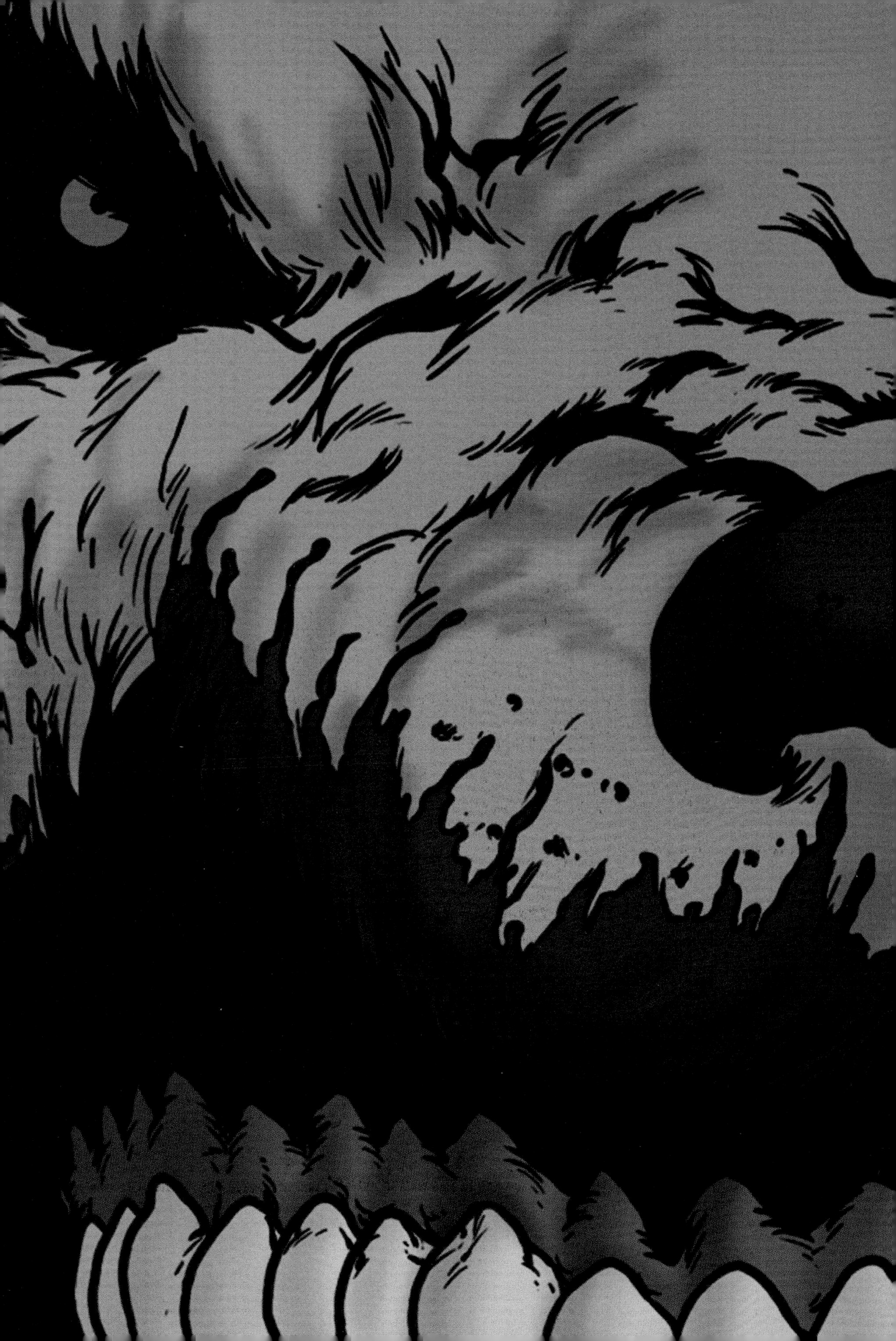

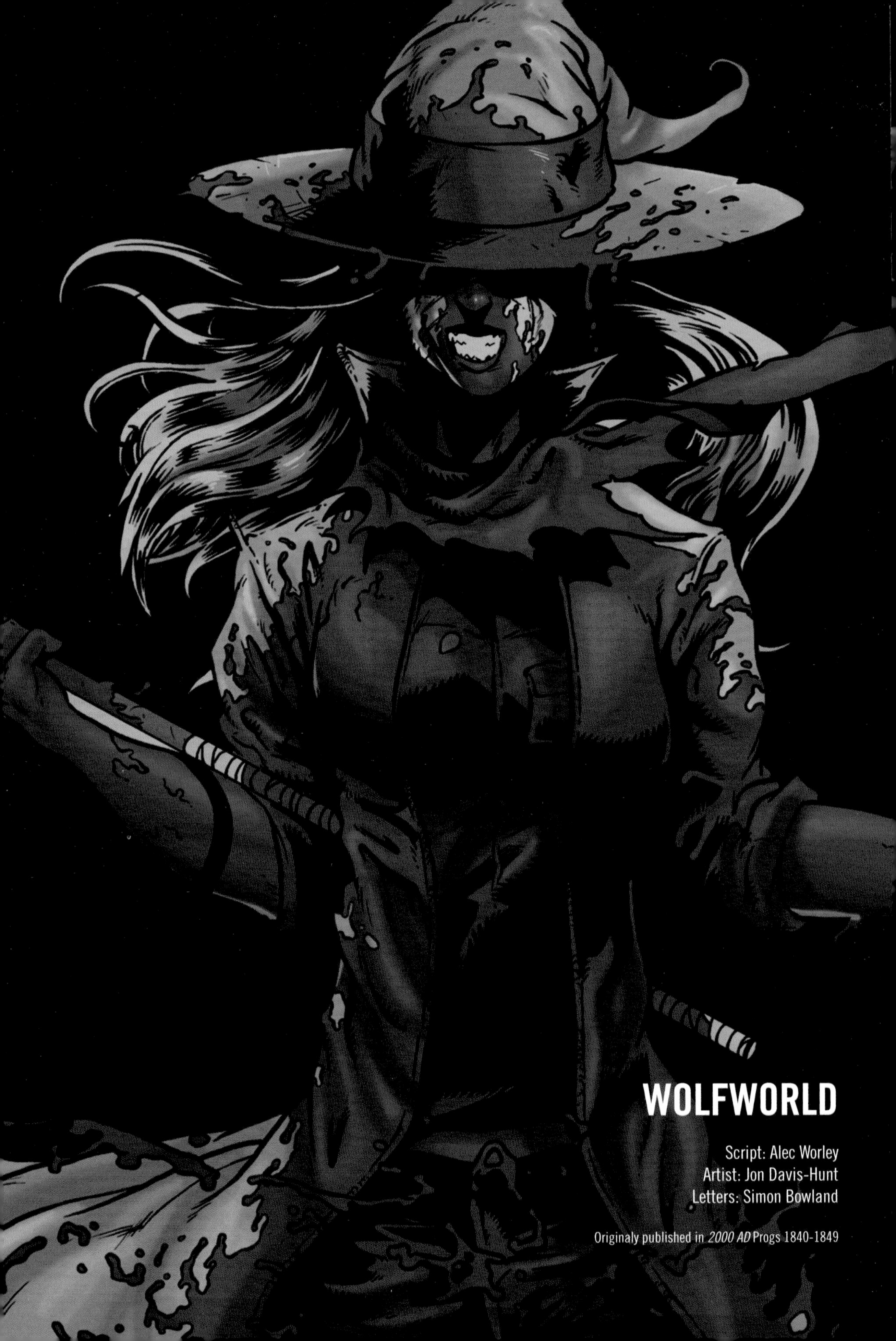

WOLFWORLD

Script: Alec Worley
Artist: Jon Davis-Hunt
Letters: Simon Bowland

Originaly published in *2000 AD* Progs 1840-1849

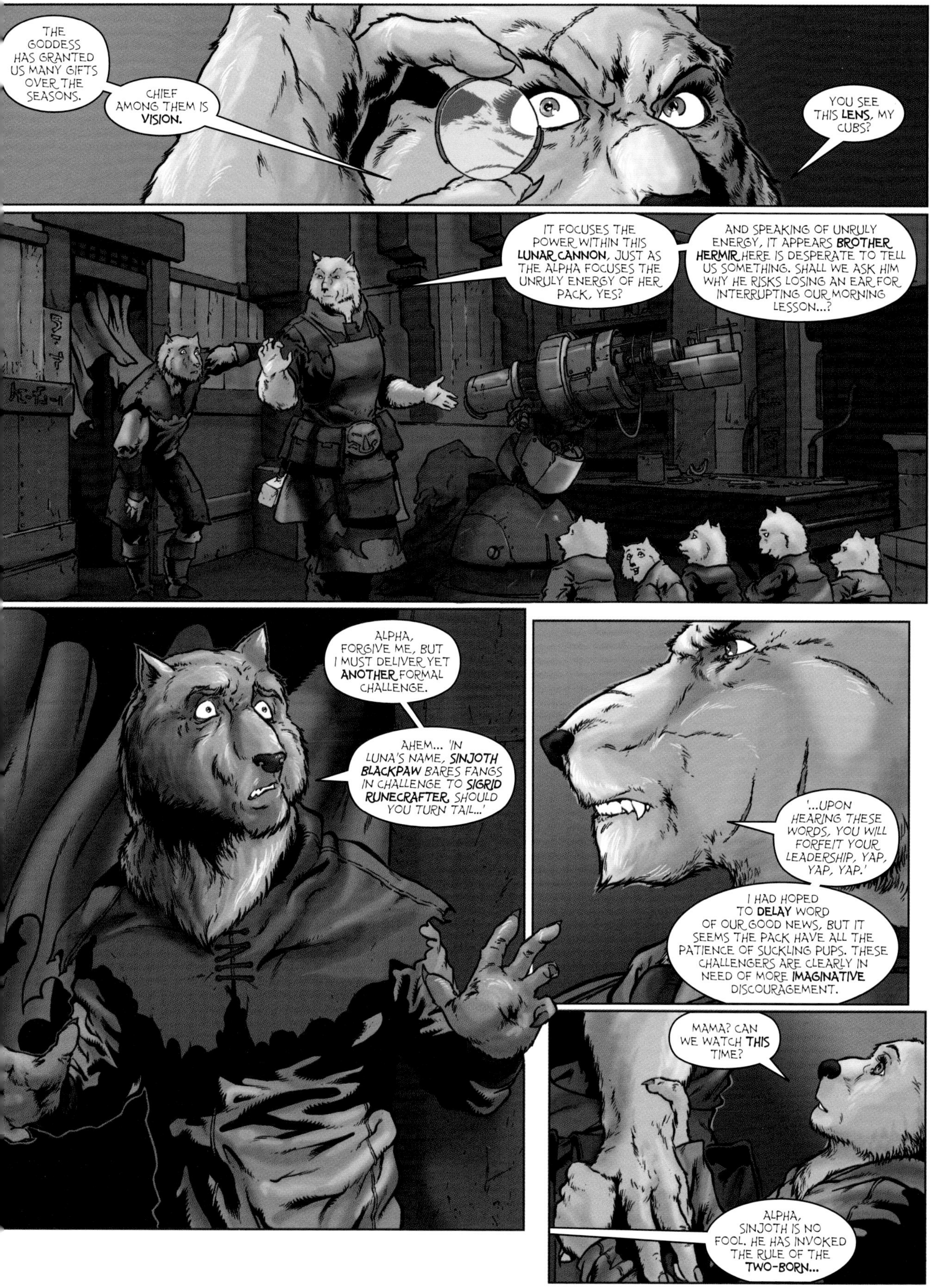
THE GODDESS HAS GRANTED US MANY GIFTS OVER THE SEASONS.
CHIEF AMONG THEM IS VISION.
YOU SEE THIS LENS, MY CUBS?
IT FOCUSES THE POWER WITHIN THIS LUNAR CANNON, JUST AS THE ALPHA FOCUSES THE UNRULY ENERGY OF HER PACK, YES?
AND SPEAKING OF UNRULY ENERGY, IT APPEARS BROTHER HERMIR HERE IS DESPERATE TO TELL US SOMETHING. SHALL WE ASK HIM WHY HE RISKS LOSING AN EAR FOR INTERRUPTING OUR MORNING LESSON...?
ALPHA, FORGIVE ME, BUT I MUST DELIVER YET ANOTHER FORMAL CHALLENGE.
AHEM... 'IN LUNA'S NAME, SINJOTH BLACKPAW BARES FANGS IN CHALLENGE TO SIGRID RUNECRAFTER. SHOULD YOU TURN TAIL...'
'...UPON HEARING THESE WORDS, YOU WILL FORFEIT YOUR LEADERSHIP, YAP, YAP, YAP.'
I HAD HOPED TO DELAY WORD OF OUR GOOD NEWS, BUT IT SEEMS THE PACK HAVE ALL THE PATIENCE OF SUCKLING PUPS. THESE CHALLENGERS ARE CLEARLY IN NEED OF MORE IMAGINATIVE DISCOURAGEMENT.
MAMA? CAN WE WATCH THIS TIME?
ALPHA, SINJOTH IS NO FOOL. HE HAS INVOKED THE RULE OF THE TWO-BORN...

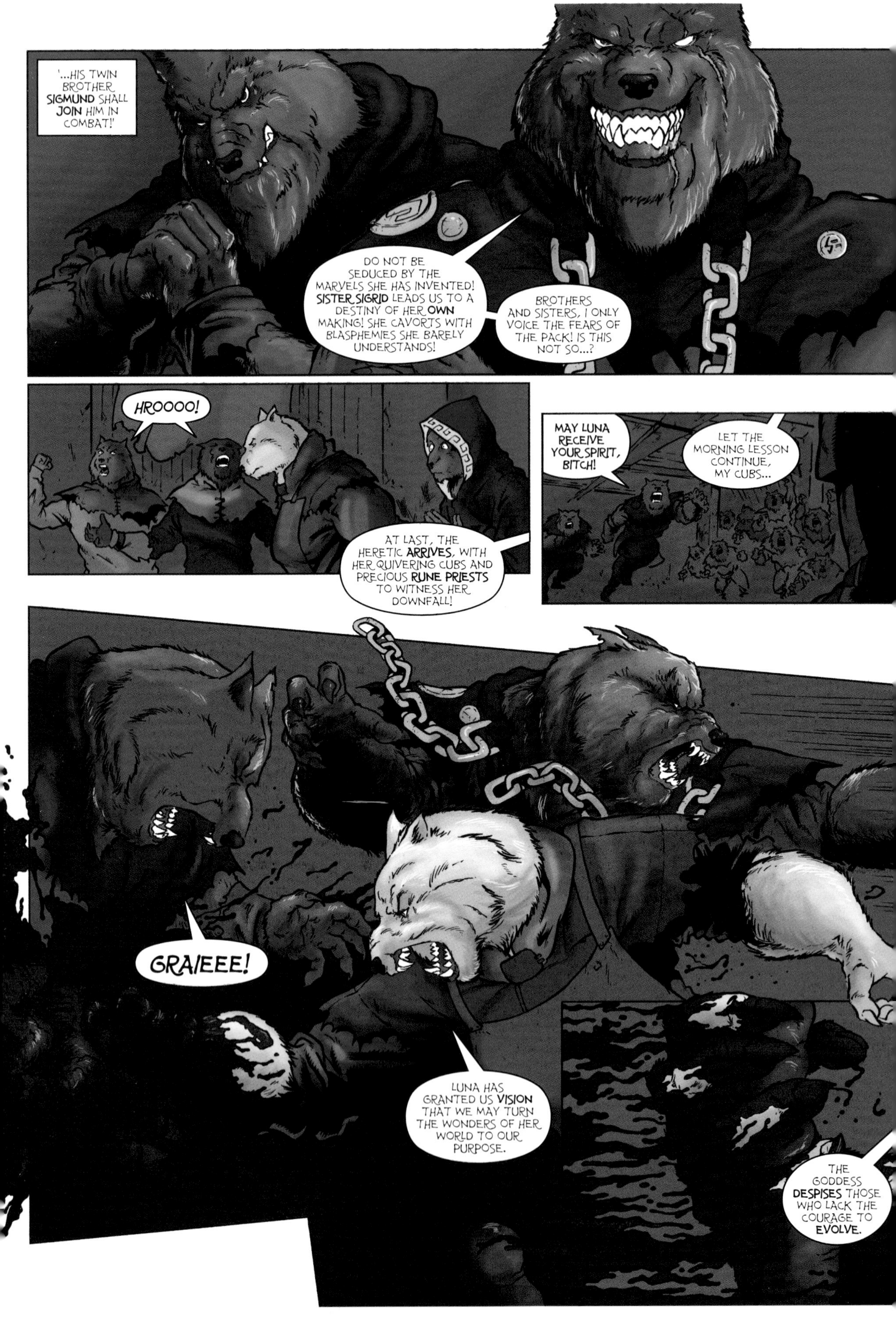
'...HIS TWIN BROTHER **SIGMUND** SHALL **JOIN** HIM IN COMBAT!'
DO NOT BE SEDUCED BY THE MARVELS SHE HAS INVENTED! **SISTER SIGRID** LEADS US TO A DESTINY OF HER **OWN** MAKING! SHE CAVORTS WITH BLASPHEMIES SHE BARELY UNDERSTANDS!
BROTHERS AND SISTERS, I ONLY VOICE THE FEARS OF THE PACK! IS THIS NOT SO...?
HROOOO!
AT LAST, THE HERETIC **ARRIVES**, WITH HER QUIVERING CUBS AND PRECIOUS **RUNE PRIESTS** TO WITNESS HER DOWNFALL!
MAY LUNA RECEIVE YOUR SPIRIT, BITCH!
LET THE MORNING LESSON CONTINUE, MY CUBS...
GRAIEEE!
LUNA HAS GRANTED US **VISION** THAT WE MAY TURN THE WONDERS OF HER WORLD TO OUR PURPOSE.
THE GODDESS **DESPISES** THOSE WHO LACK THE COURAGE TO **EVOLVE**.

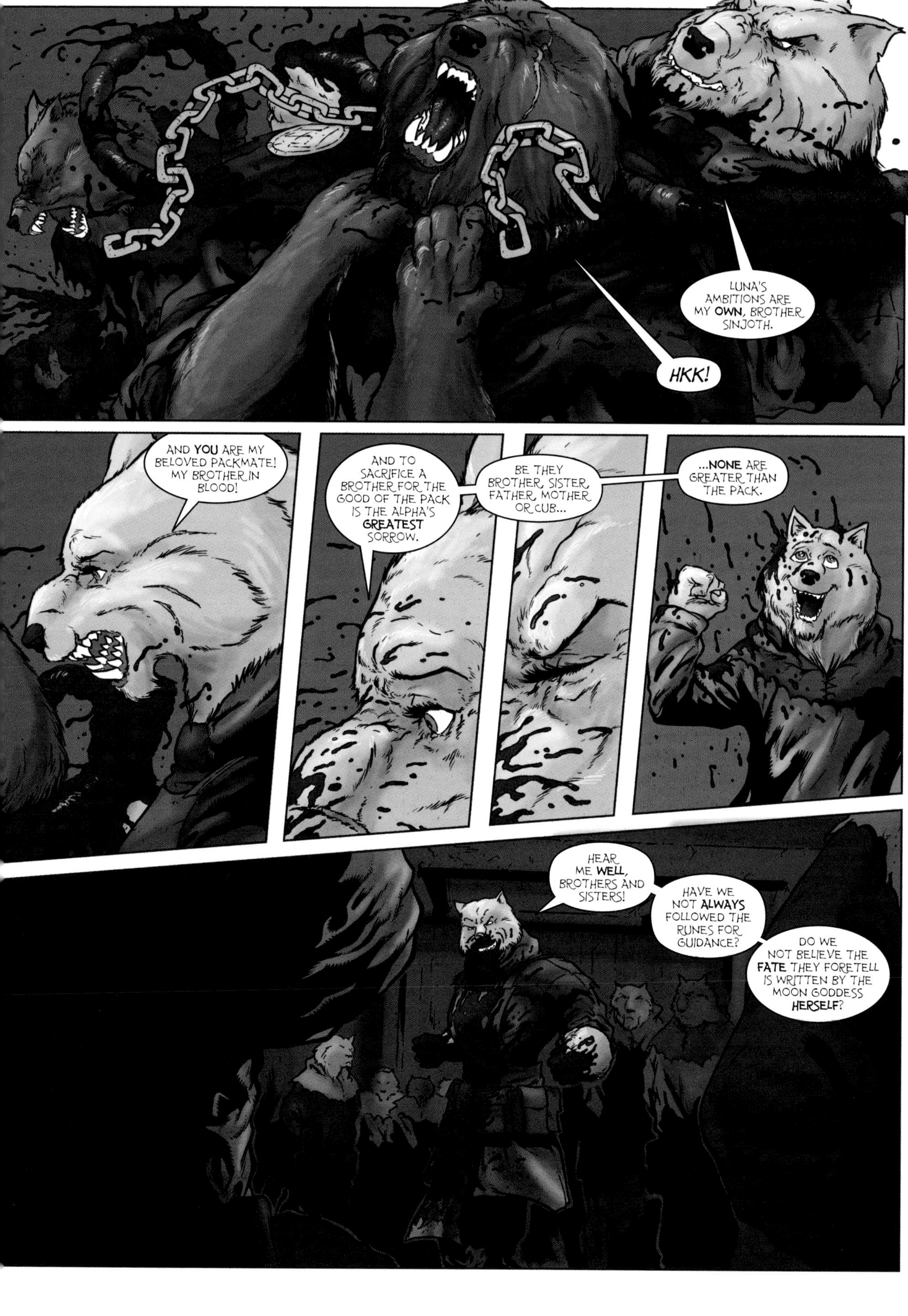
LUNA'S AMBITIONS ARE MY **OWN**, BROTHER SINJOTH.
HKK!
AND **YOU** ARE MY BELOVED PACKMATE! MY BROTHER IN BLOOD!
AND TO SACRIFICE A BROTHER FOR THE GOOD OF THE PACK IS THE ALPHA'S **GREATEST** SORROW.
BE THEY BROTHER, SISTER, FATHER, MOTHER OR CUB...
...**NONE** ARE GREATER THAN THE PACK.
HEAR ME **WELL**, BROTHERS AND SISTERS!
HAVE WE NOT **ALWAYS** FOLLOWED THE RUNES FOR GUIDANCE?
DO WE NOT BELIEVE THE **FATE** THEY FORETELL IS WRITTEN BY THE MOON GODDESS **HERSELF**?

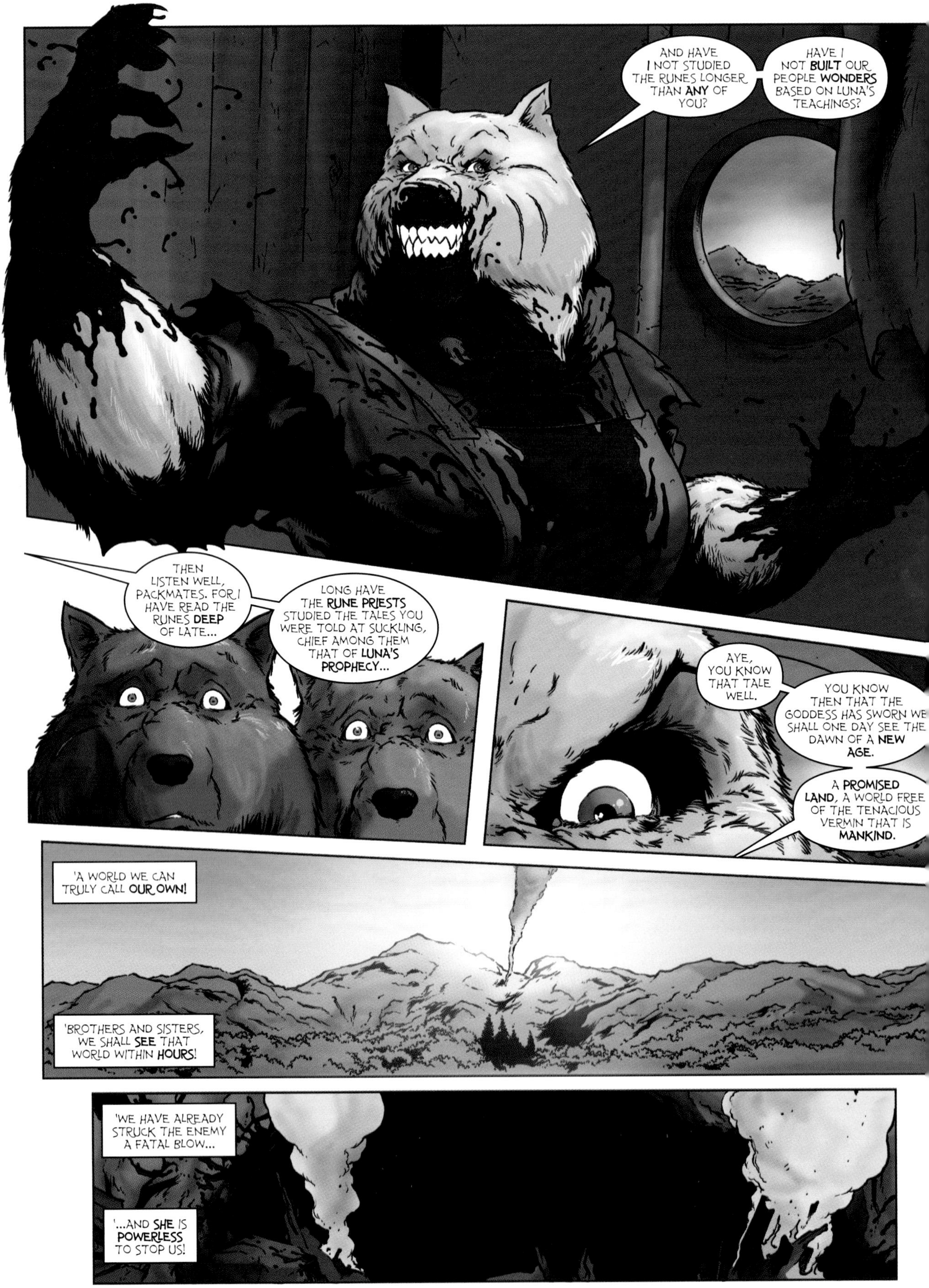
AND HAVE I NOT STUDIED THE RUNES LONGER THAN ANY OF YOU?
HAVE I NOT BUILT OUR PEOPLE WONDERS BASED ON LUNA'S TEACHINGS?
THEN LISTEN WELL, PACKMATES. FOR I HAVE READ THE RUNES DEEP OF LATE...
LONG HAVE THE RUNE PRIESTS STUDIED THE TALES YOU WERE TOLD AT SUCKLING, CHIEF AMONG THEM THAT OF LUNA'S PROPHECY...
AYE, YOU KNOW THAT TALE WELL.
YOU KNOW THEN THAT THE GODDESS HAS SWORN WE SHALL ONE DAY SEE THE DAWN OF A NEW AGE.
A PROMISED LAND, A WORLD FREE OF THE TENACIOUS VERMIN THAT IS MANKIND.
'A WORLD WE CAN TRULY CALL OUR OWN!
'BROTHERS AND SISTERS, WE SHALL SEE THAT WORLD WITHIN HOURS!
'WE HAVE ALREADY STRUCK THE ENEMY A FATAL BLOW...
'...AND SHE IS POWERLESS TO STOP US!

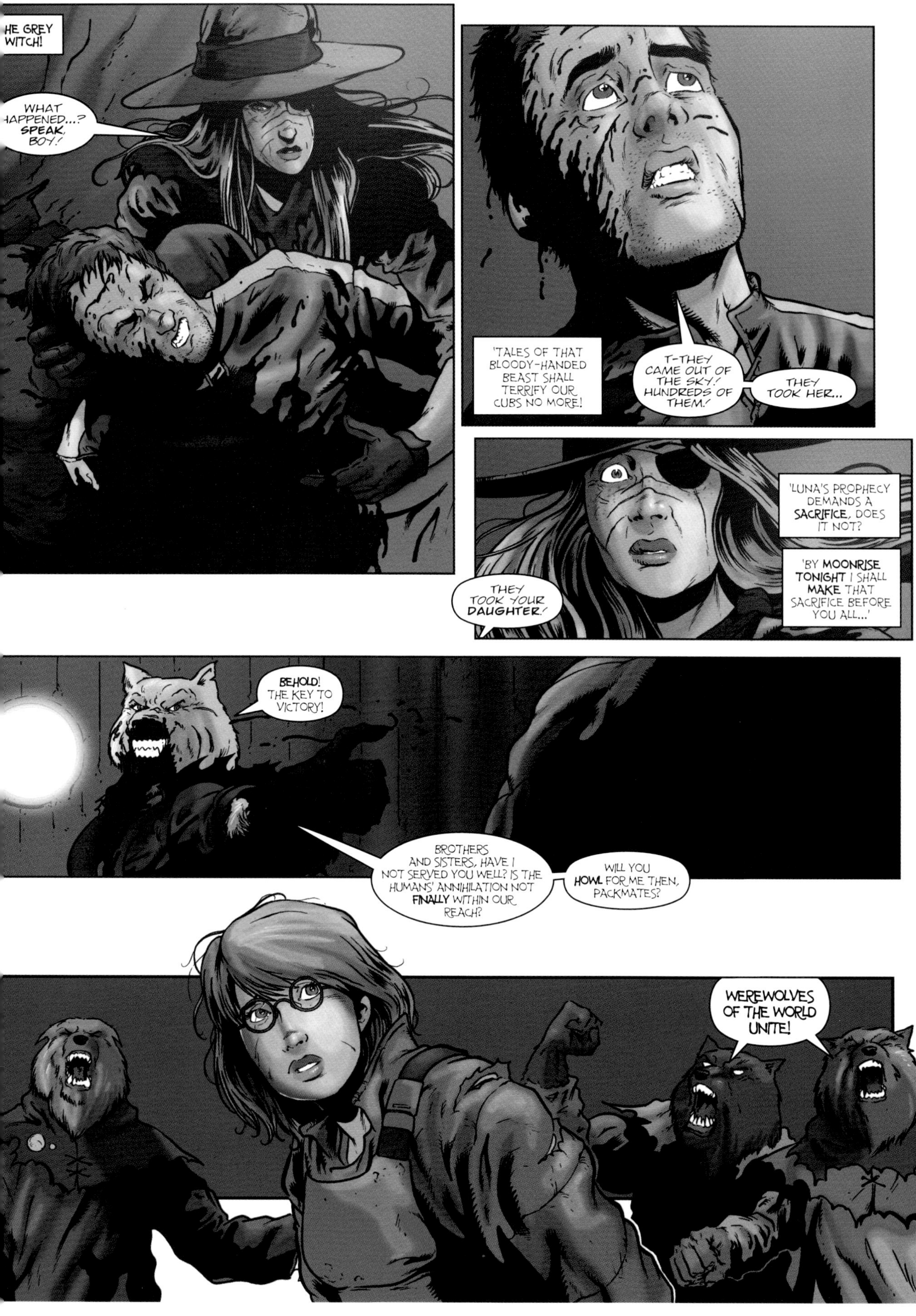
HE GREY WITCH!
WHAT HAPPENED...? SPEAK, BOY!
'TALES OF THAT BLOODY-HANDED BEAST SHALL TERRIFY OUR CUBS NO MORE!
T-THEY CAME OUT OF THE SKY! HUNDREDS OF THEM!
THEY TOOK HER...
'LUNA'S PROPHECY DEMANDS A SACRIFICE, DOES IT NOT?
'BY MOONRISE TONIGHT I SHALL MAKE THAT SACRIFICE BEFORE YOU ALL...'
THEY TOOK YOUR DAUGHTER!
BEHOLD! THE KEY TO VICTORY!
BROTHERS AND SISTERS, HAVE I NOT SERVED YOU WELL? IS THE HUMANS' ANNIHILATION NOT FINALLY WITHIN OUR REACH?
WILL YOU HOWL FOR ME THEN, PACKMATES?
WEREWOLVES OF THE WORLD UNITE!

FIFTEEN YEARS AGO:

ROWAN...?

KEIRA, HONEY, THE LESS QUESTIONS YOU KEEP ASKING, THE QUICKER I CAN STOP THIS STINGING.

I HEARD YOU TALKING TO CHIEF BYRNE. YOU TOLD HIM YOU WERE GOING AWAY AGAIN...

PEOPLE NEED MY **HELP** KEIRA.

THE WEREWOLVES ARE **EVOLVING**, THE MOON'S MAKING THEM CHANGE EVEN MORE.

IF I DON'T HELP PEOPLE PREPARE, A LOT OF THEM ARE GOING TO **DIE**.

WHAT LITTLE PLACE WE HAVE LEFT IN THIS WORLD WON'T BE AROUND MUCH LONGER.

THAT'S WHY I NEED YOU TO STAY RIGHT HERE INSIDE THIS MOUNTAIN, OUT OF REACH.

BUT YOU SAID YOU WERE GOING TO FIND OUT ABOUT MY... MY **REAL** MUM. YOU SAID YOU COULD READ THE RUNES AND —

KEIRA, I DON'T HAVE **TIME!**

I NEED TO FIND A WAY TO TURN THE MOON BACK TO NORMAL AND DESTROY THE WEREWOLVES BEFORE THEY WIPE US OUT!

I'M NOT LEAVING YOU, KEIRA. NOT REALLY.

THIS TATTOO'S A **PROTECTION RUNE**. IT'LL STOP YOU GETTING SICK OR TURNING INTO A WEREWOLF IF YOU GET HURT.

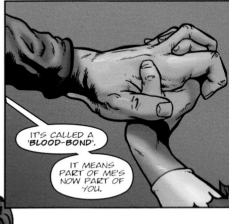

IT'S CALLED A **'BLOOD-BOND'**.

IT MEANS PART OF ME'S NOW PART OF YOU.

AND IT MEANS I CAN **FIND** YOU WHEREVER YOU ARE.

LIKE A **REAL** MUM...?

FOR NOW, SWEETHEAR

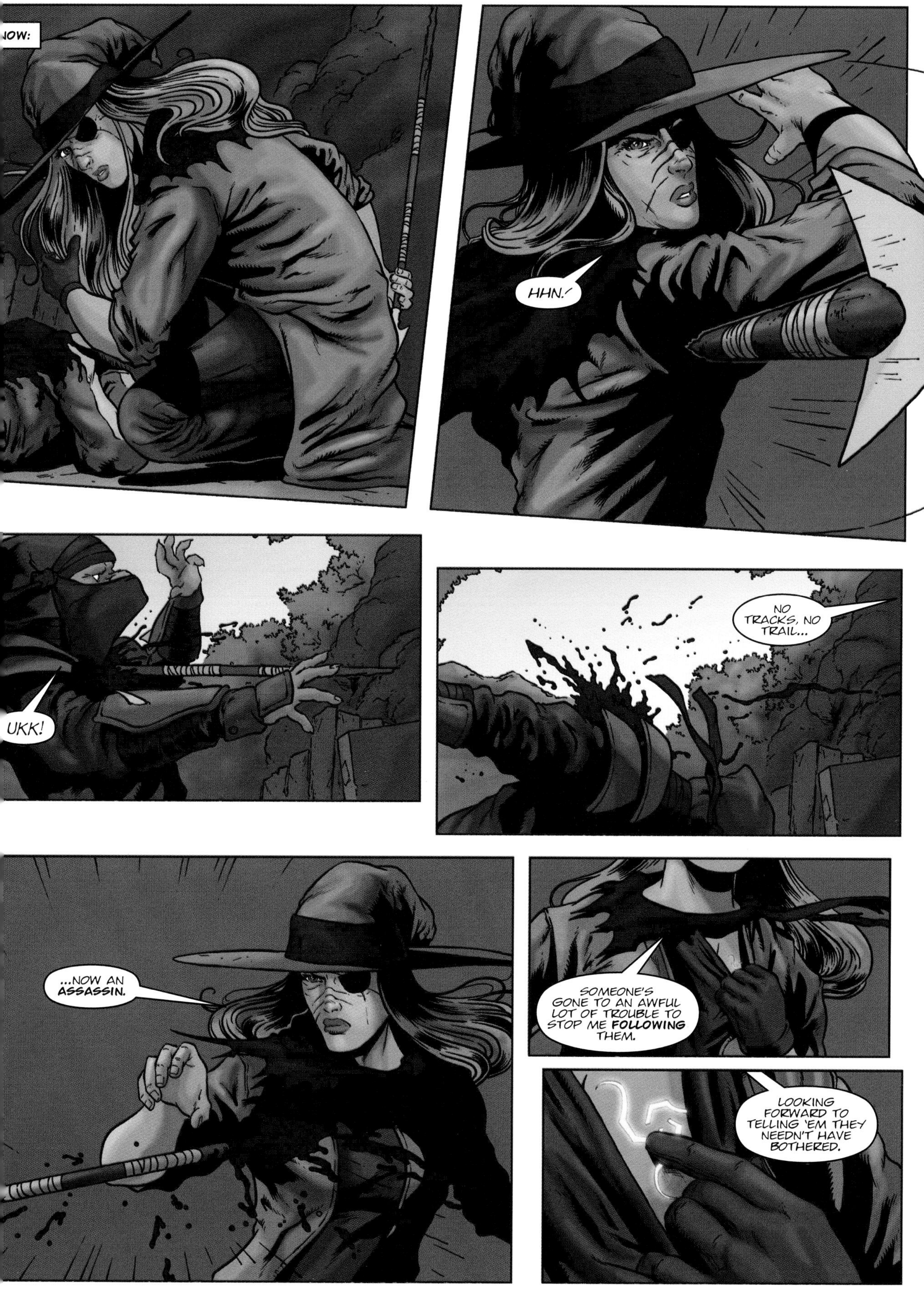
NOW:
HHN!
UKK!
NO TRACKS, NO TRAIL...
...NOW AN **ASSASSIN.**
SOMEONE'S GONE TO AN AWFUL LOT OF TROUBLE TO STOP ME **FOLLOWING** THEM.
LOOKING FORWARD TO TELLING 'EM THEY NEEDN'T HAVE **BOTHERED.**

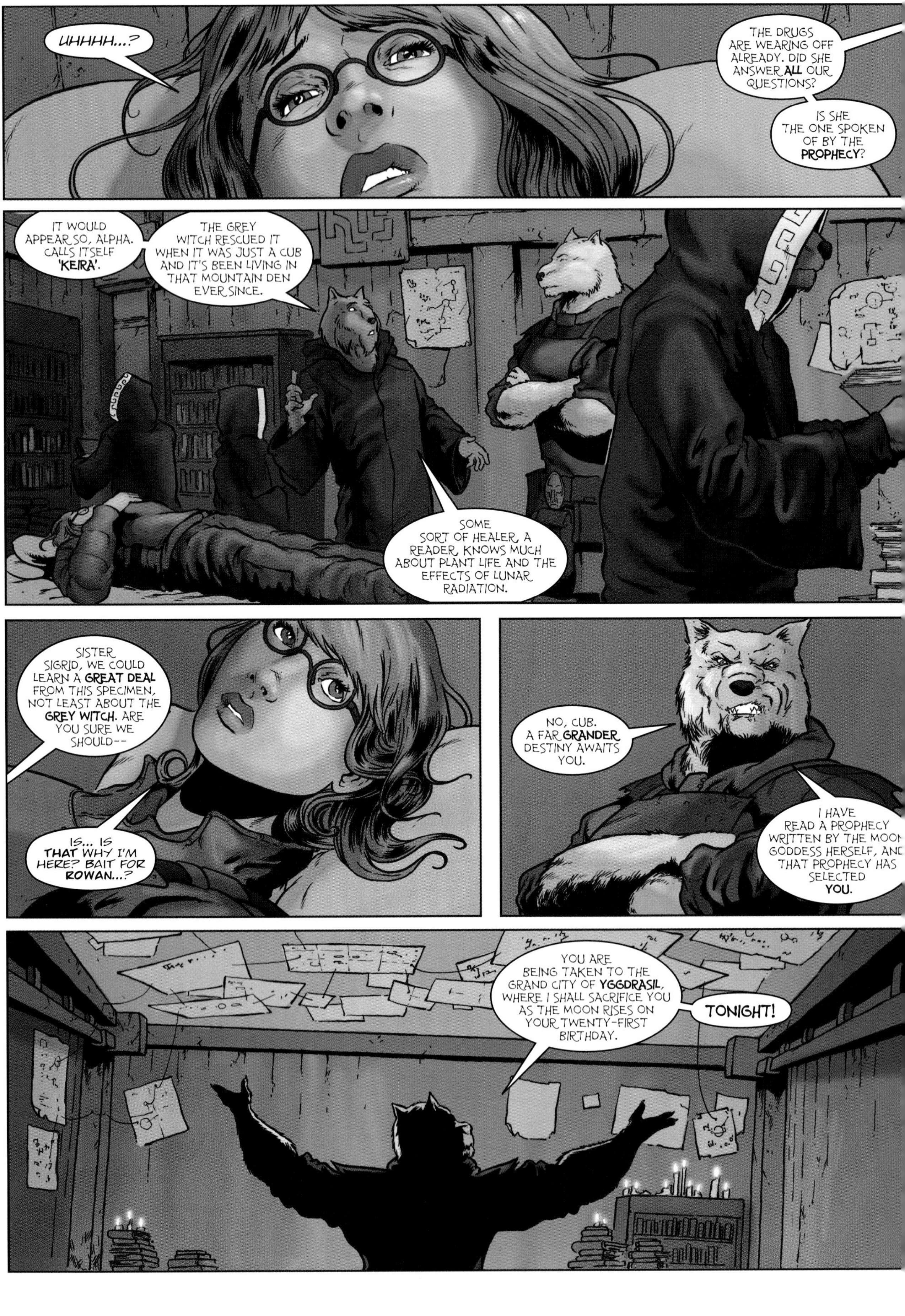
UHHHH...?
THE DRUGS ARE WEARING OFF ALREADY. DID SHE ANSWER ALL OUR QUESTIONS?
IS SHE THE ONE SPOKEN OF BY THE PROPHECY?
IT WOULD APPEAR SO, ALPHA. CALLS ITSELF 'KEIRA'.
THE GREY WITCH RESCUED IT WHEN IT WAS JUST A CUB AND IT'S BEEN LIVING IN THAT MOUNTAIN DEN EVER SINCE.
SOME SORT OF HEALER, A READER, KNOWS MUCH ABOUT PLANT LIFE AND THE EFFECTS OF LUNAR RADIATION.
SISTER SIGRID, WE COULD LEARN A GREAT DEAL FROM THIS SPECIMEN, NOT LEAST ABOUT THE GREY WITCH. ARE YOU SURE WE SHOULD--
IS... IS THAT WHY I'M HERE? BAIT FOR ROWAN...?
NO, CUB. A FAR GRANDER DESTINY AWAITS YOU.
I HAVE READ A PROPHECY WRITTEN BY THE MOON GODDESS HERSELF, AND THAT PROPHECY HAS SELECTED YOU.
YOU ARE BEING TAKEN TO THE GRAND CITY OF YGGDRASIL, WHERE I SHALL SACRIFICE YOU AS THE MOON RISES ON YOUR TWENTY-FIRST BIRTHDAY.
TONIGHT!

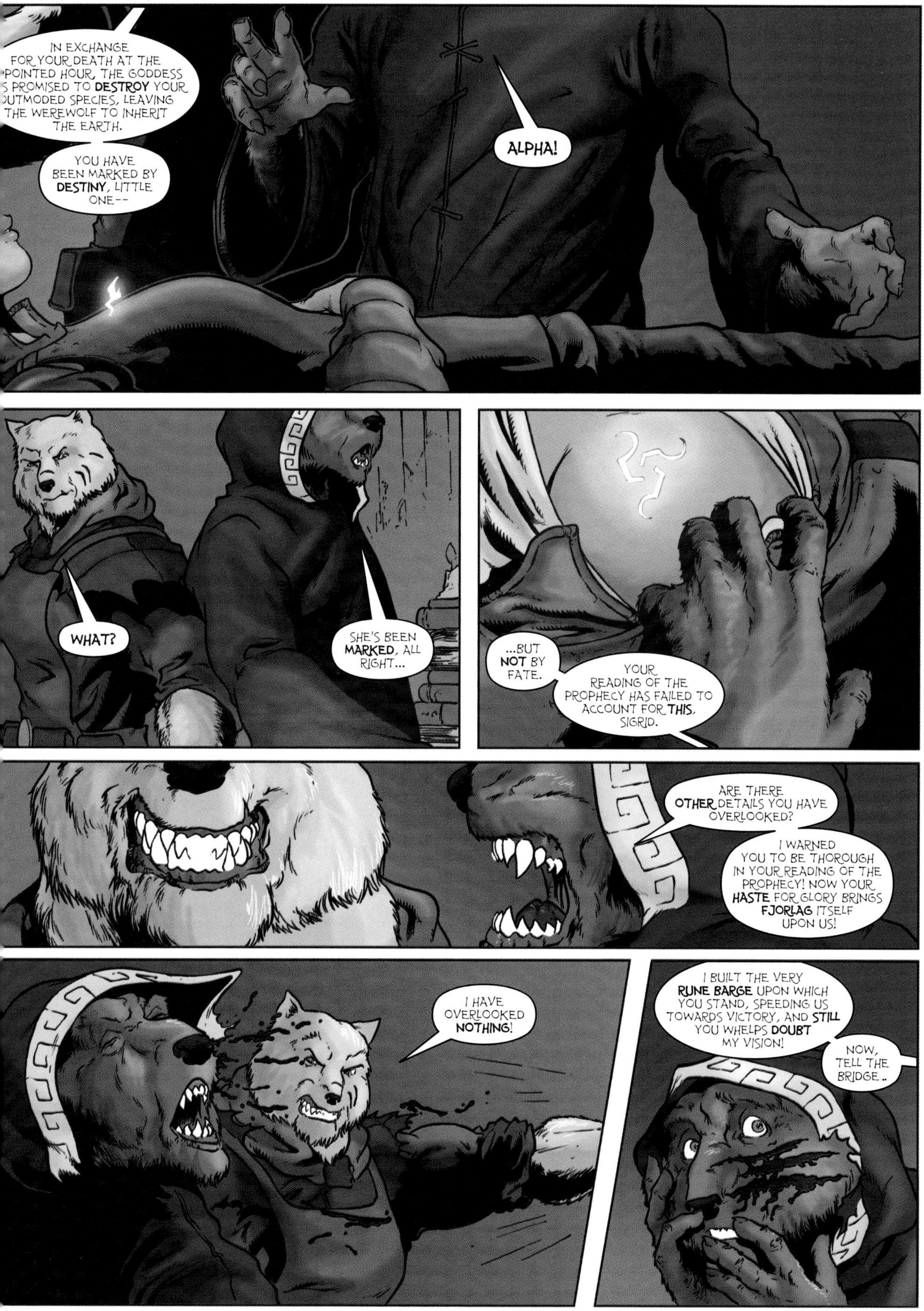
IN EXCHANGE FOR YOUR DEATH AT THE POINTED HOUR, THE GODDESS S PROMISED TO DESTROY YOUR OUTMODED SPECIES, LEAVING THE WEREWOLF TO INHERIT THE EARTH.
YOU HAVE BEEN MARKED BY DESTINY, LITTLE ONE--
ALPHA!
WHAT?
SHE'S BEEN MARKED, ALL RIGHT...
...BUT NOT BY FATE.
YOUR READING OF THE PROPHECY HAS FAILED TO ACCOUNT FOR THIS, SIGRID.
ARE THERE OTHER DETAILS YOU HAVE OVERLOOKED?
I WARNED YOU TO BE THOROUGH IN YOUR READING OF THE PROPHECY! NOW YOUR HASTE FOR GLORY BRINGS FJORLAG ITSELF UPON US!
I HAVE OVERLOOKED NOTHING!
I BUILT THE VERY RUNE BARGE UPON WHICH YOU STAND, SPEEDING US TOWARDS VICTORY, AND STILL YOU WHELPS DOUBT MY VISION!
NOW, TELL THE BRIDGE..

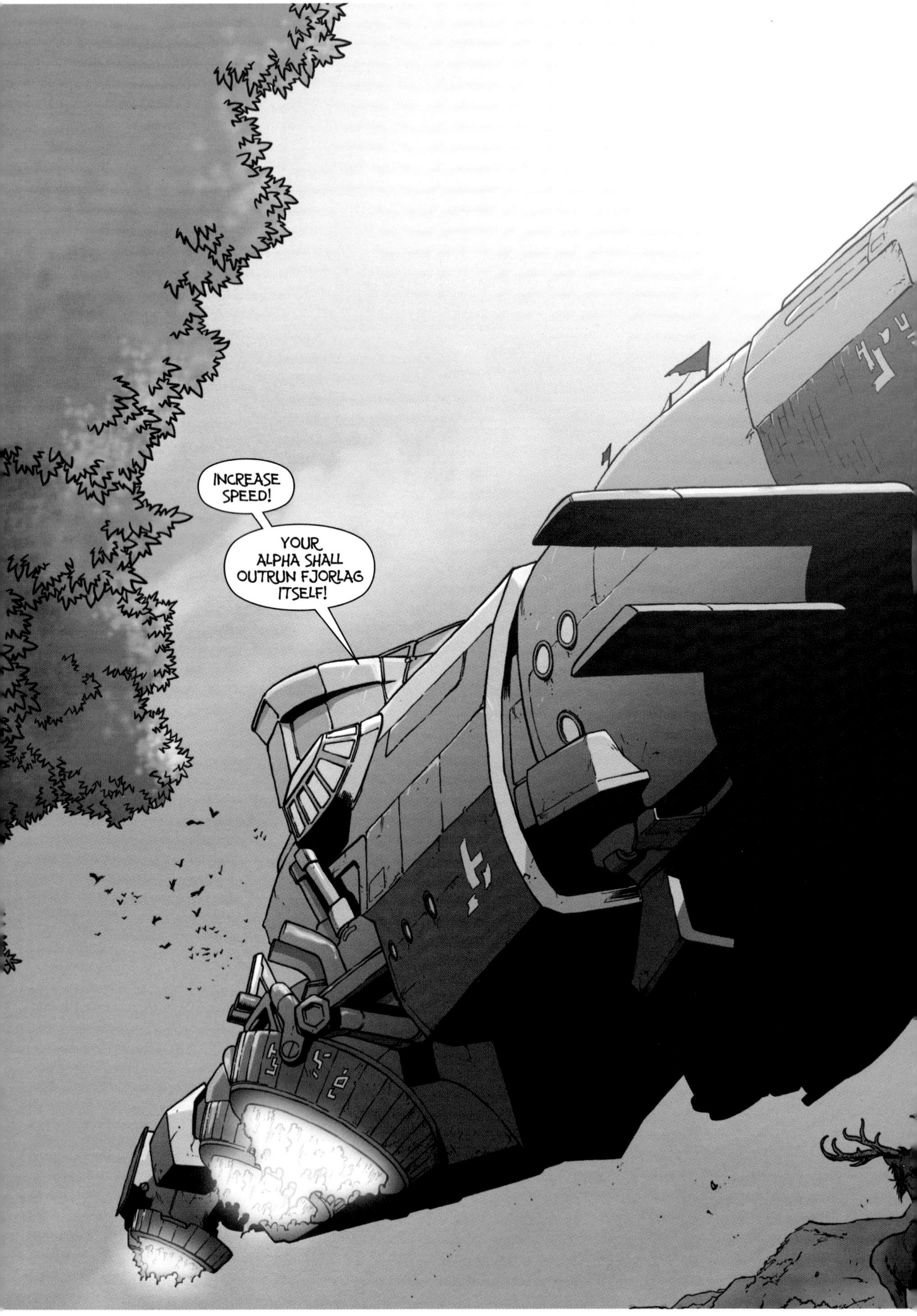
INCREASE SPEED!
YOUR ALPHA SHALL OUTRUN FJORLAG ITSELF!

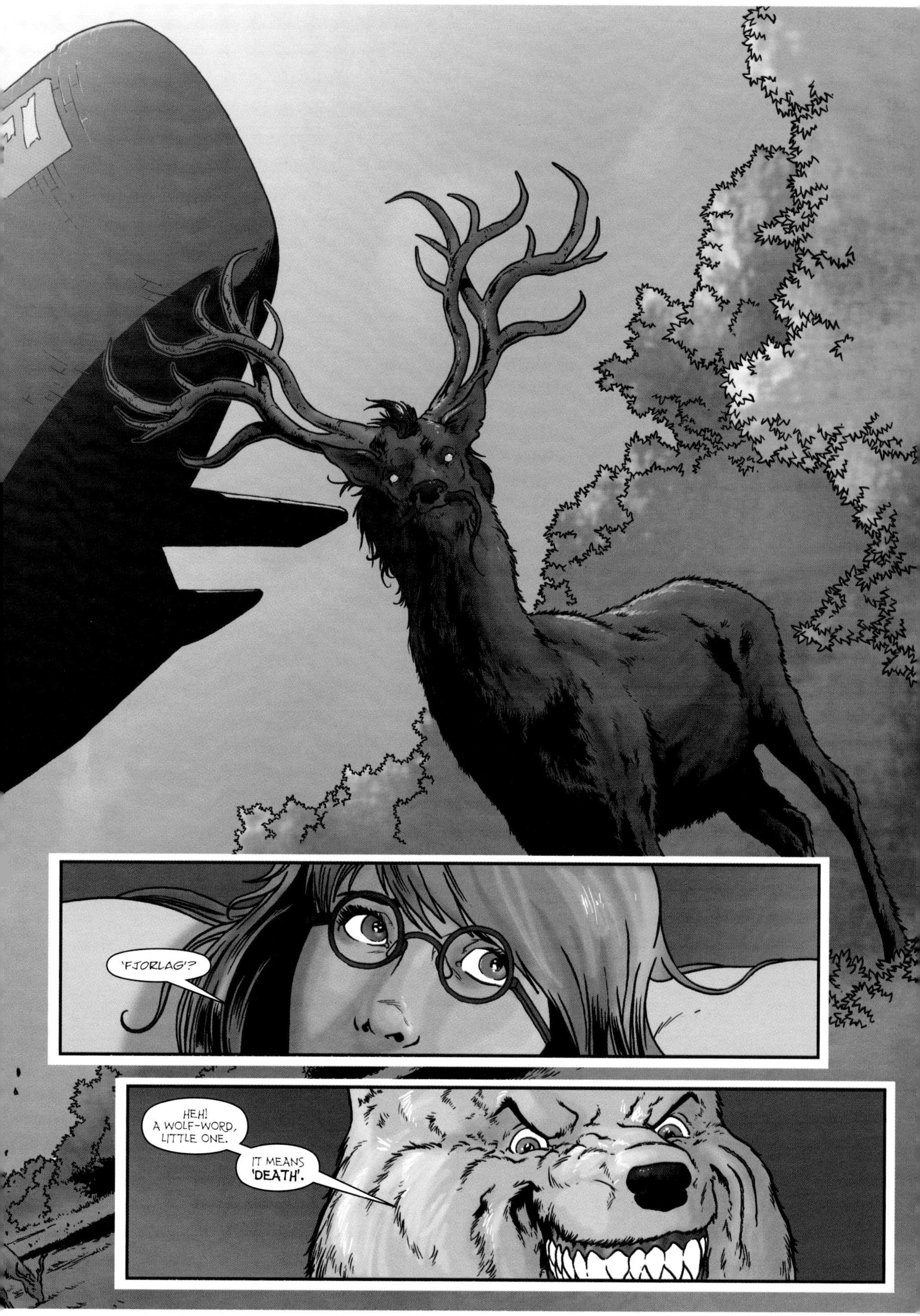
'FJORLAG'?
HEH! A WOLF-WORD, LITTLE ONE.
IT MEANS 'DEATH'.

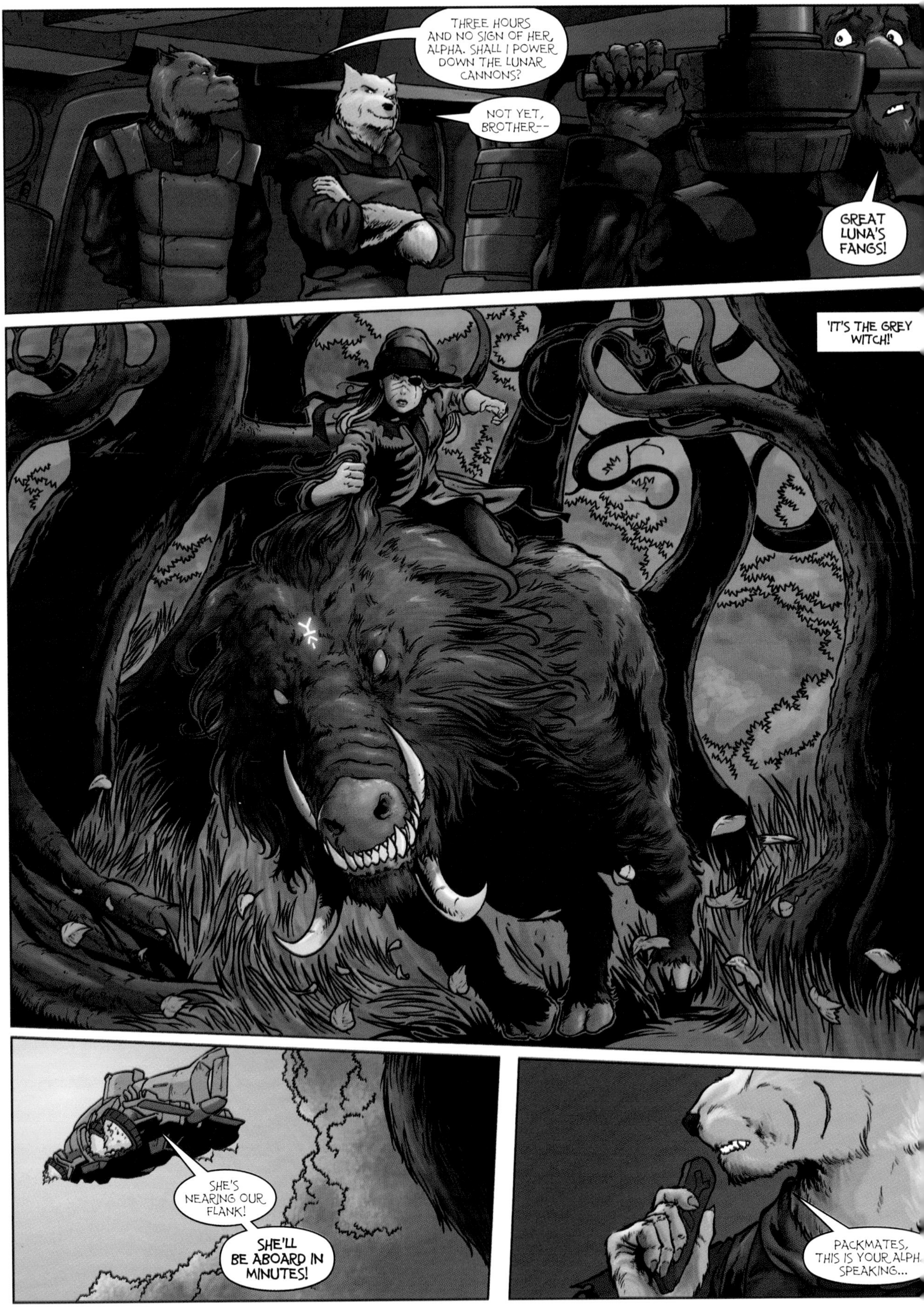
THREE HOURS AND NO SIGN OF HER, ALPHA. SHALL I POWER DOWN THE LUNAR CANNONS?
NOT YET, BROTHER--
GREAT LUNA'S FANGS!
'IT'S THE GREY WITCH!'
SHE'S NEARING OUR FLANK!
SHE'LL BE ABOARD IN MINUTES!
PACKMATES, THIS IS YOUR ALPH SPEAKING...

LUNA HAS ALREADY PROPHESISED OUR VICTORY.

TONIGHT WE SHALL ENTER OUR HOLY CITY, WHERE I SHALL SACRIFICE THE **HUMAN CUB** AND ENACT THE RITE THAT WILL **DESTROY** HER WRETCHED SPECIES.

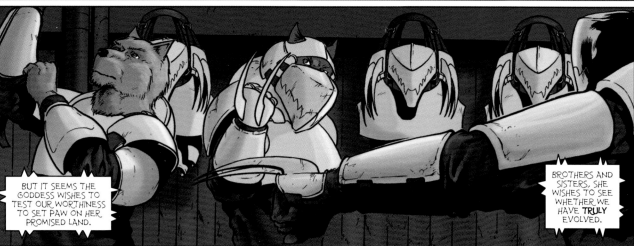

BUT IT SEEMS THE GODDESS WISHES TO TEST OUR WORTHINESS TO SET PAW ON HER PROMISED LAND.

BROTHERS AND SISTERS, SHE WISHES TO SEE WHETHER WE HAVE **TRULY** EVOLVED.

SHE HAS THEREFORE SENT OUR MOST TERRIBLE FOE AGAINST US, SO THAT WE MAY **PROVE** OUR VALOUR.

BUT FANG AND CLAW ARE NOT REQUIRED **THIS** DAY -- NOT WHEN YOUR ALPHA CAN BRING TO BEAR WEAPONS SUCH AS **THESE**...

'I HAVE JUST ACTIVATED A **SONIC WEAPON** CAPABLE OF DRIVING LESSER SPECIES INTO A KILLING FRENZY.

'THE EFFECTS CAN BE QUITE SPECTACULAR,'

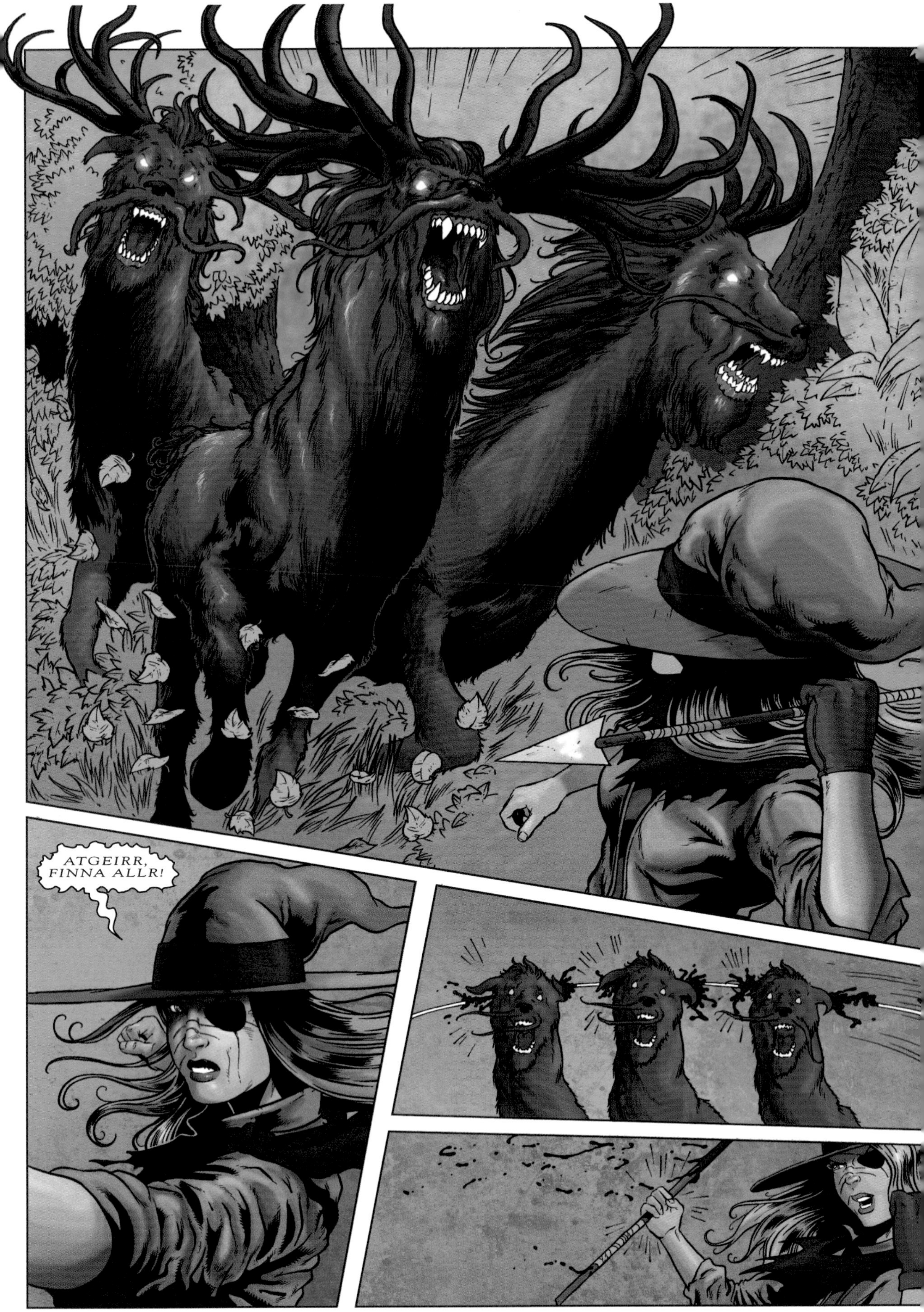
ATGEIRR, FINNA ALLR!

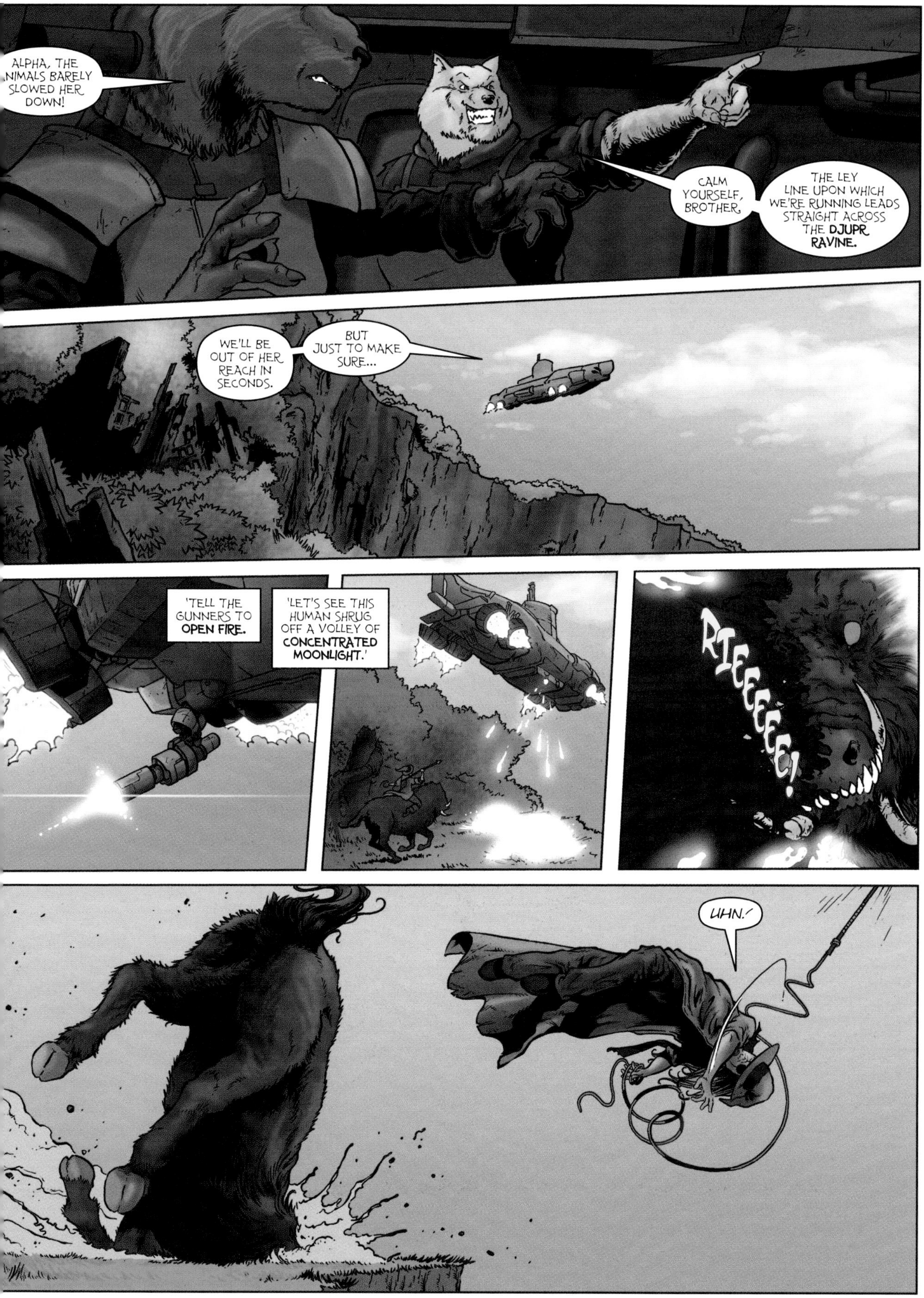
ALPHA, THE NIMALS BARELY SLOWED HER DOWN!
CALM YOURSELF, BROTHER.
THE LEY LINE UPON WHICH WE'RE RUNNING LEADS STRAIGHT ACROSS THE DJUPR RAVINE.
WE'LL BE OUT OF HER REACH IN SECONDS.
BUT JUST TO MAKE SURE...
'TELL THE GUNNERS TO OPEN FIRE.
'LET'S SEE THIS HUMAN SHRUG OFF A VOLLEY OF CONCENTRATED MOONLIGHT.'
RIEEEEEE!
UHN!

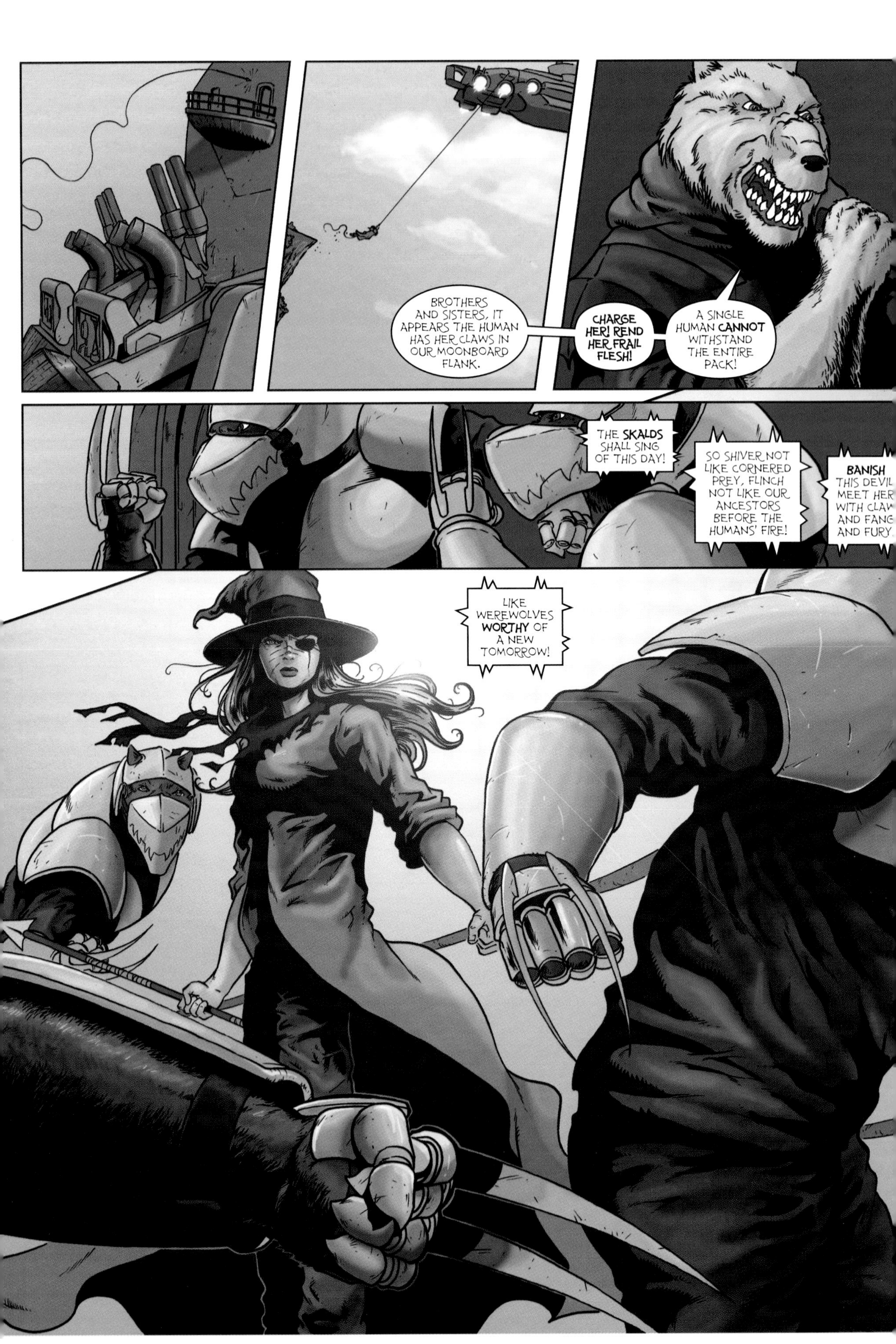
BROTHERS AND SISTERS, IT APPEARS THE HUMAN HAS HER CLAWS IN OUR MOONBOARD FLANK.
CHARGE HER! REND HER FRAIL FLESH!
A SINGLE HUMAN CANNOT WITHSTAND THE ENTIRE PACK!
THE SKALDS SHALL SING OF THIS DAY!
SO SHIVER NOT LIKE CORNERED PREY, FLINCH NOT LIKE OUR ANCESTORS BEFORE THE HUMANS' FIRE!
BANISH THIS DEVIL MEET HER WITH CLAW AND FANG AND FURY.
LIKE WEREWOLVES WORTHY OF A NEW TOMORROW!

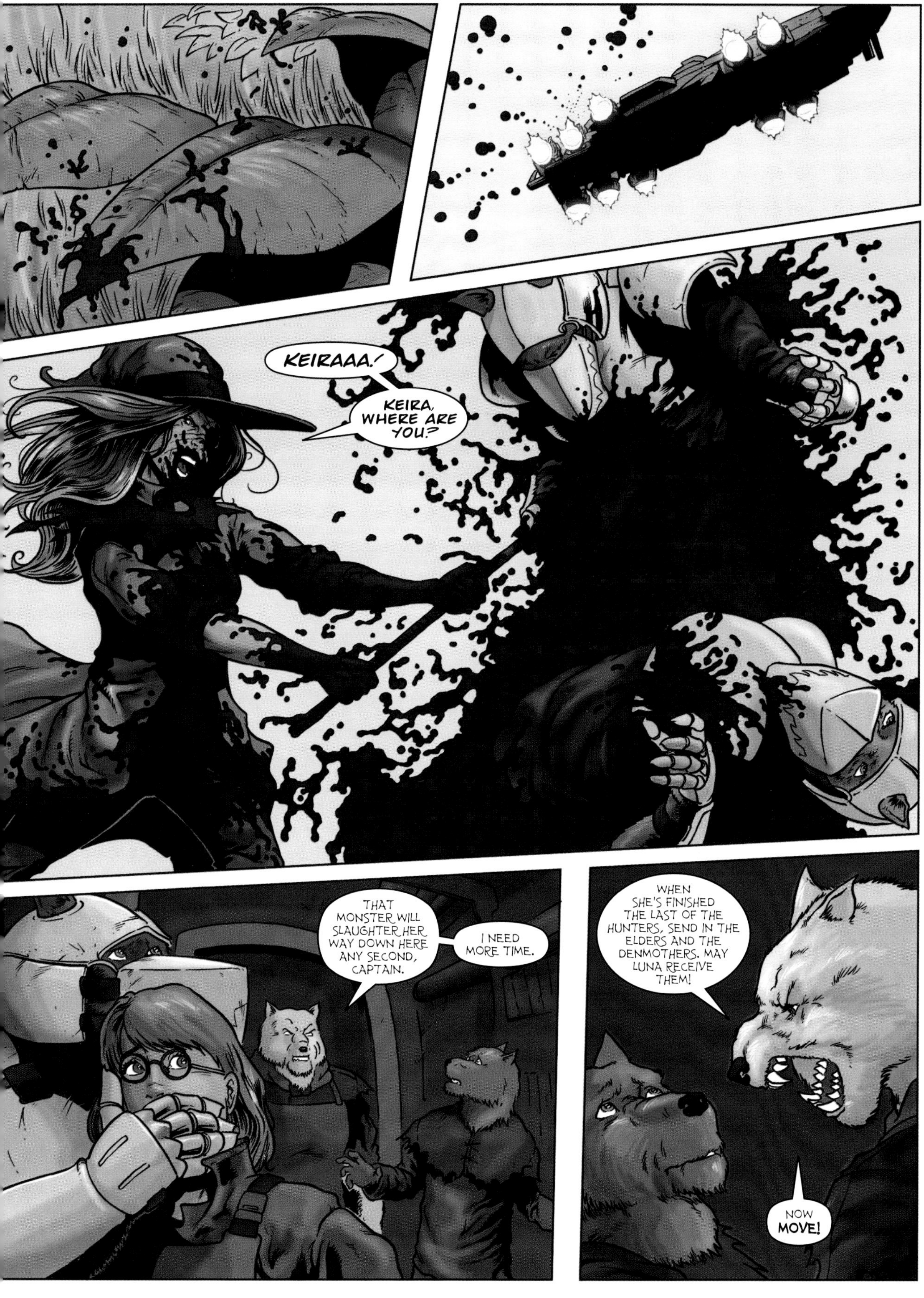
KEIRAAA!
KEIRA, WHERE ARE YOU?
THAT MONSTER WILL SLAUGHTER HER WAY DOWN HERE ANY SECOND, CAPTAIN.
I NEED MORE TIME.
WHEN SHE'S FINISHED THE LAST OF THE HUNTERS, SEND IN THE ELDERS AND THE DENMOTHERS. MAY LUNA RECEIVE THEM!
NOW MOVE!

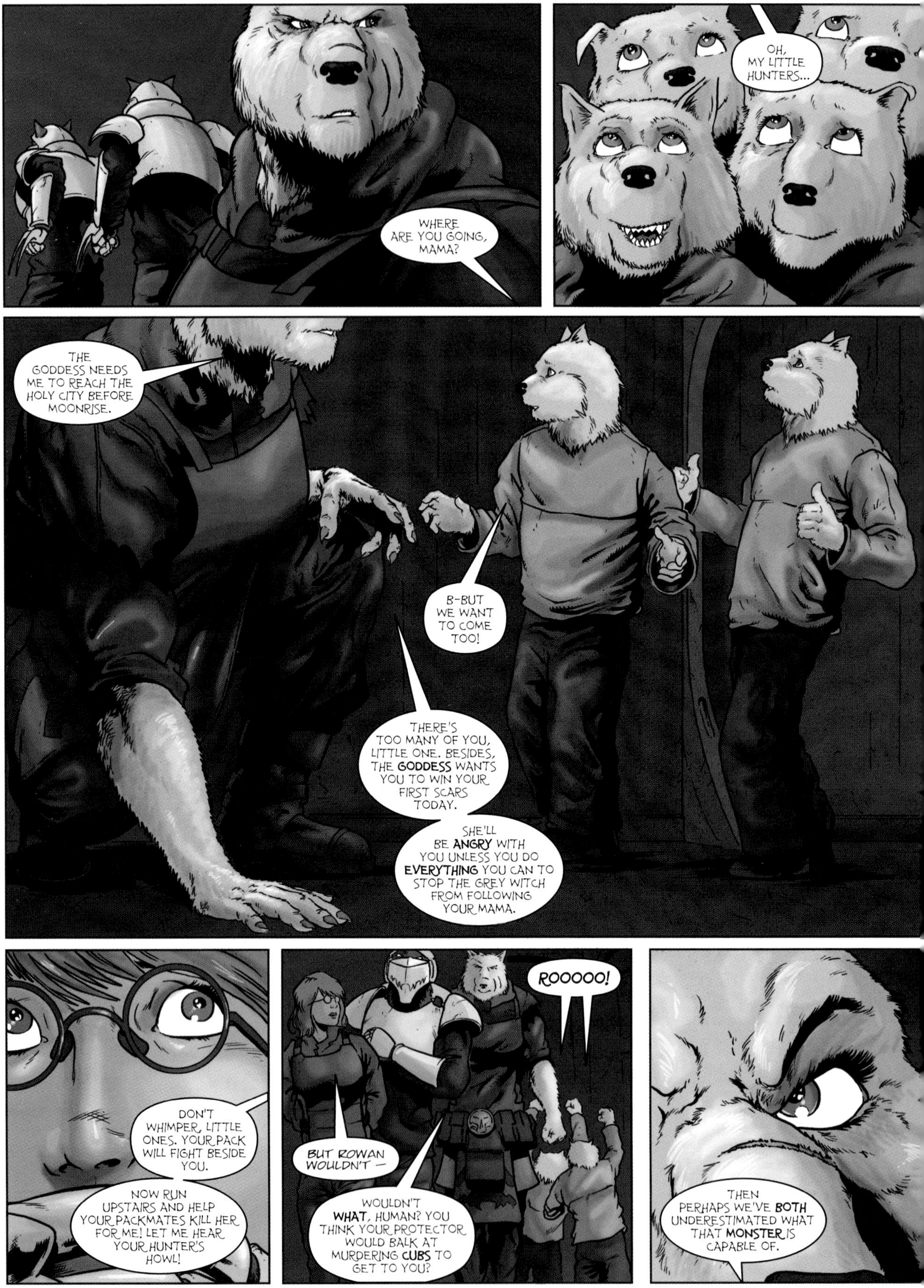
WHERE ARE YOU GOING, MAMA?
OH, MY LITTLE HUNTERS...
THE GODDESS NEEDS ME TO REACH THE HOLY CITY BEFORE MOONRISE.
B-BUT WE WANT TO COME TOO!
THERE'S TOO MANY OF YOU, LITTLE ONE. BESIDES, THE GODDESS WANTS YOU TO WIN YOUR FIRST SCARS TODAY.
SHE'LL BE ANGRY WITH YOU UNLESS YOU DO EVERYTHING YOU CAN TO STOP THE GREY WITCH FROM FOLLOWING YOUR MAMA.
DON'T WHIMPER, LITTLE ONES. YOUR PACK WILL FIGHT BESIDE YOU.
NOW RUN UPSTAIRS AND HELP YOUR PACKMATES KILL HER FOR ME! LET ME HEAR YOUR HUNTER'S HOWL!
ROOOOO!
BUT ROWAN WOULDN'T —
WOULDN'T WHAT, HUMAN? YOU THINK YOUR PROTECTOR WOULD BALK AT MURDERING CUBS TO GET TO YOU?
THEN PERHAPS WE'VE BOTH UNDERESTIMATED WHAT THAT MONSTER IS CAPABLE OF.

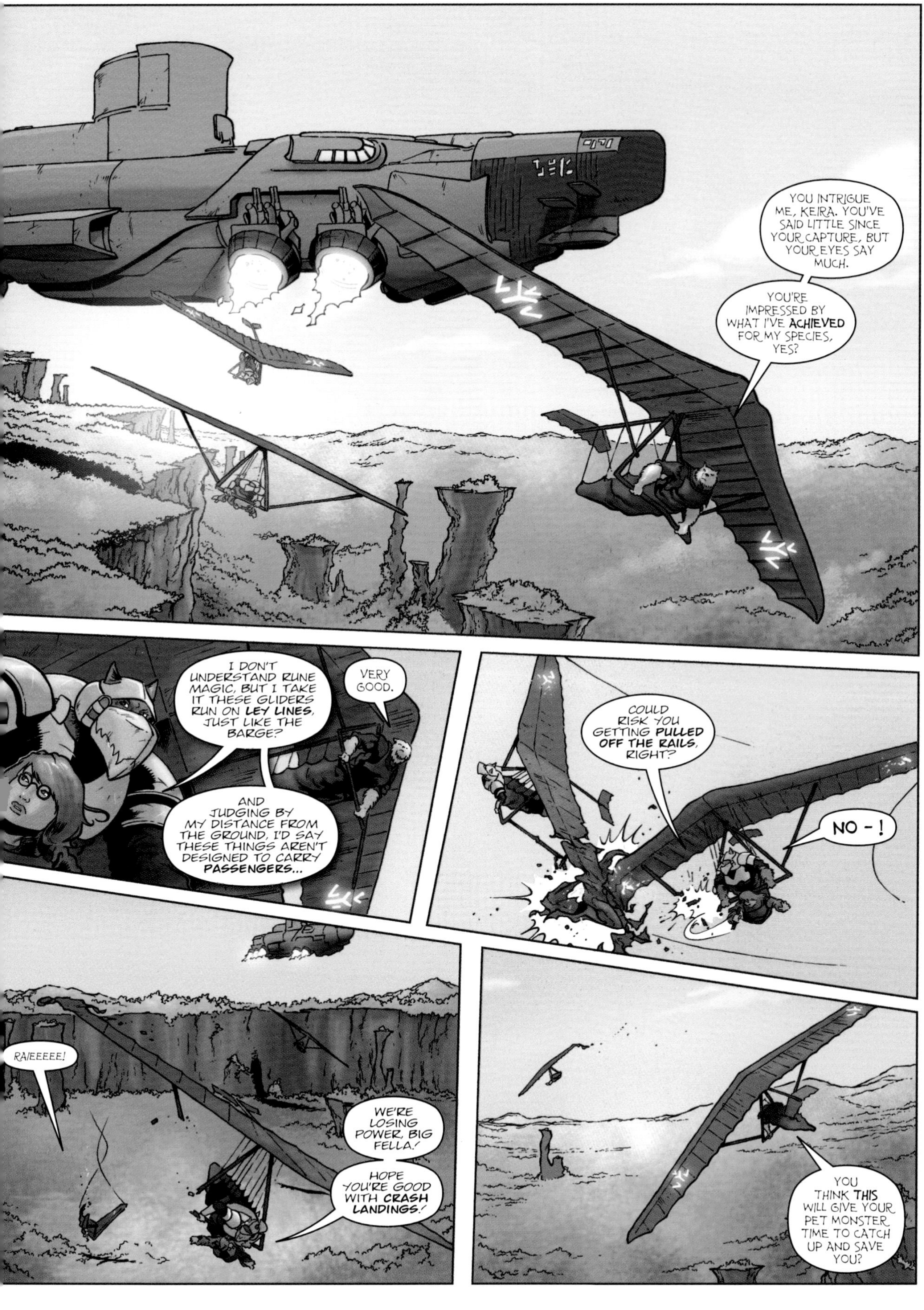
YOU INTRIGUE ME, KEIRA. YOU'VE SAID LITTLE SINCE YOUR CAPTURE, BUT YOUR EYES SAY MUCH.
YOU'RE IMPRESSED BY WHAT I'VE **ACHIEVED** FOR MY SPECIES, YES?
I DON'T UNDERSTAND RUNE MAGIC, BUT I TAKE IT THESE GLIDERS RUN ON **LEY LINES**, JUST LIKE THE BARGE?
VERY GOOD.
AND JUDGING BY MY DISTANCE FROM THE GROUND, I'D SAY THESE THINGS AREN'T DESIGNED TO CARRY **PASSENGERS...**
COULD RISK YOU GETTING **PULLED OFF THE RAILS**, RIGHT?
NO - !
RAIEEEEE!
WE'RE LOSING POWER, BIG FELLA!
HOPE YOU'RE GOOD WITH **CRASH LANDINGS**!
YOU THINK **THIS** WILL GIVE YOUR PET MONSTER TIME TO CATCH UP AND SAVE YOU?

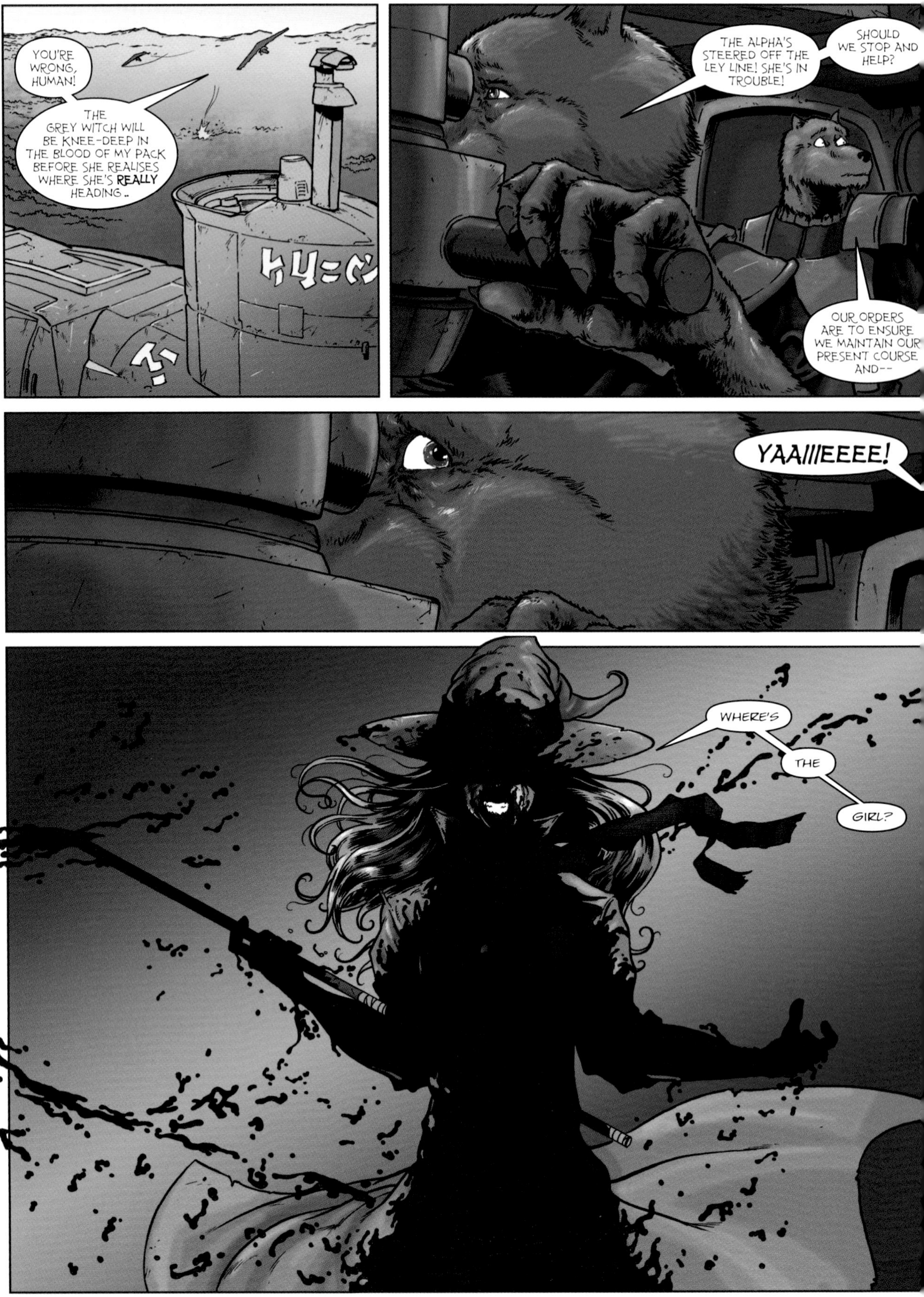
YOU'RE WRONG, HUMAN!
THE GREY WITCH WILL BE KNEE-DEEP IN THE BLOOD OF MY PACK BEFORE SHE REALISES WHERE SHE'S **REALLY** HEADING..
THE ALPHA'S STEERED OFF THE LEY LINE! SHE'S IN TROUBLE!
SHOULD WE STOP AND HELP?
OUR ORDERS ARE TO ENSURE WE MAINTAIN OUR PRESENT COURSE AND--
YAAIIIEEEE!
WHERE'S
THE
GIRL?

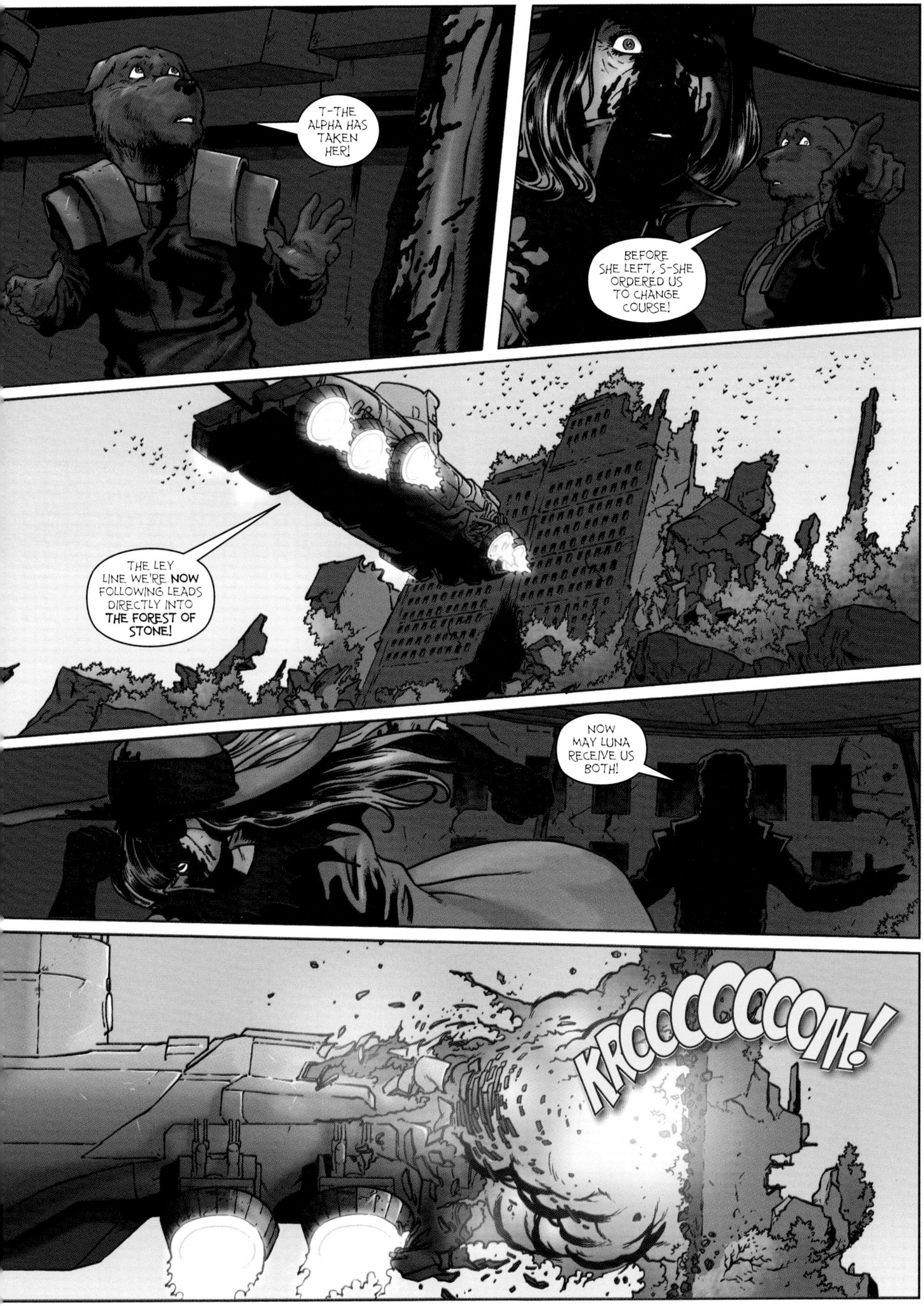
T-THE ALPHA HAS TAKEN HER!
BEFORE SHE LEFT, S-SHE ORDERED US TO CHANGE COURSE!
THE LEY LINE WE'RE **NOW** FOLLOWING LEADS DIRECTLY INTO **THE FOREST OF STONE!**
NOW MAY LUNA RECEIVE US BOTH!
KRCCCCCCCOM!

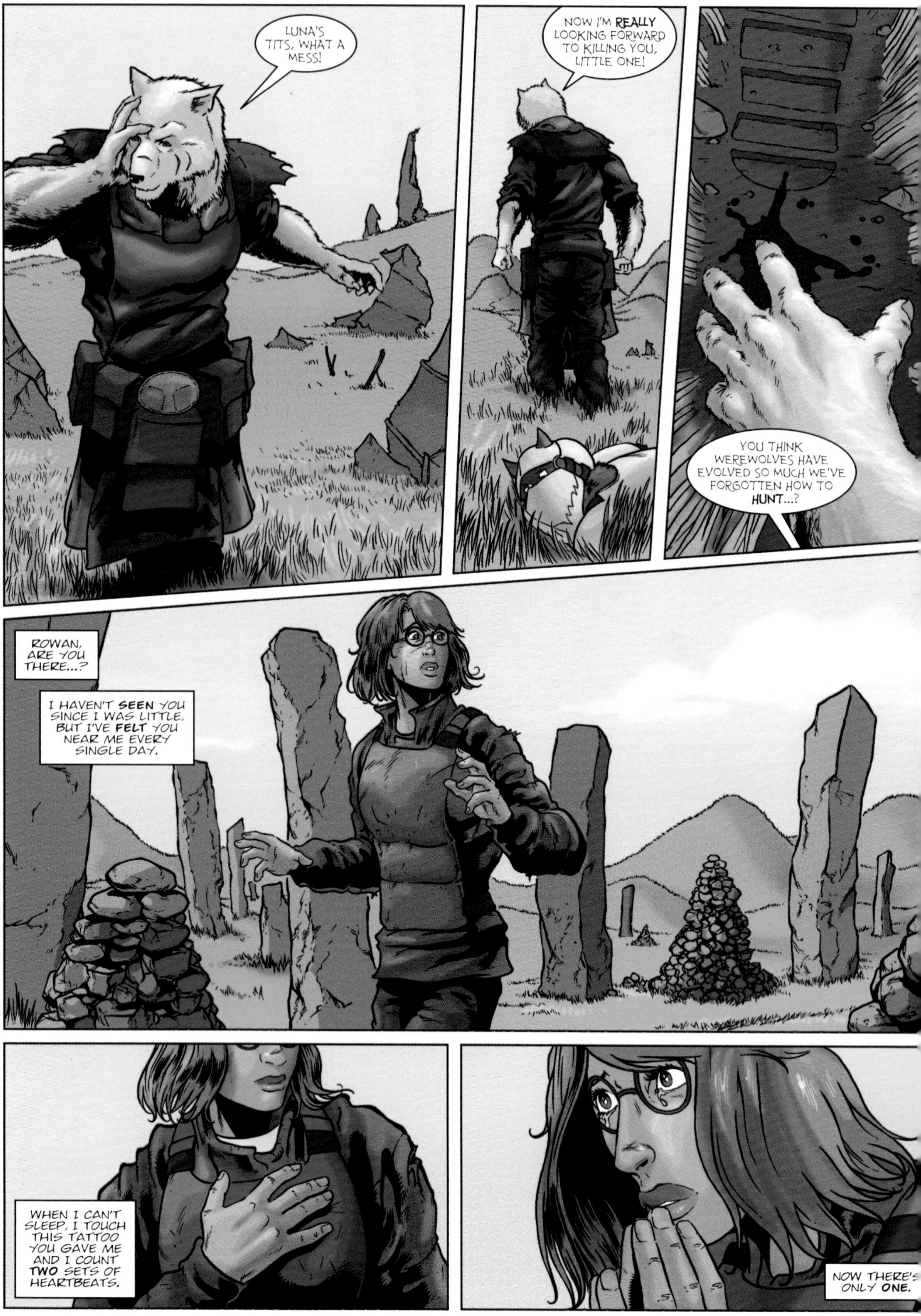
LUNA'S TITS, WHAT A MESS!
NOW I'M **REALLY** LOOKING FORWARD TO KILLING YOU, LITTLE ONE!
YOU THINK WEREWOLVES HAVE EVOLVED SO MUCH WE'VE FORGOTTEN HOW TO **HUNT**...?
ROWAN, ARE YOU THERE...?
I HAVEN'T **SEEN** YOU SINCE I WAS LITTLE, BUT I'VE **FELT** YOU NEAR ME EVERY SINGLE DAY.
WHEN I CAN'T SLEEP, I TOUCH THIS TATTOO YOU GAVE ME AND I COUNT **TWO** SETS OF HEARTBEATS.
NOW THERE'S ONLY **ONE**.

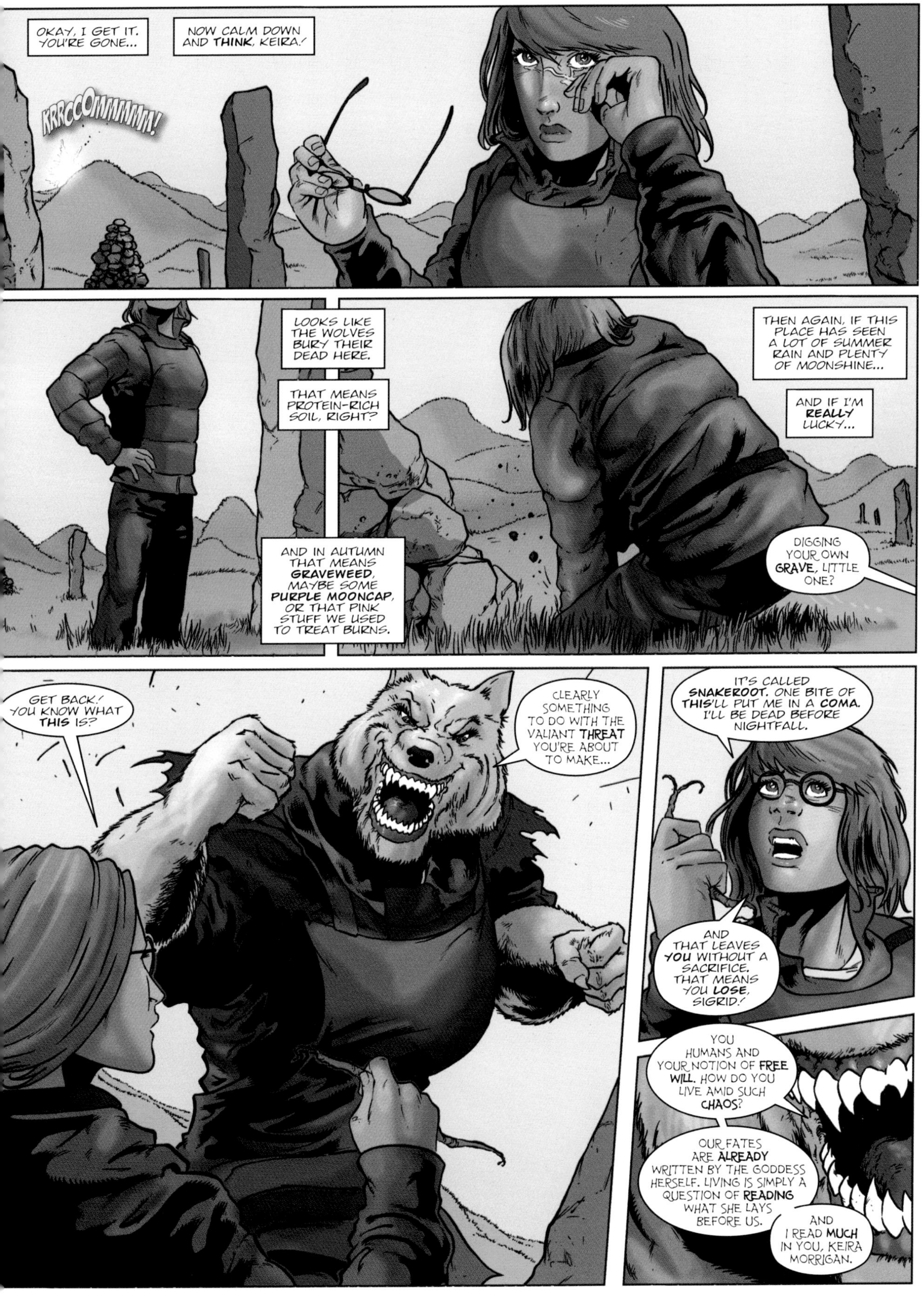
OKAY, I GET IT. YOU'RE GONE...
NOW CALM DOWN AND THINK, KEIRA!
KRRCCOMMMMM!
LOOKS LIKE THE WOLVES BURY THEIR DEAD HERE.
THAT MEANS PROTEIN-RICH SOIL, RIGHT?
AND IN AUTUMN THAT MEANS GRAVEWEED, MAYBE SOME PURPLE MOONCAP, OR THAT PINK STUFF WE USED TO TREAT BURNS.
THEN AGAIN, IF THIS PLACE HAS SEEN A LOT OF SUMMER RAIN AND PLENTY OF MOONSHINE...
AND IF I'M REALLY LUCKY...
DIGGING YOUR OWN GRAVE, LITTLE ONE?
GET BACK! YOU KNOW WHAT THIS IS?
CLEARLY SOMETHING TO DO WITH THE VALIANT THREAT YOU'RE ABOUT TO MAKE...
IT'S CALLED SNAKEROOT. ONE BITE OF THIS'LL PUT ME IN A COMA. I'LL BE DEAD BEFORE NIGHTFALL.
AND THAT LEAVES YOU WITHOUT A SACRIFICE. THAT MEANS YOU LOSE, SIGRID!
YOU HUMANS AND YOUR NOTION OF FREE WILL. HOW DO YOU LIVE AMID SUCH CHAOS?
OUR FATES ARE ALREADY WRITTEN BY THE GODDESS HERSELF. LIVING IS SIMPLY A QUESTION OF READING WHAT SHE LAYS BEFORE US.
AND I READ MUCH IN YOU, KEIRA MORRIGAN.

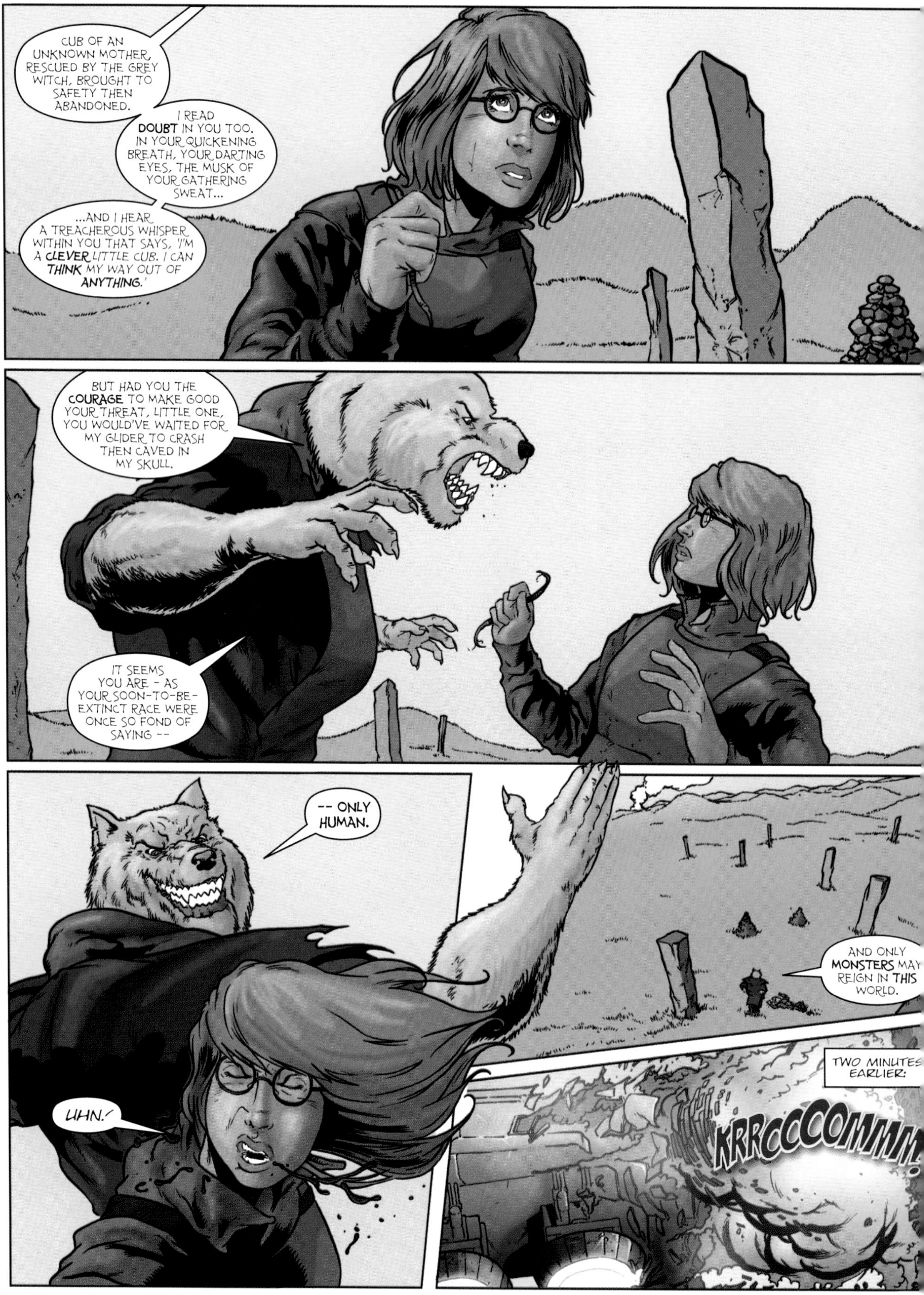
CUB OF AN UNKNOWN MOTHER, RESCUED BY THE GREY WITCH, BROUGHT TO SAFETY THEN ABANDONED.
I READ DOUBT IN YOU TOO. IN YOUR QUICKENING BREATH, YOUR DARTING EYES, THE MUSK OF YOUR GATHERING SWEAT...
...AND I HEAR A TREACHEROUS WHISPER WITHIN YOU THAT SAYS, 'I'M A CLEVER LITTLE CUB. I CAN THINK MY WAY OUT OF ANYTHING.'
BUT HAD YOU THE COURAGE TO MAKE GOOD YOUR THREAT, LITTLE ONE, YOU WOULD'VE WAITED FOR MY GLIDER TO CRASH THEN CAVED IN MY SKULL.
IT SEEMS YOU ARE - AS YOUR SOON-TO-BE-EXTINCT RACE WERE ONCE SO FOND OF SAYING --
-- ONLY HUMAN.
UHN.'
AND ONLY MONSTERS MAY REIGN IN THIS WORLD.
TWO MINUTES EARLIER:
KRRCCCOMMM!

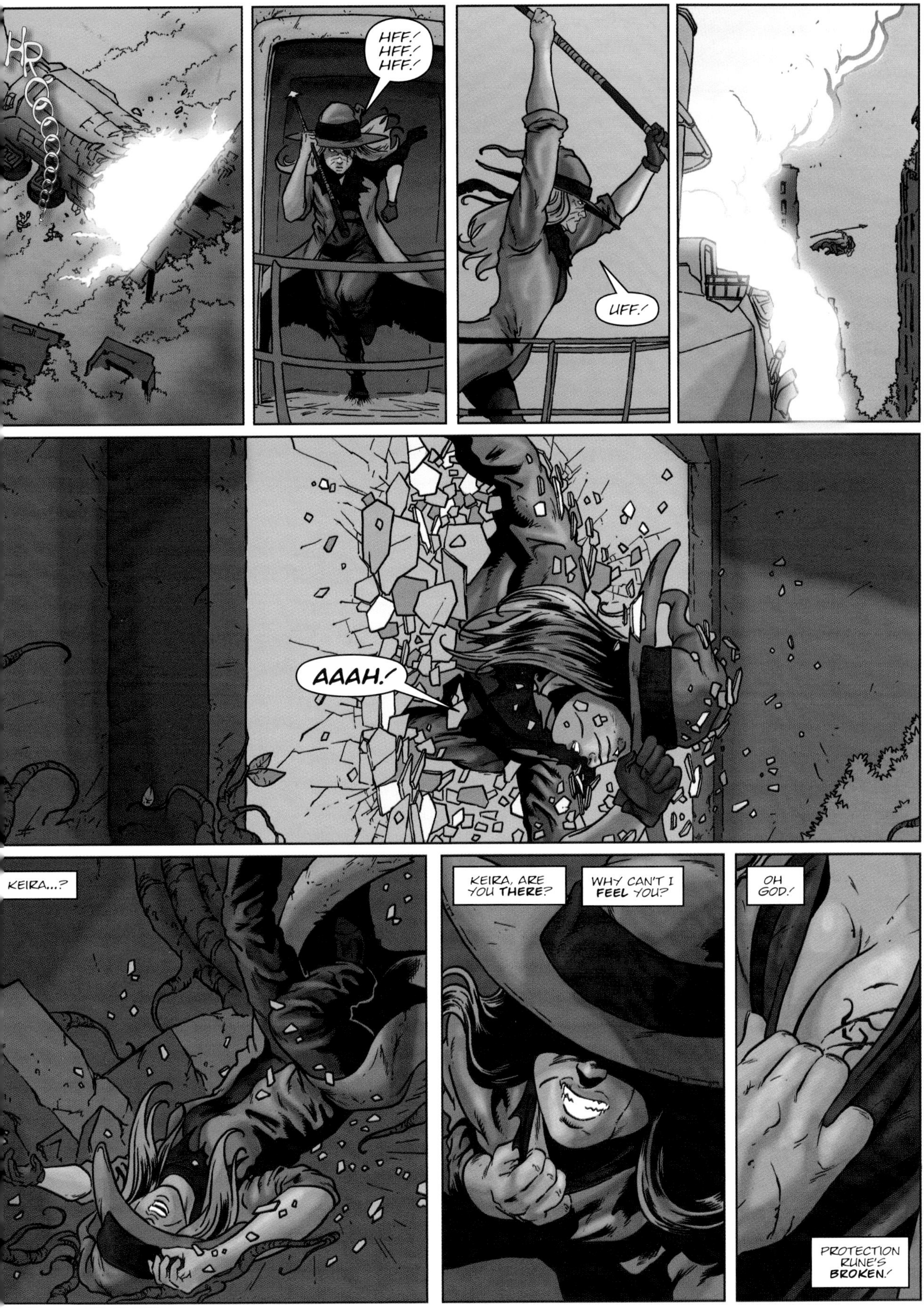

HRCOOOOO
HFF! HFF! HFF!
UFF!
AAAH!
KEIRA...?
KEIRA, ARE YOU THERE?
WHY CAN'T I FEEL YOU?
OH GOD!
PROTECTION RUNE'S BROKEN!

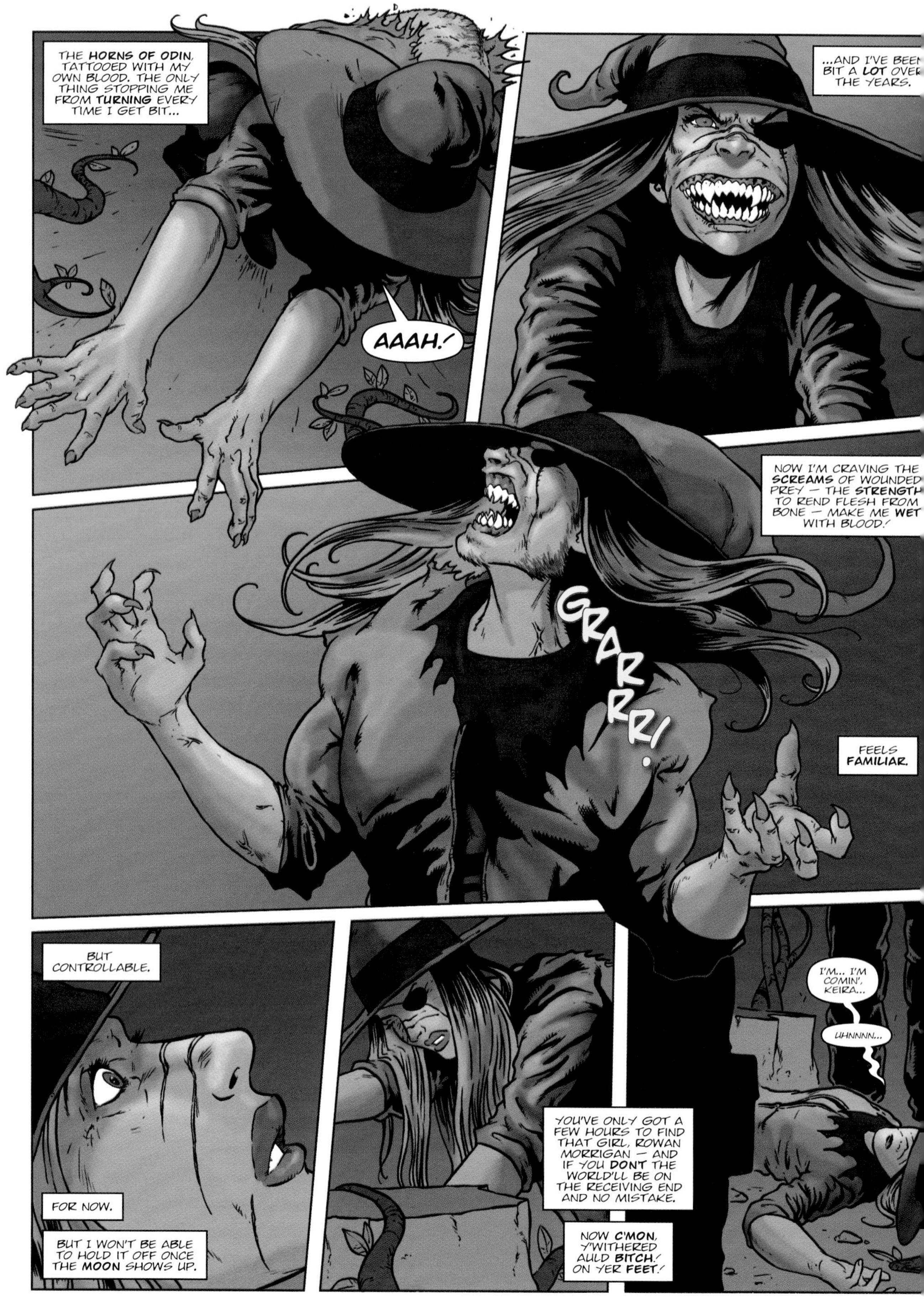
THE HORNS OF ODIN, TATTOOED WITH MY OWN BLOOD. THE ONLY THING STOPPING ME FROM TURNING EVERY TIME I GET BIT...
AAAH!
...AND I'VE BEEN BIT A LOT OVER THE YEARS.
NOW I'M CRAVING THE SCREAMS OF WOUNDED PREY — THE STRENGTH TO REND FLESH FROM BONE — MAKE ME WET WITH BLOOD!
GRARRR!
FEELS FAMILIAR.
BUT CONTROLLABLE.
FOR NOW.
BUT I WON'T BE ABLE TO HOLD IT OFF ONCE THE MOON SHOWS UP.
YOU'VE ONLY GOT A FEW HOURS TO FIND THAT GIRL, ROWAN MORRIGAN — AND IF YOU DON'T THE WORLD'LL BE ON THE RECEIVING END AND NO MISTAKE.
NOW C'MON, Y'WITHERED AULD BITCH! ON YER FEET!
I'M... I'M COMIN', KEIRA...
UHNNNNN...

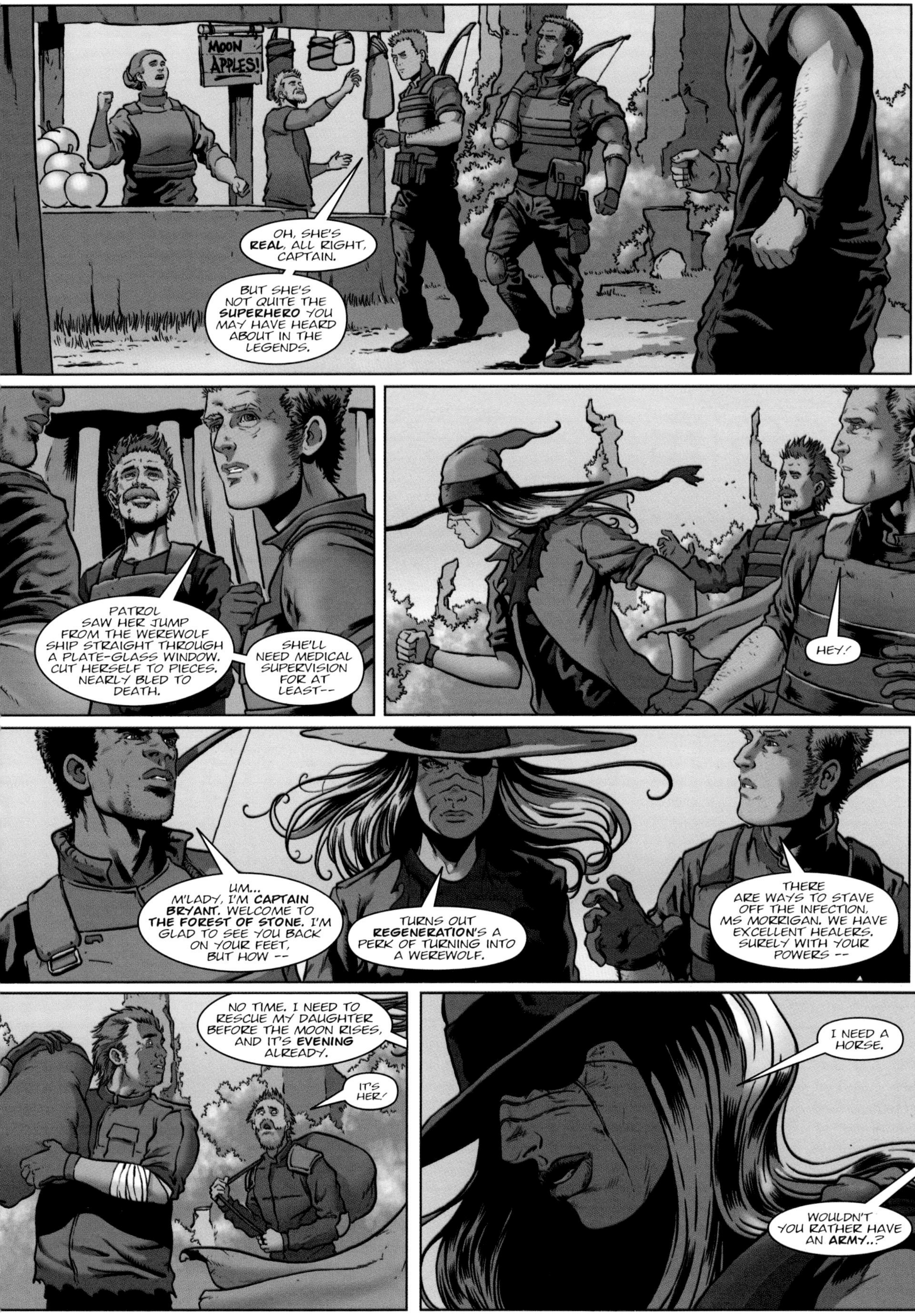
MOON APPLES!
OH, SHE'S **REAL**, ALL RIGHT, CAPTAIN.
BUT SHE'S NOT QUITE THE **SUPERHERO** YOU MAY HAVE HEARD ABOUT IN THE LEGENDS.
PATROL SAW HER JUMP FROM THE WEREWOLF SHIP STRAIGHT THROUGH A PLATE-GLASS WINDOW. CUT HERSELF TO PIECES. NEARLY BLED TO DEATH.
SHE'LL NEED MEDICAL SUPERVISION FOR AT LEAST--
HEY!
UM... M'LADY, I'M **CAPTAIN BRYANT**. WELCOME TO **THE FOREST OF STONE**. I'M GLAD TO SEE YOU BACK ON YOUR FEET, BUT HOW --
TURNS OUT **REGENERATION**'S A PERK OF TURNING INTO A WEREWOLF.
THERE ARE WAYS TO STAVE OFF THE INFECTION, MS MORRIGAN. WE HAVE EXCELLENT HEALERS. SURELY WITH YOUR POWERS --
NO TIME. I NEED TO **RESCUE** MY DAUGHTER BEFORE THE MOON RISES, AND IT'S **EVENING** ALREADY.
IT'S HER!
I NEED A HORSE.
WOULDN'T YOU RATHER HAVE AN **ARMY**..?

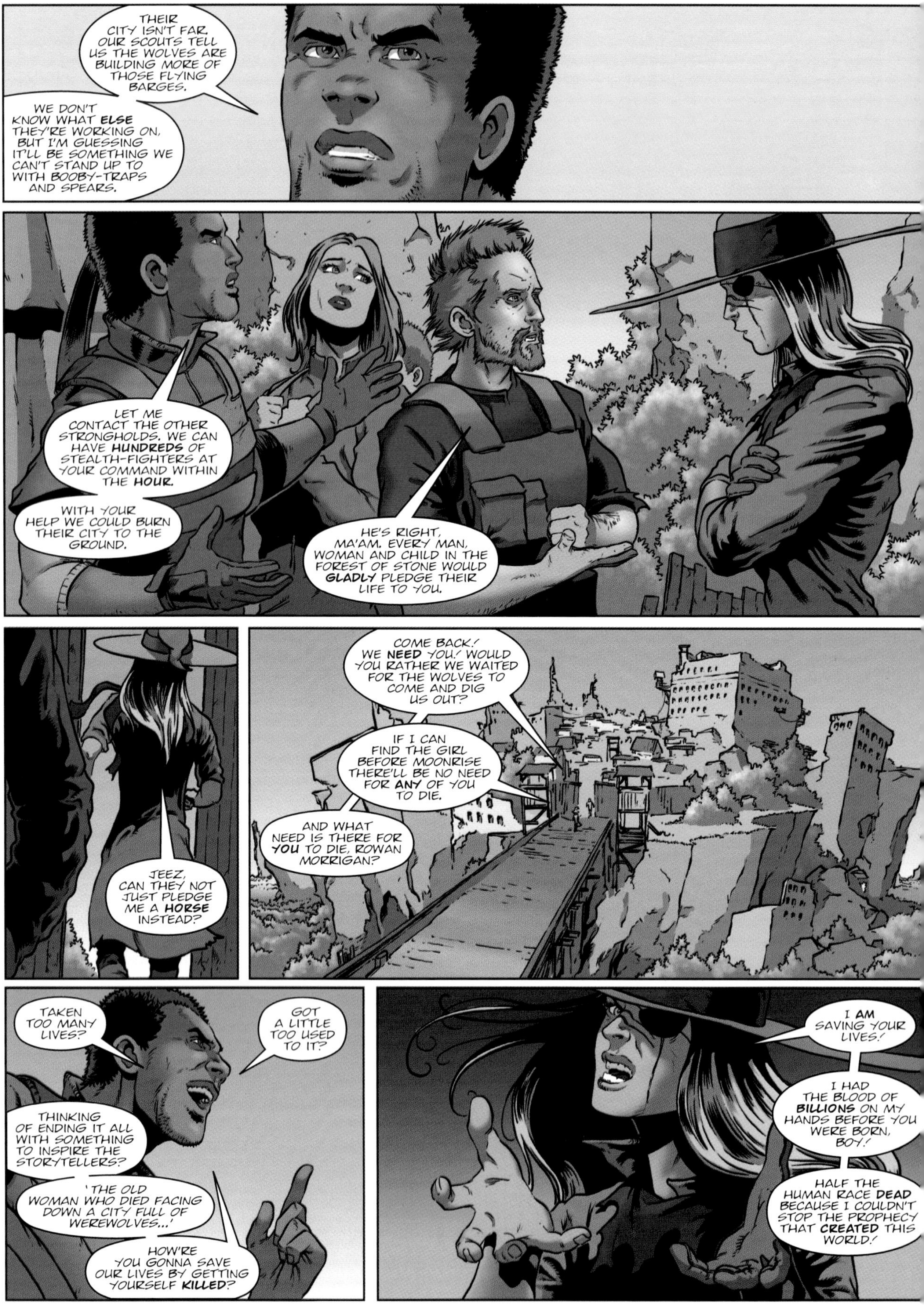
THEIR CITY ISN'T FAR. OUR SCOUTS TELL US THE WOLVES ARE BUILDING MORE OF THOSE FLYING BARGES.
WE DON'T KNOW WHAT **ELSE** THEY'RE WORKING ON, BUT I'M GUESSING IT'LL BE SOMETHING WE CAN'T STAND UP TO WITH BOOBY-TRAPS AND SPEARS.
LET ME CONTACT THE OTHER STRONGHOLDS. WE CAN HAVE **HUNDREDS** OF STEALTH-FIGHTERS AT YOUR COMMAND WITHIN THE **HOUR**.
WITH YOUR HELP WE COULD BURN THEIR CITY TO THE GROUND.
HE'S RIGHT, MA'AM. EVERY MAN, WOMAN AND CHILD IN THE FOREST OF STONE WOULD **GLADLY** PLEDGE THEIR LIFE TO YOU.
JEEZ, CAN THEY NOT JUST PLEDGE ME A **HORSE** INSTEAD?
COME BACK! WE **NEED** YOU! WOULD YOU RATHER WE WAITED FOR THE WOLVES TO COME AND DIG US OUT?
IF I CAN FIND THE GIRL BEFORE MOONRISE THERE'LL BE NO NEED FOR **ANY** OF YOU TO DIE.
AND WHAT NEED IS THERE FOR **YOU** TO DIE, ROWAN MORRIGAN?
TAKEN TOO MANY LIVES?
GOT A LITTLE TOO USED TO IT?
THINKING OF ENDING IT ALL WITH SOMETHING TO INSPIRE THE STORYTELLERS?
'THE OLD WOMAN WHO DIED FACING DOWN A CITY FULL OF WEREWOLVES...'
HOW'RE YOU GONNA SAVE OUR LIVES BY GETTING YOURSELF **KILLED**?
I **AM** SAVING YOUR LIVES!
I HAD THE BLOOD OF **BILLIONS** ON MY HANDS BEFORE YOU WERE BORN, BOY!
HALF THE HUMAN RACE **DEAD** BECAUSE I COULDN'T STOP THE PROPHECY THAT **CREATED** THIS WORLD!

HOW MANY **MORE** LIVES D'YOU WANT ME TO ADD TO MY 'LEGEND'?

THEN WE'LL MARCH ALONE, BEFORE THE WOLVES ATTACK US FIRST.

HMPH! HOW MANY FIGHTERS DID YOU SAY YOU HAD?

HUNDREDS! AND THAT'S NOT ALL.

ONCE **THE RED HOODS** HEAR YOU'RE LEADING THEM THEY'LL COME RUNNING ASTRIDE A PRIDE OF **ARMOURED HORN-CATS.**

THE DAUGHTERS OF MORRIGAN WILL BRING A CLOUD OF **STORMCROWS.**

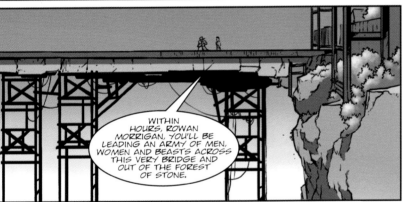

WITHIN HOURS, ROWAN MORRIGAN, YOU'LL BE LEADING AN ARMY OF MEN, WOMEN AND BEASTS ACROSS THIS VERY BRIDGE AND OUT OF THE FOREST OF STONE.

THE STUFF OF **LEGEND,** RIGHT?

WHAT D'YA SAY TO THAT..?

BRJÓTA!

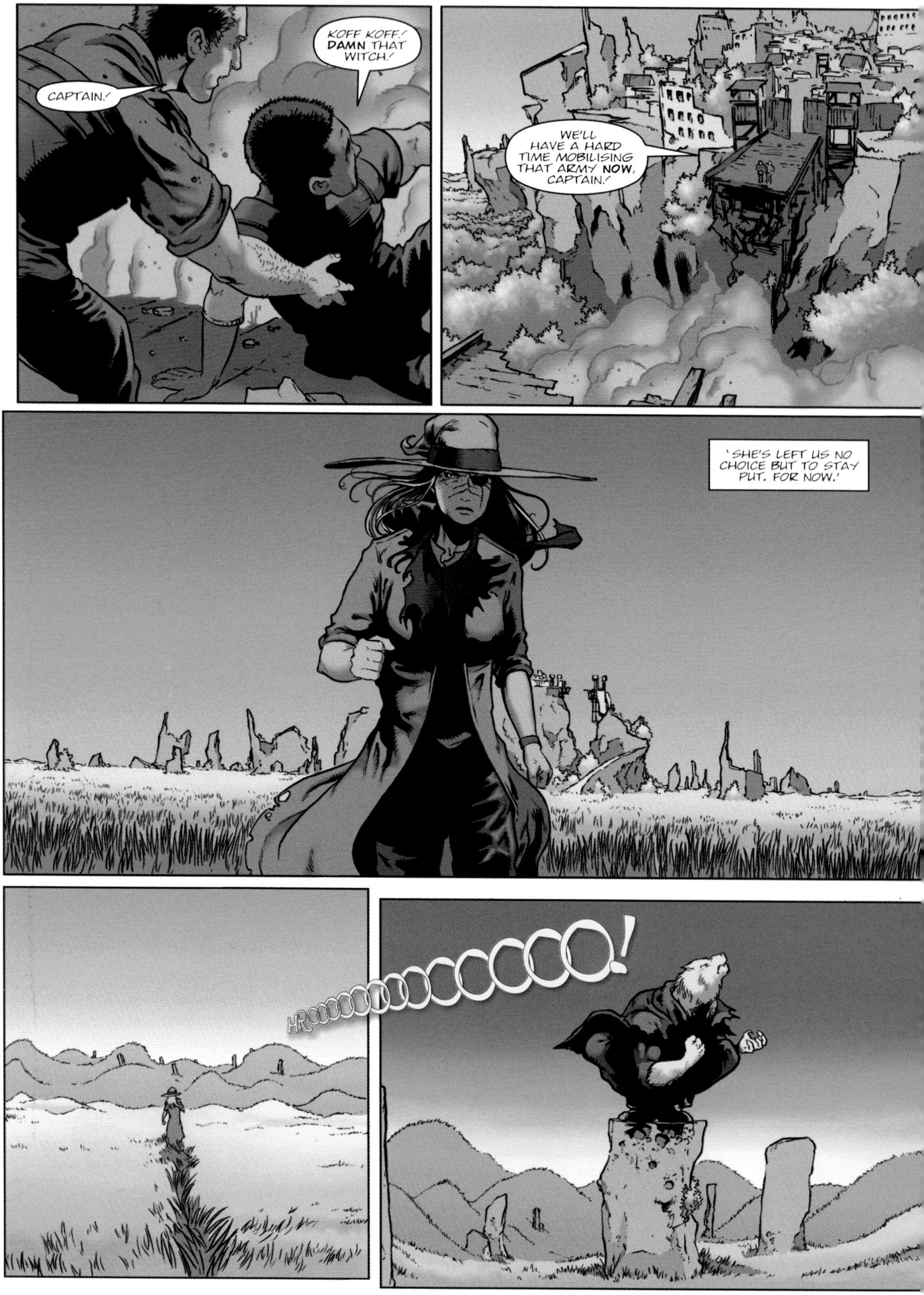
CAPTAIN.!
KOFF KOFF! DAMN THAT WITCH!
WE'LL HAVE A HARD TIME MOBILISING THAT ARMY NOW, CAPTAIN.!
'SHE'S LEFT US NO CHOICE BUT TO STAY PUT. FOR NOW.'
HROOOOOOOOOOOOOO!

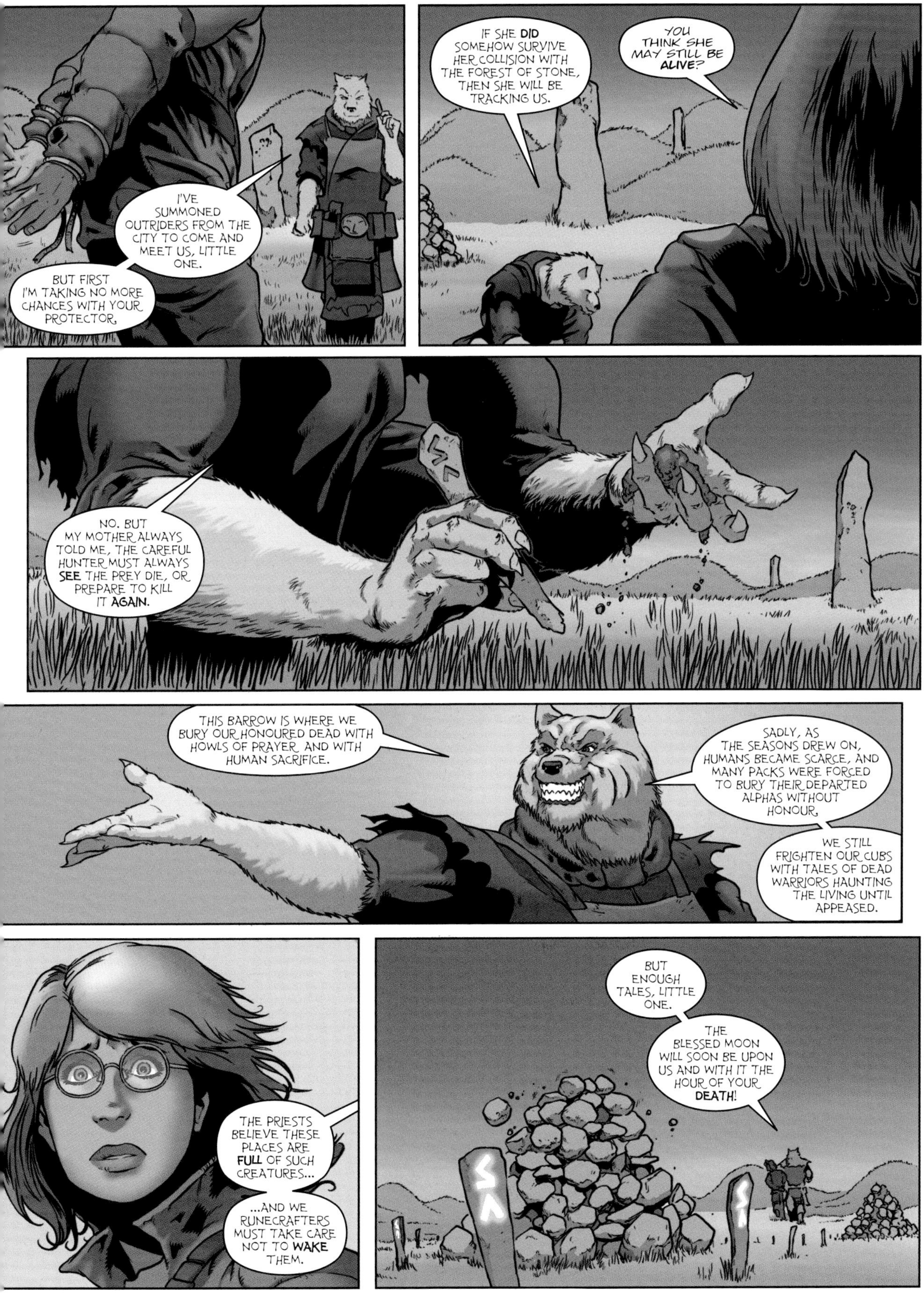
I'VE SUMMONED OUTRIDERS FROM THE CITY TO COME AND MEET US, LITTLE ONE.
BUT FIRST I'M TAKING NO MORE CHANCES WITH YOUR PROTECTOR.
YOU THINK SHE MAY STILL BE ALIVE?
IF SHE DID SOMEHOW SURVIVE HER COLLISION WITH THE FOREST OF STONE, THEN SHE WILL BE TRACKING US.
NO. BUT MY MOTHER ALWAYS TOLD ME, THE CAREFUL HUNTER MUST ALWAYS SEE THE PREY DIE, OR PREPARE TO KILL IT AGAIN.
THIS BARROW IS WHERE WE BURY OUR HONOURED DEAD WITH HOWLS OF PRAYER AND WITH HUMAN SACRIFICE.
SADLY, AS THE SEASONS DREW ON, HUMANS BECAME SCARCE, AND MANY PACKS WERE FORCED TO BURY THEIR DEPARTED ALPHAS WITHOUT HONOUR.
WE STILL FRIGHTEN OUR CUBS WITH TALES OF DEAD WARRIORS HAUNTING THE LIVING UNTIL APPEASED.
THE PRIESTS BELIEVE THESE PLACES ARE FULL OF SUCH CREATURES...
...AND WE RUNECRAFTERS MUST TAKE CARE NOT TO WAKE THEM.
BUT ENOUGH TALES, LITTLE ONE.
THE BLESSED MOON WILL SOON BE UPON US AND WITH IT THE HOUR OF YOUR DEATH!

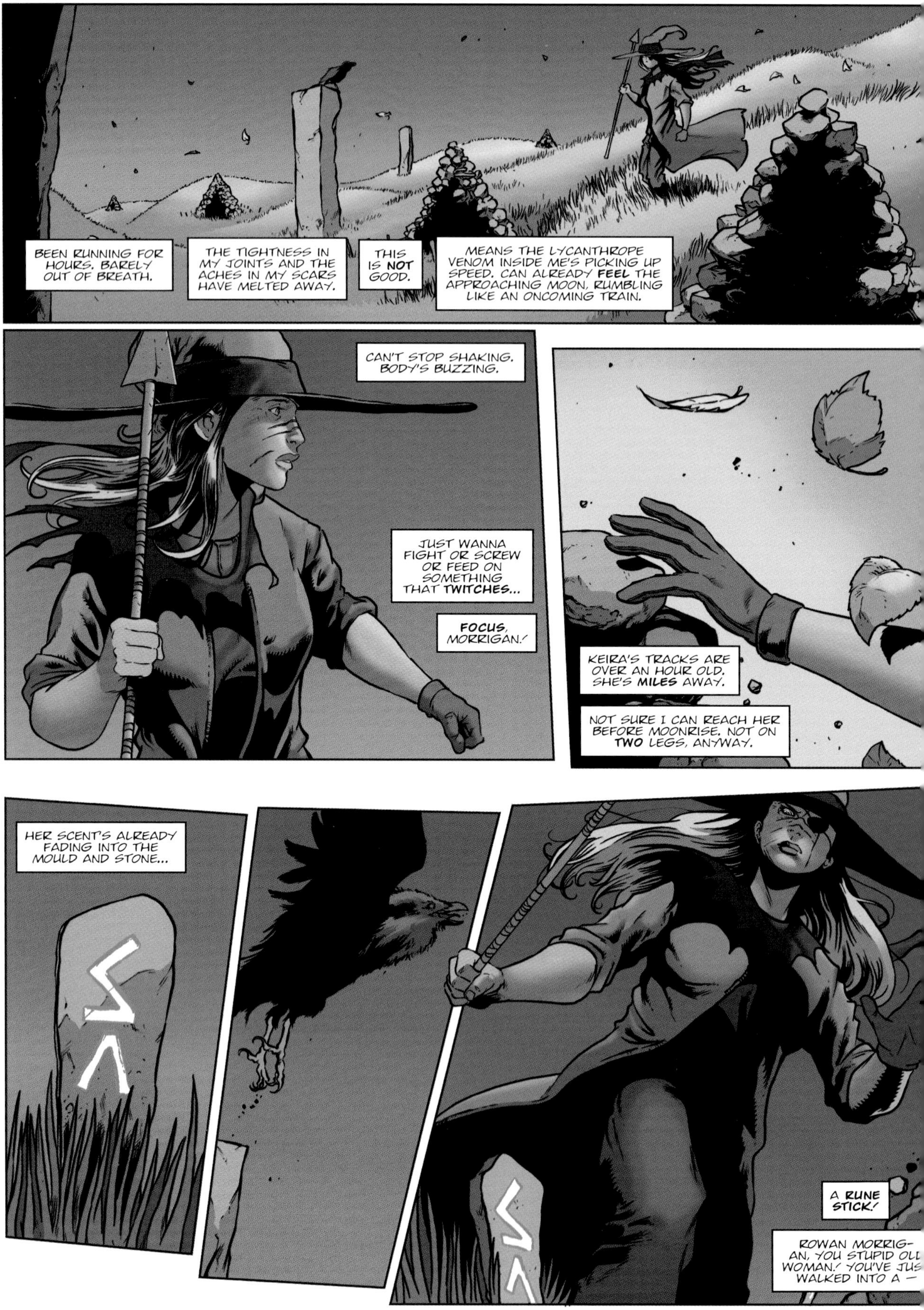
BEEN RUNNING FOR HOURS. BARELY OUT OF BREATH.
THE TIGHTNESS IN MY JOINTS AND THE ACHES IN MY SCARS HAVE MELTED AWAY.
THIS IS **NOT** GOOD.
MEANS THE LYCANTHROPE VENOM INSIDE ME'S PICKING UP SPEED. CAN ALREADY **FEEL** THE APPROACHING MOON, RUMBLING LIKE AN ONCOMING TRAIN.
CAN'T STOP SHAKING. BODY'S BUZZING.
JUST WANNA FIGHT OR SCREW OR FEED ON SOMETHING THAT **TWITCHES...**
FOCUS, MORRIGAN!
KEIRA'S TRACKS ARE OVER AN HOUR OLD. SHE'S **MILES** AWAY.
NOT SURE I CAN REACH HER BEFORE MOONRISE. NOT ON **TWO** LEGS, ANYWAY.
HER SCENT'S ALREADY FADING INTO THE MOULD AND STONE...
A **RUNE STICK!**
ROWAN MORRIGAN, YOU STUPID OLD WOMAN! YOU'VE JUST WALKED INTO A —

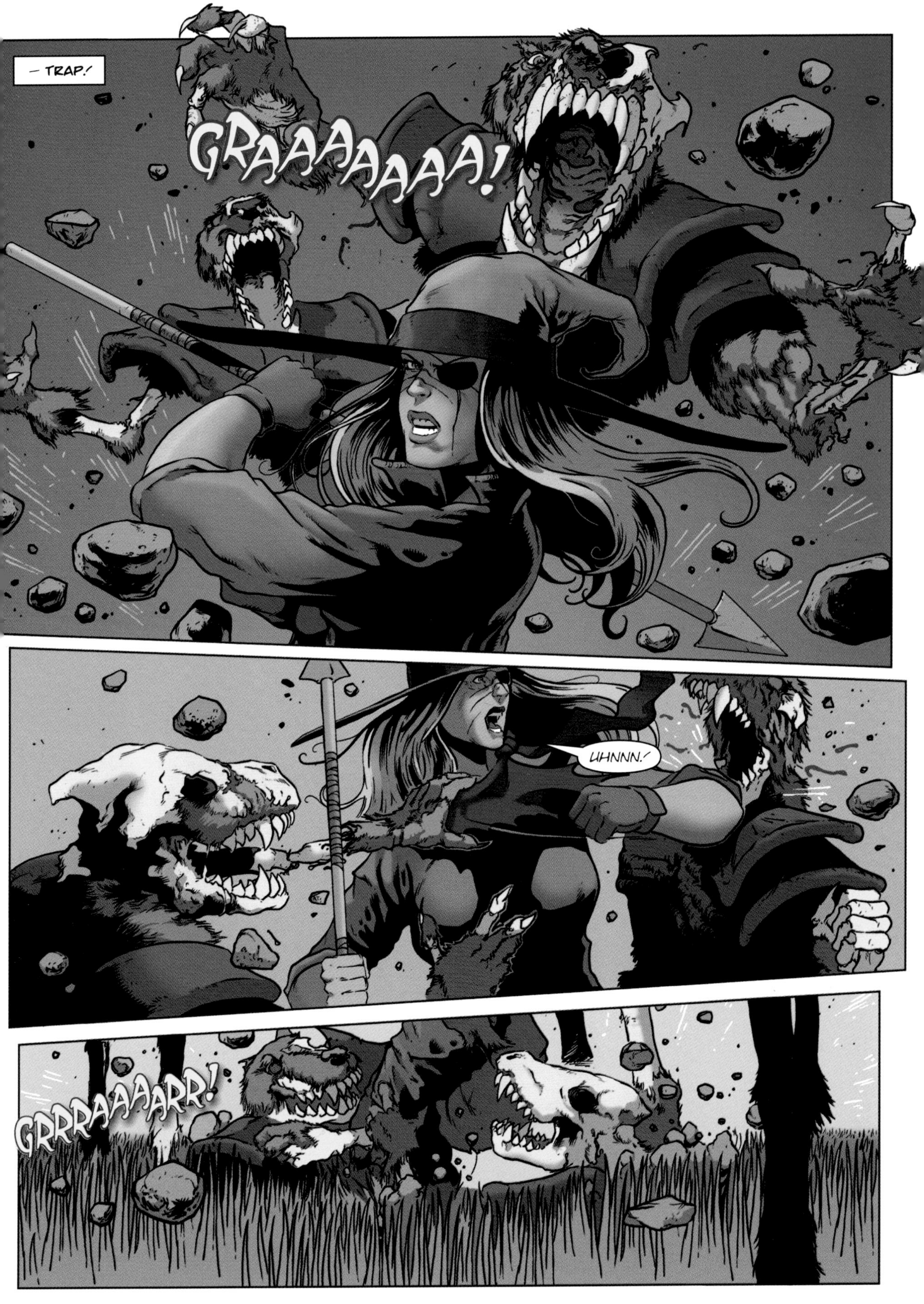

– TRAP!
GRAAAAAAAA!
UHNNN.!
GRRRAAAARR!

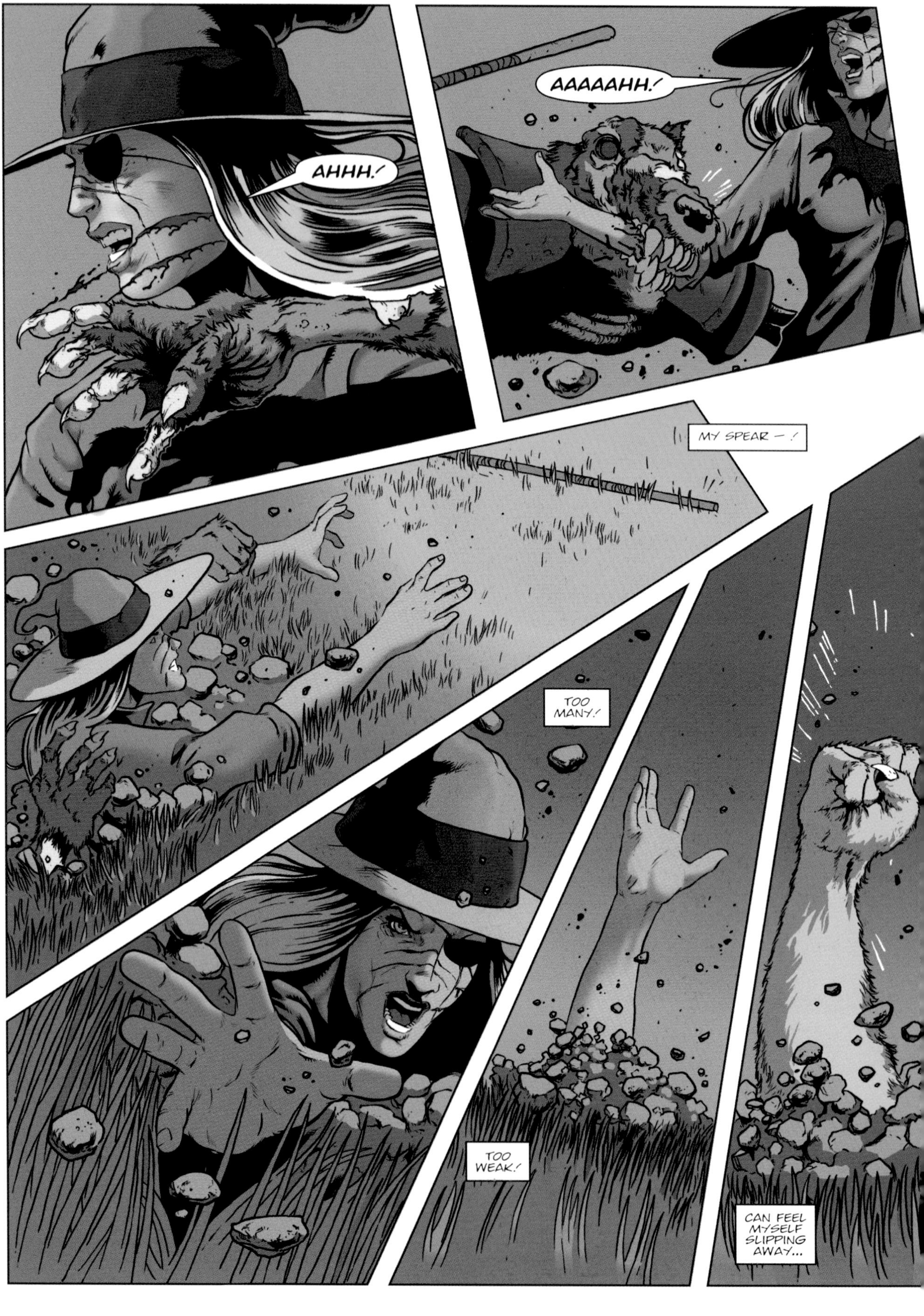
AHHH!
AAAAAHH!
MY SPEAR — !
TOO MANY!
TOO WEAK!
CAN FEEL MYSELF SLIPPING AWAY...

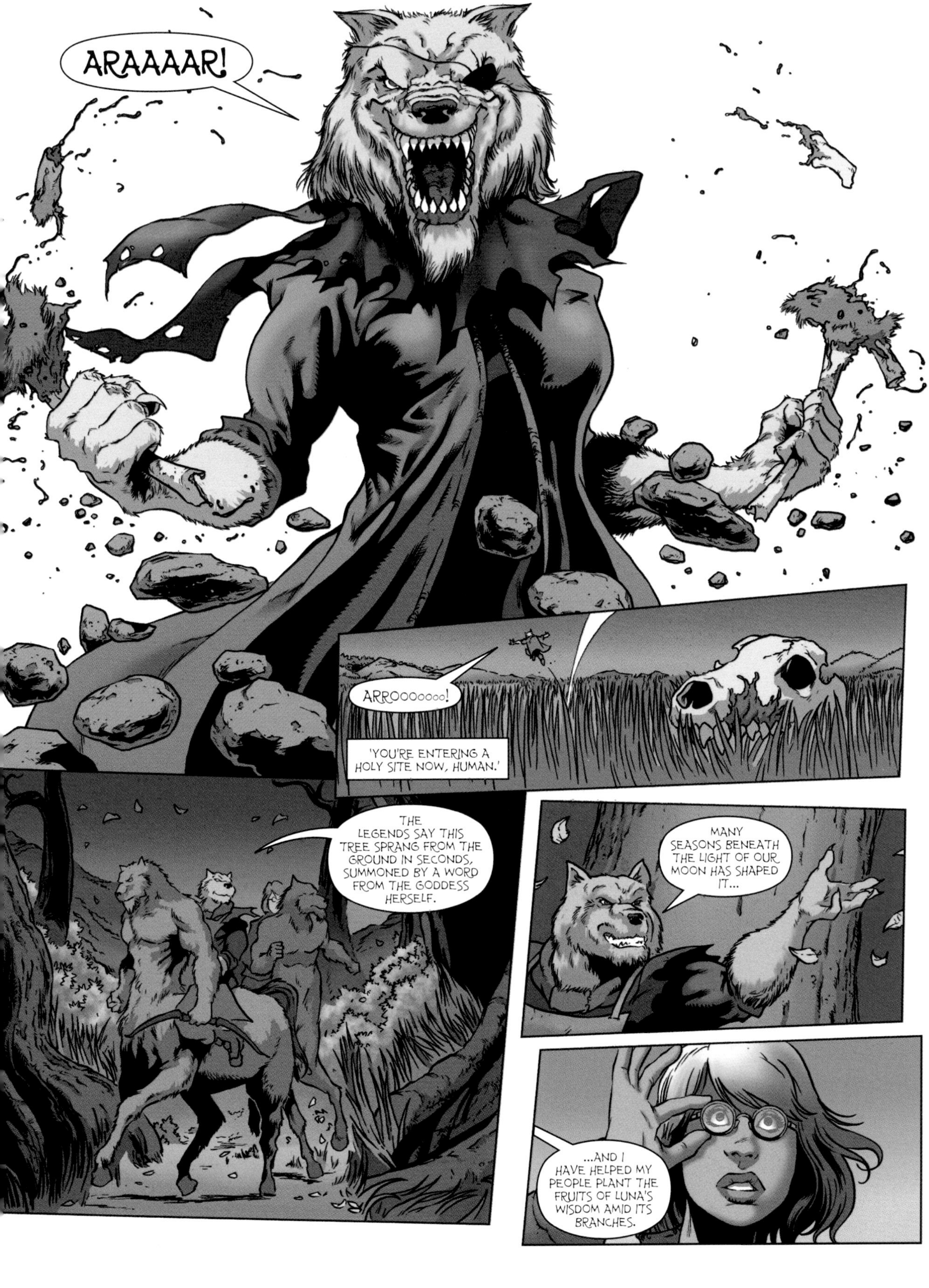
ARAAAAR!
ARROOOOOOOO!
'YOU'RE ENTERING A HOLY SITE NOW, HUMAN.'
THE LEGENDS SAY THIS TREE SPRANG FROM THE GROUND IN SECONDS, SUMMONED BY A WORD FROM THE GODDESS HERSELF.
MANY SEASONS BENEATH THE LIGHT OF OUR MOON HAS SHAPED IT...
...AND I HAVE HELPED MY PEOPLE PLANT THE FRUITS OF LUNA'S WISDOM AMID ITS BRANCHES.

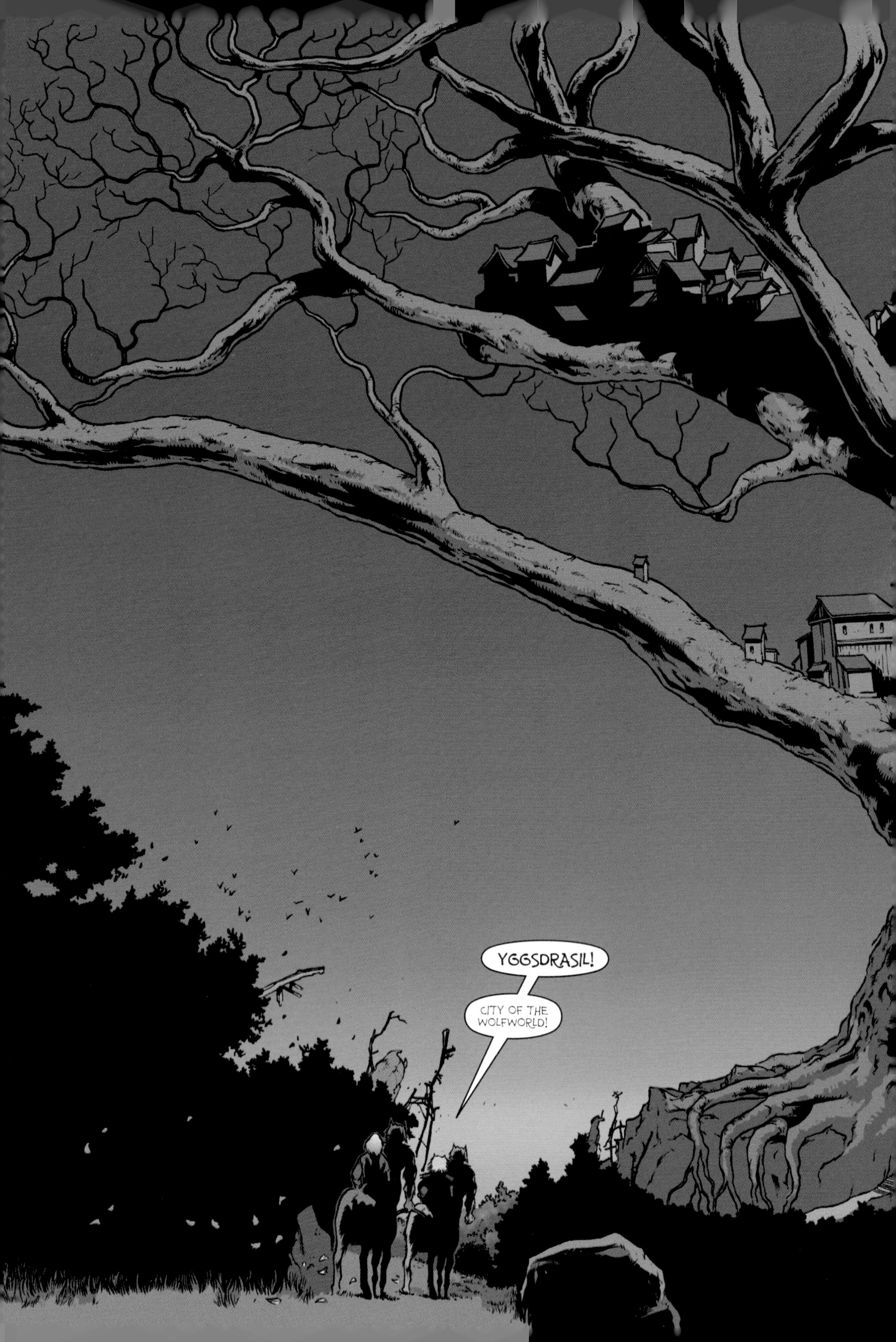
YGGSDRASIL!
CITY OF THE WOLFWORLD!

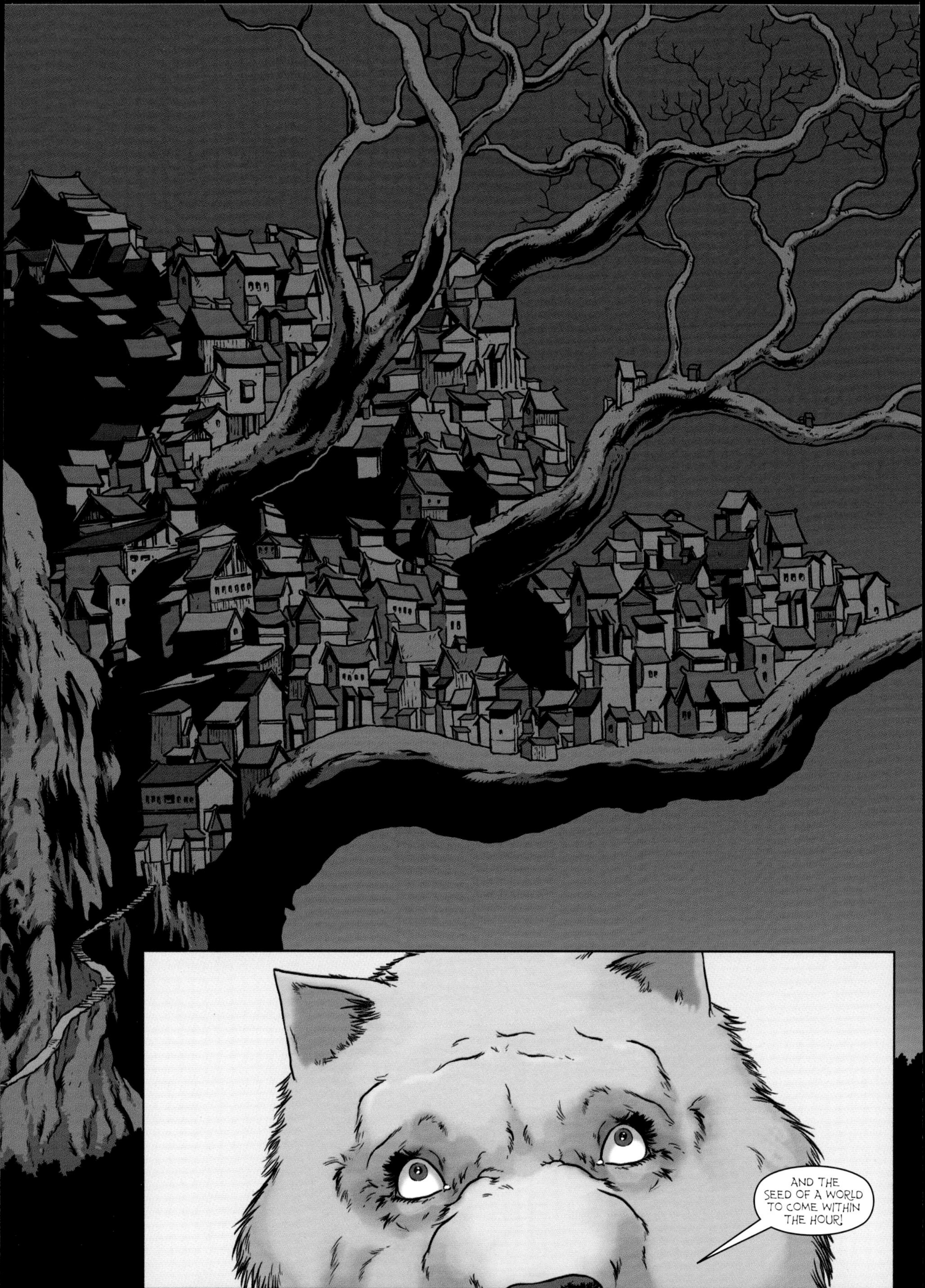
AND THE SEED OF A WORLD TO COME WITHIN THE HOUR!

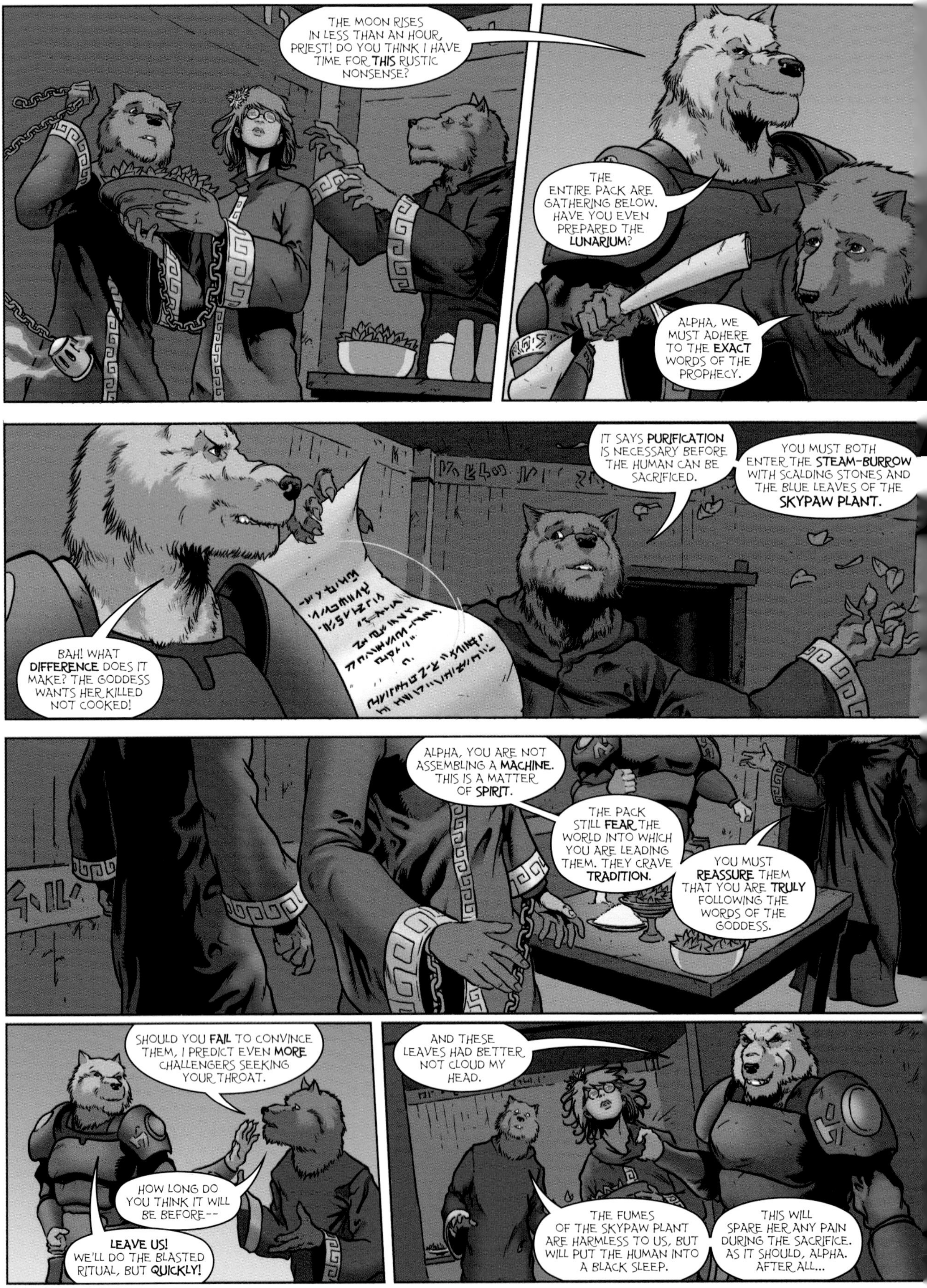
THE MOON RISES IN LESS THAN AN HOUR, PRIEST! DO YOU THINK I HAVE TIME FOR THIS RUSTIC NONSENSE?
THE ENTIRE PACK ARE GATHERING BELOW. HAVE YOU EVEN PREPARED THE LUNARIUM?
ALPHA, WE MUST ADHERE TO THE EXACT WORDS OF THE PROPHECY.
IT SAYS PURIFICATION IS NECESSARY BEFORE THE HUMAN CAN BE SACRIFICED.
YOU MUST BOTH ENTER THE STEAM-BURROW WITH SCALDING STONES AND THE BLUE LEAVES OF THE SKYPAW PLANT.
BAH! WHAT DIFFERENCE DOES IT MAKE? THE GODDESS WANTS HER KILLED NOT COOKED!
ALPHA, YOU ARE NOT ASSEMBLING A MACHINE. THIS IS A MATTER OF SPIRIT.
THE PACK STILL FEAR THE WORLD INTO WHICH YOU ARE LEADING THEM. THEY CRAVE TRADITION.
YOU MUST REASSURE THEM THAT YOU ARE TRULY FOLLOWING THE WORDS OF THE GODDESS.
SHOULD YOU FAIL TO CONVINCE THEM, I PREDICT EVEN MORE CHALLENGERS SEEKING YOUR THROAT.
HOW LONG DO YOU THINK IT WILL BE BEFORE--
LEAVE US! WE'LL DO THE BLASTED RITUAL, BUT QUICKLY!
AND THESE LEAVES HAD BETTER NOT CLOUD MY HEAD.
THE FUMES OF THE SKYPAW PLANT ARE HARMLESS TO US, BUT WILL PUT THE HUMAN INTO A BLACK SLEEP.
THIS WILL SPARE HER ANY PAIN DURING THE SACRIFICE. AS IT SHOULD, ALPHA. AFTER ALL...

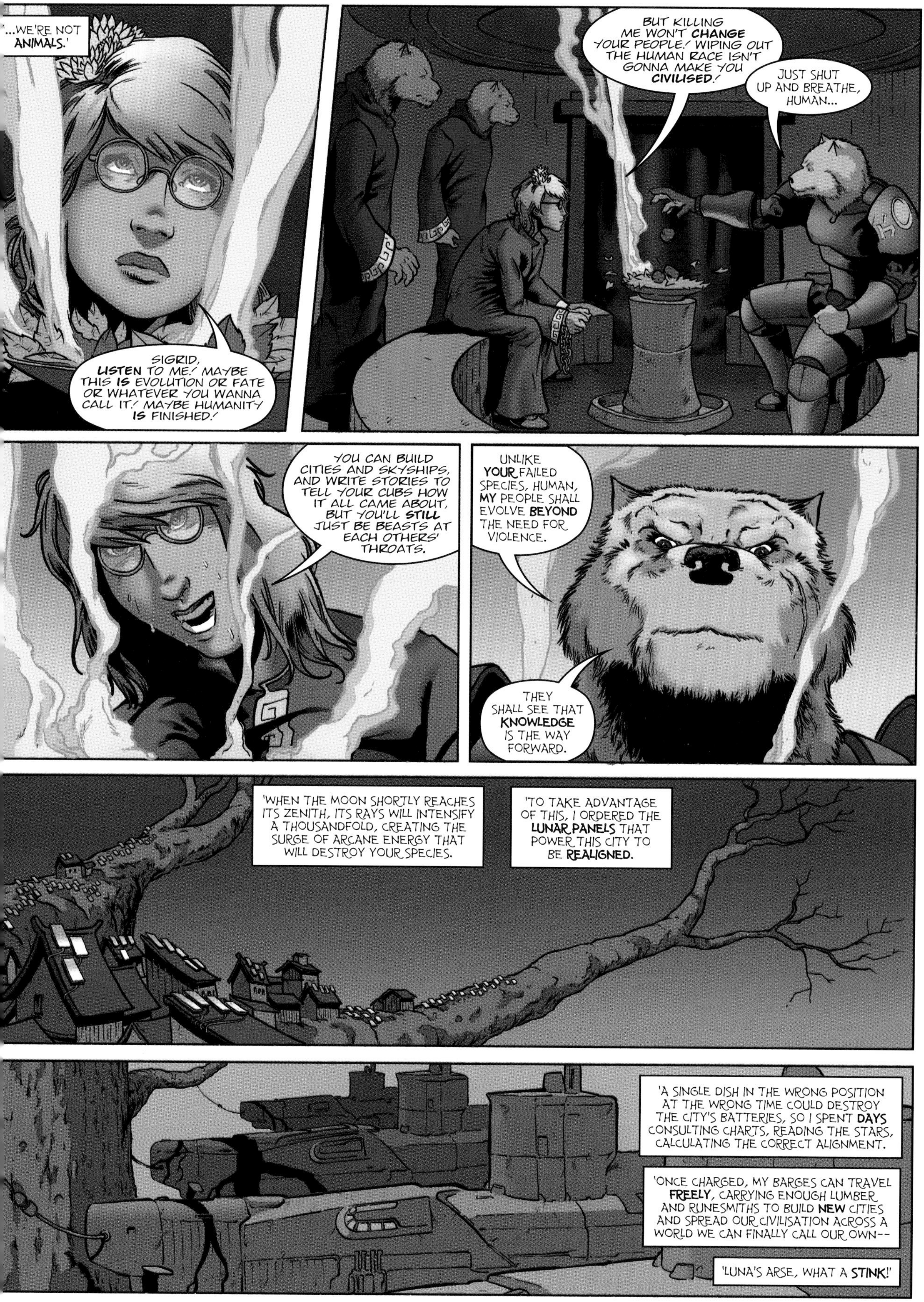
'...WE'RE NOT ANIMALS.'
SIGRID, LISTEN TO ME! MAYBE THIS IS EVOLUTION OR FATE OR WHATEVER YOU WANNA CALL IT! MAYBE HUMANITY IS FINISHED!
BUT KILLING ME WON'T CHANGE YOUR PEOPLE! WIPING OUT THE HUMAN RACE ISN'T GONNA MAKE YOU CIVILISED!
JUST SHUT UP AND BREATHE, HUMAN...
YOU CAN BUILD CITIES AND SKYSHIPS, AND WRITE STORIES TO TELL YOUR CUBS HOW IT ALL CAME ABOUT, BUT YOU'LL STILL JUST BE BEASTS AT EACH OTHERS' THROATS.
UNLIKE YOUR FAILED SPECIES, HUMAN, MY PEOPLE SHALL EVOLVE BEYOND THE NEED FOR VIOLENCE.
THEY SHALL SEE THAT KNOWLEDGE IS THE WAY FORWARD.
'WHEN THE MOON SHORTLY REACHES ITS ZENITH, ITS RAYS WILL INTENSIFY A THOUSANDFOLD, CREATING THE SURGE OF ARCANE ENERGY THAT WILL DESTROY YOUR SPECIES.
'TO TAKE ADVANTAGE OF THIS, I ORDERED THE LUNAR PANELS THAT POWER THIS CITY TO BE REALIGNED.
'A SINGLE DISH IN THE WRONG POSITION AT THE WRONG TIME COULD DESTROY THE CITY'S BATTERIES, SO I SPENT DAYS CONSULTING CHARTS, READING THE STARS, CALCULATING THE CORRECT ALIGNMENT.
'ONCE CHARGED, MY BARGES CAN TRAVEL FREELY, CARRYING ENOUGH LUMBER AND RUNESMITHS TO BUILD NEW CITIES AND SPREAD OUR CIVILISATION ACROSS A WORLD WE CAN FINALLY CALL OUR OWN--
'LUNA'S ARSE, WHAT A STINK!'

I FEEL SICK...

THANK GOD! WHILE YOU WERE ARGUING WITH YOUR PRIEST I ADDED A HANDFUL OF THAT **YELLOW SLUMPWEED** THEY HAD LYING AROUND.

WASN'T SURE IT WOULD WORK.

OUR SCOUTS USED IT TO SMOKE OUT WEREWOLF DENS YEARS AGO.

UNNNNH!

HARMLESS TO HUMANS, BUT MAKES YOU GUYS PRETTY DROWSY.

FIGURED I NEEDED TO COUNTER THE SKYPAW LEAVES, SO I ADDED A FAIR BIT.

HUMAAAAAN--

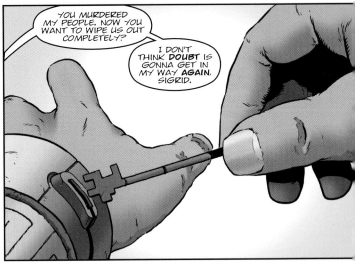

YOU MURDERED MY PEOPLE. NOW YOU WANT TO WIPE US OUT COMPLETELY?

I DON'T THINK **DOUBT** IS GONNA GET IN MY WAY **AGAIN**, SIGRID.

NOW LET'S SEE WHAT **ELSE** A LITTLE **KNOWLEDGE** CAN DO...

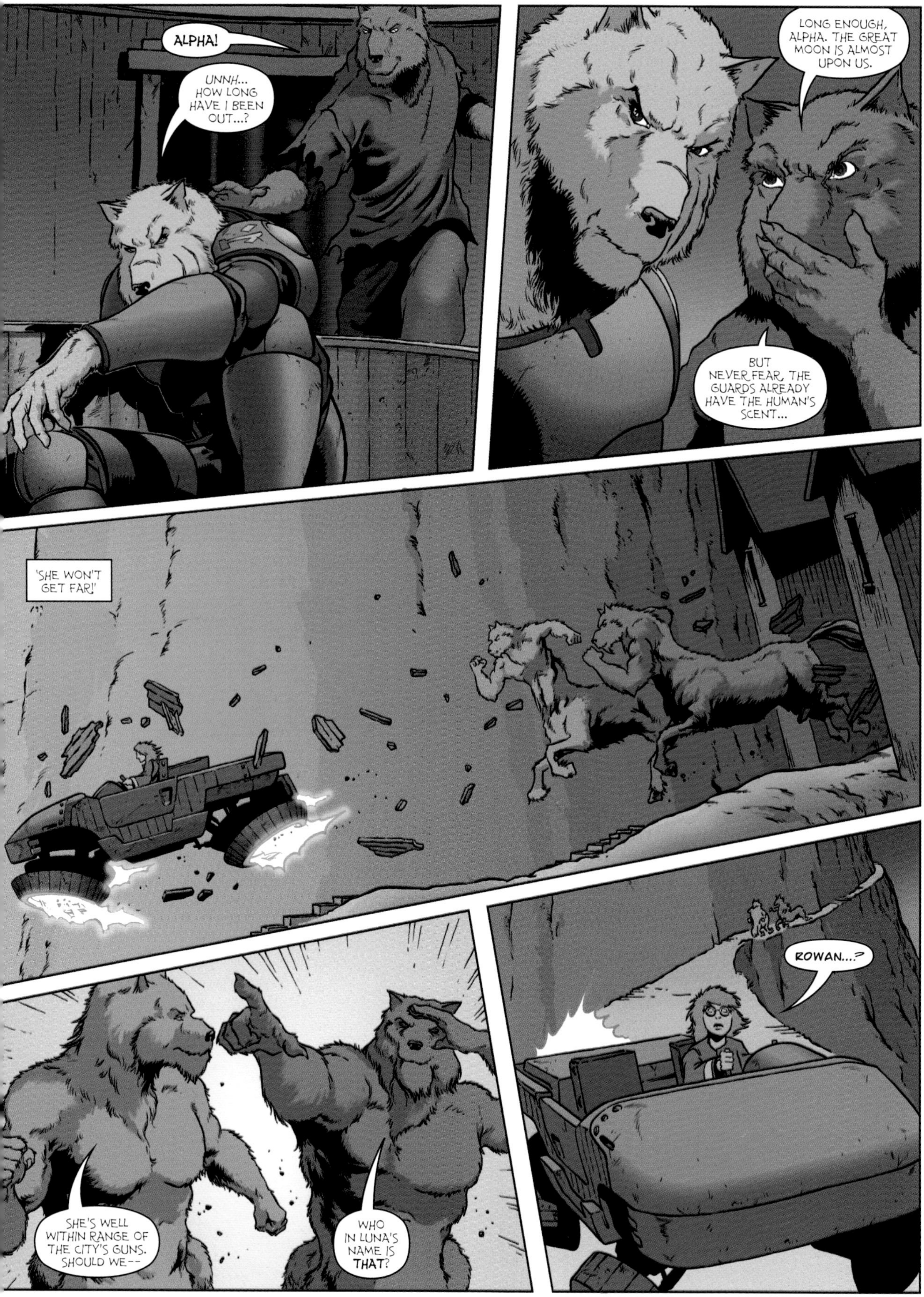
ALPHA!
UNNH... HOW LONG HAVE I BEEN OUT...?
LONG ENOUGH, ALPHA. THE GREAT MOON IS ALMOST UPON US.
BUT NEVER FEAR, THE GUARDS ALREADY HAVE THE HUMAN'S SCENT...
'SHE WON'T GET FAR!'
SHE'S WELL WITHIN RANGE OF THE CITY'S GUNS. SHOULD WE--
WHO IN LUNA'S NAME IS THAT?
ROWAN...?

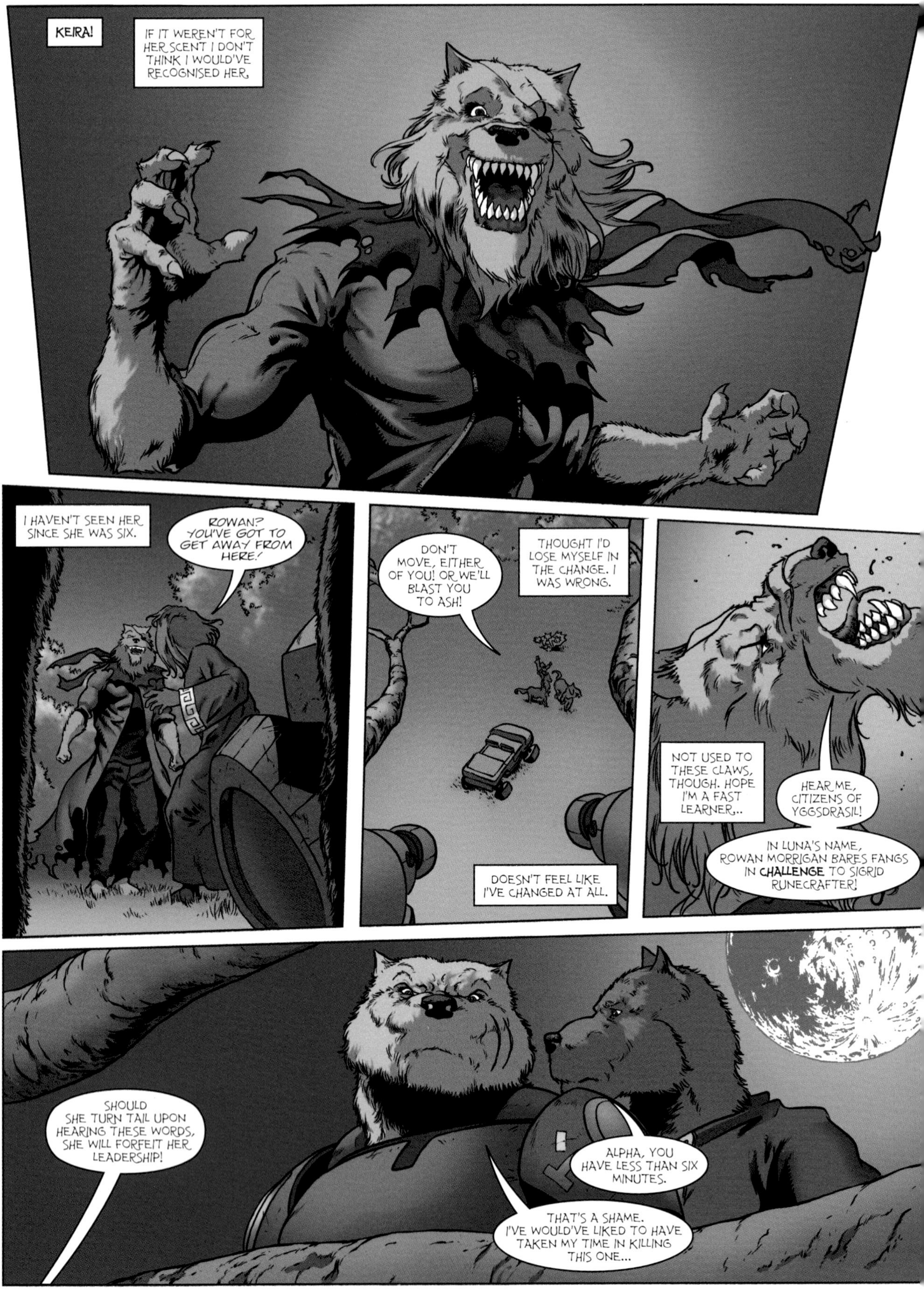
KEIRA!
IF IT WEREN'T FOR HER SCENT I DON'T THINK I WOULD'VE RECOGNISED HER.
I HAVEN'T SEEN HER SINCE SHE WAS SIX.
ROWAN? YOU'VE GOT TO GET AWAY FROM HERE!
DON'T MOVE, EITHER OF YOU! OR WE'LL BLAST YOU TO ASH!
THOUGHT I'D LOSE MYSELF IN THE CHANGE. I WAS WRONG.
DOESN'T FEEL LIKE I'VE CHANGED AT ALL.
NOT USED TO THESE CLAWS, THOUGH. HOPE I'M A FAST LEARNER...
HEAR ME, CITIZENS OF YGGSDRASIL!
IN LUNA'S NAME, ROWAN MORRIGAN BARES FANGS IN **CHALLENGE** TO SIGRID RUNECRAFTER!
SHOULD SHE TURN TAIL UPON HEARING THESE WORDS, SHE WILL FORFEIT HER LEADERSHIP!
ALPHA, YOU HAVE LESS THAN SIX MINUTES.
THAT'S A SHAME. I'VE WOULD'VE LIKED TO HAVE TAKEN MY TIME IN KILLING THIS ONE...

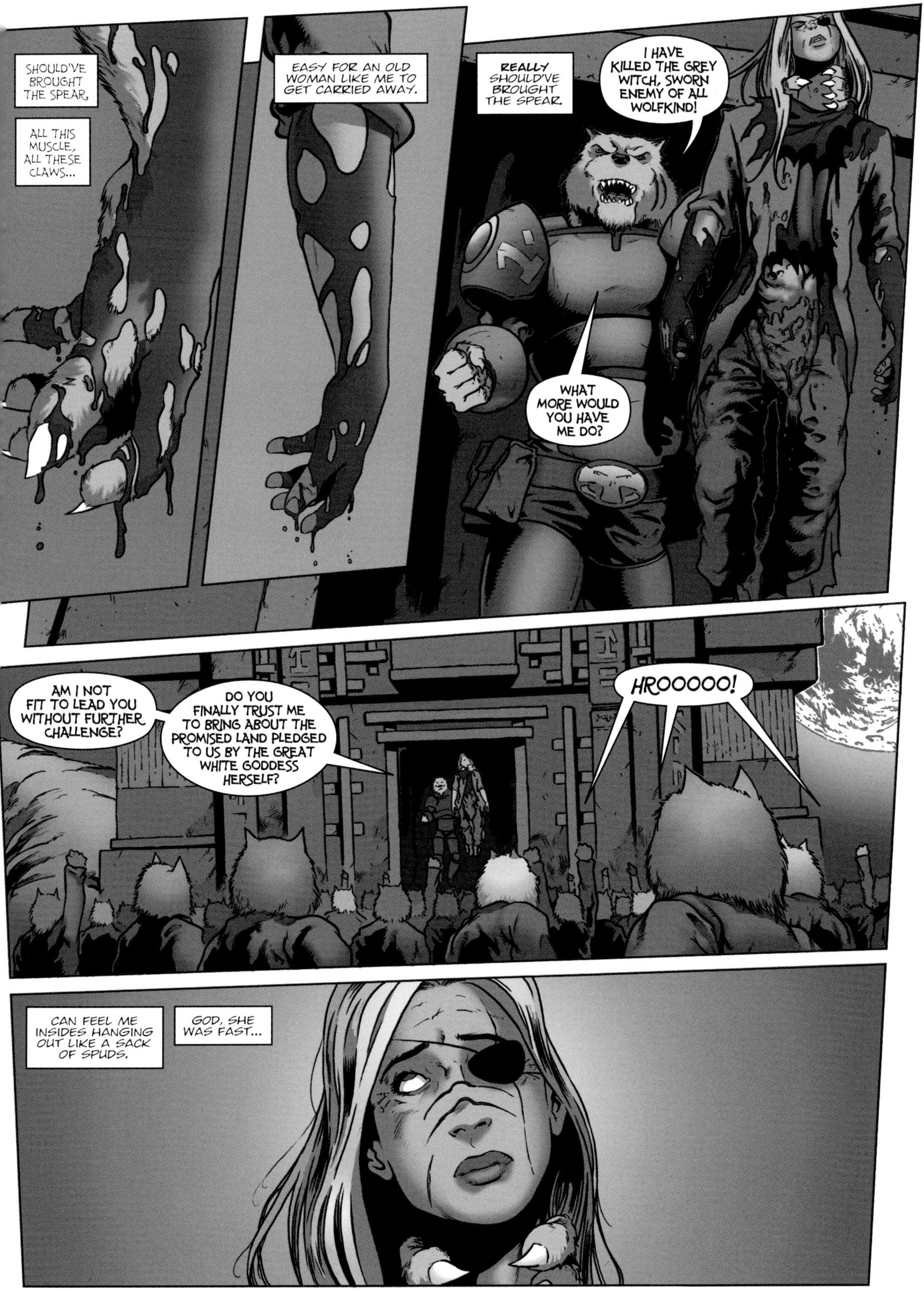
SHOULD'VE BROUGHT THE SPEAR.
ALL THIS MUSCLE, ALL THESE CLAWS...
EASY FOR AN OLD WOMAN LIKE ME TO GET CARRIED AWAY.
REALLY SHOULD'VE BROUGHT THE SPEAR.
I HAVE KILLED THE GREY WITCH, SWORN ENEMY OF ALL WOLFKIND!
WHAT MORE WOULD YOU HAVE ME DO?
AM I NOT FIT TO LEAD YOU WITHOUT FURTHER CHALLENGE?
DO YOU FINALLY TRUST ME TO BRING ABOUT THE PROMISED LAND PLEDGED TO US BY THE GREAT WHITE GODDESS HERSELF?
HROOOOO!
CAN FEEL ME INSIDES HANGING OUT LIKE A SACK OF SPUDS.
GOD, SHE WAS FAST...

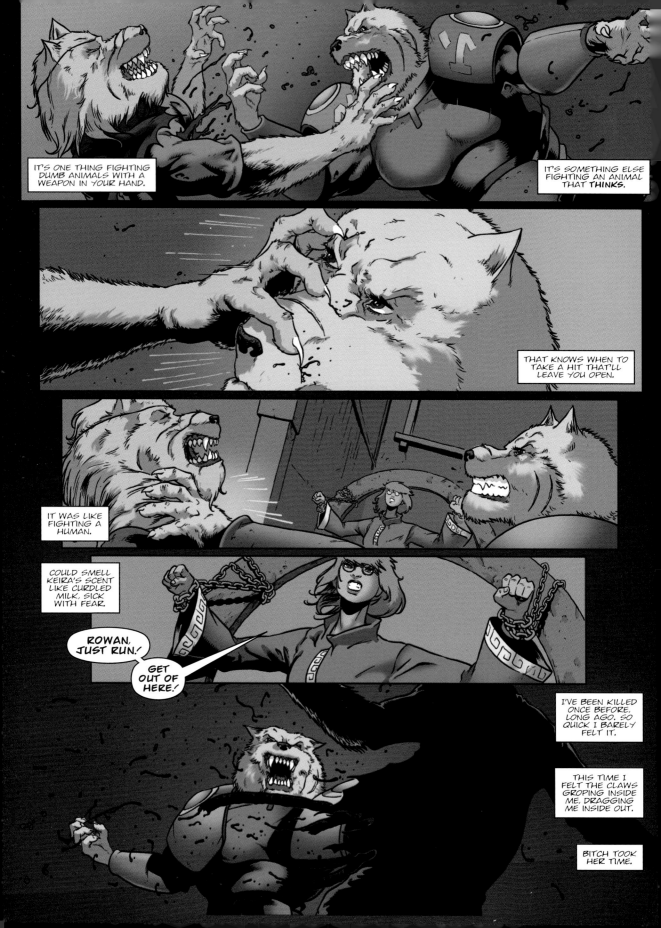

IT'S ONE THING FIGHTING DUMB ANIMALS WITH A WEAPON IN YOUR HAND.

IT'S SOMETHING ELSE FIGHTING AN ANIMAL THAT **THINKS.**

THAT KNOWS WHEN TO TAKE A HIT THAT'LL LEAVE YOU OPEN.

IT WAS LIKE FIGHTING A HUMAN.

COULD SMELL KEIRA'S SCENT LIKE CURDLED MILK, SICK WITH FEAR.

ROWAN, JUST RUN!

GET OUT OF HERE!

I'VE BEEN KILLED ONCE BEFORE, LONG AGO. SO QUICK I BARELY FELT IT.

THIS TIME I FELT THE CLAWS GROPING INSIDE ME, DRAGGING ME INSIDE OUT.

BITCH TOOK HER TIME.

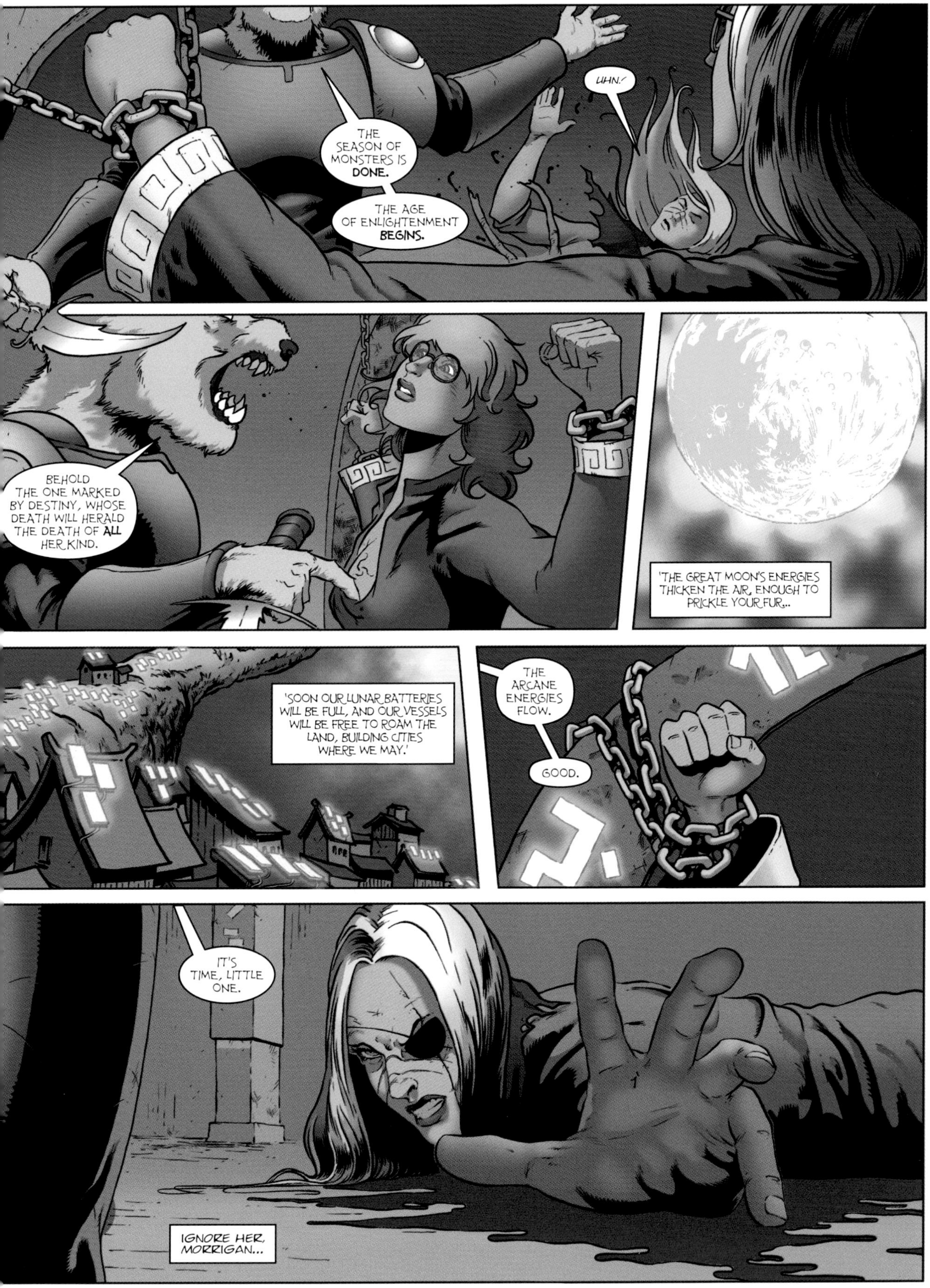
THE SEASON OF MONSTERS IS DONE.
THE AGE OF ENLIGHTENMENT BEGINS.
UHN!
BEHOLD THE ONE MARKED BY DESTINY, WHOSE DEATH WILL HERALD THE DEATH OF ALL HER KIND.
'THE GREAT MOON'S ENERGIES THICKEN THE AIR, ENOUGH TO PRICKLE YOUR FUR...
'SOON OUR LUNAR BATTERIES WILL BE FULL, AND OUR VESSELS WILL BE FREE TO ROAM THE LAND, BUILDING CITIES WHERE WE MAY.'
THE ARCANE ENERGIES FLOW.
GOOD.
IT'S TIME, LITTLE ONE.
IGNORE HER, MORRIGAN...

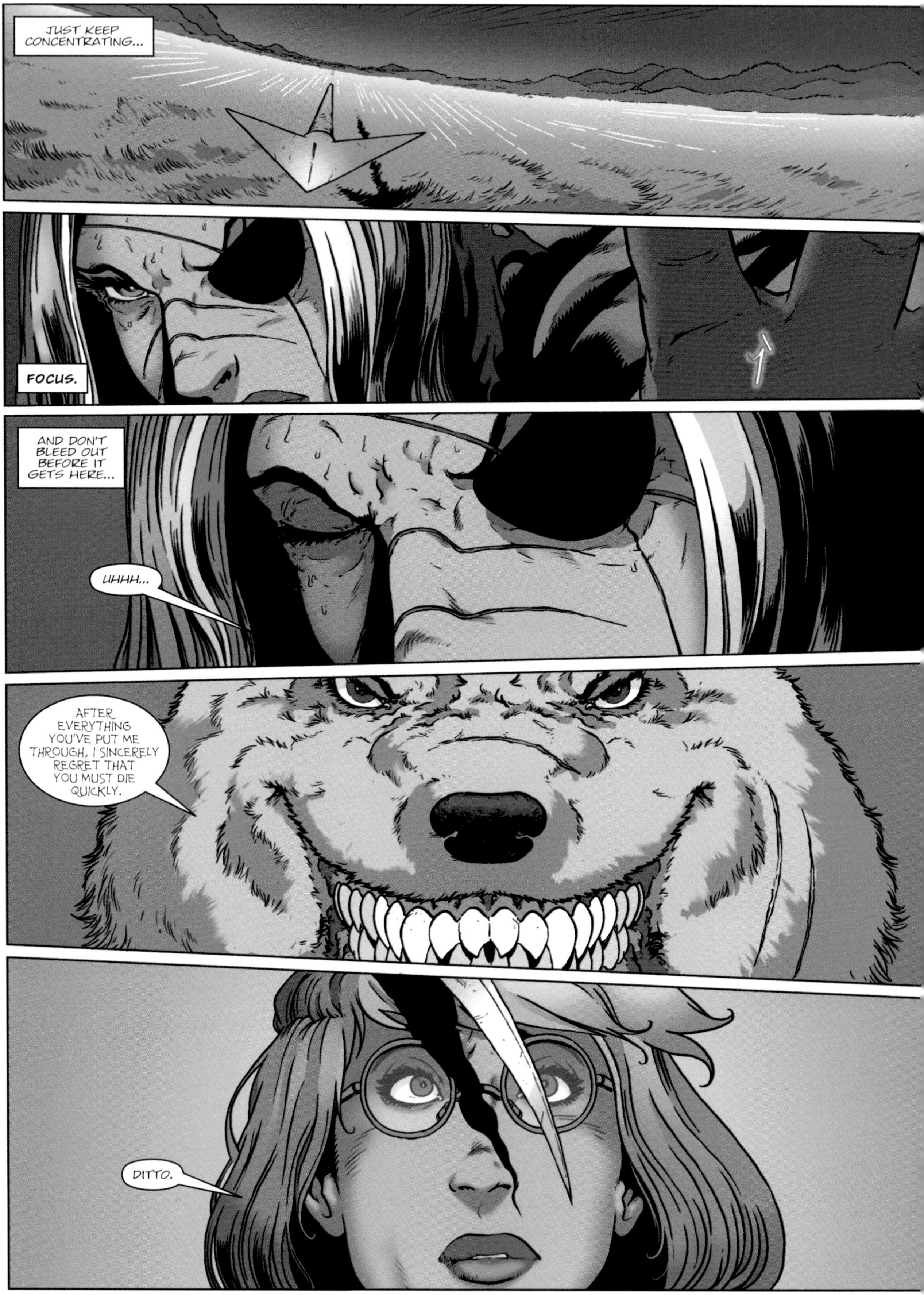
JUST KEEP CONCENTRATING...
FOCUS.
AND DON'T BLEED OUT BEFORE IT GETS HERE...
UHHH...
AFTER EVERYTHING YOU'VE PUT ME THROUGH, I SINCERELY REGRET THAT YOU MUST DIE QUICKLY.
DITTO.

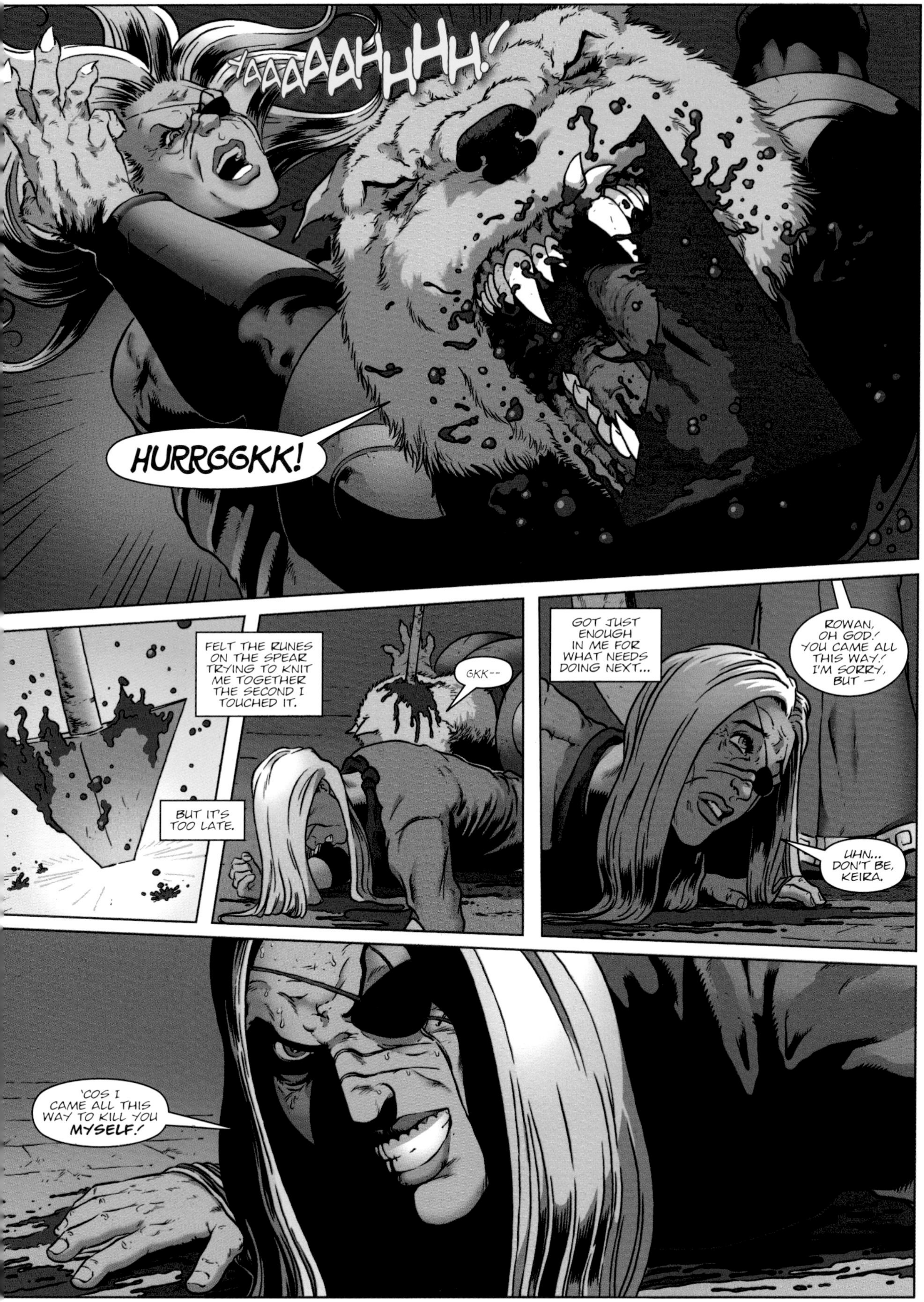
YAAAAAHHHH!
HURRGGKK!
FELT THE RUNES ON THE SPEAR TRYING TO KNIT ME TOGETHER THE SECOND I TOUCHED IT.
BUT IT'S TOO LATE.
GKK--
GOT JUST ENOUGH IN ME FOR WHAT NEEDS DOING NEXT...
ROWAN, OH GOD! YOU CAME ALL THIS WAY! I'M SORRY, BUT --
UHN... DON'T BE, KEIRA.
'COS I CAME ALL THIS WAY TO KILL YOU MYSELF!

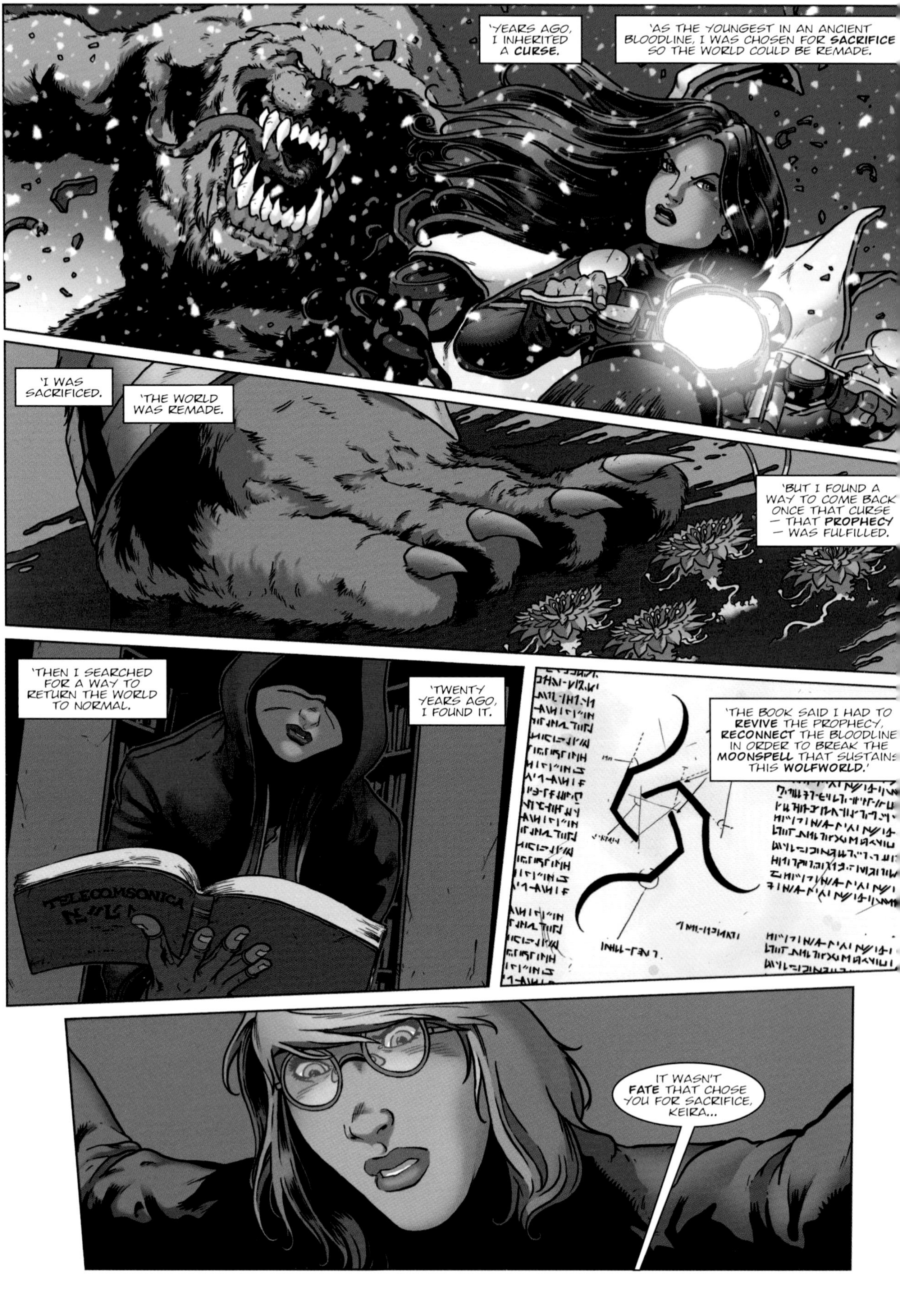
'YEARS AGO, I INHERITED A **CURSE**.
'AS THE YOUNGEST IN AN ANCIENT BLOODLINE, I WAS CHOSEN FOR **SACRIFICE** SO THE WORLD COULD BE REMADE.
'I WAS SACRIFICED.
'THE WORLD WAS REMADE.
'BUT I FOUND A WAY TO COME BACK ONCE THAT CURSE — THAT **PROPHECY** — WAS FULFILLED.
'THEN I SEARCHED FOR A WAY TO RETURN THE WORLD TO NORMAL.
'TWENTY YEARS AGO, I FOUND IT.
TELECOMSONICA
'THE BOOK SAID I HAD TO **REVIVE** THE PROPHECY, **RECONNECT** THE BLOODLINE IN ORDER TO BREAK THE **MOONSPELL** THAT SUSTAINS THIS **WOLFWORLD**.'
IT WASN'T **FATE** THAT CHOSE YOU FOR SACRIFICE, KEIRA...

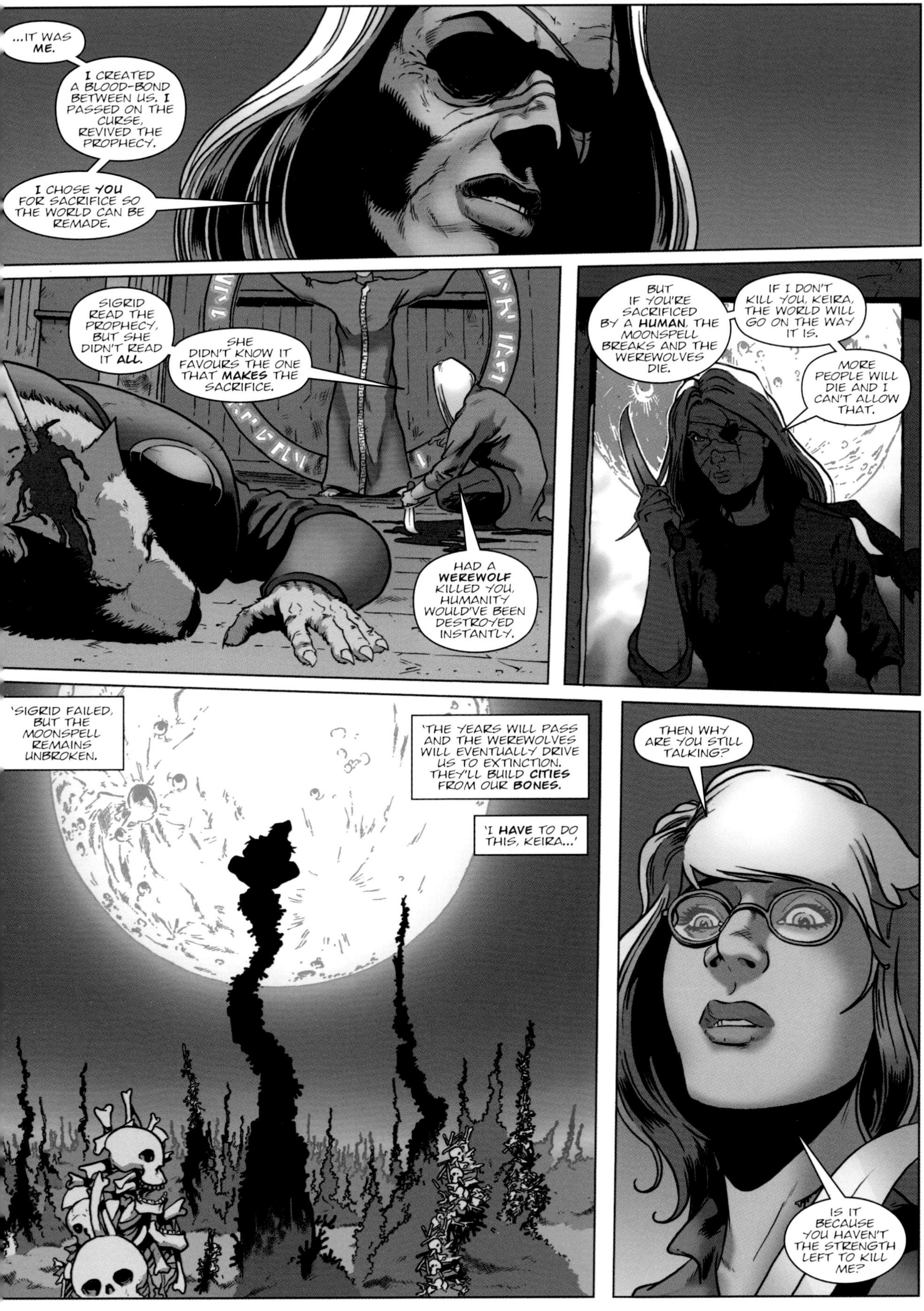
...IT WAS ME.
I CREATED A BLOOD-BOND BETWEEN US. I PASSED ON THE CURSE, REVIVED THE PROPHECY.
I CHOSE YOU FOR SACRIFICE SO THE WORLD CAN BE REMADE.
SIGRID READ THE PROPHECY, BUT SHE DIDN'T READ IT ALL.
SHE DIDN'T KNOW IT FAVOURS THE ONE THAT MAKES THE SACRIFICE.
HAD A WEREWOLF KILLED YOU, HUMANITY WOULD'VE BEEN DESTROYED INSTANTLY.
BUT IF YOU'RE SACRIFICED BY A HUMAN, THE MOONSPELL BREAKS AND THE WEREWOLVES DIE.
IF I DON'T KILL YOU, KEIRA, THE WORLD WILL GO ON THE WAY IT IS.
MORE PEOPLE WILL DIE AND I CAN'T ALLOW THAT.
'SIGRID FAILED, BUT THE MOONSPELL REMAINS UNBROKEN.
'THE YEARS WILL PASS AND THE WEREWOLVES WILL EVENTUALLY DRIVE US TO EXTINCTION. THEY'LL BUILD CITIES FROM OUR BONES.
'I HAVE TO DO THIS, KEIRA...'
THEN WHY ARE YOU STILL TALKING?
IS IT BECAUSE YOU HAVEN'T THE STRENGTH LEFT TO KILL ME?

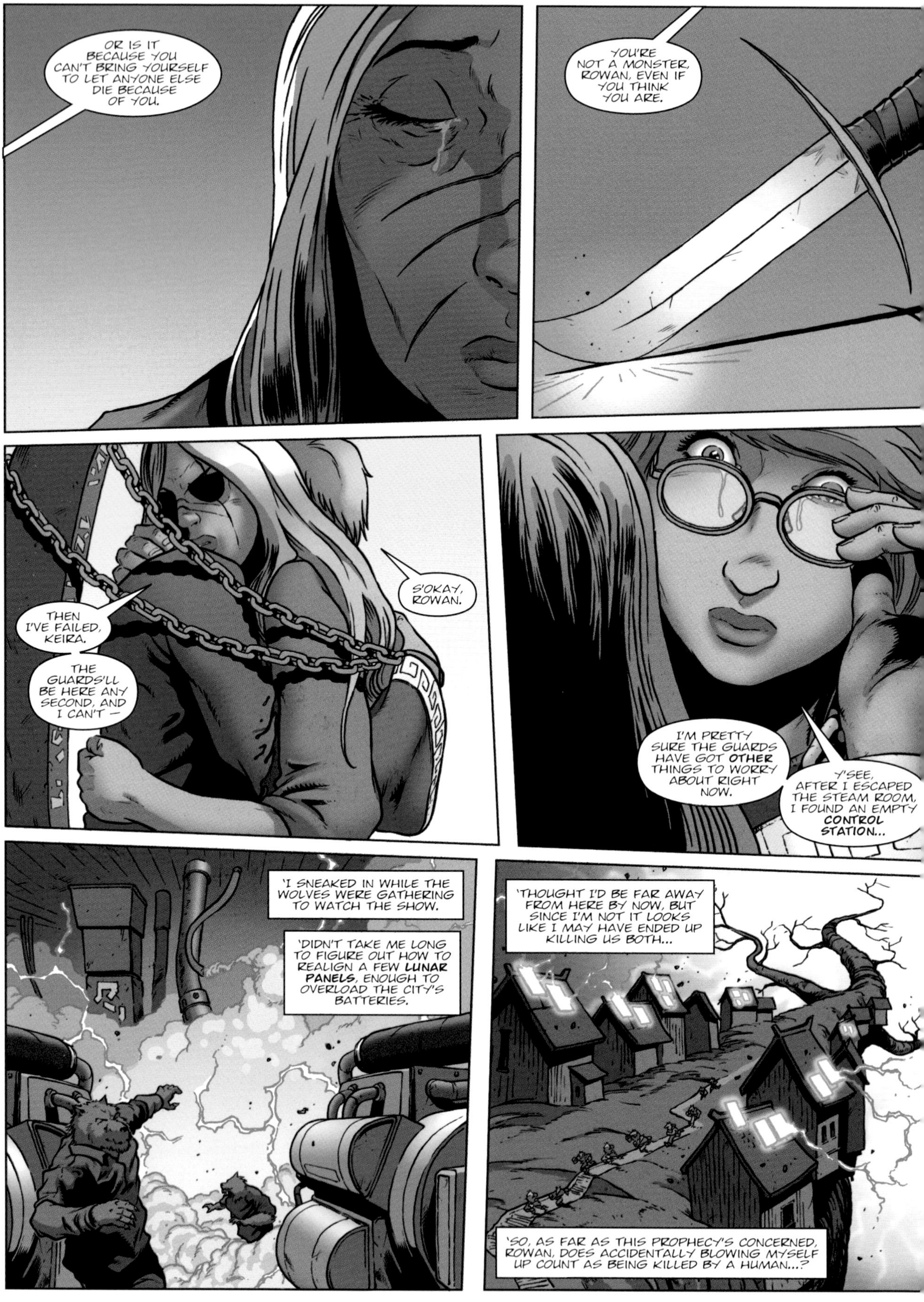
OR IS IT BECAUSE YOU CAN'T BRING YOURSELF TO LET ANYONE ELSE DIE BECAUSE OF YOU.
YOU'RE NOT A MONSTER, ROWAN, EVEN IF YOU THINK YOU ARE.
THEN I'VE FAILED, KEIRA.
THE GUARDS'LL BE HERE ANY SECOND, AND I CAN'T —
S'OKAY, ROWAN.
I'M PRETTY SURE THE GUARDS HAVE GOT **OTHER** THINGS TO WORRY ABOUT RIGHT NOW.
Y'SEE, AFTER I ESCAPED THE STEAM ROOM, I FOUND AN EMPTY **CONTROL STATION**...
'I SNEAKED IN WHILE THE WOLVES WERE GATHERING TO WATCH THE SHOW.
'DIDN'T TAKE ME LONG TO FIGURE OUT HOW TO REALIGN A FEW **LUNAR PANELS**, ENOUGH TO OVERLOAD THE CITY'S BATTERIES.
'THOUGHT I'D BE FAR AWAY FROM HERE BY NOW, BUT SINCE I'M NOT IT LOOKS LIKE I MAY HAVE ENDED UP KILLING US BOTH...
'SO, AS FAR AS THIS PROPHECY'S CONCERNED, ROWAN, DOES ACCIDENTALLY BLOWING MYSELF UP COUNT AS BEING KILLED BY A HUMAN...?

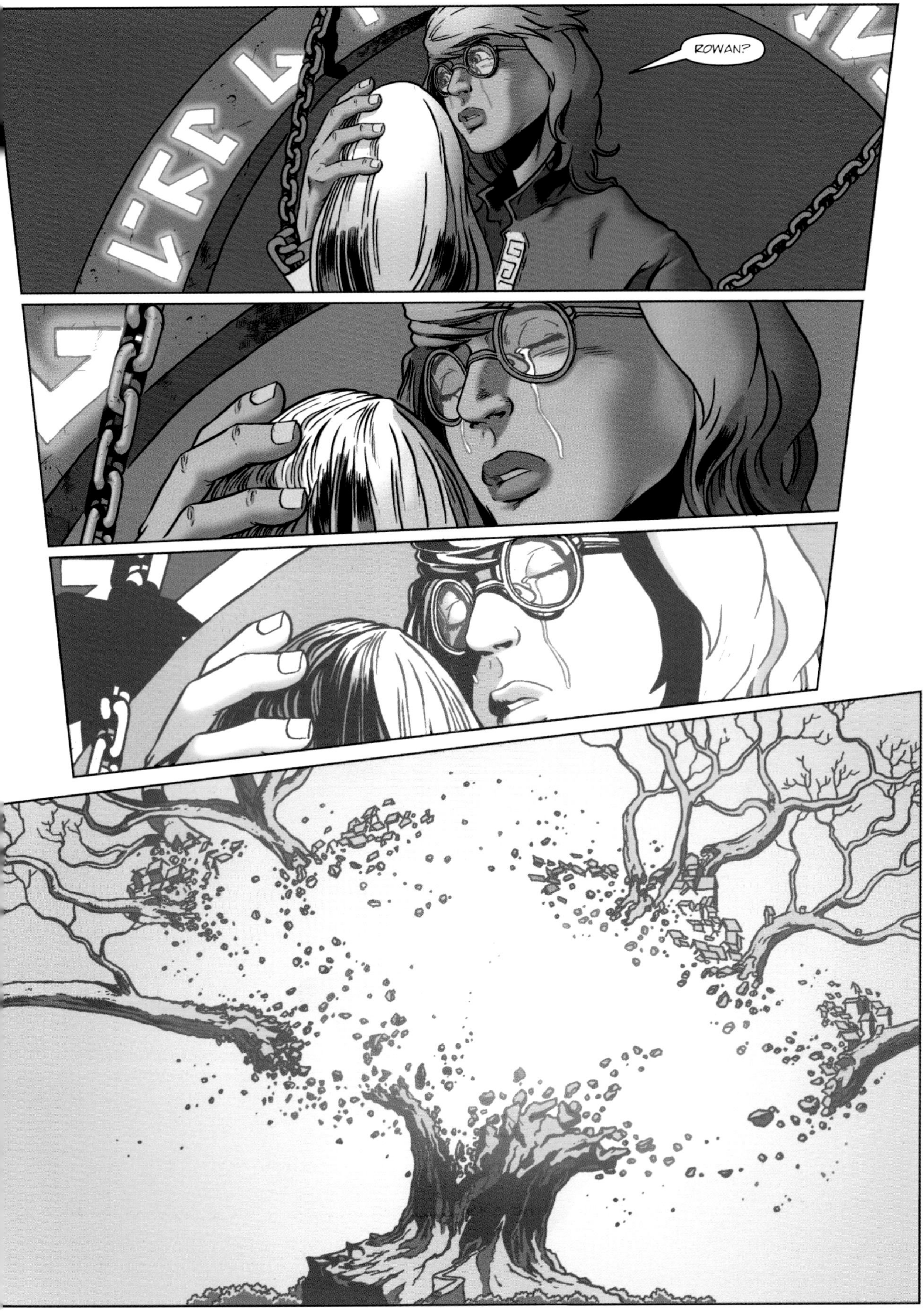
ROWAN?

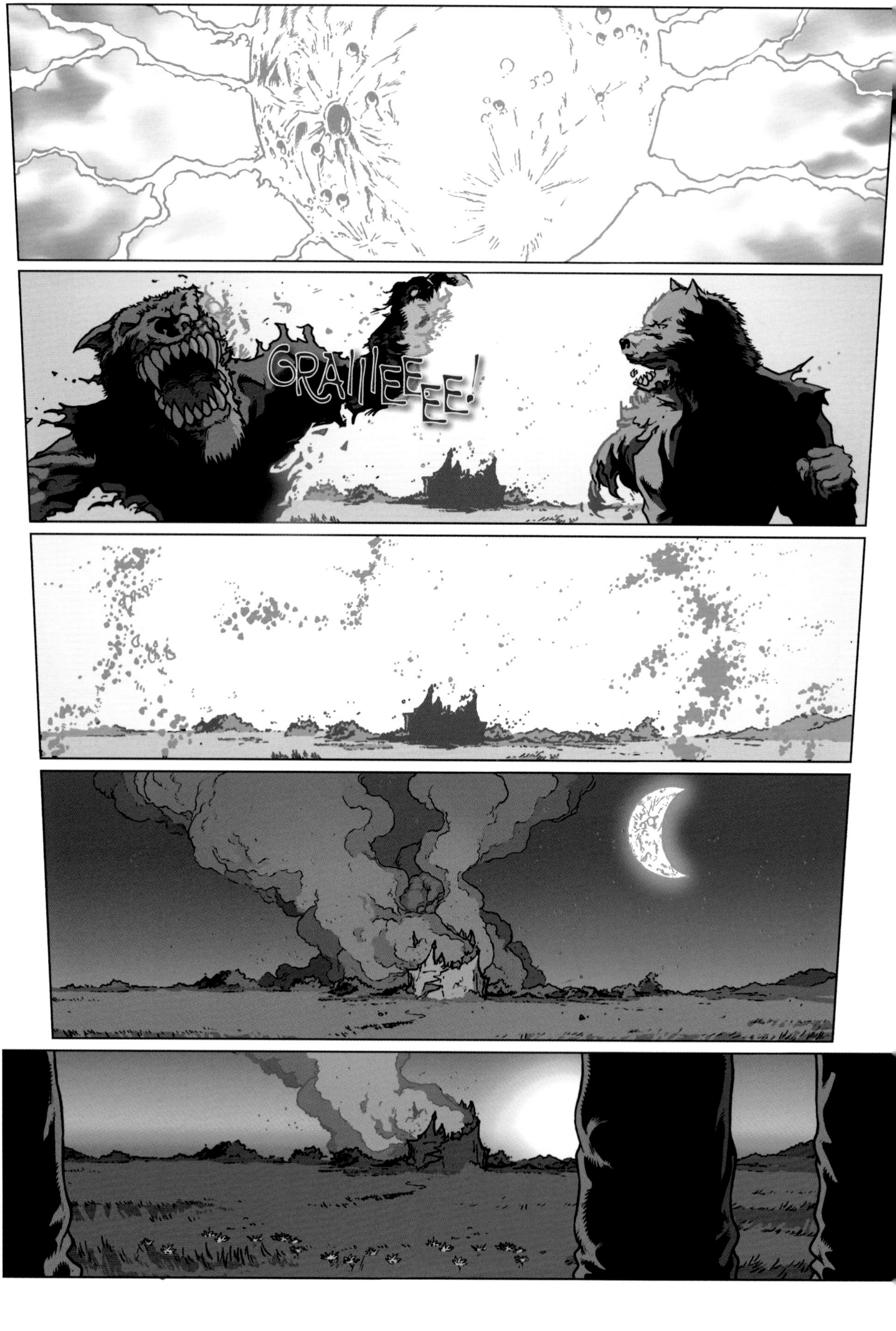
GRAIIIEEEEE!

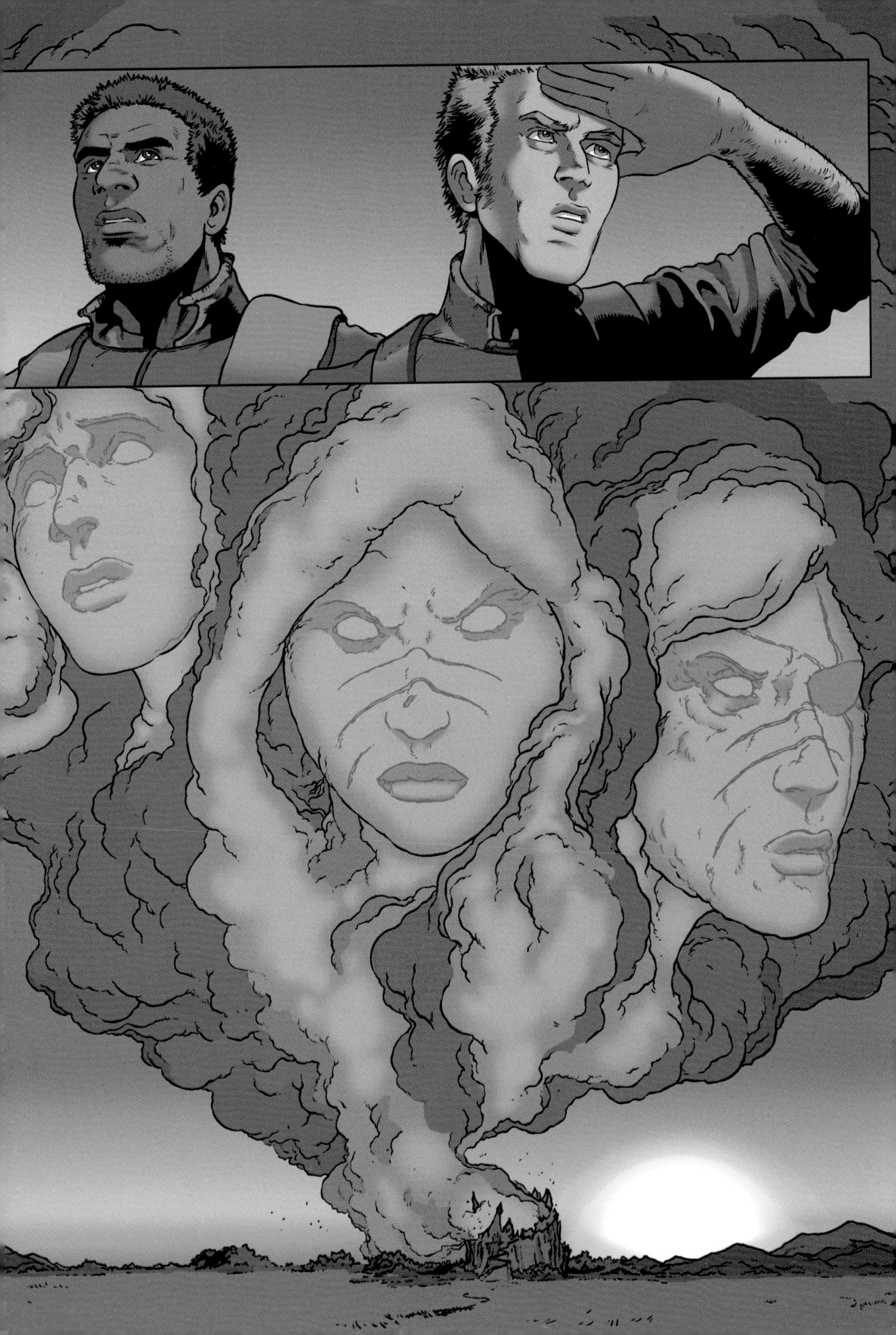

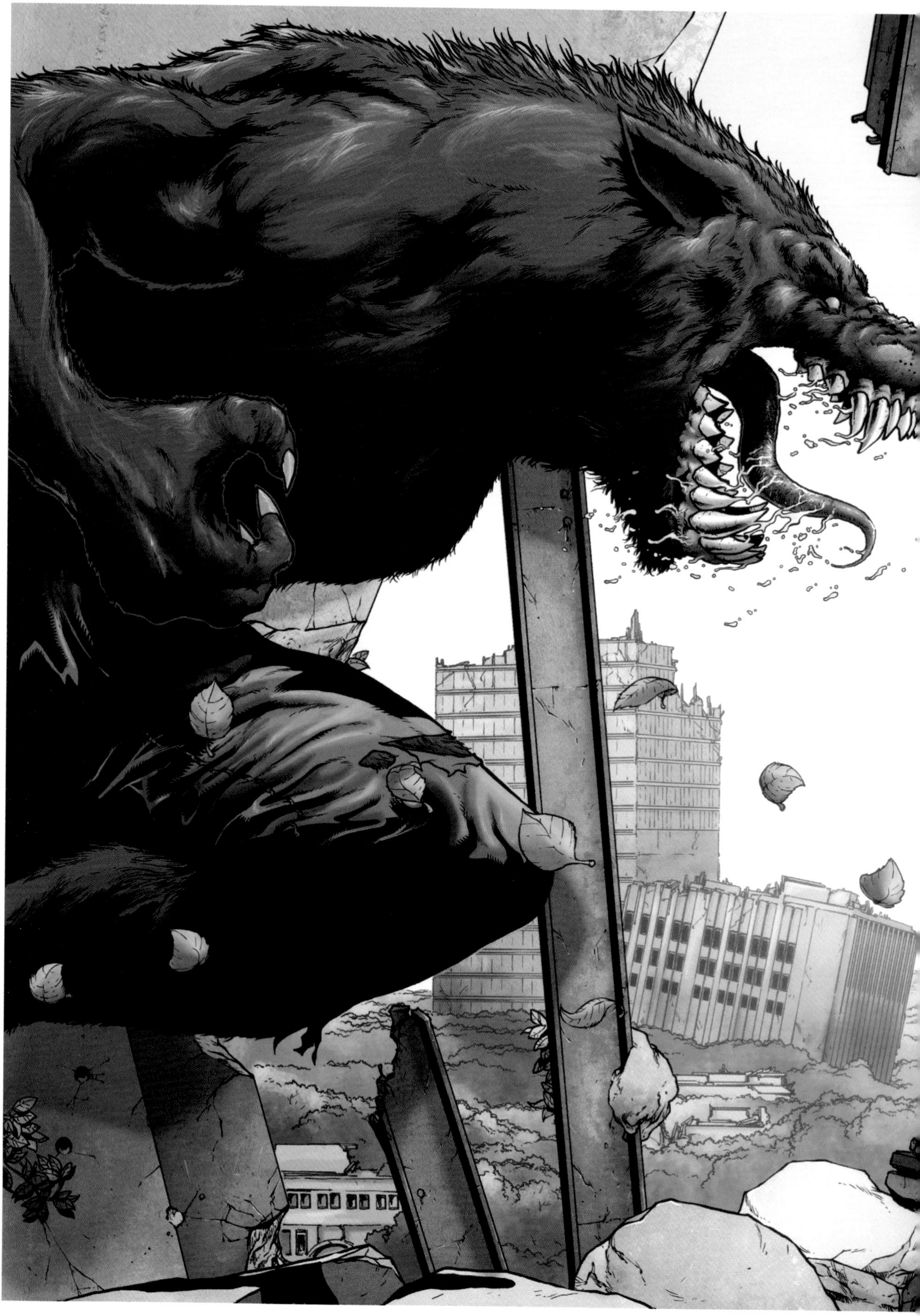

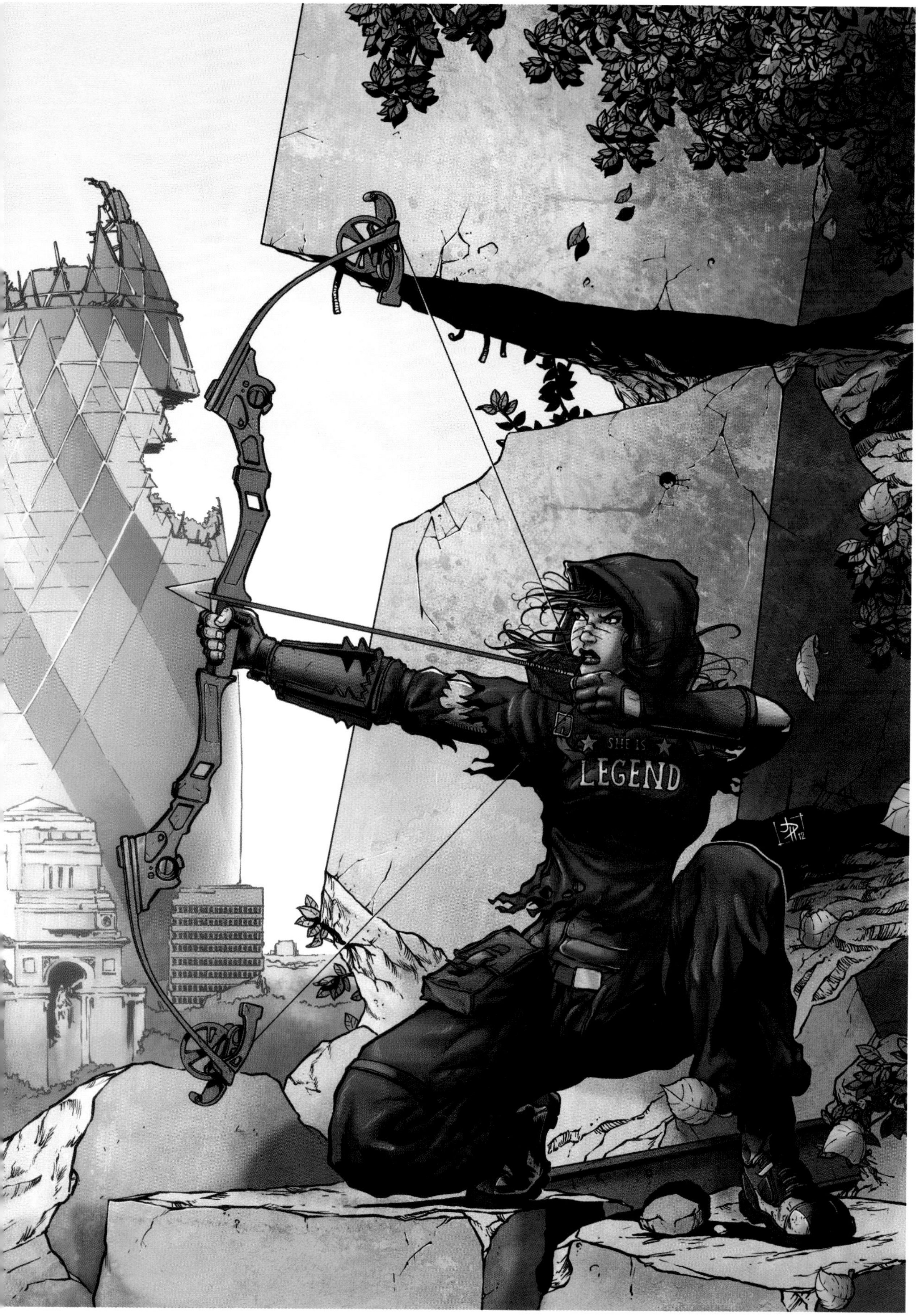
SHE IS
LEGEND

2000 AD PROG 1772: Cover by **Jon Davis-Hunt**

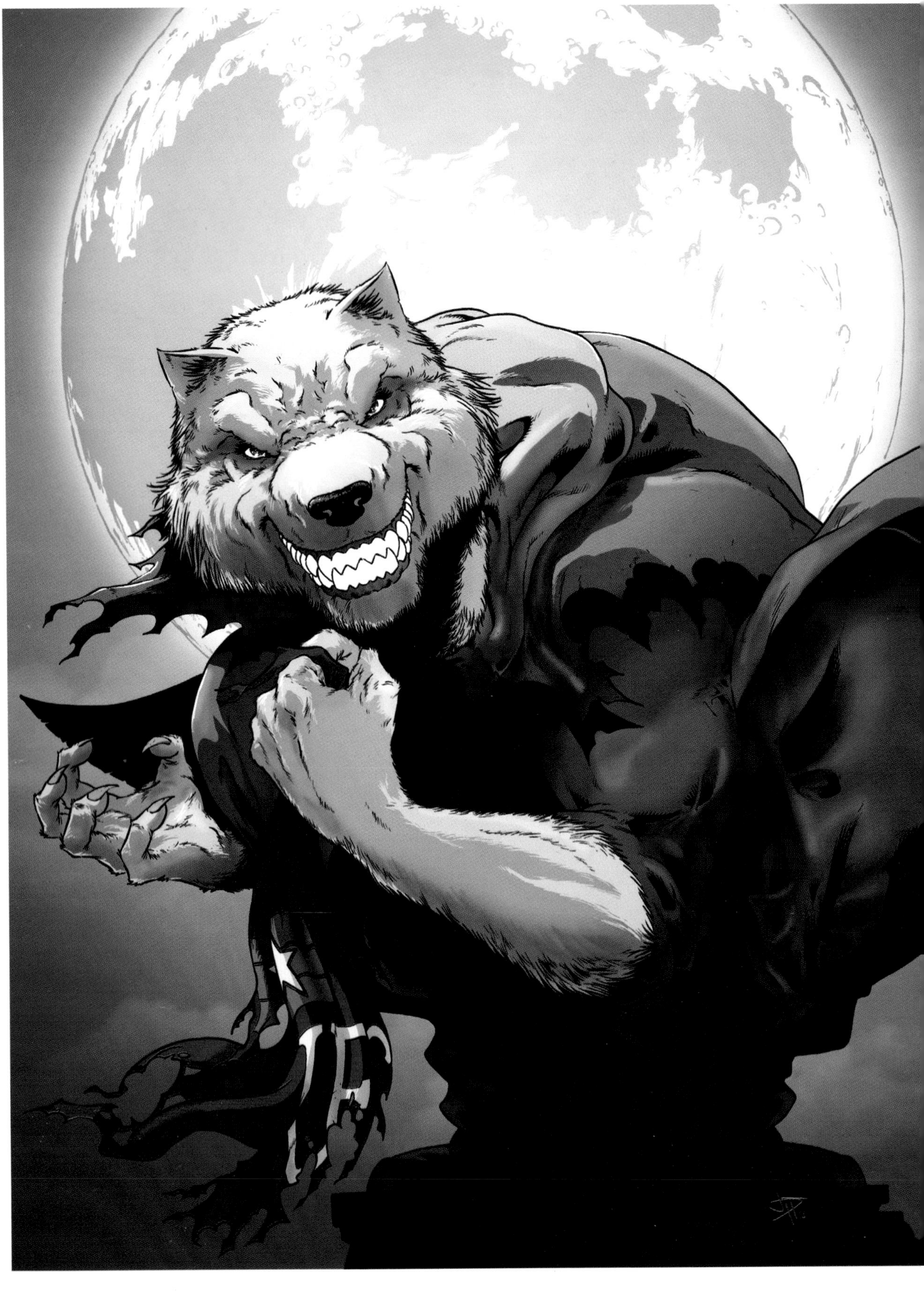

2000 AD PROG 1840: Cover by **Jon Davis-Hunt**